Lecture Notes in Computer Science 4951

Michael Luck Lin Padgham (Eds.)

Agent-Oriented Software Engineering VIII

8th International Workshop, AOSE 2007
Honolulu, HI, USA, May 14, 2007
Revised Selected Papers

Volume Editors

Michael Luck
King's College London, Department of Computer Science
Strand, London WC2R 2LS, UK
E-mail: michael.luck@kcl.ac.uk

Lin Padgham
RMIT University, School of Computer Science and Information Technology
Melbourne, VIC 3001, Australia
E-mail: lin.padgham@rmit.edu.au

Library of Congress Control Number: 2008925093

CR Subject Classification (1998): D.2, I.2.11, F.3, D.1, C.2.4, D.3

LNCS Sublibrary: SL 2 – Programming and Software Engineering

ISSN 0302-9743
ISBN-10 3-540-79487-5 Springer Berlin Heidelberg New York
ISBN-13 978-3-540-79487-5 Springer Berlin Heidelberg New York

Springer is a part of Springer Science+Business Media

springer.com

Typesetting: Camera-ready by author, data conversion by Scientific Publishing Services, Chennai, India
Printed on acid-free paper SPIN: 12262915 06/3180 5 4 3 2 1 0

Preface

The concept of an agent as an autonomous system, capable of interacting with other agents in order to satisy its design objectives, is a natural one for software designers. Just as we can understand many systems as being composed of essentially passive objects, which have state, and upon which we can perform operations, so we can understand many others as being made up of interacting, semi-autonomous agents. This paradigm is especially suited to complex systems. Software architectures that contain many dynamically interacting components, each with their own thread of control, and engaging in complex coordination protocols, are typically orders of magnitude more complex to correctly and efficiently engineer than those that simply compute a function of some input through a single thread of control, or through a limited set of stricly synchronized threads of control. Agent-oriented modelling techniques are especially useful in such applications.

Many current and emerging real-world applications—spanning scenarios as diverse as worldwide computing, network enterprises, ubiquitous computing, sensor networks, just to mention a few examples—have exactly the above characteristics. As a consequence, agent-oriented software engineering has become an important area: both as a design modelling tool, and as an interface to platforms which include specialized infrastructure support for programming in terms of semi-autonomous interacting processes. The workshop was aimed at providing a forum for discussion and debate over just these concerns.

Building on the success of the seven previous workshops, the Eighth International Workshop on Agent-Oriented Software Engineering (AOSE 2007) took place in Honolulu in May 2007 as part of the Sixth International Joint Conference on Autonomous Agents and Multi-Agent Systems (AAMAS 2007). Papers were reviewed by three members of an international Program Committee of 23 researchers and by 5 auxiliary reviewers.

This volume contains revised and improved versions of the papers presented at the workshop, together with papers resulting from discussions on tools and platforms. It is organized in four sections: methodology and processes; interacting heterogeneous agents; system development issues; tools and case studies.

1 AOSE Methodology and Processes

The first section begins with a paper by Garcia-Ojeda et al., in which they describe the organization-based multiagent system engineering (O-MaSE) process framework that aims at helping process engineers create customized agent-oriented software development processes. O-MaSE is built on the MaSE methodology and adapted from the OPEN Process Framework (OPF), which adopts a method engineering approach to process construction. O-MaSE consists of three basic structures: a metamodel, which defines the key concepts needed to design and implement multiagent systems; a set of methods fragments, which are operations or tasks that are executed to produce a set of work products, including models, documents, or code; and a set of guidelines, which define how the method fragments are related to each other. The work is illustrated by providing examples of creating such custom O-MaSE processes.

Continuing the theme, in the second paper, Gonzalez-Palacios and Luck describe work on trying to gain acceptance in industrial environments, which they argue is limited in part by drawbacks in current agent-oriented methodologies, mainly in terms of applicability and comprehensiveness. For example, while the Gaia methodology is based on organizational abstractions (which makes it suitable for the design of complex systems), and offers a simple and neutral methodological process that facilitates extensions, it neither considers agent design nor offers an iterative methodological process. Gonzalez-Palacios and Luck describe their efforts to address this by extending Gaia to include an agent design phase, and an enhanced methodological process that uses iterations.

In the third paper, Miles et al. focus on the issue of making sure that software designs include appropriate means for ensuring the quality of the processes involved. While the products of systems cannot always be judged at face value, the process by which they were obtained is also important. For instance, the rigor of a scientific experiment, the ethics with which an item was manufactured and the use of services with particular licensing all affect how the results of those processes are valued. The issue of ensuring that users are able to check these process qualities is a software engineering one: the developer must decide to ensure that adequate data are recorded regarding processes and safeguards implemented to ensure accuracy. Yet in situations in which there are multiple independent contributory organizations, the ability of autonomous agents to choose how their goals or responsibilities are achieved can hide such process qualities from users. In response, Miles et al. introduce AgentPrIMe, an adjunct to existing agent-oriented methodologies to allow system designs to be adapted so as to give users confidence in the results they generate, through documentation, corroboration, independent storage and accountability.

The next paper, by Morandini et al., addresses the problems arising from system operation in complex, heterogeneous environments, with different system users, each with different needs and preferences. They argue that software engineering methodologies need to cope with the complexity of requirements specification in such scenarios, where new requirements may emerge also at run-time and the systems goals are expected to evolve to meet new stakeholder needs. The proposed solution is to take an agent-oriented approach in the development of methods and techniques for the design of adaptive and evolvable information systems able to fulfill stakeholder objectives. Based on earlier work on a framework for the design and code of system specifications in terms of goal models, with a tool supported process that exploits the Tropos methodology JADE/Jadex, they describe how to develop a system using an iterative process, where the system execution allows the system specification to be enriched through goal models.

Finally, Nguyen et al. are concerned with a distinct aspect of software engineering: testing. As complex distributed agent-oriented systems are increasingly being applied in mission-critical services, assurances need to be given that they operate properly. Although the relevance of the link between requirements engineering and testing has long been understood, current AOSE methodologies only partially address it. While some offer specification-based formal verification, allowing software developers to correct errors at the start of the development process, others exploit object-oriented testing techniques, mapping agent-oriented abstractions into object constructs. However, a structured testing process for AOSE methodologies that complements formal verification is still missing. In response, Nguyen et al. introduce a testing framework for Tropos that includes a testing process model complementing the agent-oriented requirements and design models and strengthening the mutual relationship between goal analysis and testing. They argue that this framework provides a systematic way of deriving test cases from goal analysis, termed *goal-oriented testing*.

2 Interacting Heterogeneous Agents

The second section is concerned with software engineering in the context of interacting heterogeneous agents. As a prelude to the other papers in this section, Dignum et al. introduce and discuss some key issues in relation to open agent systems. In particular, if electronic institutions are Internet-based facilities in which agents can interact, thus forming truly open agent systems, these agents need to be able to determine whether an institution is one in which they can participate. Their solution is to use a layered approach in which, starting with a basic compatibility of message types, each extra layer ensures a higher degree of compatibility, but also requires extra sophistication.

According to German and Sheremetov, in the second paper, interaction engineering is a key issue in the effective construction of multi-agent systems, requiring software abstractions, components and control structures to manage interactions among agents and to improve infrastructures at runtime. In support of these aims, they describe a framework for the automatic processing of interactions generated using FIPA-ACL, and including three parts: an agent interaction architecture to systematize interaction processing tasks; interaction models to build reusable validated code for checking different phases of interaction processing associated with message semantics; and components and control structures for a particular agent platform. They also outline the implementation details of the proposed approach within the CAPNET agent platform and illustrate it with examples.

In a rather different vein, Bogdanovych et al. describe work on considering virtual worlds as open multi-agent systems with a new 3D Electronic Institutions methodology for their development. In this sense, 3D Electronic Institutions are virtual worlds with normative regulation of interactions. The methodology proposed helps to separate the development of such virtual worlds into two independent phases: specification of the institutional rules; and design of the 3D interaction environment. It also offers a set of graphical tools that support the development process at each stage from specification to deployment. The resulting system facilitates the incorporation of humans into multi-agent systems through participation as avatars in the 3D environment, and interacting with other humans or software agents, while the institution ensures the validity of their interactions.

3 System Development Issues

The third section of the book is concerned with agent systems development. In the first paper, Asnar et al. consider the role of risk in safety-critical agent-oriented applications. Currently, deliberation in agent architectures (particularly BDI) does not include any form of risk analysis. In response, they propose guidelines for *goal-risk* reasoning in Tropos so that the overall set of possible plans is evaluated with respect to risk. When the level of risk is too high, agents can consider and introduce additional plans, called *treatments*, which produce an overall reduction of risk, but may have side effects. Asnar et al. illustrate their model with a case study on the Unmanned Aerial Vehicle agent.

The second paper, by Dam and Winikoff, deals with one of the most critical problems in software maintenance and evolution, propagating changes. Although many approaches have been proposed, automated change propagation is still a significant technical challenge in software engineering. Their work provides an agent-oriented change propagation framework based on fixing inconsistencies when primary changes are made to design models. A core piece of the framework is a new method for generating repair plans from OCL constraints that restrict these models.

Finally, in the last paper of this section, Taveter and Sterling describe how prototype systems can be efficiently created from agent-oriented domain and design models, through a conceptual space that accommodates model transformations described by the model-driven architecture. They argue that the approach has the potential to further speed up and automate the process of fast prototyping, complementing other agent-oriented approaches.

4 Tools and Case Studies

The last section of the book is concerned with tools and case studies. As is indicated in the first paper, which functions as a brief introduction, this section resulted from a call for alternative agent-oriented designs of a common system, allowing for a more direct comparison between methodologies, and also from a call for demonstrations of AOSE tools. The result is a set of papers that provides a valuable resource for the community—namely, a set of designs using different methodologies, for the well-known conference management system example.

We believe that this volume provides a combination of cutting-edge research papers in agent-oriented software engineering and an important reference for the development and comparison of new and existing methodologies.

October 2007

Michael Luck
Lin Padgham

Organization

Organizing Committee

Michael Luck (Co-chair)
Department of Computer Science
King's College London, UK
E-mail: michael.luck@kcl.ac.uk

Lin Padgham (Co-chair)
School of CS and IT
RMIT University, Australia
E-mail: linpa@cs.rmit.edu.au

Steering Committee

Paolo Ciancarini, University of Bologna
Michael Wooldridge, University of Liverpool
Joerg Mueller, Siemens
Gerhard Weiss, Software Competence Center Hagenberg GmbH

Program Committee

Claudio Bartolini (USA)
Federico Bergenti (Italy)
Carole Bernon (France)
Giacomo Cabri (Italy)
Paolo Ciancarini (Italy)
Massimo Cossentino (Italy)
Keith Decker (USA)
Scott DeLoach (USA)
Klaus Fischer (Germany)
Paolo Giorgini (Italy)
Jorge Gomez Sanz (Spain)
Gaya Jayatilleke (Australia)
Juergen Lind (Germany)
Simon Miles (UK)
Haris Mouratidis (UK)
Andrea Omicini (Italy)
Juan Pavon (Spain)
Anna Perini (Italy)
Fariba Sadri (UK)
Arnon Sturm (Israel)
John Thangarajah (Australia)
Michael Winikoff (Australia)
Eric Yu (Canada)

Auxiliary Reviewers

James Atlas
Sachin Kamboj
Ambra Molesini
Cu Nguyen
Alberto Siena

Table of Contents

I AOSE Methodology and Processes

II Interacting Heterogeneous Agents

III System Development Issues

IV Tools and Case Studies

O-MaSE: A Customizable Approach to Developing Multiagent Development Processes

Juan C. Garcia-Ojeda, Scott A. DeLoach, Robby, Walamitien H. Oyenan, and Jorge Valenzuela

Department of Computing and Information Sciences, Kansas State University
234 Nichols Hall, Manhattan, KS 66506
{jgarciao,sdeloach,robby,oyenan,jvalenzu}@cis.ksu.edu

Abstract. This paper describes the Organization-based Multiagent System Engineering (O-MaSE) Process Framework, which helps process engineers define custom multiagent systems development processes. O-MaSE builds off the MaSE methodology and is adapted from the OPEN Process Framework (OPF). OPF implements a Method Engineering approach to process construction. The goal of O-MaSE is to allow designers to create customized agent-oriented software development processes. O-MaSE consists of three basic structures: (1) a metamodel, (2) a set of methods fragments, and (3) a set of guidelines. The O-MaSE metamodel defines the key concepts needed to design and implement multiagent systems. The method fragments are operations or tasks that are executed to produce a set of work products, which may include models, documents, or code. The guidelines define how the method fragments are related to one another. The paper also shows two O-MaSE process examples.

1 Introduction

The software industry is facing new challenges. Businesses today are demanding applications that can operate autonomously, can adapt in response to dynamic environments, and can interact with other applications in order to provide comprehensive solutions. Multiagent system (MAS) technology is a promising approach to these new requirements [13]. Its central notion - the intelligent agent - encapsulates all the characteristics (i.e., autonomy, proactive, reactivity, and interactivity) required to fulfill the requirements demanded by these new applications.

In order to develop these autonomous and adaptive systems, novel approaches are needed. In the last several years, many new processes for developing MAS have been proposed [1]; unfortunately, none of these processes have gained widespread industrial acceptance. Reasons for this lack of acceptance include the variety of approaches upon which these processes are based (i.e., object-oriented, requirements engineering, and knowledge engineering) and the lack of Computer Aided Software Engineering (CASE) tools that support the process of software design. There have been some approaches suggested for increasing the change of industry acceptance. For instance, Odell et al. suggest presenting

M. Luck and L. Padgham (Eds.): AOSE 2007, LNCS 4951, pp. 1–15, 2008.

new techniques as an incremental extension of known and trusted methods [14], while Bernon et al. suggest the integration of existing agent-oriented processes into one highly defined process [3]. Although these suggestions may be helpful in gaining industrial acceptance of agent-oriented techniques, we believe that a more promising way is to provide more flexibility in the approaches offered. The main problem with these approaches is that they do not provide assistance to process engineers on how to extend or tailor these processes. In this vein, Henderson-Sellers suggests the use of method engineering using a well-defined and accepted metamodel in order to allow users to construct and to customize their own processes that fit their particular approaches to systems development [11]. Henderson-Sellers argues that by defining method fragments based on a common underlying metamodel, new custom processes can be created that support user defined goals and preferences.

The goal of this paper is to present an overview of the Organization-based Multiagent System Engineering (O-MaSE) Process Framework. The goal of the O-MaSE Process Framework is to allow process engineers to construct custom agent-oriented processes using a set of method fragments, all of which are based on a common metamodel. To achieve this, we define O-MaSE in terms of a metamodel, a set of method fragments, and a set of guidelines. The O-MaSE metamodel defines a set of analysis, design, and implementation concepts and a set of constraints between them. The method fragments define how a set of analysis and design products may be created and used within O-MaSE. Finally, guidelines define how the method fragment may be combined to create valid O-MaSE processes, which we refer to as O-MaSE compliant processes.

The rest of the paper is organized as follows. Section 2 discusses the background material on O-MaSE. Section 3 presents a brief overview of the O-MaSE Process Framework as defined by the proposed metamodel, method fragments, and guidelines. Section 4 presents examples of two O-MaSE-compliant processes that can be used for developing a simulated cooperative robotic system. Finally, Section 5 concludes and describes future work.

2 Background

One of the major problems faced by agent-oriented software engineering is the failure to achieve a strong industry acceptance. One of the reasons hindering this acceptance is a lack of an accepted process-oriented methodology for developing agent-based systems. An interesting solution to this problem is the use of approaches that allow us to customize processes based on different types of applications and development environments. One technique that provides such an approach for the construction of tailored methods is Method Engineering [5].

Method Engineering is an approach by which process engineers construct processes (i.e., methodologies) from a set of method fragments instead of trying to modify a single monolithic, "one-size-fits-all" process. These fragments are generally identified by analyzing these "one-size-fits-all" processes and extracting useful tasks and techniques. The fragments are then redefined in terms of a common metamodel and are stored in a repository for later use. To create a new process, a process engineer selects appropriate method fragments from the repository and assembles them into a complete process based on project requirements [5]. However, the application of Method Engineering in the development of agent-oriented applications is non-trivial. Specifically, there is no consensus on the common elements of multiagent systems. Thus, it is has been suggested that prior to developing a set of method fragments, a well-defined metamodel of common agent-oriented that are typical of most varieties of MAS (e.g., adaptive, competitive, self-organizing, etc.) should be developed [4].

Fortunately, we can leverage the OPEN Process Framework (OPF), which provides an industry-standard approach for applying Method Engineering to the production of custom processes [9]. The OPF uses an integrated metamodel-based framework that allows designers to select method fragments from a repository and to construct a custom process using identified construction and tailoring guidelines. This metamodel-based framework is supported by a three-layer schema as shown in Fig. 1. The M2 layer includes the OPF metamodel, which is a generic process metamodel defining the types of method fragments that can be used in M1. Thus a process (such as OPEN) can be created in M1 by instantiating method fragments from the M2 metamodel.

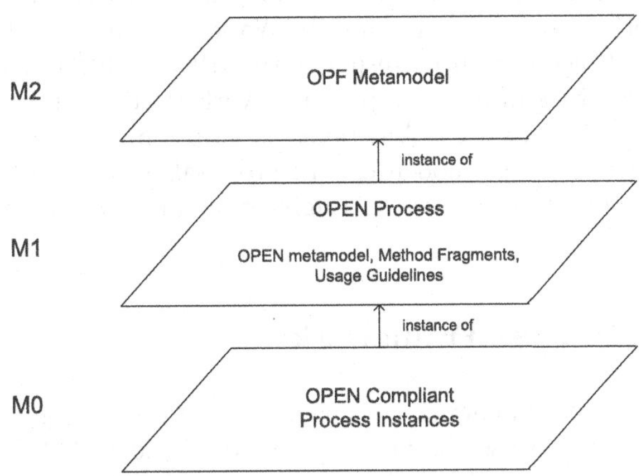

Fig. 1. OPEN Process Framework (adapted from [12])

The OPF metamodel consists of Stages, Work Units (Activities, Tasks, and Techniques), Producers, Work Products, and Languages. A Stage is defined as a "formally identified and managed duration within the process or a point in time at which some achievement is recognized" [9, pp. 55]. Stages are used to organize Work Units, which are defined as operations that are carried out by a Producer. There are three kinds of Work Units in OPF: Activities, Tasks, and Techniques. Activities are a collection of Tasks. Tasks are small jobs performed by one or more Producers. Techniques are detailed approaches to carrying out various Tasks. Producers use Techniques to create, evaluate, iterate, and maintain Work Products. Work Products are pieces of information or physical entities produced (i.e., application, document, model, diagram, or code) and serve as the inputs to and the outputs of Work Units. Work Products are documented in appropriate Languages. The M1 layer serves as a repository of method fragments instantiated from the M2 metamodel. A set of rules governing the relationship between these concepts (i.e., a process-specific metamodel and a set of reusable method fragments) is also defined in M1. Basically, the process engineer uses the guidelines to extend, to instantiate, and to tailor the predefined method fragments for creating a custom process in the M1 layer. These custom processes are then instantiated at the M0 level on specific projects; the actual custom process as enacted on a specific project is termed a process instance.

Alternatively, the FIPA (Foundation for Physical Agents) Technical Committee (TC) methodology group is working on defining reusable method fragments in order to allow designers to specify custom agent-oriented processes [17]. Although this approach is quite similar to OPF (they are both based on method engineering), its metamodel is derived from the Object Management Group (OMG) Software Process Engineering Metamodel (SPEM). SPEM is based on three basic process elements that encapsulate the main features of any development process: Activities, Process Roles, and Work Products. Development processes are assembled from a set of SPEM Activities, which represent tasks that must be done. An Activity is essentially equivalent to an OPF Work Unit and is performed by one or more Process Roles (which corresponds to OPF Producers). Process Roles carry out the Activities in order to produce Work Products (the same term is used here by SPEM and OPF). A detailed description of this metamodel and a comparison with other method fragment proposals can be found in [6]. The next section focuses on using Method Engineering and the OPF metamodel to specify O-MaSE.

3 O-MaSE Process Framework

The O-MaSE Process Framework as shown in Fig. 2, is analogous to the OPF from Fig. 1. In fact, we use the OPF metamodel in level M2. Level M1 contains the definition of O-MaSE in the form of the O-MaSE metamodel, method fragments, and guidelines. In the remainder of the section, we present the three components of the O-MaSE contained in the M1. We first describe the O-MaSE metamodel followed by a description of the method fragments obtained. Finally, we discuss the guidelines that govern the construction of O-MaSE compliant processes.

3.1 Metamodel

The O-MaSE metamodel defines the main concepts we use to define multiagent systems. It encapsulates the rules (grammar) of the notation and depicts those graphically using object-oriented concepts such as classes and relationships [9].

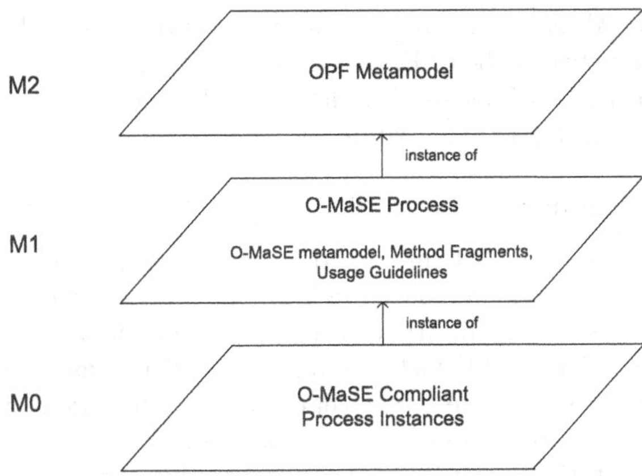

Fig. 2. O-MaSE Process Framework (adapted from [12])

The O-MaSE metamodel is based on an organizational approach [7, 8]. As shown in Fig. 3, the Organization is composed of five entities: Goals, Roles, Agents, Domain Model, and Policies. A Goal defines the overall function of the organization and a Role defines a position within an organization whose behavior is expected to achieve a particular goal or set of goals.

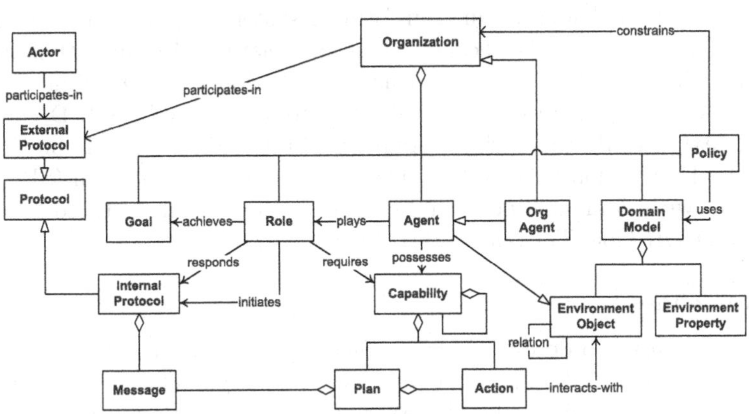

Fig. 3. O-MaSE Metamodel (adapted from [8])

Agents are human or artificial (hardware or software) entities that perceive their environment and can perform actions upon it. In order to perceive and to act in an environment, agents possess Capabilities, which define the percepts/actions the agents have at their disposal. Capabilities can be soft (i.e., algorithms or plans) or hard (i.e., hardware related actions). Plans capture algorithms that agents use to carry out specific tasks, while Actions allows agents to perceive or sense objects in the environment. This environment is modeled using the Domain Model, which defines the types of objects in the environment and the relations between them. Each organization is governed by rules, which are formally captured as Policies. A Policy describes how an organization may or not may behave in a particular situation.

3.2 Method Fragments

As mentioned above, the OPF metamodel defines Stages, Work Units, Work Products, Producers, and Languages, which are used to construct tailorable processes. In our work, the initial set of method fragments are derived from an extended version of the MaSE methodology [5]. O-MaSE assumes an iterative cycle across all phases with the intent that successive iterations will add detail to the models until a complete design is produced. This nicely fits the OPF's Iterative, Incremental, Parallel Life Cycle model. Our current work focuses on analysis and design. In O-MaSE, we have identified three main activities: (1) requirements engineering, (2) analysis, and (3) design. As shown in Table 1, we decompose each Activity into a set of Tasks and identify a set of Techniques that can be used to accomplish each Task. We also show the different Work Products, and Producers related to the associated Work Units. Due to the page limitations, we cannot discuss each of these separately . However, to illustrate our basic approach, we describe the details of the requirements engineering activity.

In the Requirement Engineering activity, we seek to translate systems requirement into system level goals by defining two tasks: Model Goals and Goal Refinement. The first focuses on transforming system requirements into a system level goal tree while the second refines the relationships and attributes for the goals. The goal tree is captured as a Goal Model for Dynamic Systems (GMoDS) [7]. The Goal Modeler must be able to: (1) use AND/OR Decomposition and Attribute-Precede-Trigger Analysis (APT) techniques, (2) understand the System Description (SD) or Systems Requirement Specification (SRS), and (3) interact with domain experts and customers. The result of these two tasks are an AND/OR Goal Tree and GMoDS tree.

3.3 Guidelines

Guidelines are used to describe how the method fragments can be combined in order to obtain O-MaSE compliant processes. These guidelines are specified in terms of a set of constraints related to Work Units and Work Products, which are specified as Work Unit preconditions and postconditions. We formally specify these guidelines as a tuple Input, Output, Precondition, Postcondition where Input is a set of Work Products that may be used in performing a work unit, Output is a set of Work Products that may be produced from the Work Unit, Precondition specifies valid Work Product/Producer states, and Postcondition specifies the Work Product State (see Table 1) that is guaranteed to be true after successfully performing a work unit (if the precondition was true). To formally specify pre and postconditions, we use first order predicate logic statements defined over the Work Products (WP) and Producers (P), the Work Products states, and the iteration (n) and version (m) of the Work Products.

Table 1. O-MaSE Method Fragments

Work Units				
Activity	**Task**	**Technique**	**Work Products**	**Producer**
Requirements Engineering	Model Goals	AND/OR Decomposition	AND/OR Goal Tree	Goal Modeler
	Goal Refinement	Attribute-Precedes-Triggers Analysis	Refined GMoDS	Goal Modeler
Analysis	Model Organizational Interfaces	Organizational Modeling	Organization Model	Organizational Modeler
	Model Roles	Role Modeling	Role Model	Role Modeler
	Define Roles	Role Description	Role Description Document	Role Modeler
	Model Domain	Traditional UML notation	Domain Model	Domain Expert
Design	Model Agent Classes	Agent Modeling	Agent Class Model	Agent Class Modeler
	Model Protocols	Protocol Modeling	Protocol Model	Protocol Modeler
	Model Plans	Plan Specification	Agent Plan Model	Plan Modeler
	Model Policies	Policy Specification	Policy Model	Policy Modeler
	Model Capabilities	Capability Modeling	Capability Model	Capability Modeler
	Model Actions	Action Modeling	Action Model	Action Modeler
	Model Services	Service Modeling	Service Model	Service Modeler

Table 2. Work Product States

No.	State	Definition
1	inProcess()	True if the work product is in process
2	completed()	True if the work product has been finished
3	exists()	exists() = inProcess() $\vee$ completed()
4	previousIteration()	True if the work product's iteration is any previous one
5	available()	True if producer specified is available to perform

Figs. 4–8 illustrate a set of guidelines for a few of the Tasks defined in Table 1. Fig. 4 defines the Model Goals task. Inputs to the task may include the Systems Description (SD), the Systems Requirement Specification (SRS), the Role Description Document (RD), or a previous version of the Goal Model (GM). Actually, only one of these inputs is required, although as many as are available may be used. The inputs are used by the Goal Model Producer (GMP) to identify goals. As a result of this task, the Work Product GM is obtained.

Fig. 5 depicts the task Goal Refinement. Generally, this task only requires as input a GM from the Model Goals task and produces a refined GMoDS model.

Fig. 6 shows the task Model Agent Classes, which requires as input a Refined Goal Model (RG), an Organization Model (OM), or a Role Model (RM). As output an Agent Class Model (AM) is obtained. In the task, the Agent Class Modeler

TASK NAME: Model Goals			
Input	Output	Precondition	Postcondition
SD, SRS, RD, GM	GM	((exists($\langle SD, n, m\rangle$) ∨ exists($\langle SRS, n, m\rangle$) ∨ previousIteration($\langle GM\rangle$)) ∧ available(GMP)	completed($\langle GM, n, m\rangle$)

Fig. 4. Model Goals Task Constraints

TASK NAME: Goal Refinement			
Input	Output	Precondition	Postcondition
GM	RG	completed($\langle GM, n, m\rangle$) ∧ available(GMP)	exists($\langle RG, n, m\rangle$)

Fig. 5. Goal Refinement Task Constraints

TASK NAME: Model Agent Classes			
Input	Output	Precondition	Postcondition
RG, RM, OM, AC, CM, PrM	AC	(exists($\langle RG, n, m\rangle$) ∨ exists($\langle RM, n, m\rangle$) ∨ exists($\langle OM, n, m\rangle$) ∨ exists($\langle SM, n, m\rangle$) ∨ previousIteration($\langle AM\rangle$)) ∧ available(ACM)	completed($\langle AC, n, m\rangle$)

Fig. 6. Model Agent Classes Task Constraints

TASK NAME: Model Plans			
Input	Output	Precondition	Postcondition
RG, RM, AC, PrM, AM, CM	PlM	((exists($\langle RG, n, m\rangle$) ∧ exists($\langle AC, n, m\rangle$)) ∨ exists($\langle PrM, n, m\rangle$) ∨ exists($\langle AM, n, m\rangle$) ∨ previousIteration($\langle PlM\rangle$)) ∧ available(PlP)	completed($\langle PlM, n, m\rangle$)

Fig. 7. Model Plans Task Constraints

TASK NAME: Model Protocols			
Input	Output	Precondition	Postcondition
RM, AC, DM, OM, AM	PrM	((exists($\langle RM, n, m\rangle$) ∧ exists($\langle AC, n, m\rangle$)) ∨ previousIteration($\langle PrM\rangle$)) ∧ available(PrP)	completed($\langle PrM, n, m\rangle$)

Fig. 8. Model Protocols Task Constraints

(ACM) identifies the types of agents in the system. A Capability Model (CM) may provide useful insight into the process however, the CM is not sufficient nor mandatory and thus is an optional input (and is not part of the Precondition). The Protocol Model (PrM) may be useful in identifying relationships between agents and thus, it is also optional.

The Model Plan task is defined in Fig. 7. The inputs can include a RG, RM, or an AC, which allow the Plan Modeler (PlM) to define plans used by agents to satisfy organization goals. In addition, a PrM, Action Model (AM), and CM are required as input because such plans may require the interaction with other entities using some defined protocol.

Finally, the Model Protocols task is defined in Fig. 8. To document a PrM, the Protocol Modeler (PrP) requires the RM and the AC or a previous iteration of the PrM. The Domain Model (DM), OM, and AM are optional inputs.

4 WMD Search Example

Next, we present two examples of applying the O-MaSE to derive custom processes. We combine O-MaSE method fragments to create a custom process for a Weapon of Mass Destruction (WMD) system in which agents detect and identify WMD in a given area. There are three types of WMD that can be identified: radioactive, chemical, and biological. Once a suspicious object is found, it must be tested to determine the concentration of radioactivity and nerve agents (chemical and biological). If the object is indeed a WMD, it is removed. The mission is successful when the area has been entirely searched and all the WMD have been removed. In the subsequent subsections, we present two custom processes for the WMD Search application.

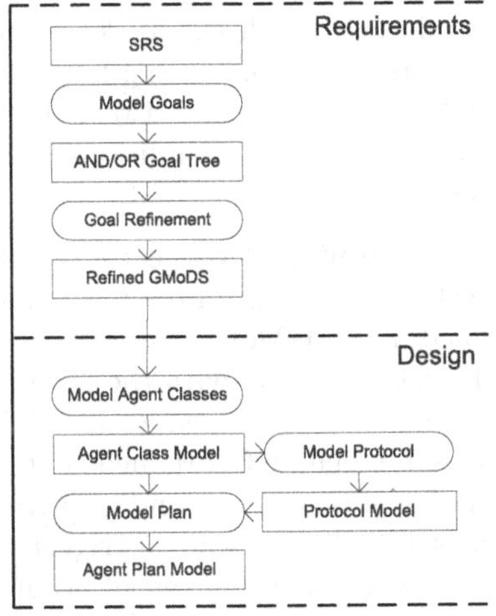

Fig. 9. Basic O-MaSE Process

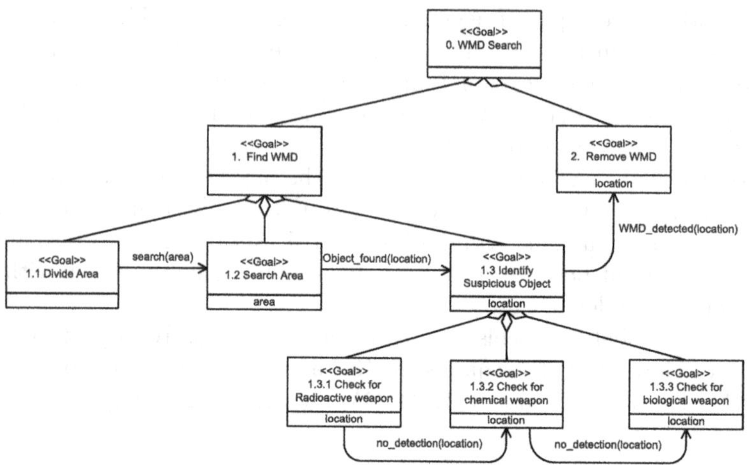

Fig. 10. AND/OR Goal Model

4.1 Basic O-MaSE Process

The first process we derive is appropriate for a small agent-oriented project in which reactive agents achieve goals that have been assigned at design time. Essentially, the only products required for this type of system are the system goals, agent classes, agent plans, and inter-agent protocols. This type of process leads to a rigid MAS but is very easy and fast to develop. This process may also be suitable for prototyping, where a simple and rapid process is needed. Fig. 9 shows the result of applying O-MaSE guidelines to the creation of our custom process. (Tasks are represented by rounded rectangles while Work Products are represented by rectangles.) The Work Products associated with the products identified above are included, along with the Tasks required to produce them. (We do not show the Producers to simplify the figure, but we assume the appropriate Producers are available.) Connections between Tasks and Work Products are drawn and the preconditions and postconditions of each Task are verified. Each Task will be discussed below:

Model Goals/Goal Refinement. From the System Description, the Goal Modeler defines a set of system level goals in the form of an AND/OR goal tree. The AND/OR tree is refined into a GMoDS goal tree as shown in Fig. 10. The syntax uses standard UML class notation with the keyword "Goal". The aggregation notation is used to denote AND refined goals (conjunction), whereas the generalization notation is used to denote OR refined goals (disjunction). GMoDS models include the notion of goal precedence and goal triggering [7]. A precedes determines which goals must be achieved while a trigger relation signifies that a new goal may be instantiated when a specific event occurs during the pursuit of the another goal. Fig. 10 captures a goal-based view of the system operation.

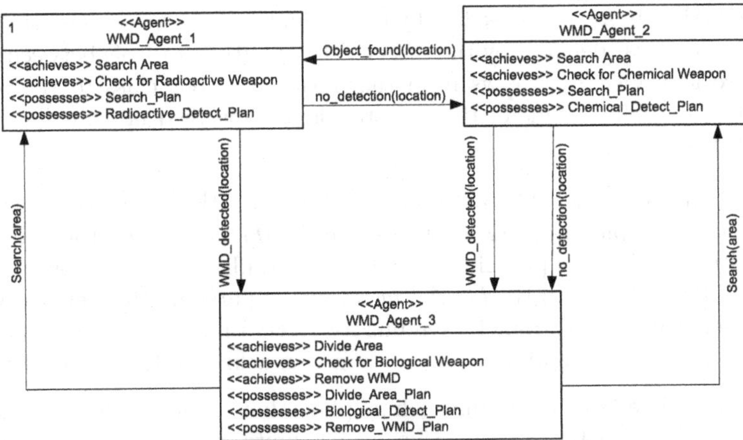

Fig. 11. Agent Class Model

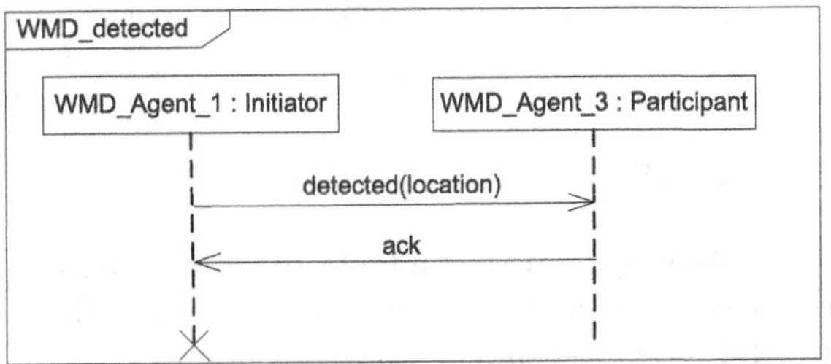

Fig. 12. Protocol Model

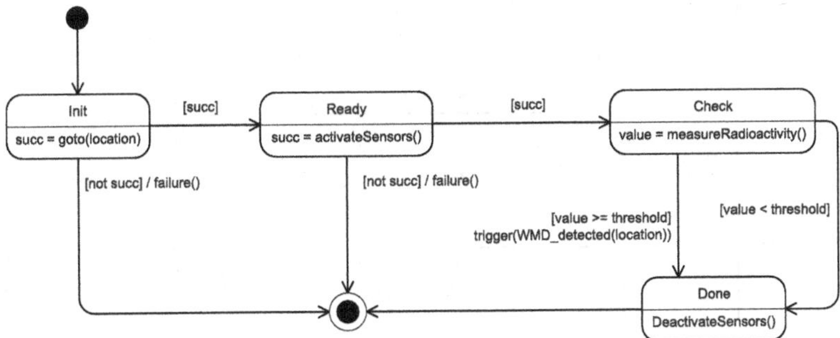

Fig. 13. Plan Model

Model Agent Class. The purpose of this task is to identify the type of agents in the organization and to document them in an Agent Class Model (Fig. 11). In our example, agents are defined based on the goals they can achieve and the capabilities they possess as specified by the "achieves" and "possesses" keywords in each agent class (denoted by the "Agent" keyword). Protocols between agent classes are identified by arrows from the initiating agent class to the receiving agent class. The details of these protocols are specified later in the Model Protocols task.

Model Protocol. The Model Protocol task defines the interactions between agents. For example, Fig. 12 captures the *WMD_detected* protocol where *WMD_Agent_1*, (who is pursuing the Check for Radioactive Weapon goal) detects a WMD and notifies *WMD_Agent_3* (who is pursuing the Remove WMD goal). The notification is done by sending a detected message with the location as parameter. Upon reception of this message, an acknowledgment is returned.

Model Plan. The Model Plan task defines plans that agents can follow to satisfy the organization's goals. To model this, we use finite state automata to capture both internal behavior and message passing between agents. Fig. 13 shows the *Radioactive_Detect_Plan* possessed by *WMD_Agent_2* to achieve the Check For Radioactive Weapon goal. The plan uses the goal parameter, location, as input. Notice that, a plan produced in this task should correspond to all related protocols.

4.2 Extended O-MaSE Process

To produce a more robust system that adapts to changes and internal failures, it is necessary to have a process that can produce additional information such as roles and policies. Roles define behavior that can be assigned to various agents

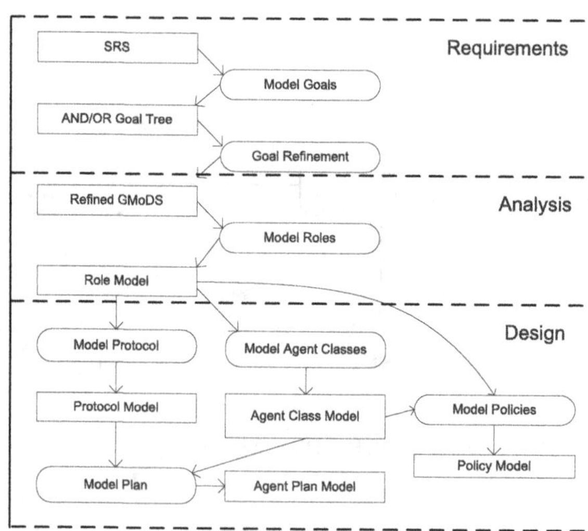

Fig. 14. Extended O-MaSE Process

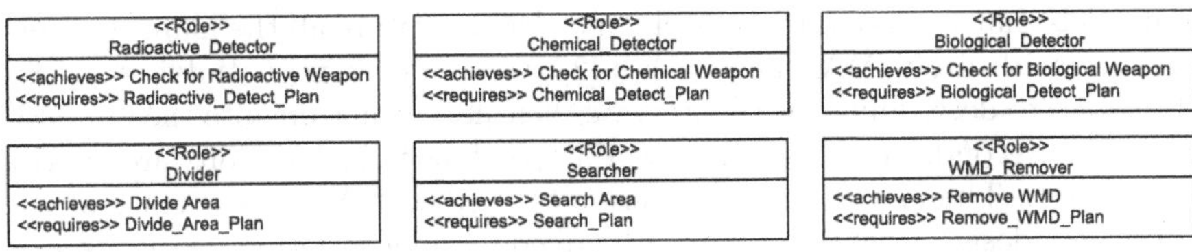

Fig. 15. Role Model

while policies guide and constrain overall system behavior. To accommodate such a system, additional Tasks must be introduced into the process to produce a Role Model and a Policy Model. This type of process will allow designer to produce a flexible, adaptive, and autonomous system. Fig. 14 shows the custom process for this example.

Model Roles. The Model Roles task identifies the roles in the organization and their interactions. Role Modelers focus on defining roles that accomplish one or more goals For example, each role in the Role Model shown in Fig. 15 achieves specific goals from Fig. 10; to do this, each role also requires specific capabilities.

Model Policies. The Model Policy task defines a set of rules that describe how an organization may or may not behave in particular situations [10]. For example, a policy "An agent may only play one role at a time" can be translated as

$$\forall a1, a2 : agent, r : role | a1.plays(r1) \wedge a1.plays(r2) \Longrightarrow r1 = r2.$$

5 Conclusions and Future Work

In this paper we have presented the O-MaSE Process Framework[1], which allows users to construct custom agent-oriented processes from a set of standard methods fragments. The main advantages of our approach is that: (1) all O-MaSE fragments are based on a common metamodel that ensures the method fragments can be combined in a coherent fashion, (2) each method fragment uses only concepts defined in the metamodel to produce work products that can be used as input to other method fragments; and, (3) the associated guidelines constrain how method fragments may be combined in order to assemble custom O-MaSE compliant processes that produce an appropriate set of products without producing unnecessary products.

Although we believe the O-MaSE is headed in the right direction with this approach [11], there is a considerable additional work that must be done in order to create a process amenable to industrial application. First, although the O-MaSE metamodel covers the most basic MAS concepts (i.e., agents, interaction, organization, and interactions), there are other agent-oriented methods and

[1] This work was supported by grants from the US National Science Foundation (0347545) and the US Air Force Office of Scientific Research (FA9550-06-1-0058).

metamodels that deserve further study in order to capture all the main concepts associated with other MAS approaches [2]. We are currently studying several metamodels to determine how to integrate their novel concepts into the O-MaSE metamodel. Second, we are currently working on how to include software metrics into O-MaSE. The aim of these metrics is to predict MAS performance at the analysis and design level [15]. Third, we are continuing to formalize our process guidelines in order to avoid ambiguities between the metamodel and the method fragments used to assembly the agent-oriented applications.[2]

Finally, we are integrating our working into agentTool III (aT3)[3], which is an analysis and design tool that supports the use of O-MaSE and exists as a plugin for the Eclipse platform[4]. Eventually, we envision adding a module to aT3 that allows process designers to create and to use custom O-MaSE compliant processes. Future plans for aT3 also include code generation for various platforms and integration with the Bogor model checking framework for verification and providing predictive metrics [16].

References

1. Bergenti, F., Gleizes, M.-P., Zambonelli, F. (eds.): Methodologies and Software Engineering for Agent Systems: The Agent-Oriented Software Engineering Handbook. Kluwer Academic Publishers, Dordrecht (2004)
2. Bernon, C., Cossentino, M., Pavón, J.: Agent Oriented Software Engineering. The Knowledge Engineering Review 20, 99–116 (2005)
3. Bernon, C., Cossentino, M., Gleizes, M., Turci, P., Zambonelli, F.: A study of some multi-agent meta-models. In: Odell, J.J., Giorgini, P., Müller, J.P. (eds.) AOSE 2004. LNCS, vol. 3382, pp. 62–77. Springer, Heidelberg (2005)
4. Beydoun, G., Gonzalez-Perez, C., Henderson-Sellers, B., Low, G.: Developing and Evaluating a Generic Metamodel for MAS Work Products. In: Garcia, A., et al. (eds.) Software Engineering for Multi-Agent Systems IV. LNCS, vol. 3194, pp. 126–142. Springer, Heidelberg (2005)
5. Brinkkemper, S.: Method Engineering: Engineering of Information Systems Development Methods and Tools. Jnl of Information and Software Technology 38(4), 275–280 (1996)
6. Cossentino, M., Gaglio, S., Henderson-Sellers, B., Seidita, V.: A metamodelling-based approach for method fragment comparison. In: Proceedings of the 11th International Workshop on Exploring Modeling Methods in Systems Analysis and Design (EMMSAD 2006), Luxembourg (June 2006)
7. DeLoach, S.A., Oyenan, W.H.: An Organizational Model and Dynamic Goal Model for Autonomous, Adaptive Systems. Technical Report No. MACR-TR-2006-01. Kansas State University (March 2006)
8. DeLoach, S.A., Valenzuela Jorge, L.: An Agent-Environment Interaction Model. In: Padgham, L., Zambonelli, F. (eds.) AOSE 2006. LNCS, vol. 4405, Springer, Heidelberg (2007)

[2] A detailed description of the current set of O-MaSE Tasks, Techniques, Work Products, and Producers can be found at http://macr.cis.ksu.edu/O-MaSE/

[3] See http://agenttool.projects.cis.ksu.edu/

[4] See http://www.eclipse.org/

9. Firesmith, D.G., Henderson-Sellers, B.: The OPEN Process Framework: An Introduction. Addison-Wesley, Harlow-England (2002)
10. Harmon, S.J., DeLoach, S.A., Robby: Guidance and Law Policies in Multiagent Systems. Multiagent & Cooperative Robotics Laboratory Technical Report No. MACR-TR-2007-02. Kansas State University (March 2007)
11. Henderson-Sellers, B., Giorgini, P. (eds.): Agent-Oriented Methodologies. Idea Group Inc. (2005)
12. Henderson-Sellers, B.: Process Metamodelling and Process Construction: Examples Using the OPEN Process Framework (OPF). Annals of Software Engineering 14(1-4), 341–362 (2002)
13. Luck, M., McBurney, P., Shehory, O., Willmott, S.: Agent Technology: Computing as Interaction (A Roadmap for Agent Based Computing), AgentLink (2005)
14. Odell, J., Parunak, V.D., Bauer, B.: Representing Agent Interactions Protocols in UML. In: Ciancarini, P., Wooldridge, M.J. (eds.) AOSE 2000. LNCS, vol. 1957, pp. 121–140. Springer, Heidelberg (2001)
15. Robby, DeLoach, S.A., Kolesnikov, V.A.: Using Design Metrics for Predicting System Flexibility. In: Baresi, L., Heckel, R. (eds.) FASE 2006 and ETAPS 2006. LNCS, vol. 3922, pp. 184–198. Springer, Heidelberg (2006)
16. Robby, Dwyer, M.B., Hatcliff, J.: Bogor: A Flexible Framework for Creating Software Model Checkers. In: Proceedings of the Testing: Academic & industrial Conference on Practice and Research Techniques, pp. 3–22. IEEE Comp. Society, Washington
17. Seidita, V., Cossentino, M., Gaglio, S.: A repository of fragments for agent systems design. In: Proceedings of the 7th Workshop from Objects to Agents (WOA 2006), Catania, Italy, pp. 130–137 (2006)

Extending Gaia with Agent Design and Iterative Development

Jorge Gonzalez-Palacios[1] and Michael Luck[2]

[1] School of Electronics and Computer Science, University of Southampton SO17 1BJ, UK
jlgp02r@ecs.soton.ac.uk
[2] Department of Computer Science, King's College London, Strand, London WC2R 2LS, UK
michael.luck@kcl.ac.uk

Abstract. Agent-oriented methodologies are an important means for constructing agent-based systems in a controlled repeatable form. However, agent-oriented methodologies have not received much acceptance in industrial environments, which can be partially explained by drawbacks in current agent-oriented methodologies, mainly in terms of applicability and comprehensiveness. Specifically, Gaia, one of the most cited methodologies, does not consider agent design, nor exhibits an agile methodological process. On the other hand, Gaia is based on organisational abstractions (which makes it suitable to cope with the design of complex systems) and possesses a simple methodological process whose neutrality makes it suitable for extensions. In this paper, we extend Gaia in two directions: we incorporate an agent design phase, and we enhance the methodological process with the use of iterations.

1 Introduction

Emergent technologies such as the Grid, peer-to-peer computing and ubiquitous computing, require systems that are open, highly distributed, and whose components exhibit some level of autonomy and pro-activeness. It has been claimed [12, 4] that the combined use of the multi-agent approach and organisational abstractions is a suitable means to model such systems. More specifically, organisational abstractions provide agent-oriented methodologies with the necessary design abstractions to cope with the development of complex systems in a systematic and controlled form.

Among agent-oriented methodologies based on organisational abstractions [13, 9, 3, 1], Gaia [13] is arguably the most used. The popularity of Gaia can be explained by the characteristics of its methodological process, which is simple to understand, has a good separation of development phases, and is neutral to any specific implementation technique or platform. However, Gaia focuses only on the *organisational* aspect of multi-agent systems (or macro level), leaving the actual design of agents (the micro level) unconsidered. This results in the absence of key development phases in the methodological process, such as agent design and implementation, both essential for the development of real world systems. Additionally, there is a propensity of the methodological process in general to construct systems once and for all, rather than part by part. This constitutes another drawback of Gaia, since it is very difficult to accomplish in a single opportunity the complete and detailed design of a whole complex system.

M. Luck and L. Padgham (Eds.): AOSE 2007, LNCS 4951, pp. 16–30, 2008.

Similarly, other development activities such as implementation and testing are also complicated if no explicit mechanism for decomposing the development is present.

In order to address these drawbacks, in this paper we present two extensions to the Gaia methodology. The first extension consists of incorporating a phase for agent design, based on the use of well-known *agent architectures* [11]. The second provides the Gaia process with a mechanism that decomposes the development of a system into *iterations*, an approach that has been used successfully in mature object-oriented methodologies, for example in the Unified Software Development Process [7].

The rest of this paper is organised in the following way. In Section 2 we briefly describe the main aspects of the Gaia methodology. In Section 3 we present the models and activities of our proposed agent design phase, and show how this phase fits in the Gaia methodology. In Section 4 we describe how we enhance the Gaia process to incorporate the agent design phase, and use iterations to decompose the development of a system. Finally, in Section 5 we present our conclusions.

2 Gaia Overview

Gaia [13] is an agent-oriented methodology based on the organisational concepts of roles, interactions, and organisations, and is divided into analysis, *architectural* design, and *detailed* design. A brief description of these concepts and phases is presented below.

2.1 Roles

Roles in Gaia represent well defined positions in the organisation, and the behaviour expected from them. Roles are characterised by: a *name* that identifies the role; a brief *description*; the *protocols* through which it interacts with other roles; the *activities* that the role performs without interacting with other roles; the *responsibilities* that express the functionality of the role (divided into *liveness properties* and *safety properties*, which relate to states of affairs that a role must bring about, and the conditions whose compliance the role must ensure, respectively); and the *permissions* to access the resources that the role needs for fulfilling its responsibilities. A role is depicted graphically by means of a *role schema*, an example of which is shown in Figure 1. As can be observed in the figure, boxes in the schema correspond to the characterisation of roles, and the names of activities are underlined to distinguish them from names of protocols. Additionally, the responsibilities are expressed in a purpose-built language that includes operators to represent sequence (.), alternatives (|) and indefinite repetition (^{w}).

2.2 Interactions

Interactions in Gaia are characterised by means of *protocol definitions*, which consist of: a *purpose*, that provides a brief description of the interaction; a list of *initiators*, that enumerates the roles that can start the interaction (usually a single element); a list of *responders* that enumerates the roles involved in the interaction; a list of *inputs* and *outputs* that provides the information required or produced during the interaction; and a brief *description* of the purpose of the interaction. This characterisation is represented graphically using a diagram like that shown in Figure 2.

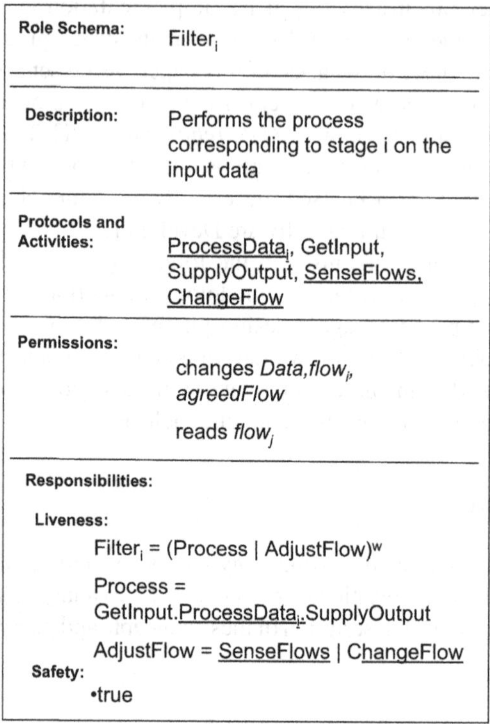

Fig. 1. Example of a role schema

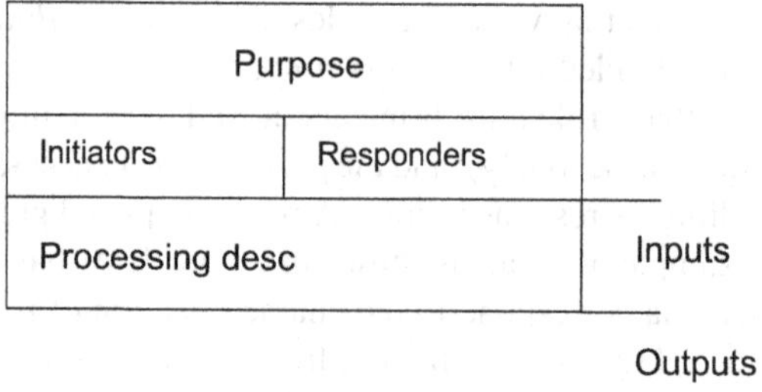

Fig. 2. Example of generic protocol definition

2.3 Organisations

An organisation in Gaia is formed of an organisational structure and a set of organisational rules. The former consists of a topology (the set of communication paths between the roles), and a control regime (relationships of authority between the roles). Organisational rules are constraints about how the different elements of the organisation interact, and either express situations that agents try to bring about, or express conditions that must be kept invariable.

2.4 Phases

The Analysis Phase. The analysis phase deals with collecting the features needed to understand the system, and consists of five activities: decomposition of the system into sub-organisations, which aims to partition the system into more manageable units; identification of environmental entities, which deals with creating a list of the resources used by agents while carrying out their activities and the rights of access to them (such as *read* or *change*); creation of the preliminary role model, which consists of the construction of all role schemata; creation of the preliminary interaction model, consisting in the creation of protocol definitions; and determining the organisational rules. It must be noted that, for the preliminary models, the emphasis is placed on the identification of roles and protocols, rather than in providing a complete description of their features.

The Architectural Design Phase. The next phase, architectural design, consists of two parts: the selection of an organisational structure, and the completion of the role and interaction models. The organisational structure plays an important part in the development of the system because it impacts on the way agents are coordinated, and on how the organisational rules are implemented. The completion of the role and interaction models deals with detailing the roles and protocols with the information obtained once the structure is determined. This activity includes the incorporation of new roles and interactions which may have resulted from the application of the previous step.

The Detailed Design Phase. The final phase of Gaia, the design phase, consists of producing the agent model, which involves determining which roles will be played by which agents, based on considerations such as efficiency and physical distribution.

3 Agent Design

In addition to what Gaia provides, we also need to consider the design of the internal composition of agents. However, since no agent design phase is included in Gaia, we have constructed one which takes its inputs from the organisational design and its output is a specification of *how* agents fulfil their requirements, which in turn serves as input to the implementation phase. Our proposed agent design phase complements the organisational design, in which agents are considered to be black boxes, and their detailed composition is ignored. Although, in general agents can play more than one role, in the following we assume that each agent plays exactly one role. At the end of the section, however, we provide guidelines for the general case in which an agent implements more than one role. The design phase consists of models and activities to produce these models, and is applied for each role of the system. These models and activities are described below.

3.1 Models

The agent design considers two models, the *structure model* and the *functionality model*, the former providing a structural decomposition of a role into classes, and the latter specifying how these classes collaborate to achieve the expected behaviour of the role.

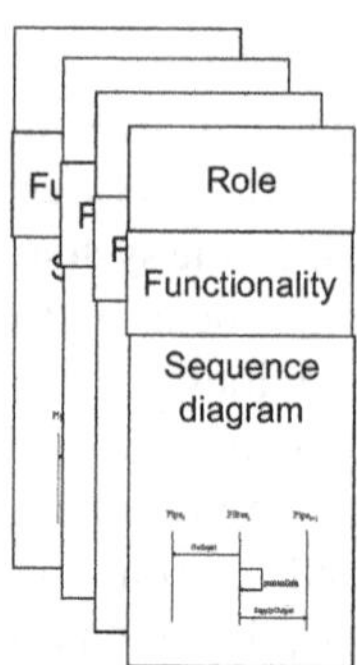

Fig. 3. The functionality model

The Structure Model. The structure model decomposes a role into classes, with each class encompassing data and functionality. In this way, the structure model is formed of class diagrams [5], one diagram for each role in the system. Although a class diagram is common in object-based techniques, it is used to represent different concepts — depending on the stage of the process in which it is used — so it is worth explaining the way in which we use it here. In the structure model, we use a class diagram to describe the main internal components of a role (as classes), and the static relationships between them, such as *dependence*, *part-of* and *inheritance*. The level of detail in the description must be sufficient to identify the core classes, and for each of these classes, the operations necessary to achieve the functionality of the role, and the internal information required to implement these methods (attributes). However, it is not necessary that the diagram includes all the classes needed to implement the role, nor all the attributes and methods to implement each class.

The Functionality Model. The functionality model consists of a set of *scenarios*, each of which represents a piece of functionality of the role, and contains a sequence diagram [5] showing how the role executes the functionality. The classes involved in the sequence diagram are those of the class diagram corresponding to the role. For example, in a market application, a possible scenario for the buyer role would represent the functionality *find the best price seller for a given product* by means of a sequence diagram showing how the classes of the buyer interact to achieve it. Figure 3 depicts a generic functionality model, and the composition of the scenarios.

Thus, any role in the system has an associated class diagram and a number of scenarios, each referring to a piece of functionality and described by means of a sequence diagram. This association is illustrated in Figure 4 for a generic role *i*, and a generic scenario *j*.

3.2 Activities

The activities involved in agent design consist of selecting an appropriate agent architecture and building the models described above. These activities are illustrated in

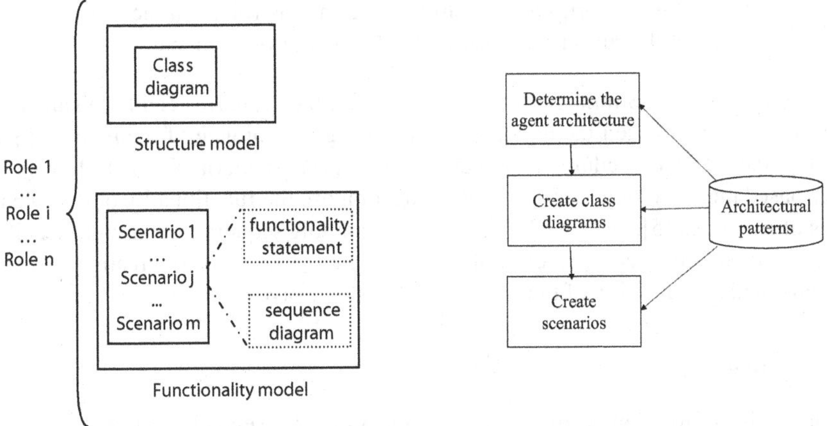

Fig. 4. The models (left) and activities (right) of the agent design

Figure 4, together with indications of those stages in which the use of architectural patterns is valuable. Architectural patterns [6] are design patterns that correspond to well established agent architectures, and include a class diagram, scenarios, and situation in which their use is advisable, and methodological guidelines for their use. In this way, for every role in the system, the following activities are performed.

Determining the Agent Architecture. In this activity, the architecture for the role is determined. In order to do this, several factors must be considered. The most important factor deals with the complexity of the behaviour expected from the role. For example, a simple behaviour can be more easily implemented through reactive architectures, whereas a complex behaviour may require the use of deliberative or hybrid architectures. A second factor deals with the level of pro-activeness required. Reactive architectures typically produce agents which are not pro-active, but operate on request of other agents, whereas BDI architectures are suitable for constructing pro-active agents. Other factors that affect the decision are the level of familiarity of developers with a specific architecture, and the support that different development tools provide for specific architectures. This activity can be facilitated by a catalogue of design patterns showing, for each architecture, its characteristics, advantages, limitations and applicability.

Creating Class Diagrams. In order to create the class diagram, two different methods can be used. The first is to employ an object-based methodology. The second consists of using a catalogue of *architectural patterns*, together with guidelines for selecting an appropriate pattern for a specific role. Regardless of which method is used to construct the class diagram, the inputs are taken from the organisational design models of Gaia. Specifically, the role model provides three inputs: the liveness responsibilities (which describe the functionality that the role is expected to exhibit), the safety responsibilities (describing the conditions that must hold during the lifetime of the role), and the permissions (which contain the environmental entities employed by the role, together with the rights to access them). Additionally, the interaction model of Gaia provides the inputs and outputs of the protocols in which a role participates, the organisational structure provides the authority relationships involving the role, and the organisational rule model provides the rules that constrain the behaviour of the agent.

Creating Scenarios. Similarly to the class models, the scenarios can be obtained by following an object-based methodology, or by using a catalogue of architectural patterns together with procedures to select the appropriate pattern. When following an object-based methodology, it is advisable to decompose the functionality of the role by means of *use cases* [5], and then build the corresponding sequence diagram for each of them. The inputs for creating the set of scenarios are the same as for creating the class diagrams, with the addition of the class diagrams themselves.

3.3 Example

In order to illustrate agent design, we consider a system for segmenting users according to common interests. This system is based on [8], used to illustrate the INGENIAS methodology. It deals with a segmentation of users in groups of common interests, and is meant to be used for marketing purposes, such as for offering specific products only to potentially interested users. The system is conceived as a multi-agent system in which each (human) user is represented by a *personal clerk*, which groups with other personal clerks to form a community. Such a community is represented by a *clerk of community*, and relates to one subject. This segmentation of interests helps to control the quality of documents provided to users, as explained below.

A community can be seen as a source of information to which users subscribe to obtain relevant information for their interests. Once subscribed, a user begins to receive information from the community. This information originates from members of the community or from other sources of information such as forums of news and other communities (different communities can exchange information as long as it is authorised by the administrator of the system). The information that the users receive passes through a series of filters to ensure its quality.

When a user suggests information to the community, the community first compares the suggestion with the *community profile*. If the information matches the community profile, the document is evaluated by a set of members of the community. However, before being evaluated by their users, each of their personal clerks decides, on their own, whether the document is interesting to its user. In the affirmative case, the evaluation request is presented to the user, so that he evaluates the document. In the negative case, a vote against the document is produced. The suggested document is approved only if most of the consulted members vote in favour of the document, and the positive and negative evaluations are registered and used in the acceptance of future suggestions.

The permanence of members in a community is subject to the following restrictions: first, users who have suggested many documents evaluated negatively are expelled, since their interests are not in accordance with those of the community; and second, users who evaluate too many documents negatively are also expelled, since they have not shown interest in the type of information provided by the community.

Community clerks and personal clerks describe their interests by means of a *profile*, which can take the form of a set of documents (the last documents evaluated positively), keywords or categories. The keywords and categories of a clerk can be modified by its

Role Schema:	Profiler
Description:	Decides if a document is relevant to a community
Protocols and Activities:	MatchDoc, ApproveDoc, matchProfileDoc, CountVotes
Permissions :	read s document, profile change s evaluation.
Responsibilities: Liveness:	
	Profiler = ((MatchDoc . matchProfileDoc) | (ApproveDoc . CountVotes))^{w}
Safety :	.

Fig. 5. The *Profiler* role

user. Users connect with their clerks by means of a Web interface that allows them to: suggest documents, evaluate documents, see documents, and see statistics of operation.

In the following, we assume that the analysis and organisational design have identified a role in charge of determining if a proposed document is relevant to a community, hereafter called the *Profiler*, and whose role schema is shown in Figure 5. Additionally, we assume that, according to the organisational structure of the system, the *Profiler* role is completely subordinated to the authority of the community clerk, so that its behaviour can be modelled as a process of receiving orders, performing activities related to accomplishing these orders, and replying with the results produced by the activities. Considering its purely reactive behaviour, we conclude that the *Profiler* role can be modelled by means of the subsumption architecture [2].

The Subsumption Architecture. The subsumption architecture [2, 10] is a reactive architecture developed by Brooks, that bases its function on the existence of *behaviours* and their relationships of *inhibition*. Each behaviour is intended to achieve a specific task and associates perceptual inputs with actions. For example, in the case of a vehicle control application, the behaviour, *changing direction if an obstacle is found in front*, associates the perceptual input, *an obstacle is in front*, with the task, *change direction*. To pursue its aim, each behaviour continually senses the environment until the environmental state matches its associated perceptual input, in which case the associated action is performed. In this example, the environment is continually sensed until an obstacle is detected in front of the vehicle, in which case the action of changing direction is performed. However, since an environment state may match more than one behaviour, an *inhibition relation* is used to specify priorities. According to this inhibition relation, the behaviours are arranged into layers, with lower layers capable of inhibiting upper layers, and the higher the layer the more abstract its behaviour. For example, in the case of vehicle control, the behaviour corresponding to *collision avoidance* occupies a lower layer than that of the behaviour corresponding to *reach the destination*, since avoiding an obstacle has priority over reaching the destination. Therefore, using the subsumption architecture, we construct the structure and functionality models corresponding to the *Profiler* role, as described below.

Structure Model. The *Profiler* interacts with its environment by means of interaction protocols. As can be observed in its schema (Figure 5), the *Profiler* role participates in two protocols: *MatchDoc* and *ApproveDoc*. According to this, the environment perceived by the *Profiler* can be described as the set of tuples, *(command, content1, content2)*, where: *command* is an identifier of the type of protocol (for example, *Match* for the *MatchDoc* protocol, or *Approve* for the *ApproveDoc* protocol); *content1* is a document; and *content2* is an *evaluation* if *command* is *Match*, or *nil* otherwise (this corresponds to the outputs of these protocols, as stated in the interaction model). Accordingly, there are two behaviours for this role, as described below.

b1. *if (Match, d, e) is perceived then execute MatchProfileDoc(d) and continue the execution of protocol MatchDoc.*

b2. *if (Approve, d, e) is perceived then execute IsApproved(d, e) and continue the execution of protocol ApproveDoc.*

Here, *MatchProfileDoc* and *IsApproved* are activities of the *Profiler* role, dealing with matching a document to the community profile, and approving a document, respectively, as is stated in its role description. Note that, in this particular case, the inhibition relationship is irrelevant, since no perceived state can match both *b1* and *b2*.

The class diagram for the structural model is obtained by enhancing the class diagram of the subsumption pattern, with the particular characteristics of the *Profiler* role, resulting in the diagram shown in Figure 6. The enhancements consist in the elimination

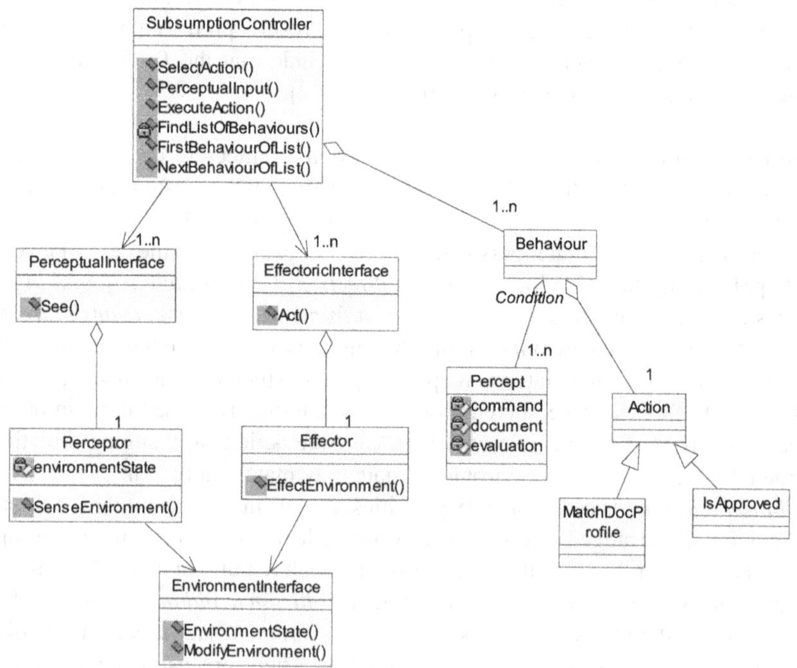

Fig. 6. Class diagram of the structure model

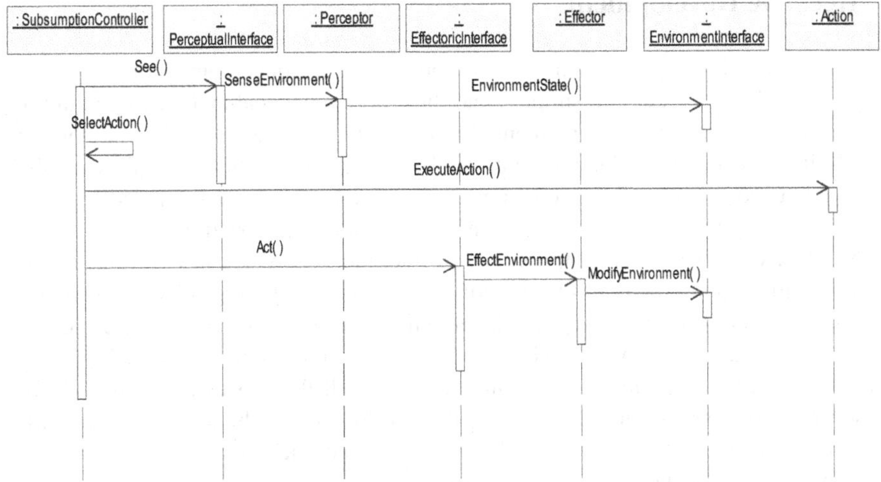

Fig. 7. Sequence diagram of the functionality model

of the original *Inhibitor* class (since no inhibition relationship is required), the description of the information perceived (*Percept* class), and the representation of the *Inhibitor* activities as actions of behaviours.

Functionality Model. The operation of the *Profiler* is so simple that only one scenario is needed to describe its functionality. Such a scenario describes the dynamics followed by the classes to accomplish the functionality of the role, and is expressed by a sequence diagram adapted from the subsumption pattern. This sequence diagram, which is shown in Figure 7, is easier to interpret if we consider that the *Profiler* perceives the environment by receiving messages and interpreting their content, and affects the environment by sending messages.

3.4 Agents that Play More Than One Role

In the previous description of the agent design phase, the agent in question encompasses only one role. However, in general this is not the case, since a given agent may encompass more than one role for reasons of efficiency, physical distribution and facility of implementation. When more than one role is included in one agent, the agent design is applied to each of the roles, and the resulting models analysed to identify common classes. These common classes can then be merged, resulting in a reduction of the number of classes, particularly when the roles are modelled by the same agent architecture. However, an excessive merging of classes increases the coupling between the roles, and can bring some difficult problems. For example, in the case of the subsumption architecture, when merging the behaviours of two different roles, a new inhibition relationship (that considers the behaviours of the two roles) must be determined.

Now that we have described the agent design phase, we also need to consider how it might be incorporated into the methodological process. We do this below.

4 Iterative Development

The main idea behind applying an *iterative* approach to the development of a system is to divide the development into simpler, and thus more manageable, units. Each unit is then analysed, designed and implemented to produce an executable deliverable which extends, in functionality, the previous deliverable, in such a way that the final executable deliverable encompasses all the functionality expected from the system. This reduces the risk of producing the *wrong* system, and of exceeding delivery times.

The iterative approach decomposes the development activities in two dimensions. The first dimension corresponds to the typical ways of developing software, which in our case consists of decomposing the development into analysis, architectural design, detailed design, and agent design. The second dimension relies on the use of *iterations*, which consist of the application, to some degree, of all the phases mentioned above, and several iterations are carried out during the development of the whole system. Early iterations focus on the first phases, analysis and architectural design, while subsequent iterations focus on the last phase, agent design.

While the decomposition into phases is common for all applications, iteration decomposition varies from application to application, in terms of work dedicated to each phase, number of iterations, and, more importantly, purpose. As a general rule, the larger the system, the more iterations are needed. In addition, the actual decomposition of the development cycle into iterations is guided by the functionality of the system. This means that the functionality of the system is divided into parts, one or more of which are assigned to an iteration, whose purpose is to accomplish that part of the functionality. The order in which the iterations must be carried out is important and must be established as part of the iteration decomposition, since the most critical and important parts of functionality must be considered first, to obtain earlier user feedback and foresee possible changes in delivery times.

Some guidelines for iteration decomposition are as follows: the set of iterations must cover all the functionality expected from the system; the early iterations in the decomposition must be occupied by those functionalities that form the core of the system (such as critical processes that are poorly described), or by those functionalities that involve a high risk of creating the wrong system or delaying the delivery of the system (such as the employment of new technology); early iterations must provide insight of most of the system; and it is desirable to achieve a balance in the iterations, so that no iteration is too big nor too small.

To illustrate all this, we apply the iterative process to the problem described in Section 3.3. First, the functionality of the system can be divided into several parts.

Part 1. Approve new information: receiving, filtering, and disseminating documents suggested by users.

Part 2. Exchange information: the part dealing with the exchange of information between different communities or other sources of information.

Part 3. Create communities: the process of creating new communities in the system.

Part 4. Eliminate communities: elimination of unwanted communities from the system.

Part 5. Register new users: the process of accepting new users in the communities.
Part 6. Expel users: the part dealing with expelling unwanted users from communities.

This partition is used as the basis for the iteration decomposition of the system, which also takes into account the following two factors. First, it considers the potential size of each of the parts, and tries to keep a balance in the sizes of the iterations. Second, it prioritises the parts by their importance in the functionality of the system. In particular, it recognises *Part 1* as the core of the system, since it directly supports the accomplishment of the goal of the system, and is also the most complex part, involving several components of the system. The decomposition of the system into iterations is presented in Table 1, and the next section describes the first of these iterations.

Table 1. Iteration decomposition of the case study

Iteration	Parts	Functionalities
1	Part 1	Approve new information
2	Part 5 and Part 6	Register new users and expel users
3	Part 3 and Part 4	Create communities and Eliminate communities
4	Part 2	Exchange information

4.1 First Iteration

For the first iteration, the following are the roles that form the role model: the *Profiler*, which decides if a document is relevant to a community; the *PersonalClerk*, in charge of interacting with a user; the *CommunityClerk*, that act as the representative of a community; and the *Evaluator*, which decides if a document is interesting to a particular user. The role schema for the *Profiler* was presented previously in Figure 5, but lack of space prevents us from including the other schemas.

The interaction model consists of six protocols, which are summarised in Table 2. In this table, note the existence of the environmental entities *Recommender*, *Reader* and *Voter*. The resulting organisational structure is a tree with the CommunityClerk at the root, and a peer branch to the PersonalClerk, and authority branches to the Profiler and to the Evaluator. Lastly, and assuming that each role is implemented by a different agent, the first iteration ends with the design of each of the four corresponding agents. In Section 3.3 we presented the design of the *Profiler*, but space constraints prevent us from presenting the design of the other agents.

Table 2. Interactions in the first iteration

Protocol	Initiator	Collaborators	Description
ProposeDoc	Recommender	PersonalClerk	a user suggests a document
DisseminateDoc	CommunityClerk	PersonalClerk, Reader	an approved document is distributed
EvaluateDoc	CommunityClerk	Evaluator, Voter	a user and her clerk evaluate a document
MatchDoc	CommunityClerk	Profiler	a document is checked against a profile
ApproveDoc	CommunityClerk	Profiler	acceptance or rejection of a document
ChangeProfile	Reader	PersonalClerk	a user changes her profile

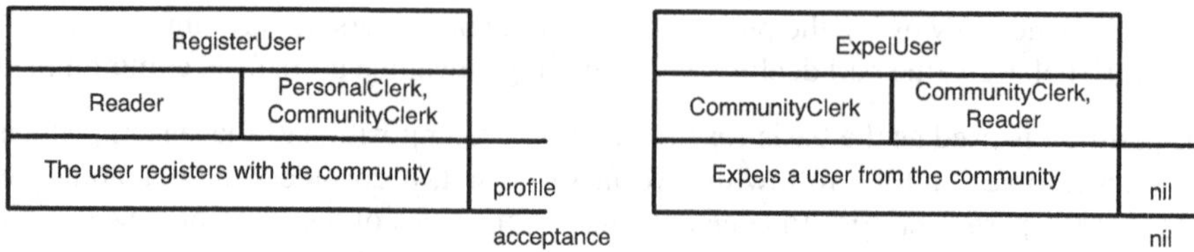

Fig. 8. Preliminary protocol description of registering and expelling users

4.2 Second Iteration

The second iteration addresses another part of the functionality of the system, and consists of enhancing the results of the previous iteration in terms of adding elements to the models, extending elements or modifying them. For example, in the case of the preliminary role model, new roles can be added and existing roles can be modified to include interaction with the new roles. In this example, the second iteration deals with the registration of new users and the expulsion of inadequate users, as described below.

In order to incorporate the functionality of the second iteration, no new roles are required, since it can be carried out by the *PersonalClerk* and *CommunityClerk*. However, the incorporation of new protocols to the preliminary interaction model is necessary to cope with these tasks. Such protocol descriptions are shown in Figure 8, the first of which refers to the registration of new users and the second to the expulsion of users.

The role model obtained in the first iteration is updated to incorporate these introduced protocols, specifically, the *PersonalClerk* and *CommunityClerk* schemas should be modified to include them. In contrast, the organisational structure needs no modification, since the introduced protocols do not change either the communication paths or the authority relationships between the roles. Finally, since no new roles were introduced in the second iteration, the agent design phase consists only of updating the design of those roles that were affected, namely the *PersonalClerk* and *CommunityClerk*.

The completion of the example would require the accomplishment of the rest of the iterations, but since they are very similar, they are not included in this paper.

5 Conclusions

Gaia has been recognised as a valuable methodology for the development of open complex systems based on the multi-agent approach. However, in order to be used in the development of real world systems, Gaia needs to be extended in several respects. In this paper, we have extended the Gaia methodology in two directions. The first extension deals with the design of the internal composition of agents in a multi-agent system. For this, we have presented an agent design phase that follows the organisational design phase of Gaia and produces an object-based specification from which an implementation can follow. This agent design phase relies on the use of agent architectures as a means to specify the classes that form an agent and the way they interact to fulfil its behaviour. As an example of the application of the design phase, we have presented the design of a reactive agent which is based on the subsumption architecture. Although simple, this example shows how entities acting as service providers can be agentified, which can also be applied to legacy software.

The benefits of this approach are that the resulting design phase does not depend on a specific agent architecture, but developers are free to select the architecture that best models a given agent. Nevertheless, the drawback of this approach is that agent architectures are not based on organisational concepts (like those on which Gaia's organisational design is based), so it is necessary to *adapt* them. However, since this process is essentially independent of the domain, it can be pre-determined and then reused.

The second extension to Gaia presented in this paper provides Gaia with a flexible methodological process that facilitates the development of large systems. This enhancement consists of decomposing the development into iterations, each of which corresponds to a part of the functionality of the system and consists of the analysis, organisational design and agent design phases.

The benefits of this iterative process are multiple. First, it enables the production of executable deliverables from early stages of the development. Second, it explicitly prioritises those parts of the system that are critical, unclear or involve technological risks. Finally, it speeds up the development by incrementing the parallelism in development tasks. The full potential of this iterative process, however, is limited by the lack of an implementation phase, which is subject of further work.

References

1. Bresciani, P., Perini, A., Giorgini, P., Giunchiglia, F., Mylopoulos, J.: Tropos: An agent-oriented software development methodology. Autonomous Agents and Multi-Agent Systems (8), 203–236 (2004)
2. Brooks, R.A.: A robust layered control system for a mobile robot. IEEE Journal of Robotics and Automation 2(1), 14–23 (1986)
3. DeLoach, S.A.: Modeling organizational rules in the multiagent systems engineering methodology. In: Cohen, R., Spencer, B. (eds.) Canadian AI 2002. LNCS (LNAI), vol. 2338, Springer, Heidelberg (2002)
4. Ferber, J., Gutknecht, O., Michel, F.: From agents to organisations: An organizational view of multi-agent systems. In: Giorgini, P., Müller, J.P., Odell, J.J. (eds.) AOSE 2003. LNCS, vol. 2935, pp. 214–230. Springer, Heidelberg (2004)
5. Fowler, M., Scott, K.: UML Destilled: Applying the Standard Object Modeling Language. Addison-Wesley, Reading (1997)
6. Gonzalez-Palacios, J.: Increasing Accessibility in Agent-Oriented Methodologies. PhD thesis, University of Southampton (to appear, 2006)
7. Jacobson, I., Rumbaugh, J., Booch, G.: The Unified Software Development Process. Addison-Wesley, Reading (1999)
8. Mestras, J.P., Sanz, J.G., Fuentes, R.: (1999), `http://grasia.fdi.ucm.es/ingenias/`
9. Omicini, A.: SODA: Societies and infraestructures in the analysis and design of agent-based systems. In: Ciancarini, P., Wooldridge, M.J. (eds.) AOSE 2000. LNCS, vol. 1957, pp. 185–194. Springer, Heidelberg (2001)
10. Wooldridge, M.: Multiagent Systems: a Modern Approach to Distributed Artificial Intelligence, chapter Intelligent Agents. MIT Press, Cambridge (1999)

11. Wooldridge, M., Jennings, N.R.: Intelligent agents: theory and practice. The Knowledge Engineering Review 10(2), 115–152 (1995)
12. Zambonelli, F., Jennings, N.R., Wooldridge, M.: Organisational abstractions for the analysis and design of multi-agent systems. In: First International Workshop on Agent-Oriented Software Engineering, pp. 127–141 (2000)
13. Zambonelli, F., Jennings, N.R., Wooldridge, M.: Developing multiagent systems: The Gaia methodology. ACM Transactions on Software Engineering and Methodology 12(3), 317–370 (2003)

AgentPrIMe: Adapting MAS Designs to Build Confidence

Simon Miles[1], Paul Groth[2], Steve Munroe[2], Michael Luck[1], and Luc Moreau[2]

[1] Department of Computer Science, King's College London, UK
{simon.miles,michael.luck}@kcl.ac.uk
[2] School of Electronics and Computer Science, University of Southampton, UK
lavm@ecs.soton.ac.uk

Abstract. The products of systems cannot always be judged at face value: the process by which they were obtained is also important. For instance, the rigour of a scientific experiment, the ethics with which an item was manufactured and the use of services with particular licensing all affect how the results of those processes are valued. However, in systems of autonomous agents, and particularly those with multiple independent contributory organisations, the ability of agents to choose how their goals or responsibilities are achieved can hide such *process qualities* from users. The issue of ensuring that users are able to check these process qualities is a software engineering one: the developer must decide to ensure that adequate data is recorded regarding processes and safeguards implemented to ensure accuracy. In this paper, we describe AgentPrIMe, an adjunct to existing agent-oriented methodologies that allows system designs to be adapted to give users confidence in the results they produce. It does this by adaptations to the design for *documentation, corroboration, independent storage* and *accountability*.

1 Introduction

Agent-based systems have particular qualities that require their activity to be justified to their users. First, since they are based on autonomous components, decisions that make use of expert knowledge or have significant consequences can be handled by software, and so the decisions made by such software must be seen to be reliable if the software is to be widely adopted. In addition, by having multiple, distributed points of control, an application may rely on services not under the authority of the user, and whose side-effects may not be apparent to the user: a user may wish to know that the services do not produce their results in an undesirable way, such as being illegal, unethical, etc. Finally, in systems where agents represent localised concerns of distributed users, it is important to know that agents have not released private information more widely than desired.

At some level, this problem has been well researched. There are already approaches to formally specify a multi-agent system, enabling developers to verify its desirable properties [9]. However, this does not in itself inform developers about what factors need to be considered, nor is it (commercially) realistic to

M. Luck and L. Padgham (Eds.): AOSE 2007, LNCS 4951, pp. 31–43, 2008.

assume fine-grained knowledge of third-party services used in an application. Mechanisms have been designed to guide agent behaviour towards reliable results or to constrain agent behaviour to only desirable results, including contracts, norms, protocols, trust evaluations etc.

Nevertheless, we argue that, even with this breadth of beneficial technology, there are significant outstanding issues. First, agent-based systems must be designed not just to be reliable but to make their reliability apparent to users if they are to have *confidence* in the system. Second, the above mechanisms concentrate on the value or otherwise of *results* or the *cost* of achieving those results, both aspects of the system that can be immediately judged by the user or an agent acting on their behalf. Because of this emphasis, other, hidden but still important, aspects are ignored. In particular, the mechanisms do not address how to determine *process qualities* that are not immediately apparent in the result returned by an agent but have an impact on its worth. Examples of important process qualities occur in many domains, such as the following.

- The rigour of the scientific experiment that produced some result.
- The ethics (fair trade, environmental impact, etc.) of the process that led to the sale of an item.
- The use of services with licenses that make a result unpatentable.
- The actual inter-dependence of two apparently independent recommendations.

The qualities of the process that led to a result are all evident in the *provenance* of that result, i.e. everything that caused the result to be as it is. For the provenance of a result, and process qualities evident from it, to be made apparent to a user requires that an agent-based system be engineered to *record* adequate information to determine both *(1)* what has occurred in the system prior to the result being produced, and *(2)* which of those events are causally related to the eventual result.

However, in a system of flexible autonomous agents, such agents may lie or collude to hide the actions they have taken where it is in their interests to do so (as is true in the four process examples above). Similarly, without specifically designing a system that prevents agents' inaccuracy, a user can be misled. Therefore, we argue that agent-oriented designs must be specifically adapted to mitigate for inaccuracy and provide confidence that users can determine exactly how a multi-agent system came to produce a result.

In this paper, we describe *AgentPrIMe*, an additional stage for existing methodologies. It is used, firstly, for determining what information needs recording and how to adapt the relevant agents to do so. Then, it tackles what must be established of an agent owned by a third-party in order to rely on it to provide compatible and verifiable information regarding provenance.

2 AgentPrIMe

A *methodology fragment* [8] is a software engineering procedure that is used in addition to the usual stages of a methodology when designing an application. It aims to add or ensure some functionality of the system, that may otherwise not be guaranteed by the original methodology. Aspect-oriented software engineering [6] provides an example of methodology adjuncts that provide functionality pervading across a design (usually object-oriented). Others have applied aspect-orientation to agent-based systems [3], but we do not use the aspect concept here because, while it is not entirely inappropriate, it carries connotations of cutting across agents in a way that pre-supposes that the process they are involved in is fixed at design-time. Process qualities are concerned with processes that have already occurred in a system that may be flexible, open and unreliable.

A desirable quality of a methodology adjunct is *methodology-neutrality*, so that it is general and sufficiently well-defined to be applied as part of as many methodologies as possible. This is a distinct quality from the comparable requirement of methodologies (and their adjuncts) of being *widely applicable* to a range of applications.

AgentPrIMe is a methodology adjunct for agent-oriented software engineering methodologies. We will refer to the methodology to which it is acting as an adjunct as the *extended methodology*. The outcome of applying AgentPrIMe is a set of *adaptations* to be applied to a system design, so that queries regarding provenance can be reliably answered. It builds on an existing methodology adjunct, Provenance Incorporation Methodology (PrIMe), described elsewhere [11], which is concerned with adapting software to help users determine provenance of results, but considers only service-oriented systems. In particular, PrIMe does not address issues relevant to an agent-oriented design, where autonomous components choose their own methods to achieve their goals and so may be dishonest.

There are two aims of AgentPrIMe: *(1)* to make the provenance of results available to users of the system, and *(2)* to ensure that, as far as possible, the provenance is accurate even when agents in the system may be unreliable. Specifically, AgentPrIMe has two phases, described in detail in the following sections.

- Identify the causes of agent actions in the design, instances of which are recorded as the agents act. This phase results in adaptations to agents so that they record such causes for users to later query.
- Identify where additional guarantees of accuracy are required, so as to be able to rely on what agents have recorded. This phase results in adaptations to the interactions between agents, so that users can have more confidence that what agents have recorded is accurate.

AgentPrIMe relies on understanding the types of agents that will exist within a system, so that their effects in processes and the interactions possible between those agents can be understood. It can affect both how those agents are ultimately implemented, and may alter the possible interactions between them, as will be seen in the subsequent sections. These dependencies mean that AgentPrIMe is ideally applied at a particular point in the extended methodology, when the design is sufficiently well developed to adapt but not so far developed that effort is wasted. To be more concrete, we specify below at which point

AgentPrIMe would apply when using various methodologies that the reader may be familiar with.

- In Gaia [14], AgentPrIMe must be applied after the *agent model* and *acquaintance model* have been completed. This is because it applies to *agent types*, where the functionality of an agent of each type is well-defined, and the interactions between them dictated by the acquaintance model.
- In MaSE [2], AgentPrIMe must be applied after the *agent classes* and *conversations* have been created, for analogous reasons to those given for Gaia.
- In Prometheus [13], AgentPrIMe operates on the *agent overview*, after the architecture design and before the detailed design.
- In SODA [12], AgentPrIMe requires the data from the *interaction* and *agent models*, so applies after SODA has completed.

3 Causality in Multi-Agent Systems

In this section, we describe the first phase of AgentPrIMe, where system designs are adapted to document the causal relationships between agent actions. This gives users the facilities to determine the provenance of agent actions and outputs. We consider the unreliability of agents in the next section.

3.1 Causality within Agents

A key part of AgentPrIMe is to allow agents to document the *causes* of their actions, so that this information can later be used to determine what occurred in a process. The possible causes in a model depend on the extended methodology, but we discuss some examples in this section and then show how these can be generalised in a well-defined way for methodology-neutrality.

A variety of factors influence an agent's behaviour at a given instant, as illustrated in the examples summarised in Figure 1. Here, we are concerned with behaviour that affects the environment, i.e. actions, shown as the *output* of the agent. Depending on the agent model used by the extended methodology, the influencing factors can include the agent's *goals*, *responsibilities* or *rights*. Often, the latter factors are due to the *roles* that the agent is playing within a system at that instant, with the goals and responsibilities having been allocated to the roles in applying the extended methodology [7]. Additionally, triggers from the environment, which include messages from other agents, shown as *input* in the figure, influence how an agent acts.

AgentPrIMe, and its supporting technologies, allow an agent to assert the *causal relationship* between two *occurrences*. These assertions, called *relationship p-assertions*, can be stored for later interrogation by a user, as discussed further below. Applied to an agent design, this means that relationships can be asserted between an output (the effect) and the inputs, goals, responsibilities, and so on that caused it to take place. These relationships are depicted in Figure 2. Using the examples already described, these causal relationships can be used to assert:

- that an output message was sent in response to an input message;
- that an action was taken to attempt to fulfil a goal;
- that an action was taken because it was part of the reponsibilities of the agent; or
- that an action was taken because it was allowed for by a right of the agent.

In recent work [10], we have discussed one particular example of this: how the documentation of the causal effects of goals can be used to make applications more robust.

However, the concepts described above are only a subset of those used in agent-oriented methodologies. Others include motivations, beliefs, intentions, adherence to protocols and so on, and many of these may be asserted as causes of an agent's action. In order for AgentPrIMe to be methodology-neutral, we need a general definition of whether something specified as part of applying a

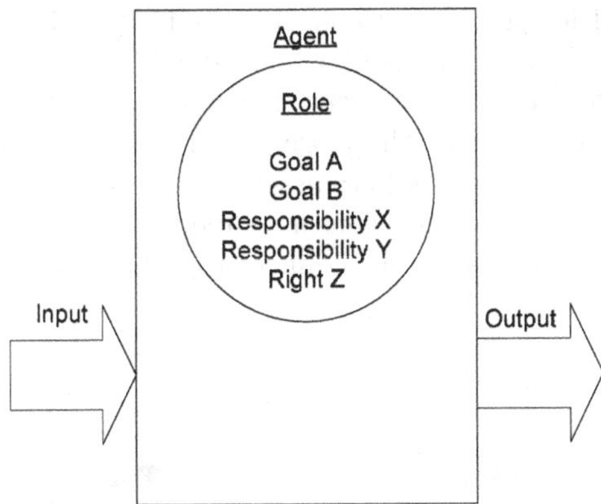

Fig. 1. Potential causes of an agent's actions

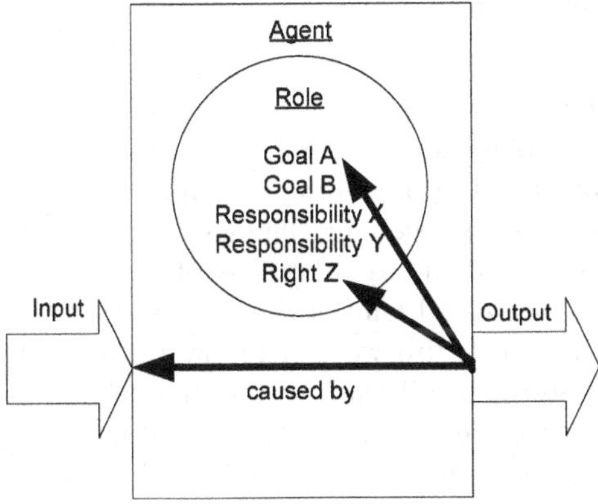

Fig. 2. Causal relationships between an agent's action and its causes

methodology is a causal relationship, and adopt the following definition derived from work in the philoshopy of mind [5].

> E was caused by C, if E would not have occurred without C not having occurred, all else being equal.

By applying this definition, we can determine whether a particular factor influenced an action regardless of the methodology extended. For example, we can say that a particular action would not have been taken if the agent didn't have a responsibility to do so, or that an action would not have occurred (because it could not) if the agent did not have the right to do so. The important quality of this definition is that it is *system independent*, relying only on a notion of occurrence.

3.2 Causality between Agents

One of the causes of an agent's actions discussed above is a message received from another agent. This is of particular interest when examining process qualities: it is not the actions of a single agent that matter but of a set of agents that ultimately produce some result. Therefore, in addition to asserting causal relationships, AgentPrIMe allows agents to assert the inputs it receives and outputs it sends to other agents. These assertions are called *interaction p-assertions*, and, along with relationship p-asssertions, connect together the actions of one agent to those of another.

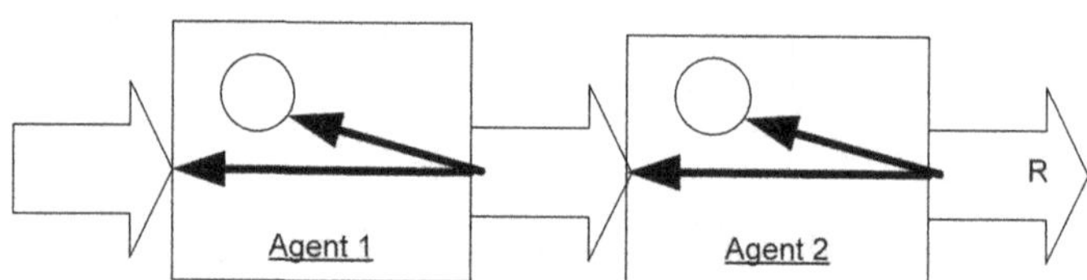

Fig. 3. A chain of interactions and causal relationships between agents

A chain of two agents is shown in Figure 3. In this figure, Agent 1 sends a message to Agent 2. This behaviour by Agent 1 is caused by the factors discussed in the previous section, possibly including communications from other agents. Agent 2 may act on the basis of receiving the message, possibly sending messages to other agents. Thus, an adequate collection of interaction and relationship p-assertions provides a connected trail of the process that led to a result. From the result, R, shown in the figure we can follow the causal relationships and interactions back to determine all the factors that ultimately caused it to be as it is. Note that here, we are describing the actual interactions that an agent engages in at run time. How to design agent interactions to best meet system requirements has been addressed by others [1].

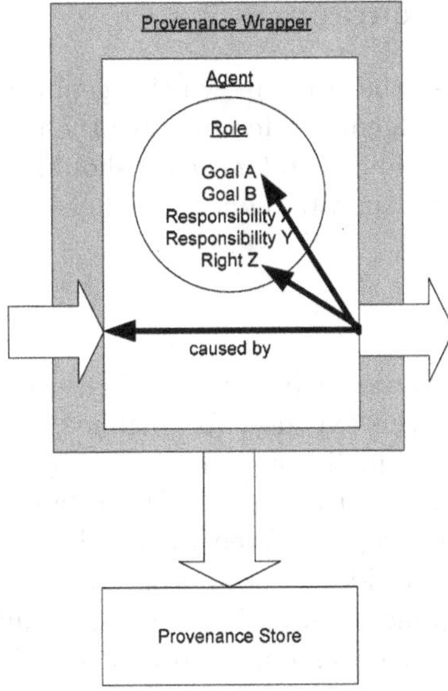

Fig. 4. Wrappers are adaptations to agents that automatically document incoming and outgoing messages, and causal relationships, and send them to a provenance store

3.3 The Wrapper Adaptation

The p-assertions described above must be recorded in repositories so that users can later query them. We call such repositories *provenance stores*. Such recording of interaction and relationship p-assertions can be realised in a system by applying a *wrapper* to each agent that is doing the recording, as shown in Figure 4. As messages come into or leave an agent, the wrapper records interaction p-assertions regarding their content, and relationship p-assertions regarding their causes.

3.4 Provenance

An important part of our approach is to use a common, open data model for p-assertions. This means that all agents can independently and autonomously record documentation of their activities in the same format, and a user can examine and interpret this documentation without relying on implementation details of those agents. The full data model is documented elsewhere [4].

By examining the provenance of a result, we can therefore determine the procedure that was followed to produce it. In theory, this would allow us to check such process qualities as the rigour of a scientific result, or whether businesses with dubious ethical records were used in manufacturing a good. However, doing so depends on the agents involved in a process accurately documenting what they do, an unreasonable assumption in many domains. In the following section, we show how AgentPrIMe tackles the problem of potentially dishonest agents.

4 Designing for Accuracy

In this section, we discuss the ways in which agents' inaccuracy can obscure process qualities, and how AgentPrIMe mitigates these problems through *third-party storage*, *accountability* and *corrobration*. It should be emphasised that these solutions do not *guarantee* accurate, honest documentation, but merely reduce the possibilities for deception.

4.1 Design Levels

Mitigating for inaccuracy can be expensive, and not every application of AgentPrIMe needs to incur all of this expense. For instance, a multi-agent system may be completely trusted not to maliciously produce incorrect assertions, e.g. if all agents are owned by a single trusted organisation, but still may do so through error. It is important, therefore, that AgentPrIMe allows developers to apply the degree of mitigation they consider most appropriate for a given application.

We classify types of application, and the design requirements due to them, into three levels, increasing in development cost. A *reliable system* is one in which the agents are assumed always to record complete and accurate documentation, or at least sufficiently complete and accurate that any mitigation would be more costly than it is worth. A *transparent system* is one in which the agents cannot always be trusted to assert correct information but for which there exist ways to corroborate what they have asserted. An *exploitable system* is one in which some agents are free to withold information about their activities or give false information without being detectable. The latter two types of system will be characterised more concretely in the following section.

It is important to note that the systems that need to be adapted to mitigate inaccuracy are exactly those systems that users may suspect of recording inaccurate documentation. The incentive for the designers of such systems to apply the adaptations is that users can check whether they have been applied and will trust the results produced by such systems on that basis. That is, regardless of whether a system is reliable or not, a user can choose to trust results from that system only if it is both *(i)* clear from a result's provenance that it was produced in a legitimate way, and *(ii)* clear from the provenance and other system components described below that the designs were adequate to prevent inaccuracy. AgentPrIMe, therefore, provides benefits to two parties:

- for the user, it provides a way to check that adequate safeguards were in place to ensure the provenance is reliable; and
- for the system designer, it provides a way to give the necessary guarantees of accuracy to a user.

4.2 Corroboration

We now characterise the difference between transparent and exploitable unreliable systems, and show how AgentPrIMe requires more adaptations to be applied to the latter.

Returning to the causal chain shown in Figure 3, we note that for every message in the system, two agents are involved: the *sender* and the *receiver*. If both agents record interaction p-assertions documenting the fact and content of the message they sent/received, then one agent's assertion can be used to verify the correctness of the other's assertion. We say that each agent's *view* of the interaction provides *corroboration* of the other view. Therefore, where an interaction involves one reliable agent and one unreliable agent, the latter's view of what occurred can be checked. Note, that this cannot apply to the internal causal relationships: only an agent knows whether its actions were caused by a particular goal, responsibility etc. We argue that the actions that are taken in a system will tend to be more important than the intent behind them for the end user, so that the lack of ability to corroborate internal information is not critical.

The kinds of process that cause most problems are those that involve multiple *organisations*, where each organisation owns a set of agents involved in the process. This is problematic because one organisation can provide an honest facade for another; for example, an apparently reliable shop may use an unethical supplier. We depict such a scenario in Figure 5, in which Agent 3 in Organisation 2 produces result R partly on the basis of the operations of Agents 1 and 2 in Organisation 1.

Organisations provide a unit of trust: agents can be grouped into organisations such that all agents in an organisation are trusted independently from those in any other organisation. If, in the process shown in Figure 5, Organisation 1 is trusted, then the system as a whole can be said to be transparent. This is because every agent is either trusted or, if not, every interation they have in a process is with a trusted agent and can therefore be corroborated by examining the p-assertions of the trusted agent.

An alternative situation arises when Organisation 2 is trusted, but Organisation 1 is not. In this case, one of the agents' assertions cannot be corroborated.

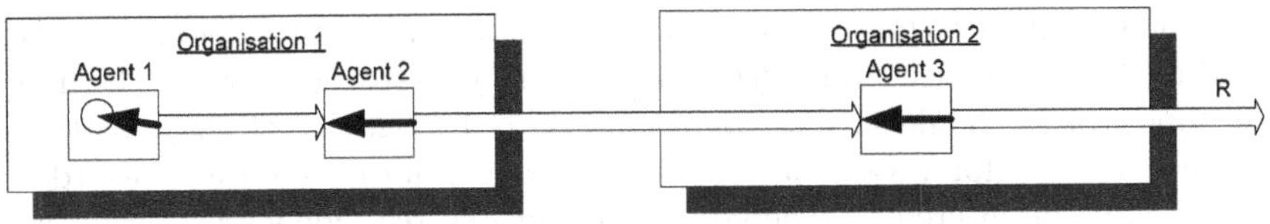

Fig. 5. Multiple organisations involved in a process

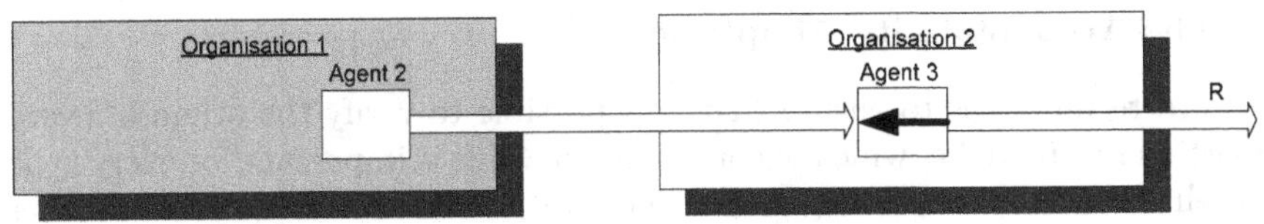

Fig. 6. Opaque organisations involve actions that cannot be verified

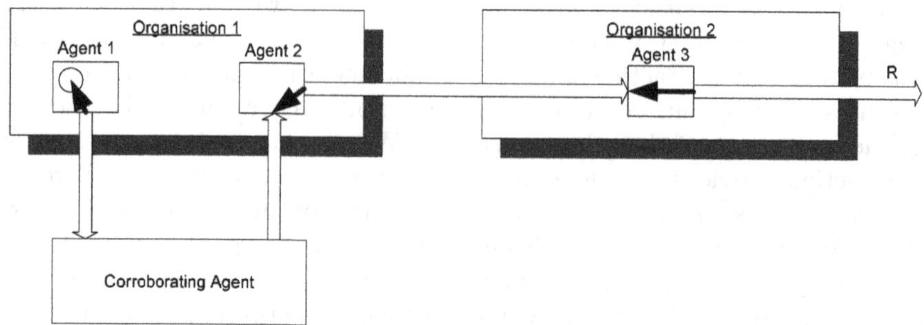

Fig. 7. Corroborating agents can be introduced to ensure a process remains transparent

The situation, from a user's point of view, is shown in Figure 6: only Agents 2 and 3 produce p-assertions that can be relied on. In this case, we say that Organisation 1 is *opaque* because part of its process, possibly a significant part from the user's perspective, is not reliably documented.

4.3 The Corroboration Adaptation

Applying AgentPrIMe to the case above causes additional agent interactions to be introduced to the application process. As shown in Figure 7, the *corroborating agent* is introduced into the process, so that instead of a direct interaction between Agents 1 and 2, this corroborating agent acts as a redirecting intermediary. The corroborating agent must record its own documentation of its interactions, and be trusted by a user to be of value. The agent may be part of an existing trusted organisation, such as Organisation 2, or may in a new organisation created by the user.

4.4 The Third-Party Storage Adaptation

The second technique to mitigate inaccuracy is for agents to store documentation in third-party provenance stores, trusted by both the system owner and the user. These repositories should ensure immutability and longevity of the assertions they contain. Therefore, users have assurance that if accurate data is recorded, it cannot later be altered or deleted. Provenance stores independent from the agents recording documentation is recommended for all types of system, even reliable ones.

4.5 The Accountability Adaptation

The third technique is to ensure that it is possible to verify the origin of every p-assertion recorded, i.e. which agent created it. This is important for every type of unreliable system, including those that are unreliable through error rather than malice, as it allows the faulty agents to be pinpointed within a system. Accountability can be achieved by each agent applying a digital signature to each p-assertion, with users able to validate a p-assertion's signature when they retrieve it from a provenance store (the store may also do its own checks).

This guards against a particular type of deception that applies to both transparent and exploitable systems: an agent may assert something false but attempt to make it appear that the assertion comes from another, trusted, agent. Without accountability, agents are free to give a completely false view of a process without detection.

5 Applying AgentPrIMe

Applying the AgentPrIMe methodology fragment in the context of an agent-oriented methodology requires that the developer knows both at which point to apply it and what steps to take in doing so. With regard to the former point, we have already said that AgentPrIMe is ideally applied at a particular point in the extended methodology, when the design is sufficiently well developed to adapt, but not so far developed that effort is wasted. In practice, given the adaptations described above, this means the point at which (types of) agents have been defined well enough to know the (types of) interactions they will take part in and the causal chains their actions lead to. Depending on the methodology, some adaptations may be best applied even later, when an agents internal structure is defined.

Once a reasonable point in the methodology has been determined, the developer should consider each agent in turn and determine how to wrap the agent to record p-assertions about its activity in a provenance store, preferably a third party one. The form that such wrapping takes depends on technology: the aim is for the agents logic to trigger the recording of p-assertions and anything that achieves this aim is considered to be an instantiation of a wrapper adaptation. Consideration of ensuring accuracy can then begin. First, where possible, an agent should be adapted to sign its p-assertions. Second, each interaction between agents should be considered and, where no agent would be able to corroborate the contents of the interaction, a third party should be added and interactions redirected through it. The choice of third party is based on the developers best guess as to what will be trusted by those others the system is likely to interact with.

In terms of tool support, if an agents internal operations are made explicit, for example as an architecture with plans, then it may be possible to automate the modelling of causation in that agent.

6 Conclusions

AgentPrIMe is an extension applicable to existing agent-oriented methodologies that gives users confidence in the results produced by designed systems. Developers applying AgentPrIMe to a design must determine how that design needs to be adapted, firstly to record adequate documentation that exposes the qualities of the process that produced some output of the system, and then to ensure that the documentation itself is reliable through corroboration, independent storage and accountability of agents.

The approach aims to be as *methodology-neutral* as possible, being applicable regardless of the agent-oriented concepts that have been used in designing a system. It does this by relying only on the agents and their interactions, that are present in any multi-agent system, and then defining the *causal relationships*, which define the processes they are involved in, in a system-independent way.

Four design adaptations are defined in this paper:

Wrapper Adaptation. Adapting agents (or agents of a given type) to record documentation on what they have done and why.

Corroboration Adaptation. Adapting agent interactions that may be seen as collusion so that an intermediary can provide collaborating evidence of the communications.

Third-Party Storage Adaptation. Providing storage of documentation that is trusted by both recording agents and users.

Accountability Adaptation. Adapting agents to sign data before recording it for users to query.

In future work, we will investigate further uses of process documentation recorded by multi-agent systems. For instance, it may be possible to determine whether agents have fulfilled their responsibilities and do not prevent other agents exercising their rights, by examining the documentation recorded. Additionally, we will investigate how the assurances provided by our adaptations can be integrated with the quantitative trust models prevalent in other agent-based research to give an informative measure of reliability to users.

Acknowledgements

This work was supported in part by the Southampton-Chicago Activity (SOCA) project (EPSRC reference EP/C528131/1). It was also supported in part by the CONTRACT project, which is co-funded by the European Commission under the 6th Framework Programme for RTD with project number FP6-034418. Notwithstanding this fact, this paper and its content reflects only the authors' views. The European Commission is not responsible for its contents, nor liable for the possible effects of any use of the information contained therein.

References

1. Cheong, C., Winikoff, M.: Hermes: Designing goal-oriented agent interactions. In: Müller, J.P., Zambonelli, F. (eds.) AOSE 2005. LNCS, vol. 3950, pp. 16–27. Springer, Heidelberg (2006)
2. DeLoach, S.A., Wood, M.F., Sparkman, C.H.: Multiagent systems engineering. International Journal of Software Engineering and Knowledge Engineering 11(3), 231–258 (2001)

3. Garcia, A., Kulesza, U., Sant'Anna, C., Chavez, C., de Lucena, C.J.P.: Aspects in agent-oriented software engineering: Lessons learned. In: Müller, J.P., Zambonelli, F. (eds.) AOSE 2005. LNCS, vol. 3950, pp. 231–247. Springer, Heidelberg (2006)
4. Groth, P., Jiang, S., Miles, S., Munroe, S., Tan, V., Tsasakou, S., Moreau, L.: An architecture for provenance systems. Technical report, Electronics and Computer Science, University of Southampton (October 2006), `http://eprints.ecs.soton.ac.uk/12023/`
5. Guttenplan, S.: Introduction to Philosophy of Mind, chapter An Essay on Mind. Oxford University Press, Oxford (1994)
6. Jacobson, I., Ng, P.-W.: Aspect-Oriented Software Development with Use Cases. Addison Wesley, Reading (2004)
7. Jureta, I.J., Faulkner, S., Schobbens, P.-Y.: Allocating goals to agent roles during mas requirements engineering. In: Padgham, L., Zambonelli, F. (eds.) AOSE 2006. LNCS, vol. 4405, Springer, Heidelberg (2007)
8. Kumar, K., Welke, R.J.: Methodology engineering: a proposal for situation-specific methodology construction. In: Challenges and strategies for research in systems development, pp. 257–269. John Wiley & Sons Inc., New York (1992)
9. Luck, M., d'Inverno, M.: Engagement and cooperation in motivated agent modelling. In: Zhang, C., Lukose, D. (eds.) DAI 1995. LNCS, vol. 1087, pp. 70–84. Springer, Heidelberg (1996)
10. Miles, S., Munroe, S., Luck, M., Moreau, L.: Modelling the provenance of data in autonomous systems. In: Proceedings of Autonomous Agents and Multi-Agent Systems 2007, Honolulu, Hawai'i, May 2007, p. 8 (2007)
11. Munroe, S., Miles, S., Moreau, L., Valquez-Salceda, J.: Prime: A software engineering methodology for developing provenance-aware applications. In: Proceedings of the Software Engineering and Middleware Workshop (SEM 2006), ACM Digital (to appear, 2006)
12. Omicini, A.: SODA: Societies and infrastructures in the analysis and design of agent-based systems. In: Ciancarini, P., Wooldridge, M.J. (eds.) AOSE 2000. LNCS, vol. 1957, pp. 185–193. Springer, Heidelberg (2001)
13. Padgham, L., Winkoff, M.: Prometheus:a methodology for developing intelligent agents. In: Giunchiglia, F., Odell, J.J., Weiss, G. (eds.) AOSE 2002. LNCS, vol. 2585, pp. 174–185. Springer, Heidelberg (2003)
14. Wooldridge, M., Jennings, N.R., Kinny, D.: The gaia methodology for agent-oriented analysis and design. Automous Agents and Multi-Agent Systems 3, 285–312 (2000)

Refining Goal Models by Evaluating System Behaviour

Mirko Morandini, Loris Penserini, Anna Perini, and Angelo Susi

Fondazione Bruno Kessler - IRST, Via Sommarive 18, I-38050, Trento, Italy
{morandini,penserini,perini,susi}@itc.it

Abstract. Nowadays, information systems have to perform in complex, heterogeneous environments, considering a variety of system users with different needs and preferences. Software engineering methodologies need to cope with the complexity of requirements specification in such scenarios, where new requirements may emerge also at run-time and the system's goals are expected to evolve to meet new stakeholder needs.

Following an agent-oriented approach, we are studying methods and techniques to design adaptive and evolvable information systems able to fulfill stakeholders' objectives.

In a previous work we defined an Agent-Oriented framework to design and code system specifications in terms of goal models and we instantiated it in a tool supported process which exploits the Agent-Oriented Software Engineering methodology *Tropos* and the Multi-Agent Platform JADE/Jadex [11].

In this paper, we show how to use this framework to develop a system following an iterative process, where the system execution allows enriching the system specification given in terms of goal models.

Experimental evaluation has been performed on a simple example and lead to the refinement of the designed goal model upon the analysis of the system's run-time behaviour.

1 Introduction

Information systems are today expected to perform in complex environments which make computing resources available to anyone, at any time and anywhere. In these scenarios, complexity comes from the variety of system users (including organizations) with their needs and preferences, which tend to evolve according to the dynamic nature of users in the network, and from the heterogeneity of the environment a system is deployed in. Therefore, systems should be aware of users' goals and able to choose the most suitable behaviour from various alternatives.

These scenarios motivate research on practices and methodologies for software development. Traditional software development models, which assume that the requirements specification has been finalized before proceeding to design and then to implementation, need to be replaced by more flexible iterative models, able to take into account that new requirements may emerge also at run-time. Moreover, the traditional concept of software maintenance has to be revised since systems are expected to evolve to meet the needs of the changing environment rather than to preserve their original structure [8].

Multi-Agent Systems (MAS) provide candidate technologies for building software with adaptivity and evolvability qualities [6], while recently proposed Agent-Oriented

M. Luck and L. Padgham (Eds.): AOSE 2007, LNCS 4951, pp. 44–57, 2008.

Software Engineering (AOSE) methodologies offer a complementary paradigm for the analysis of system requirements and design [4]. Some of them, such as GAIA [17] and *Tropos* [1] offer concepts and models to analyse the system and its environment in terms of agent organizations. Moreover, *Tropos* has been recently proposed as a methodology to support "high-variability software design" through the explicit modelling of the different alternative design solutions to a given stakeholder goal (requirement) [7].

We are studying methods and techniques to design information systems with qualities such as adaptivity and evolvability, following an Agent-Oriented approach. That is, we conceive an information system as an open network of software agents who interact with each other and with human/organizational agents in their operational environment in order to fulfil stakeholder objectives. Concretely, we propose a development framework which adopts MAS technology as implementation platform and agent-oriented methods and techniques for the analysis and the specification of system requirements and design. In [11,12] we instantiate this framework with respect to the *Tropos* methodology and to the Jadex/JADE platform [14], and propose a tool-supported process to derive agents that base on a Belief-Desire-Intention architecture [15] from *Tropos* goal models.

In this paper, we show how this framework can be used to develop a system following an iterative process, in which the system execution allows to enrich the system specification expressed in terms of goal models. From a goal-oriented system model we derive agent skeletons automatically in a tool-based process. We execute the modelled system, simulating system users and observing system behaviour in correspondence to variability in user desires and in environmental conditions. The different MAS behaviours can then be traced back to the specification of the alternatives in the goal model, giving experimental evidence of the effectiveness of the proposed framework in supporting traceability between run-time and design-time artefacts. Moreover, run-time observations could lead to a refinement of the design. For instance contribution relationships between model elements can be further qualified or quantitative analysis of system qualities, which have been defined at design time in terms of system (soft)goals, can be performed. We consider this work as a first step towards setting up feedback mechanisms from run-time to the design, a core aspect in the development of adaptive systems.

The paper is structured as follows. In Section 2, we recall basic concepts of the proposed development framework and describe the tool-supported process, which exploits the *Tropos* methodology and the JADE/Jadex MAS platform. A simple travel agency system is used as example to illustrate the approach. The system handles requests from different customer categories and gives proposals for a full travel package, according to user preferences. Experimental evaluations, based on a run-time simulation, are described and discussed in Section 3. Related work is presented in Section 4 and concluding remarks in Section 5.

2 Background

2.1 Conceptual Framework

We adopt concepts from recently proposed AOSE methodologies [4] and from BDI MAS research [6] to define an Agent-Oriented approach to system design and coding. The

Belief-Desire-Intention (BDI) architecture, as proposed in [15], bases on three mental concepts: *beliefs* which model the knowledge of an agent about himself and about its environment, *goals* the agent can try to achieve, and *intentions*, sets of plans an agent commits for execution to achieve a goal. Within our framework, we further use knowledge level concepts such as those of *agent*, which can be social, organizational, human or software and *social dependency* that defines the obligations of an agent to others.

The key part in the analysis and design stages is the so called *Goal Model (GM)*. Like in other approaches [5,16], in our framework a *GM* is a goal graph consisting of a forest of AND/OR decomposed goals, along with inter-dependency links between goals and means-end relationships between leaf-level goals and plans that represent a way to achieve these goals. During requirements analysis, *GM*s make easier to model stakeholders' goals and their relationships, showing how they really affect the system functionalities. Moreover, deriving an agent *GM* at architectural design allows designers to model dependencies between the system agent goals and stakeholder goals.

More operative concepts are needed during software agents specification. We define a *capability* as the sub-graph rooted in a leaf goal containing a set of *means-end* plans with their inter-dependency relationships towards other goals. We call *knowledge-level* design the process of building the higher level part of a *GM* and *capability-level* design the process of refining leaf goals into plan means-end and inter-dependency relationships. This last design step represents a way to operationalize goals, that is, to define the possible behaviours of an agent. Therefore, a *GM* can be also seen as a schema for the possible behaviours an agent can use to fulfil its goals.

More formally, let E be the set of events[1] an agent can perceive, C the set of constraints (e.g. user preferences and system QoS), G the set of goals an agent can achieve, Cp a set of capabilities an agent can exploit, and $G_L \subseteq G$ the set of leaf-level goals an agent can operationalize, we give the following definitions:

Behaviour-Schema. *BS is the set of all possible type of behaviours an agent can play $BS = \{Bh_1(X), ..., Bh_n(X)\}$, where each Bh_i is a sub-schema representing a set of behaviours associated to a specific set of events and constraints. Formally, X is a list of attributes $X = \{Events, Constraints, Goals\}$, where $Events$ assumes values in 2^E; $Constraints$ assumes values in 2^C, and $Goals$ assumes values in 2^{G_L}.*

Behaviour-Schema Function. *A behaviour-schema function f_{Bh} associates a set of events and constraints to a set of leaf-level goals: $f_{Bh} : 2^E \times 2^C \rightarrow 2^{G_L}$. It allows to build the $Bh(X)$ specific to an occuring event and the constraints perceived.*

Capability Function. *For each sub-schema Bh, there exists a capability function $f_{Cp} : Bh \rightarrow 2^{Cp}$ such that, giving in input a behaviour b_i, retrieves the different sets of Capabilities an agent can execute to exhibit this behaviour.*

Behaviour-schema- and capability-functions allow to query the behaviour-schema and a *GM* structure about agent properties with reference to concrete instances of behaviours and capabilities, each time an event occurs or environmental conditions change. For example, each time an agent receives a request message (an event), it

[1] Examples are goal triggering messages.

interprets it in order to extract the goals to be triggered, and concurrently perceives environmental conditions (C) to better choose the right behaviour.

2.2 Tool Supported Framework

In [11,12] we instantiate the described framework using the *Tropos* methodology for analysis and design, and JADE and the Jadex BDI agent platform for the implementation. The *Tropos* agent-oriented methodology borrows modelling and analysis techniques from goal-oriented requirements engineering approaches and integrates them into an agent-oriented paradigm (see [1] for details). The main idea in *Tropos* is to support knowledge level specification by providing a conceptual modelling language which offers concepts like *actor*, *goal*, *plan*, *resource*, *capability*, and *social dependency* between actors. The methodology provides a graphical notation to depict views of a model, along with analysis techniques and supporting tools [13].

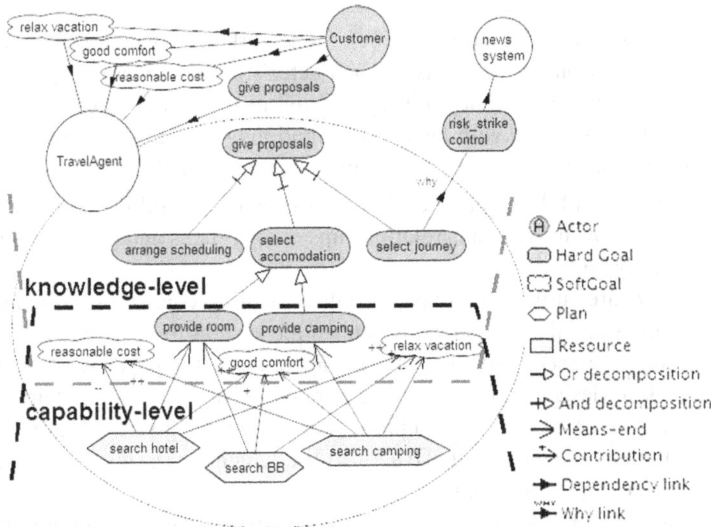

Fig. 1. *Tropos* architectural design: a fragment of knowledge and capability levels from the goal model of agent TravelAgent

In the rest of this section, we give an overview of the framework by defining basic process artefacts and their role in the main process stages, as depicted in Figure 2. Moreover, we give more details on how a *GM* is automatically mapped into a BDI agent specification that can, at execution time, give useful feedback to refine the original design. To illustrate our approach we take as an example a simple travel agency system, TravelAgent. The system handles requests from several classes/categories of customers (e.g. business customers, vacation customers or students) and gives proposals for a full travel package, according to the users' preferences. These preferences are modelled through softgoals. For example, as illustrated in Figure 1, possible softgoals to characterize a customer category are reasonable cost, good comfort, and relax

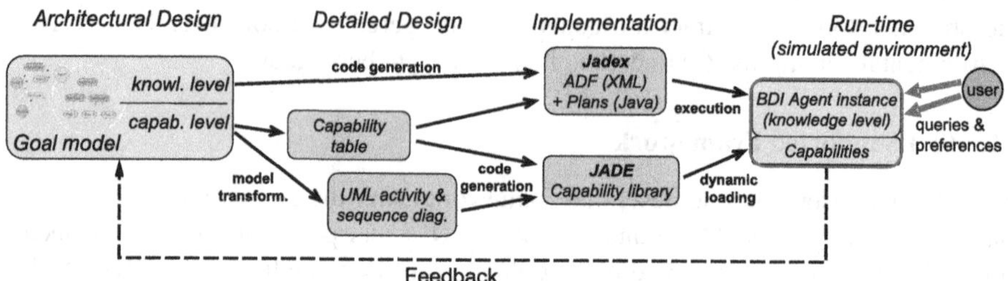

Fig. 2. Process's artefacts and their role in *Tropos*. Feedback from system execution to design can be obtained upon observing the system behaviour.

vacation. The agent tries to achieve them exploiting different alternatives for journey and accommodation and selecting suitable additional activities.

Process Artefacts. Adopting *Tropos* in our framework allows us to represent MAS with *GM*s, resulting from the analysis of each actor's point of view. *Tropos GM*s are based on the $i*$ notation [16]. They are represented in terms of a forest of AND- and OR-decomposed goals, along with lateral contributions labelled $+$, $-$ (for partial positive or negative contribution to the satisfaction of a goal) or $++$ (for strong positive or negative contribution). For example, if $g_1 \xrightarrow{++} g_2$ and g_1 is fulfilled, so is g_2. Additionally a *GM* contains means-ends relationships among plans and goals, to define the means to satisfy a goal.

In *Tropos*, *GM*s are built during requirements analysis to characterize domain stakeholders, their needs and their dependencies from the system-to-be. In the architectural design phase they are used to detail software agents. As this paper work focuses on getting feedback to design-time from the generated agents, here we consider mainly *GM*s at the *Tropos* architectural design phase. An example is given in Figure 1, which illustrates a fragment of a *GM* for the TravelAgent, which represents the main actor of the software system under development.

At *Tropos* architectural design phase, a *GM* represents the agent intentionality in terms of how the agent perceives the environment, applies strategies to fulfil its responsibilities, and chooses alternative ways to adapt to requirements changes. In other words, like a human being, the agent perceives the environment and chooses a suitable behaviour. Notice that the set of possible agent behaviours can be characterized in terms of perceivable events, environmental conditions and agent goals by applying the behaviour-schema function, f_{Bh}, to the *GM*. The actual behaviour results from the execution of the specific capabilities thanks to the capability function, f_{Cp}.

Figure 1 depicts the two different abstraction levels that characterize the agent design: *knowledge level* and *capability level*. The knowledge level refers to the goal AND/OR decomposition part of the *GM* that contributes to the description of the behaviours the specific agent role can play. The capability level brings about the executable part of an agent and its connection to the agent's leaf goals.

Capabilities ($cp \in Cp$, where Cp is the set of all capabilities of the agent) represent the glue between the two agent modelling levels. A capability is defined by the concepts of *ability* and *opportunity*. The *ability* refers to the plans for achieving a given goal and is specified by a means-end relationship between the goal and the plan. The *opportunity* represents user preferences (contributions between goals and plans to softgoal, $c \in 2^C$) and environmental conditions represented by message events $e \in 2^E$ that affect the agent's beliefs. At run time, these preferences and conditions can enable or disable the execution of an ability.

Following the design process sketched in Figure 2, a *capability table* extracted from the *GM*, and UML 2.0 diagrams, extracted by model transformation from the *GM*s capability level, are used to generate JADE code in a capability library. The structure of an agent's reasoning part, that relies on a BDI architecture, can be automatically generated from the knowledge level of the *GM*.

Table 1. Fragment of TravelAgent capability Table

Capabilities	Means_End(goal,plan)	List of Contributions
cp_1	`provide room, search hotel`	`{reasonable cost --;good comfort ++; relax vacation --}`
cp_2	`provide room, search BB`	`{good comfort +;relax vacation +}`
cp_3	`provide camping, search camping`	`{reasonable cost ++;good comfort --; relax vacation --}`
...	...	{...}

Table 1 depicts a fragment of the capability table for the TravelAgent example, which was obtained from the *GM* in Figure 1. If the goal select accommodation is triggered, as this is OR-decomposed in the two sub-goals, the agent TravelAgent has two possible behaviours to satisfy the triggered goal: one that can achieve the goal provide room (by cp_1 or cp_2) and one that can achieve the goal provide camping (by cp_3).

The design artefacts (*GM*s, capability table, activity- and sequence diagrams) drive agent code generation. Specifically, our tool supported framework allow us to generate a *library of capabilities* from the capability table and the activity- and sequence diagrams, as detailed in [12]. Executable skeletons for the *BDI agents*, which are able to use the capabilities in this library, can be automatically generated from the knowledge level specification contained in the *GM*, through a mapping of the *GM* structures into a BDI agent description for the *Jadex* framework, specified by an Agent Description File (ADF) in XML format, augmented with some Java code[2].

The implementation consists of Jadex BDI agent definitions along with their capabilities. For the simulation we run instances of these agent definitions. The agents are queried by simulated users sending request-messages and the resulting behaviour is then used to give feedback to the design artefacts.

Coding the GM into BDI Agents. In order to endow the generated BDI agents with all the information included in the *GM*, the specification for the mapping process has been conducted along two phases: basic concept mappings (goals, softgoals, plans, resources) and structure mappings (AND/OR goal dependencies, means-end links,

[2] Further details can be found in [14].

contribution links, delegation and dependency links). A sketch of the mapping is given below, while we remind the interested reader to see [11] for more details.

Goal. As a Jadex-goal can be only triggered by a Jadex-plan, a *Tropos* goal is mapped to a pair of $< goal, plan >$ in Jadex.

Softgoal. Softgoals are considered as abstract entities related more to beliefs and desires than to goals and plans. In our prototype they are mainly used to define opportunities for the selection of the next goals or plans to pursue along the *GM*. That is, they model domain constraints $c \in C$ to drive the selection of the most convenient behaviour $b \in Bh(X)$, once an event $e \in 2^E$ occurs

A softgoal is therefore mapped only to a belief base entry, which contains its name and a value that may be changed by the user at run-time. This value expresses the softgoal's actual importance and may change from time to time to reflect environmental changes.

Plan. *Tropos* plans that have a direct means-end relationship to leaf goals (root-level plans) are mapped to Jadex plans according to our definition of capability.

AND-decomposition. If an AND-decomposed goal is activated, all subgoals have to be dispatched. The following Jadex solution was adopted: an AND-decomposed goal is set as trigger for exactly one plan, called AND-dispatch-plan (Figure 3). In the plan body, all subgoals have to be dispatched in (random or user defined) sequence. If one subgoal fails, the process has to be stopped and a failure has to be returned. For this first proposal, on failure no techniques for compensation of already executed actions have been considered.

An analogous mapping for the **OR-decomposition** is described in [11], while *Tropos* **means-end** relationship are mapped one-to-one to the Jadex plan triggering mechanism. Having defined no conditions, every time the associated goal is activated, plan execution is triggered. Notice that, in this case the Jadex plans are root-level plans in *Tropos*, namely those required to build up agent capabilities. Jadex supposes that every

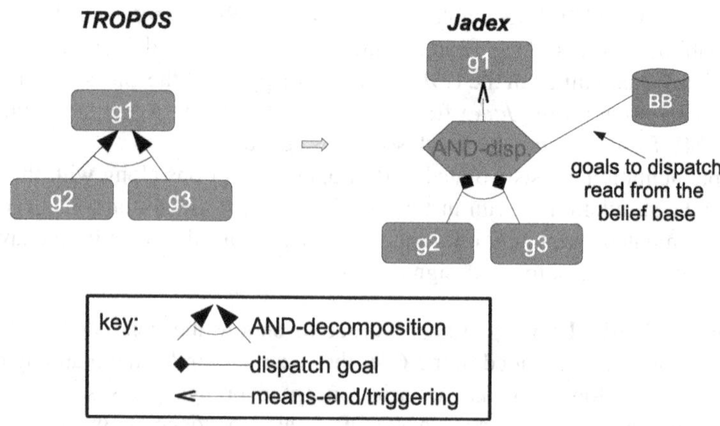

Fig. 3. Mapping of the *Tropos* goal AND-decomposition into an equivalent Jadex BDI structure

applicable plan for a goal is able to satisfy that goal completely. Therefore, if more than one plan is applicable, Jadex meta-level reasoning is exploited to select the appropriate plan, as in the case of alternative paths in OR-decomposition. The selection of alternatives can be guided by preconditions and by softgoal contributions.

The generated agent can evaluate costs for every goal and plan. They include softgoal contribution and importance: negative contributions cause higher cost, lower importance of the relative softgoal to the user can alleviate this penalty. Moreover, each generated agent endows knowledge about its goal relationships from the *GM* in its belief base: AND/OR decompositions, dependencies, delegations, and contribution links.

3 Experimental Setting and Evaluation

This Section describes a general experimental setting, suitable to be applied in several kinds of scenarios, and the results obtained.

The objective of our experiment is twofold: on one hand, we aim at verifying the behaviour of a MAS with respect to the designed specifications; on the other hand, we aim at supporting the refinement (such as the introduction of new relationships) of the *GM* by exploiting information retrieved from the simulation.

We refer to the TravelAgent example, partially depicted in Figure 1. The main idea is to focus on the preferences of different customer categories recognized by the system at run-time by profiling users from the set of queries they submitted. We observe the system while it is adapting to each category, trying to maximize customer satisfaction (customer's softgoals delegated to the TravelAgent system) and providing evidence of how such softgoals have different impact to the system's own internal softgoals (e.g. maximize profit).

3.1 Experimental Setting

We refer to the fragment of *GM* shown in Figure 1. Suppose that a generic Customer could be distinguished into three categories: *business customer* (BC), *vacation customer* (VC) and *student customer* (SC), each one composed by individuals having similar preferences and similar requests to the travel agency system. The simulation assumes that these categories will be recognized by the system only at run-time.

In the simulation, the Customer (in the following also *user*) interacts with the system by submitting sets of queries that correspond to set of activation events for system goals (belonging to 2^E). Moreover, the system is supposed to acquire information from the environment in order to provide user profiling. This would allow to activate sets of softgoals that represent the users' preferences (belonging to 2^C). Basing on this information our system is able to assume the best-suited behaviour, activating all necessary capabilities. Table 2 shows the components for the run-time choice process of sets of capabilities. In particular, the second column represents the input elements. The former is given as a set of queries made by the different Customer Categories (i.e. $CC = \{BC, VC, SC\}$), e.g. the business customers' query will be q^{BC}, whereas the latter is given by the set of user preferences and constraints (e.g. C^{BC}) perceived by the system via an user profiling activity or by user-guided configuration. The third column

Table 2. System inputs (CC and $2^E \times 2^C$) and outputs ($Bh(X)$ and 2^{Cp}) for the simulation, following the definition recalled in Section 2.1

User class (CC)	Trigger events ($2^E \times 2^C$)	Behaviours ($Bh(X)$)	Capabilitiy sets (2^{Cp})
BC	q_1^{BC}, C^{BC} ... q_m^{BC}, C^{BC}	b_1^{BC} ... b_m^{BC}	Cp_1^{BC} ... Cp_m^{BC}
VC	q_1^{VC}, C^{VC} ... q_n^{VC}, C^{VC}	b_1^{VC} ... b_n^{VC}	Cp_1^{VC} ... Cp_n^{VC}
SC	q_1^{SC}, C^{SC} ... q_k^{SC}, C^{SC}	b_1^{SC} ... b_k^{SC}	Cp_1^{SC} ... Cp_k^{SC}

contains the set of behaviour instances suitable for each category (e.g. b_i^{BC}) related to the queries (e.g. q_i^{BC}), while the fourth column contains the capability sets (e.g. Cp_i^{BC}) able to realize the corresponding behaviours.

To choose appropriate capabilities, the system exploits the *behaviour-schema* function f_{Bh} and the *capability* function f_{Cp}, defined in Section 2. In particular, the first line of the table refers to a single query made by an user that belongs to the BC category. Let us assume that such a category is characterized by a set Q^{BC} of m possible queries ($Q^{BC} = \{q_1^{BC}, ..., q_m^{BC}\}$) and by a set C^{BC} of preferences ($C^{BC} = \{sg_1^{BC}, sg_2^{BC}, ...\}$), which are inputs for the application of the *behaviour-schema* function. With this input, the system is able to compute the set of possible behaviours b_{1-m}^{BC}, that can be exploited in order to accomplish user requests.

The application of the *capability function* f_{Cp} to a behaviour b_i allows the system to retrieve the different sets of capabilities that can be activated in order to operatively execute this behaviour. The capability to execute can then be selected according to the opportunities. This calculation process can be repeated for all user categories in the model.

A domain expert would be able to define contribution relationships between each capability and internal softgoals, such as maximize profit, but she cannot know *a-priori* which capabilities will be executed to satisfy a user query that occurs to the system.

In Table 3 sample values for the importance of the contributions to softgoals adopted to characterize the customer categories are given; those values refer to the three different classes of customers and are expressed via numeric values.

We prepared the experiments, defining a set of queries for every different customer category and identifying sets of softgoals that are typical for them. Table 4 gives examples for sets of queries for the three classes of users we considered. Moreover, for

Table 3. Softgoals used by the system to profile the user preferences. These values are supposed to be given by domain experts.

C_i	Vacation Customer	Student Customer	Business Customer
good_business_travel	0	0	1
good_comfort	0.6	0.2	1
action_vacation	0.4	1	0
good_time_utilization	0.3	0	1
reasonable_cost	0.6	1	0.1
relax_vacation	0.6	0.3	0

Table 4. Queries that characterize each customer category

Query	Vacation Customer	Student Customer	Business Customer
q_1	give proposals	give proposals	give proposals
q_2	provide camping, car journey, prop. act.	propose activities	provide room, flight journey
q_3	provide room, train journey	provide room, flight journey	select journey
q_4	select accommodation	camping, train journey	select accommodation

Table 5. Contribution values between each capability and the internal softgoals

Capability	Contribution to *maximize profit*	Contribution to *maximize travel miles*
search hotel	0.8	0
search BB	0.4	0
camping	0.3	0
eurostar train	0.2	0.3
intercity train	0.1	0.2
business flight	0.9	1
low cost flight	0.2	0
gastronomy	0	0
nightlife	0	0
...	...	...

Table 6. Contribution relationships among capability groups and internal system softgoals

Query	Sets of Capabilities	$sgint_1$	...	$sgint_l$
q_1^{BC}	Cp_1^{BC}	$val_{1,1}$	...	$val_{1,l}$
...	...	...	...	...
q_m^{BC}	Cp_m^{BC}	$val_{m,1}$	...	$val_{m,l}$
		$f_{avg}(val_{1,1}\dots val_{m,1})$	...	$f_{avg}(val_{1,l}\dots val_{m,l})$

each capability (*cp*), we define its contribution towards the internal system softgoals ($sgint_1, \dots, sgint_l$), as illustrated in Table 5.

Table 6 can be built only after running the system along with simulated inputs and getting information on which set of capabilities where executed by the system to satisfy user queries. Specifically, the table shows the schema of the relationships among sets of capabilities and internal softgoals ($sgint_1, \dots, sgint_l$), for each agent. These values are then used to compute the cumulative contribution of the run-time sets of capabilities *cp*, belonging to the selected behaviour b_i, to a given internal softgoal, via the functions $f_{avg}(val_{1,j}\dots val_{m,j})$ (at the bottom of the table). In our experimental setting we used the function:

$$avg(val_{1,J}\dots val_{m,J}) = \sum_{i=1}^{m}(val_{i,J})/m \qquad (1)$$

Notice that an analysis by simulation does not cope with the possible contribution produced by all the different capability groupings. On the contrary, the simulation will converge towards the only sets of capabilities requested by the real customer categories.

3.2 Results and Discussion

After the simulation, the set of data related to the experiment for the TravelAgent scenario has been collected. According to our first objective, we are able to monitor the system behaviour (b), each time a query (e.g. q_4^{BC}) occurs, along with some user preferences (e.g. C^{BC}={good comfort}), verifying that b belongs to the *GM* behaviour schema ($b \in Bh(X)$). Specifically, we can observe that the system has the ability to adapt its behaviour to best accommodate with the current customer category. For example, let us assume that q_4^{BC} will trigger the system goal select accommodation, along with the softgoal good comfort. Now, the system is able to navigate the *GM* in order to maximize the user preference modelled by this softgoal.

Looking at the *GM* fragment illustrated in Figure 1, we can see that the goal select accommodation has two alternative ways to be achieved, i.e. provide room and provide camping. The system will first try to select provide room, because its capabilities (characterized by the two plans search hotel and search BB) give the biggest contribution to the given user preference. The same procedure will be used in a next step to discriminate between the two available capabilities, this time resulting in the selection of search hotel.

These experiments confirmed the effectiveness of the framework in supporting traceability between run-time and design-time artefacts.

To meet our second objective, we simulate the execution of a set of user queries and preferences in order to revise softgoal relationships in the *GM*. Table 7 shows the sets of capabilities activated by the system, i.e. the behaviour instances it selected at run-time, as a response to the simulated user queries described in Table 4. In Table 7, each row specifies a query from a particular category of users (BC, VC and SC). Contributions to *maximize profit* are calculated by summing the value of each capability contribution as indicated in Table 5, e.g. in the case of Cp_1^{BC}: *eurostar train* + *search hotel* + *gastronomy* = $0.2 + 0.8 + 0 = 1$.

The results of these queries allow to observe how the real (in our case simulated) customer preferences affect system behaviour.

The capability groups corresponding to the different behaviours of the TravelAgent can then be used to add or quantify *Tropos* contribution links.

Figure 4 A), shows the values of f_{avg} computed according to 1, as shown in Table 7, considering the internal softgoal maximize profit. In Figure 4 B), a softgoal customer satisfaction was introduced to aggregate the softgoals relevant to a specific customer

Table 7. Capability groups associated to every query at run-time

Query	Sets of executed capabilities	Contribution to *maximize profit*	
q_1^{BC}	Cp_1^{BC}: eurostar train, search hotel, gastronomy	1	
q_2^{BC}	Cp_2^{BC}: business flight, search hotel	1.7	
q_3^{BC}	Cp_3^{BC}: eurostar train	0.2	
q_4^{BC}	Cp_4^{BC}: search hotel	0.8	$f_{avg} = 0.925$
q_1^{VC}	Cp_1^{VC}: low cost flight, search BB, culture	0.6	
q_2^{VC}	Cp_2^{VC}: use own car, camping	0.3	
q_3^{VC}	Cp_3^{VC}: intercity train, search BB	0.5	
q_4^{VC}	Cp_4^{VC}: search BB	0.4	$f_{avg} = 0.45$
q_1^{SC}	Cp_1^{SC}: low cost flight, search camping, nightlife	0.5	
q_2^{SC}	Cp_2^{SC}: nightlife	0	
q_3^{SC}	Cp_3^{SC}: low cost flight, search BB	0.6	
q_4^{SC}	Cp_4^{SC}: intercity train, camping	0.4	$f_{avg} = 0.375$

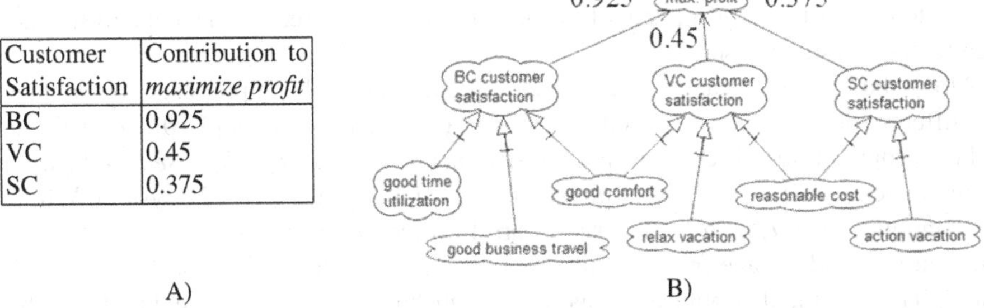

Customer Satisfaction	Contribution to *maximize profit*
BC	0.925
VC	0.45
SC	0.375

Fig. 4. A) Quantifying the contribution relationships between each customer satisfaction softgoal and the maximize profit softgoal; B) visualizing the results in terms of the *Tropos* goal model refinement. The labels define the new relationship values.

category. Contributions between them and the internal softgoal maximize profit can be drawn and quantified by the contribution values computed at run-time.

This result can contribute both to validate existing contribution links and to add new ones. In the case run-time feedback is in contrast with the design-time models, a revision of the *GM* could be required.

In a subsequent step, these new relations could be used by the system to adapt its strategic behaviours, not only according to the user preferences (i.e. softgoal customer satisfaction), but also according to its internal organizational objectives (i.e. softgoal maximize profit), following a trade-off for the achievement of this two softgoals.

4 Related Work

Different research lines are of interest to the work described in this paper. Here we focus on research in AOSE methodologies, which aims at supporting traceability between process artefacts, and research on methods for evaluating design strategies.

Along the first research line, we shall mention the Prometheus methodology [9], which makes use of goal models to describe system requirements. Analogous to [1], after building a goal model, the designer identifies those goals that are related to system functionalities (by the use of *descriptors*) and delegates them to specific system actors. Then functionalities are grouped to characterize scenarios, namely sequence of steps (functionalities) in order to achieve a goal. Notice that, this grouping mechanism is also used to determine different agent types (roles). Agents' awareness about their goal model is limited in Prometheus. For example, designed agent behaviour is mainly reactive rather than proactive and deliberative; the agent cannot automatically reason on its goal model in order to deal with failures and to choose alternative behaviours. Moreover, also traceability from and to design artefacts is not supported.

Hermes [2] aims at overcoming the weak points of the above-mentioned methodology, considering the goal model a core element of the implemented agent. In Hermes, generated BDI agents are aware of their goal model, called *Interaction Goal Hierarchy Diagram*, which is used to characterize behavioural strategies to cope with social commitments. This gives a more flexible approach in respect to traditional message-centric agent interaction approaches. Hermes needs further research in order to deal with a complete design framework, actually it does not cover the requirements analysis and architectural design phases.

Along the second research line, several approaches have been proposed to evaluate the different design strategies used in a *GM*, e.g. to achieve goals [3,10]. In [10] the authors propose three different evaluation criteria (*symbolic*, *scenario based*, and *quantitative*) to characterize the cooperation strategies of an agent-based P2P system. While the *symbolic* and *scenario based* criteria are fulfilled at design time, the *quantitative* criterion takes advantage from run-time results. In particular, the *symbolic* evaluation criterion is elaborated through analysis of the contribution links in the agent *GM*. A substantial difference to our approach is that their evaluation system has not been automatically generated from design-time artefacts (e.g. *GM*). Besides, they have not discussed how to correlate the run-time feedback to design-time *GM*.

The approach presented in [3] proposes a formal framework to reason on generic *GM*s, namely not only on those related to software systems. Specifically, the authors adopt some well-known algorithms to navigate the *GM* relationships, proposing an assessment criterion to propagate contribution values (labels) in order to verify the goal achievement. The analysis is called *qualitative* if the labels range in $\{++, +, -, --\}$, while it is called *quantitative* if the labels assume numeric values. The most significant difference to our framework is that their analysis framework works only when applied to a *GM* at design-time, while our approach considers run-time as a principal source of feedback to the design.

5 Conclusions and Future Work

In this paper we described an Agent-Oriented framework for developing systems with qualities such as adaptivity and evolvability. We showed how information gained from the execution of a system can be used to refine the original design.

As example, we modelled a simple travel agency system. The system handles requests from different customer categories and gives proposals for a full travel package, according to user preferences. We tested our approach by simulating an environment where several categories of users, which are characterized by their own preferences and typical requests, interact with the MAS. We observed the behaviour of the system in order to verify that it is compliant with the designed specifications. This confirmed the effectiveness of the framework in supporting traceability of *Tropos* concepts between run-time and design-time artefacts. Moreover, starting from the run-time behaviour of the system in response to the user queries, we described a way to refine and extend the relationships among a set of user preferences and the internal goals of the system.

We believe that this is a first step towards defining feedback mechanisms from the real execution of the system back to design.

As future work we will revise the proposed framework, formalizing it and investigating on some AI technique which will allow the system agent to automatically discriminate the customer category (i.e. by user profiling) from a set of input queries. Moreover we aim at experimenting the framework in a real environmental setting.

References

1. Bresciani, P., Giorgini, P., Giunchiglia, F., Mylopoulos, J., Perini, A.: Tropos: An Agent-Oriented Software Development Methodology. Autonomous Agents and Multi-Agent Systems 8(3), 203–236 (2004)
2. Cheong, C., Winikoff, M.: Hermes: Designing Goal-Oriented Agent Interactions. In: Müller, J.P., Zambonelli, F. (eds.) AOSE 2005. LNCS, vol. 3950, Springer, Heidelberg (2006)
3. Giorgini, P., Mylopoulos, J., Nicchiarelli, E., Sebastiani, R.: Reasoning with Goal Models. In: Spaccapietra, S., March, S.T., Kambayashi, Y. (eds.) ER 2002. LNCS, vol. 2503, Springer, Heidelberg (2002)
4. Henderson-Sellers, B., Giorgini, P. (eds.): Agent-Oriented Methodologies. Idea Group Inc. (2005)
5. Jennings, N.: Foundations of Distributed Artificial Intelligence, chapter Coordination Techniques for Distributed Artificial Intelligence. Wiley-IEEE (1996)
6. Jennings, N., Sycara, K., Wooldridge, M.: A roadmap of agent research and development. Autonomous Agents and Multi-Agent Systems 1(1), 7–38 (1998)
7. Lapouchnian, A., Liaskos, S., Mylopoulos, J., Yu, Y.: Towards Requirements-Driven Autonomic Systems Design. In: Design and Evolution of Autonomic Application Software (DEAS 2005) at ICSE 2005 (2005)
8. Norvig, P., Cohn, D.: Adaptive software. PC AI 11(1), 27–30 (1997)
9. Padgham, L., Winikoff, M.: Prometheus: A practical agent-oriented methodology. In: Henderson-Sellers, B., Giorgini, P. (eds.) Agent-Oriented Methodologies, Idea Group (2005)
10. Penserini, L., Liu, L., Mylopoulos, J., Panti, M., Spalazzi, L.: Modeling and Evaluating Cooperation Strategies in P2P Agent Systems. In: Moro, G., Koubarakis, M. (eds.) AP2PC 2002. LNCS (LNAI), vol. 2530, Springer, Heidelberg (2003)
11. Penserini, L., Perini, A., Susi, A., Morandini, M., Mylopoulos, J.: A Design Framework for Generating BDI-agents from Goal Models. In: Sheory, O., Huhns, M. (eds.) AAMAS 2007, 6th International Joint Conference on Autonomous Agents and Multi-Agent Systems, Honolulu, Hawai'i (2007), Extended version available as ITC-irst TR200601002 at: `http://sra.itc.it/images/sepapers/bdiagents_goalmodels.pdf`
12. Penserini, L., Perini, A., Susi, A., Mylopoulos, J.: From Stakeholder Intentions to Software Agent Implementations. In: Dubois, E., Pohl, K. (eds.) CAiSE 2006. LNCS, vol. 4001, pp. 465–479. Springer, Heidelberg (2006)
13. Perini, A., Susi, A.: Automating Model Transformations in Agent-Oriented Modelling. In: Müller, J.P., Zambonelli, F. (eds.) AOSE 2005. LNCS, vol. 3950, pp. 167–178. Springer, Heidelberg (2006)
14. Pokahr, A., Braubach, L., Lamersdorf, W.: Jadex: A bdi reasoning engine. In: Bordini, J.D.R., Dastani, M., Seghrouchni, A.E.F. (eds.) Multi-Agent Programming, vol. 9, pp. 149–174. Springer Science+Business Media Inc., USA (2005) (Book chapter)
15. Rao, A.S., Georgeff, M.P.: Modeling rational agents within a bdi-architecture. In: KR, pp. 473–484 (1991)
16. Yu, E.: Modelling Strategic Relationships for Process Reengineering. PhD thesis, University of Toronto, Department of Computer Science, University of Toronto (1995)
17. Zambonelli, F., Jennings, N.R., Wooldridge, M.: Developing multiagent systems: The gaia methodology. ACM Transactions on software Engineering and Methodology 12(3), 317–370 (2003)

A Goal-Oriented Software Testing Methodology

Duy Cu Nguyen, Anna Perini, and Paolo Tonella

SRA Division / ITC-irst
Via Sommarive, 18
38050 Trento, Italy
{cunduy,perini,tonella}@itc.it

Abstract. Agent-Oriented Software Engineering (AOSE) methodologies are proposed to develop complex distributed systems based upon the agent paradigm. The natural implementation for such systems has usually the form of Multi-Agent Systems (MAS). As these systems are increasingly applied in mission-critical services, assurances need to be given to their owners and users that they operate properly. Although the relevance of the link between requirements engineering and testing has long been recognized, current Agent-Oriented Software Engineering methodologies partially address it. Some of them offer specification-based formal verification, allowing software developers to correct errors at the beginning of the development process, others exploits Object-Oriented (OO) testing techniques, upon a mapping of agent-oriented abstractions into OO constructs. However, a structured testing process for AOSE methodologies that complements formal verification is still missing.

In this paper we introduce a testing framework for the AOSE methodology *Tropos*. It specifies a testing process model that complements the agent-oriented requirements and design models and strengthens the mutual relationship between goal analysis and testing. Furthermore, it provides a systematic way of deriving test cases from goal analysis. We call this approach goal-oriented testing.

1 Introduction

The changing of organizational architecture and the use of Internet-based applications make software systems more and more complex. These systems often involve variety of users and heterogeneous platforms. They need to be evolved continuously in order to meet the changes of business and technology. In some circumstances, they need to be autonomous and adaptive for dealing with different preferences and pervasive amount of information.

As these systems are increasingly taking over operations in enterprise management and financing, assurances need to be given to their owners and their users that these complex systems operate properly. This calls for an investigation of suitable software engineering frameworks, including requirements engineering and testing techniques, to provide high-quality software development processes and products.

M. Luck and L. Padgham (Eds.): AOSE 2007, LNCS 4951, pp. 58–72, 2008.

The strong link between requirements engineering and testing have been commonly recognized [11]. First, designing test cases early and in parallel with requirements helps discover problems early, thus avoiding implementing erroneous specification. Secondly, good requirements produce better tests. Moreover, early test specification produces better requirements as it helps clarify ambiguity in requirements. The link is so relevant that considerable effort has been devoted to what is called test-driven (or test-first) development. In such approach, tests are produced from requirements before implementing the requirements themselves [1].

Research in AOSE mainly addresses development issues in software agents and MAS. Several AOSE methodologies [12] have been proposed. Some of them offer specification-based formal verification, allowing software developers to detect errors at the beginning of the development process (e.g. *Formal Tropos* [10] and [7]). Others borrow Object-Oriented (OO) testing techniques to be exploited later in the development process, upon a mapping of agent-oriented abstractions into OO constructs (e.g. *PASSI [6]* and *INGENIAS [14]*). However, a structured testing process for AOSE methodologies that complements formal verification is still missing

In this paper, we propose a testing framework that takes into account the strong link between requirements and test cases, following the V-Model [16]. We describe the proposed approach with reference to *Tropos* [4] and consider MAS as a target application of the methodology. In analogy with OO approaches in which test cases are derived from use-case requirements models, we investigate how to derive test cases from *Tropos* requirements goal-models. We call this approach Goal-Oriented (GO) testing.

Specifically, the proposed methodology contributes to the existing *Tropos* methodology by providing: (*i*) a testing process model, which complements the *Tropos* methodology and strengthens the mutual relationship between goals and test cases; (*ii*) a systematic way for deriving test cases from goal analysis.

The remainder of the paper is organized as follows. Section 2 recalls basic elements of the *Tropos* methodology and introduces related work. Section 3 discusses the proposed methodology, a testing model, goal types, test types, test derivation, and structure of test suite. An example that illustrates how to derive test suites is presented in Section 4. Finally, Section 5 gives conclusion and describes our future work.

2 Background and Related Work

2.1 Background on Tropos

Tropos is an agent-oriented software engineering methodology [4] that adopts a requirement-driven approach, that is domain and system requirement analysis plays a pivotal role in the development process. In *Tropos*, the notion of agent and all related mentalistic notions (for instance goals, plans, and resources) are used in all phases of software development, from early analysis down to implementation.

The methodology provides a conceptual modeling language based on the $i*$ framework [20], a goal analysis technique and a diagrammatic notation to build views on a model. Basic constructs of the language are those of actor, goal, plan, softgoal, resource, and capabilities. Dependency links between pairs of actors allow to model the fact that one actor depends on another in order to achieve a goal, execute a plan, or acquire a resource and can be depicted in *actor diagrams.* As an example, Fig. 1 shows how those constructs are used to model a MAS that supports users (such as researchers) during bibliographic research. Both the user and the system are represented as actors (circles), user needs are represented in terms of goal dependencies from the actor *Researcher* to the system actor *BibFinder*, e.g. by the hard goal *Find Bib* and the softgoal *Fast and efficient.* Details of this example are discussed in Section 4.

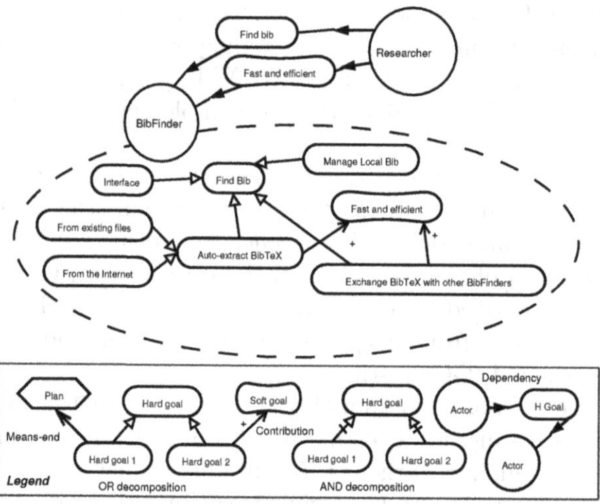

Fig. 1. An example of late requirements analysis in *Tropos*. The actor *Researcher* delegates two goals *Find Bib*, and *Fast and efficient* to the system actor *BibFinder*. *BibFinder* then analyzes those two goals in order to achieve them.

In *Tropos*, goals are classified into hardgoals and softgoals, the latter has no clear-cut definition and/or criteria as to whether they are satisfied. Softgoals are particularly useful to specify non-functional requirements. Goals are analyzed from the owner actor perspective through *AND, OR* decomposition; *means-end* analysis of *plans* and *resources* that provide means for achieving the goal (the end); contribution analysis that points out hardgoals and softgoals that contribute positively or negatively to reaching the goal being analyzed.

2.2 Related Work

Agent verification can be classified into static and dynamic verification. Among work on static verification, Bordini et al. [3] presented an approach to the verification of MAS implemented in AgentSpeak. MAS specifications were transformed into Promela or Java, and model checkers i.e. Spin and JPF (a general purpose Java model checker) were then used to verify the properties that those systems needed to satisfy. Benerecetti et al. [2] introduced a multi-agent temporal logic that extended temporal logic for formalizing BDI attitudes of agent. They then proposed MAFSM (Multi-Agent Finite State Machine) and a model-checking algorithm for verifying agent properties formalized in that logic on a MAFSM.

Recent researches on dynamic verification (testing) of MAS have mainly investigated monitoring MAS at run-time in order to observe abnormal behaviors. Coelho et al. [5] focused on unit testing (i.e. single agent testing) with the help of mock agents that simulated real agents that the agent under test communicated with. A monitoring agent has been involved to monitor the interactions among agents. Poutakidis et al. [15] used knowledge from diagrams that specified communication protocols during the architectural design phase to monitor execution and detect problems of a MAS. Dikenelli et al. [19] proposed a test-driven MAS development approach that supports iterative and incremental MAS construction. A testing framework, which is built on top of JUnit and Seagent [9], is used to support the approach. The framework allows writing automated tests for agent behaviors and interactions between agents.

3 The Methodology

3.1 A Process Model for Goal-Oriented Testing

The V-Model [16] is a representation of the system development process, which extends the traditional water-fall model. The left branch of the V represents the specification stream, and the right branch of the V represents the testing stream where the systems are being tested (against the specifications defined on the left-branch). One of the advantages of the V-model is that it describes not only construction stream but also testing stream, i.e., unit test, integration test, acceptance test, and the mutual relationships between them.

Tropos guides the software engineers in building a conceptual model, which is incrementally refined and extended, from an early requirements model to system design artifacts and then to code, according to the upper branch of the V (corresponding to the left branch of the original V) depicted in Fig. 2. We integrate testing in *Tropos* by proposing the lower branch of the V (corresponding to the right branch of the original V) and a systematic way to derive test cases from *Tropos* modeling results, i.e. the upper branch of the V, in Fig. 2.

The modeling artifacts produced along the development process are: a domain model (i.e. the organizational setting, as is), the *Early Requirements* model; a model of the system-to-be where system requirements are modeled in terms of system goal graph, *Late Requirements* model; a system architecture model, specified in terms of a set of interacting software agents, *Architectural Design* model; a specification of software agent roles, capabilities, and interactions, *Detailed Design* model; agent code *Implementation* artifact.

Two levels of testing are distinguished in the model. At the first level of the model (external test – test executed after release), stakeholders (in collaboration

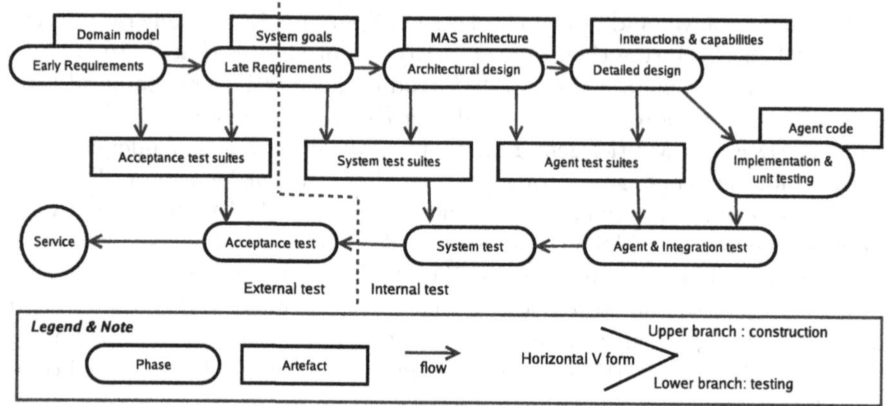

Fig. 2. V-Model for GO testing

with the analysts), during requirement acquisition time produce the specification of acceptance test suites. These test suites are one of the premises to judge whether the system fulfills stakeholders' goals.

At the second level (internal test – test executed before release), developers refer to: goals that are assigned to the system-to-be, high-level architecture, detailed design of interactions and capabilities of single agents, and implement these agents. Based on the output of the *Late Requirements* and *Architectural Design* phases, developers derive system test suites to test the system under development at system level. Similarly, based on the output of the *Architectural Design* and *Detailed Design* phases, developers derive agent test suites to test agents individually as well as to test interactions among them. The derivation of test suites is conducted in the same time as developers specify or design the system, thus helping them refine their design and uncover defects early.

3.2 Testing Types and Goal Types

Currently, we focus on the internal level of the V (the right half of Fig. 2) and consider three types of testing: *Agent testing*, *Integration testing*, and *System testing*. The objectives and scope of each type is described as follows:

- *Agent testing.* The smallest unit of testing in agent-oriented programming is an agent. Testing a single agent consists of testing its inner functionality and the functionality it exposes to other agents with respect to the assigned goals.
- *Integration testing.* An agent has been unit-tested, we have to test its integration with existing agents. In some circumstances, we have to test also the integration of that agent with the agents that will be developed and integrated subsequently. Integration testing involves making sure an agent works properly with the agents that have been integrated before it and with the "future" agents that are in the course of *Agent testing* or that are not

ready to be integrated. This often leads to developing mock agents or stubs that simulate the behaviors of the "future" agents.
- *System testing.* Agents may operate correctly when they run alone but incorrectly when they are put together. System testing involves making sure all agents in the system work together as intended. Specifically, one must test the interactions among agents (protocol, incompatible content or convention, etc.) and other concerns like security, deadlock.

Goals can be classified according to different perspectives or criteria. For instance, goals can be classified into perform goals, achieve goals, and maintain goals according to the agent's attitude toward goals [8]. Other goal types are also discussed elsewhere e.g. *KAOS* [7]. In this paper, since we are interested in separating individual agent's behavior from social behavior induced by goal delegation in *Tropos*, we consider two types of goal: *delegated goal* and *own goal.* The former goal type is delegated to one agent (dependee) by another agent (depender). This goal type often leads to interactions between the two agents: The depender demands (by sending requests to) the dependee to fulfill the goal. The later goal type requires responsibility of its owner; however, the owner agent does not necessarily run within its boundary, i.e. it can involve interactions with other agents as well.

One can reason about assigned goals of the *own* type of a single agent to come out with *agent testing* level. That is, based on these goals, developers could figure out which plans or behaviors of the agent, i.e. functionality, to test. Since *integration testing* and *system testing* involve making sure the operation of agents together in the system, the goals of type *delegated* and those goals of type *own* that involve agents interactions are good starting points for these testing types.

3.3 Test Suites Derivation

Goals are states of affair, and one must do something in order to achieve his/her goals. A very natural way of testing the achievement of a goal is to check one's work or behavior with respect to the goal. Similarly, in order to test a goal in *Tropos*, we have to check what the system does or plans to do to fulfill the goal.

When applying the *Tropos* methodology, we can find out how goals can be fulfilled by looking at their relationships with other goals and with plans. For instance, if there is a *Means-End* relationship between goal $G1$ and plan $P1$, we say $G1$ is fulfilled when $P1$ is executed successfully; if goal $G2$ contributes positively to softgoal $SG2$ (*Contribution+* relationship) then we can say $SG2$ is partially satisfied when $G2$ is fulfilled. Based on the relationships associated with a goal, we can check the fulfillment of the goal.

Goal-goal or goal-plan relationships are classified into two categories: *elementary relationships* and *intermediate relationships*. *Elementary relationships* are depicted in Fig. 3. This includes (1) *Means-End* between a plan and a hard goal; (2) *Contribution+* between a plan and a softgoal; (3) *Contribution-* between a plan and a softgoal. In order to test this kind of relationships, the execution of the plan corresponding to a goal is triggered and checked through assertions on the

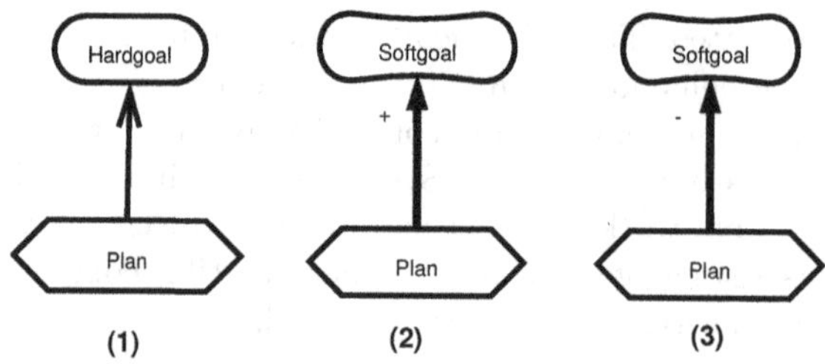

Fig. 3. Elementary relationships. (1): a *Means-End* plan-hardgoal; (2): a *Contribution+* plan-softgoal; (3): a *Contribution-* plan-softgoal.

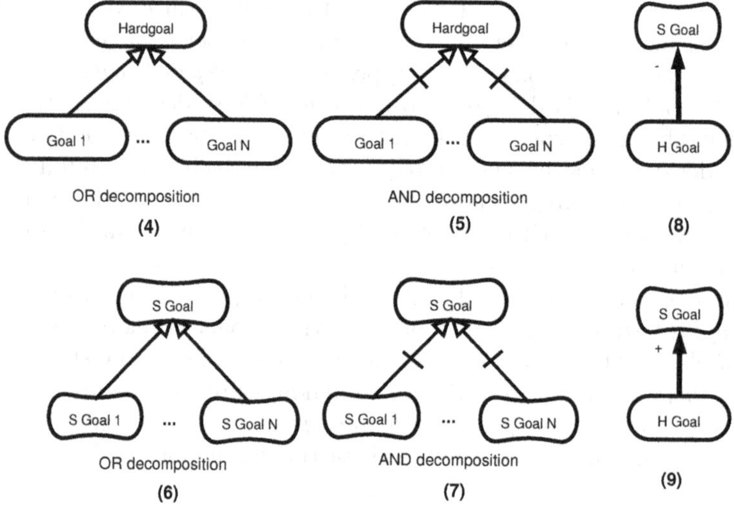

Fig. 4. Intermediate relationships

expected behavior. Developers derive test suites from goal diagrams by starting from the relationships associated with each goal. Each relationship gives raise to a corresponding test suite, consisting of a set of test cases that are used to check goal fulfillment (called positive test cases) and unfulfillment (called negative test cases). Positive test cases are aimed at verifying the fulfillment capability of an agent with regard to a given goal; negative test cases, on the other hand, are used to ensure an appropriate behavior of the system under test when it can not achieve a given goal such as error management.

Intermediate relationships are shown in Fig. 4. Six intermediate relationships are considered: (4) *OR decomposition* of a hardgoal into N sub-hardgoals; (5) *AND decomposition* of a hardgoal into N sub-hardgoals; (6) *OR decomposition* of a softgoal into N sub-softgoals; (7) *AND decomposition* of a softgoal into N sub-softgoals; (8) *Contribution-* of a hardgoal to a softgoal; and (9) *Contribution+* of a hardgoal to a softgoal. In order to test the fulfillment of the root goals that are decomposed into subgoals or of those which receive contributions from other goals, we have to test the fulfillment of their subgoals or of those that contribute

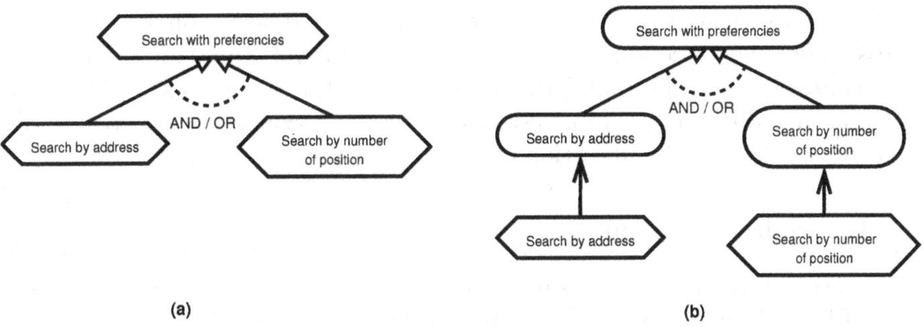

Fig. 5. An example of changing plan decomposition (a) to goal decomposition (b) alternative way of representing that decomposition: the plan decomposition is changed to a goal decomposition and two means-end relationships are added

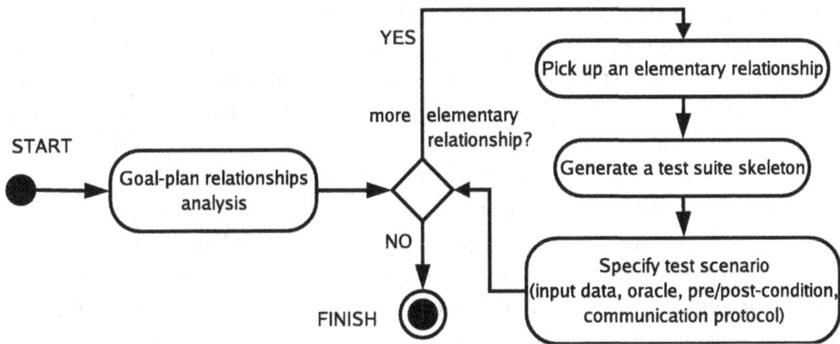

Fig. 6. Test-suites derivation steps

to them. Specifically, to test the root goal of (5) or (7), we have to test the fulfillment of N subgoals at the same time; to test the root goal of (4) or (6), we have to test the fulfillment of each subgoals; to test the root goal of (8) or (9), we have to test the corresponding hardgoals (contributing goals). The subgoals or contributing goals become, in turn, root goals of further analysis. This process continues until all considered relationships are of elementary kind. Therefore, the testing of goals in intermediate relationships is approached eventually by the testing of goals that are part of elementary relationships.

There could be additional types of relationships that differ from those presented above. For instance, a common practice is to decompose a plan into several sub-plans. This could be avoidable by replacing the original plan by a goal that is then decomposed into subgoals; the sub-plans are then means to achieve those subgoals. An example is illustrated in Fig. 5.

To this end, test-suites derivation for testing goal fulfillment is realized by investigating all relationships that lead to the goal. This ends up analyzing all elementary relationships (ER), as described above. The derivation steps for ER are shown in Fig 6. At the first step: *Goal-plan relationships analysis*, the tester has to identify all ER in the goal diagrams, i.e., *Tropos* architectural and detailed design diagrams (results of the architectural and detailed design phase, see our V process model in Subsection 3.1). Then, he/she iteratively takes an ER, creates a test suites skeleton for that ER, and completes the test suites by filling in test data, including input data, test oracle, pre/post-condition etc. Test suite structure is described in Subsection 3.4.

3.4 Test Suites Structure

The structure of the test suites is partially summarized, using a BNF-style notation, in Fig. 7. A test suite contains three parts: <*General*>, <*Functional*>, and one or more <*TestCase*>. <*General*> contains descriptive information such as ID, name, created by, version, date of creation, and textual, free-format description. <*Functional*> contains functional information about the agent under test, the goal-plan couple being tested, pre-/post-conditions, test suite setup and teardown activities. <*TestCase*>, in turn, apart from general information and test case setup/teardown activities, contains the core element of a test suite: <*Scenario*>.

A test scenario consists of an ordered set of sequences, which is in turn a communication act (<*Initiator*>, <*Responder*>, <*Message*>), a branching or sequencing condition (<*NextSequence*>, <*NextIfTrue*>, <*NextIfFalse*>), or a check point (test oracle) to validate output data (<*Condition*>). <*Scenario*> is also used to specify the interaction protocol, in which check points can be added for testing purposes. The comparison operators <*CompareOpt*> between message <*Message*> and <*ConditionData*> include *eq*: equal, *ne*: not equal, *ge*: greater or equal, etc., *contains*: message content contains condition data, $not - null$: message content is not null.

As an example of test scenario, let's assume that we have an agent acting as a tester agent, called *TA*, and an agent under test, named *BibFinder*. *TA* can

```
<TestSuite>     ::= <General> <Functional> <TestCase>+
<General>       ::= <ID> <Name> <CreatedBy> <Version> <CreatedDate> <Description>
<Functional>    ::= <AgentInCharge> <GoalPlan>+ [<PreCondition>] [<PostCondition>]
                    [<Setup>] [<Teardown>]
<GoalPlan>      ::= <Goal> <Plan> <Relationship>
<Relationship>  ::= Means-End | Contribution--| Contribution-| Contribution+| Contribution++
<TestCase>      ::= <ID> <Name> [<Type>] [<Desctiption>] [<TCSetup>] [<TCTeardown>]
                    <Scenario> [<PostCondition>] <Active> <Priotity>
<Scenario>      ::= <Sequence>+
<Sequence>      ::= <ID> <Initiator> <Responder> <SequenceType> [<NextSequence>]
                    [<NextIfTrue>] [<NextIfFalse>] [<Message>] [<Condition>] [<TimeOut>]
<Condition>     ::= <CompareOpt> <ConditionData>
<SequenceType> ::= initial | checkpoint | communication | branch | final
<Message>       ::= ACLMessage | AnyType // AnyType accepts both structured and unstructured text
<ConditionData> ::= AnyType
<CompareOpt> ::= eq | ne | ge | le | gt | lt | contains | not-contains | is-null | not-null
<Active>        ::= true | false
<Priotity>      ::= double // value between 0-1
```

Fig. 7. Test suite structure

test the search function of *BibFinder* by a test scenario having two sequences as follows: $Seq_1 \doteq$ (*Initiator* = *TA*, *Responder* = *BibFinder*, *Message* = *"search keywords: aamas"*, *SequenceType* = *initial*, *NextSequence* = Seq_2); $Seq_2 \doteq$ (*Initiator* = *BibFinder*, *Responder* = *TS*, *SequenceType* = *checkpoint*, *Condition* $\doteq$ (*CompareOpt* = *not-null*)). The scenario says that *TS* sends a request to *BibFinder* asking it to search for "aamas", and then *TS* checks the response from *BibFinder* to see if the result is not null.

The proposed structure of test suite, test case, and test scenario are designed such that they can be used at different formality levels and with different programming languages. Informally, developers can specify their test cases using descriptive text. This format can be used by human testers to manually provide input data to the system and evaluate the output results. When used formally, the specified test cases can be read by a testing tool to test the system automatically. To obtain these purposes, the elements *Pre-condition, Post-condition, Setup, Teardown, Message*, and *ConditionData* are designed to contain any user-defined data type; developers can associate their data with their own parser and grammar. An example in Section 4 will illustrate how the structure is used formally to specify a test case of a communication act and *Pre-condition.*

3.5 Agent Testing Tool

In order to facilitate test-suites derivation and execution, we propose an agent testing tool, called eCAT[1] that consists of three main components: *Test Suite Editor*, that semi-automatically generates test suites skeleton and allows human testers to specify test data from goal analysis diagrams produced by TAOM4E[2], a tool that supports *Tropos*; *Autonomous Tester Agent*, a special JADE [18] agent that is capable of executing test suites against a MAS; and *Monitoring Agent*, that monitors communications and events among agents to help debugging.

Testing execution is realized by the *Autonomous Tester Agent*, following test specification in the test suites. Depending on the <*SequenceType*> of each sequence of the specified scenario, the *Autonomous Tester Agent* either reads the defined message and sends it to the agent under test (*Responder*), or waits for a response from the agent under test to evaluate the test result with respect to the specified <*Condition*>. The later happens when <*SequenceType*> equals to *checkpoint.*

4 An Example

In scientific research and writing, bibliography search is a time-consuming activity. BibFinder is a MAS for the retrieval of bibliographic information in BibTeX format[3]. BibFinder is capable of scanning the local drivers of the host machine,

---

[1] More information about the tool: `http://dit.unitn.it/~dnguyen/ecat`

[2] `http://sra.itc.it/tools/taom4e`

[3] `http://www.ecst.csuchico.edu/~jacobsd/bib/formats/bibtex.html`

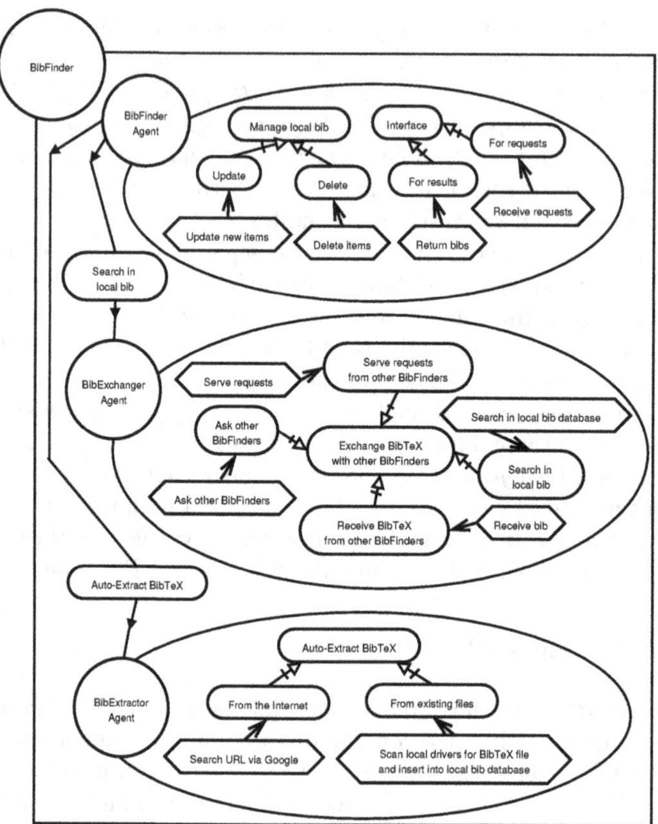

Fig. 8. Architecture of BibFinder. BibFinder contains three "physical" agents: *BibFinderAgent*, *BibExchangerAgent*, and *BibExtractorAgent*.

where it runs, to search for bibliographic data in the format of BibTeX. It consolidates databases spread over multiple devices into a unique one, where the queried item can be quickly searched. BibFinder can also exchange bibliographic information with other agents, in a peer-to-peer manner, thus augmenting its search capability with those provided by other peer agents. Moreover, BibFinder performs searches on and extracts BibTeX data from the Scientific Literature Digital Library[4], exploiting the Google search Web service[5].

Let's revisit Fig. 1 that shows the late requirements analysis of BibFinder. Basically, the actor *Researcher* depends on the BibFinder system by the hard goal *Find Bib* and the softgoal *Fast and efficient*. Inside BibFinder, the former goal is decomposed into subgoals *Interface* to external systems, *Manage local bib* database, *Auto-extract bibtex* either *From existing files* or *From the Internet*, and *Exchange bibtex with other BibFinders*. The three goals *Manage local bib*,

[4] `http://citeseer.ist.psu.edu`

[5] `http://code.google.com/apis/soapsearch`

Auto-extract bibtex, and *Exchange bibtex with other BibFinders* contribute positively to the softgoal *Fast and efficient.*

Fig. 8 shows the architecture of BibFinder. BibFinder is composed of three agents, namely: *BibFinderAgent*, *BibExtractorAgent*, and *BibExchangerAgent.* The goals identified in the late requirements analysis phase are assigned to these agents. For instance, *Manage local bib* and *Interface* are assigned to the *BibFinderAgent* agent while *Exchange bibtex with other BibFinders* is the *BibExchangerAgent*'s task.The *BibExtractorAgent* agent is in charge of the goal *Auto-extract bibtex*; and the *BibFinderAgent* depends on the *BibExtractorAgent* agent for that goal in order to serve requests from external systems.

4.1 Test Suites Derivation for BibFinder

Testing BibFinder consists of testing its three agents (*BibFinderAgent*, *BibExtractorAgent*, *BibExchangerAgent*) and the interactions among them (presented as goal dependencies). Inside each agent, we analyze the top root goal to find out all elementary relationships. A test suite will be derived for each elementary relationship by following the steps described in Fig. 6. For instance, test suite *TS1: Search-Bib* is derived from the *Means-End* relationship between the goal *Search in local bib* and the plan *Search in local bib database.* The goal is delegated by the *BibFinderAgent* agent to the *BibExchangerAgent* agent, so two sample test cases are defined to check if the latter agent is able to search for an existing BibTeX item and if it behaves properly in case of badly formatted request; and two test cases address the former agent's ability to delegate the request.

Fig. 9 in depicts the test suite *TS1* in XML format. Apart from general and functional elements, the test suite contains four test cases. The test scenario of the first test case has two sequences. The first one consists of sending a request to the *BibFinderAgent.* The request asks the *BibFinderAgent* to find BibTeX related to the keywords *Tropos Methodology* (request content is shown in Fig. 10, placed on the Fig. 9). The second sequence specifies a checkpoint where the tester agent waits for a result and then verifies if it contains "John Mylopoulos".

As an example of using pre-condition, Fig. 11 (placed on Fig. 9) illustrates a graphical presentation of the *BibFinderAgent* and shows the <*PreCondition*> of *TS1* in OCL [17]. Basically, the *BibFinderAgent* has two references to the *BibExtractorAgent* and *BibExchangerAgent*, and they must not be null whenever the *BibFinderAgent* processes a request by the method *action().* The pre-condition of *TS1* is specified to guarantee this constraint. Then, it can be transformed to executable code, e.g. Java, and used in the course of testing the *BibFinderAgent.*

4.2 Testing BibFinder Against the Derived Test Suites

BibFinder has been implemented under JADE [18] and tested by the agent testing tool introduced in Subsection 3.5. For experimenting, we derived three test suites from three *Means-End* relationships in the architectural design of BibFinder: *TS1: Search-Bib*, described in Subsection 4.1; *TS2: Search-URL-via-Google; TS3: Update-Bib.* The tool took these test suites and executed them against the BibFinder.

```
<?xml version="1.0" encoding="UTF-8" ?>
- <TestSuite xmlns="http://sra.itc.it/se/TestSuite" xmlns:tc="http://sra.itc.it/se/TestCase"
    xmlns:acl="http://www.fipa.org/ACLSchema" xmlns:tsc="http://sra.itc.it/se/TestScenario"
    xmlns:xsi="http://www.w3.org/2001/XMLSchema-instance"
    xsi:schemaLocation="http://sra.itc.it/se/TestSuite ..\xsd\TestSuite.xsd">
  + <General>
  - <Functional>
      <AgentInCharge>BibFinderAgent</AgentInCharge>
    - <GoalPlan>
        <Goal>Search in local bib</Goal>
        <Plan>Search in local bib Database</Plan>
        <Relationship>Means-End</Relationship>
      </GoalPlan>
    </Functional>
  - <tc:TestCase>
      <tc:ID>TS1-TC1</tc:ID>
      <tc:Name>Search Bib</tc:Name>
      <tc:Type>possitive</tc:Type>
      <tc:Description>Search bibtex items for a given title</tc:Description>
    - <tc:Scenario>
      - <tsc:Sequence>
          <tsc:ID>TC1001</tsc:ID>
          <tsc:Initiator>TesterAgent</tsc:Initiator>
          <tsc:Responder>BibFinderAgent</tsc:Responder>
          <tsc:SequenceType>initial</tsc:SequenceType>
          <tsc:NextSequence>TC1002</tsc:NextSequence>
        - <tsc:Message>
          + <acl:fipa-message act="REQUEST" conversation-id="C12">
          </tsc:Message>
          <tsc:Timeout>5000</tsc:Timeout>
        </tsc:Sequence>
      - <tsc:Sequence>
          <tsc:ID>TC1002</tsc:ID>
          <tsc:Initiator>BibFinderAgent</tsc:Initiator>
          <tsc:Responder>TesterAgent</tsc:Responder>
          <tsc:SequenceType>checkpoint</tsc:SequenceType>
        - <tsc:Message>
          - <acl:fipa-message act="INFORM">
            + <acl:msg-param>
            </acl:fipa-message>
          </tsc:Message>
        - <tsc:Condition>
            <tsc:compareOpt>contains</tsc:compareOpt>
          - <tsc:ConditionData>
            - <acl:fipa-message act="INFORM">
              - <acl:msg-param>
                  <acl:content>John Mylopoulos</acl:content>
                </acl:msg-param>
              </acl:fipa-message>
            </tsc:ConditionData>
          </tsc:Condition>
          <tsc:Timeout>5000</tsc:Timeout>
        </tsc:Sequence>
      </tc:Scenario>
      <tc:Active>true</tc:Active>
      <tc:Priority>0.9</tc:Priority>
    </tc:TestCase>
  + <tc:TestCase>
  + <tc:TestCase>
  + <tc:TestCase>
  </TestSuite>
```

Fig. 9. *TS1 - Search Bib* test suite

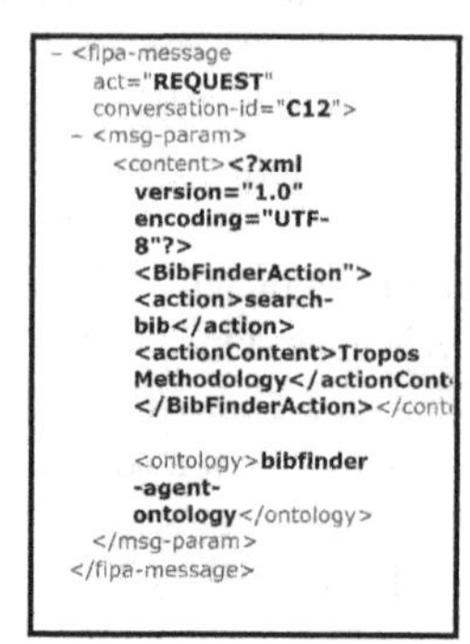

```
- <fipa-message
    act="REQUEST"
    conversation-id="C12">
  - <msg-param>
      <content><?xml
        version="1.0"
        encoding="UTF-
        8"?>
        <BibFinderAction">
        <action>search-
        bib</action>
        <actionContent>Tropos
        Methodology</actionCont
        </BibFinderAction></cont

        <ontology>bibfinder
        -agent-
        ontology</ontology>
    </msg-param>
  </fipa-message>
```

Fig. 10. Content of the request **C12**

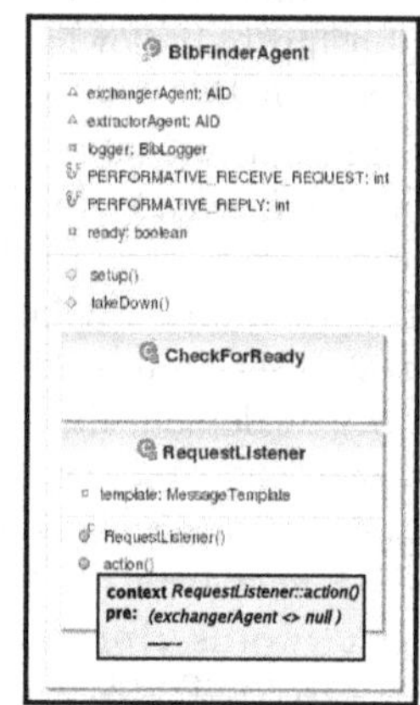

Fig. 11. Pre-condition expression of *TS1*

These test suites have revealed four moderate severity errors, related to the *BibExtractor* agent, which, in some cases, does not reply to an admissible request, replies to the wrong address or wrong performative. The last defect is related to the *BibFinder* agent, that is it raises a fatal error while updating a wrong BibTeX item.

5 Conclusion and Future Work

This paper introduced a GO testing methodology that takes design artifacts, specified as *Tropos* goal models, as central elements to derive test cases. The methodology provides a systematic guidance to generate test suites along the *Tropos* development process. These test suites, on the one hand, are used to refine goal analysis and detect problems early at the requirement phase. On the other hand, they are executed afterward to test the achievement of the goals from which they were derived. Our preliminary application of the proposed methodology in testing BibFinder, which has been introduced in Section 4, are promising in detecting errors.

Different goal types, testing types, and the connection between them were discussed. In addition, the test suite structure was also discussed. The detailed structures of test suite, test case, and test scenario in XML format are introduced separately in a technical report [13].

In the paper, the proposed methodology has focused mainly on the goal concept, leaving out other dependencies among actors like *resource dependency, plan dependency.* The methodology will be extended to cover those types of dependency as well. In addition, the internal structure of a plan has not been fully exploited. Detailed information concerning operations and interactions could facilitate detailed test generation. In the future work, we will investigate plan modeling as well in order to extract this information.

In particular, we are investigating MAS testing with respect to the properties of MAS such as autonomous and adaptive. A technique, called *continuous testing*, is being implemented. It takes test suites derived by following the proposed methodology, evolves and runs them continuously against a MAS in order to find defects.

References

1. Beck, K.: Test Driven Development: By Example. Addison-Wesley Longman Publishing Co., Inc., Boston (2002)
2. Benerecetti, M., Giunchiglia, F., Serafini, L.: Model checking multiagent systems. Journal of Logic and Computation 8(3), 401–423 (1998)
3. Bordini, R., Fisher, M., Visser, W., Wooldridge, M.: Verifying multi-agent programs by model checking. Autonomous Agents and Multi-Agent Systems 12, 239–256 (2006)
4. Bresciani, P., Giorgini, P., Giunchiglia, F., Mylopoulos, J., Perini, A.: Tropos: An Agent-Oriented Software Development Methodology. Autonomous Agents and Multi-Agent Systems 8(3), 203–236 (2004)
5. Coelho, R., Kulesza, U., von Staa, A., Lucena, C.: Unit testing in multi-agent systems using mock agents and aspects. In: SELMAS 2006: Proceedings of the 2006 international workshop on Software engineering for large-scale multi-agent systems, pp. 83–90. ACM Press, New York (2006)
6. Cossentino, M.: From requirements to code with the passi methodology. In: Henderson-Sellers, Giorgini [12]
7. Dardenne, A., van Lamsweerde, A., Fickas, S.: Goal-directed requirements acquisition. Science of Computer Programming 20(1-2), 3–50 (1993)
8. Dastani, M., van Riemsdijk, M.B., Meyer, J.-J.C.: Goal types in agent programming. In: ECAI, pp. 220–224 (2006)

9. Dikenelli, O., Erdur, R.C., Gumus, O.: Seagent: a platform for developing semantic web based multi agent systems. In: AAMAS 2005: Proceedings of the fourth international joint conference on Autonomous agents and multiagent systems, pp. 1271–1272. ACM Press, New York (2005)
10. Fuxman, A., Liu, L., Mylopoulos, J., Pistore, M., Roveri, M., Traverso, P.: Specifying and analyzing early requirements in tropos. Requir. Eng. 9(2), 132–150 (2004)
11. Graham, D.R.: Requirements and testing: Seven missing-link myths. IEEE Software 19(5), 15–17 (2002)
12. Henderson-Sellers, B., Giorgini, P. (eds.): Agent-Oriented Methodologies. Idea Group Inc. (2005)
13. Nguyen, D.C., Perini, A., Tonella, P.: A goal-oriented software testing methodology. Technical report, ITC-irst (2006), `http://sra.itc.it/images/sepapers/gost-techreport.pdf`
14. Pavon, J., Gomez-Sanz, J.J., Fuentes, R.: The ingenias methodology and tools. In: Henderson-Sellers, Giorgini [12]
15. Poutakidis, D., Padgham, L., Winikoff, M.: An exploration of bugs and debugging in multi-agent systems. In: AAMAS 2003: Proceedings of the second international joint conference on Autonomous agents and multiagent systems, pp. 1100–1101. ACM Press, New York (2003)
16. The Development Standards for IT Systems of the Federal Republic of Germany. The V-Model (2005), `http://www.v-modell-xt.de`
17. The Object Management Group. Uml ocl2 specification (2005), `http://www.omg.org`
18. TILAB. Java agent development framework, `http://jade.tilab.com/`
19. Tiryaki, A.M., Oztuna, S., Dikenelli, O., Erdur, R.: Sunit: A unit testing framework for test driven development of multi-agent systems. In: Padgham, L., Zambonelli, F. (eds.) AOSE 2006. LNCS, vol. 4405, Springer, Heidelberg (2007)
20. Yu, E.: Modelling Strategic Relationships for Process Reengineering. PhD thesis, University of Toronto, Department of Computer Science, University of Toronto (1995)

Open Agent Systems ???

Frank Dignum[1], Virginia Dignum[1], John Thangarajah[2], Lin Padgham[2], and Michael Winikoff[2]

[1] Dept. Information and Computing Sciences, Utrecht University
The Netherlands
{dignum,virginia}@cs.uu.nl
[2] RMIT University
Melbourne, Australia
{johthan,linpa,winikoff}@cs.rmit.edu.au

Abstract. E-institutions are envisioned as facilities on the Internet for heterogeneous software agents to perform their interactions and thus forming truly open agent systems. We investigate how these heterogeneous agents can determine whether an institution is one in which they can participate. We propose a layered approach which is supported through a (traditional) middle agent that is part of the environment. Starting with a basic compatibility of message types, each extra layer ensures a higher degree of compatibility, but requires also extra sophistication in both the information required and the matching algorithms. In this paper, we describe reasoning about how an agent should take on a specific role, message matching, and protocol compatibility. We explore the issues in the context of an actual accommodation agent built in JACK, and a travel agency institution built in ISLANDER.

1 Introduction

The notion of *"open agent systems"* is a popular and appealing one. However, there are many question marks associated with making such a vision a reality! Increasingly, the Internet is being viewed as an open interaction space where many heterogeneous agents co-exist. As in human societies, electronic interaction spaces must deal with issues inherent to open environments, namely heterogeneity of agents; trust and accountability; exception handling (detection, prevention and recovery from failures that may jeopardise the global operation of the system); and societal change (capability of accommodating structural changes). *Electronic Institutions* have been proposed as a way to implement interaction conventions for agents to regulate their interactions and establish commitments in an open environment [1]. In theory, such open environments have open admission policies, and therefore potentially fluid membership, and in such an environment, any agent could join a given institution. However, it is not clear how an agent should determine whether a particular institution is one that makes sense for it to join. Is the institution one in which it will be able to successfully achieve its goals? Can it successfully exchange the expected messages for a given role in the institution? Currently, in practice, agents are designed so as to be able to operate exclusively with a single given institution, thus basically defying the open nature of the institution.

M. Luck and L. Padgham (Eds.): AOSE 2007, LNCS 4951, pp. 73–87, 2008.

We consider the situation in which many different institutions and agents coexist, and where the institutions and the agents pursue their own goals, but are dependent on each other to realize them. We take as an example the domain of travel, where institutions represent travel agencies and agents can be seen as representing individuals (or enterprises) seeking or offering certain services (trips, hotels, air tickets, ...). Institutions are developed by (possibly competing) entities with the view to offering an interaction space around a certain topic (flights, tourism in Victoria, eco-tourism, etc.) enforcing certain regulations on the interaction. The institutions may be more or less regulated allowing for more or less autonomy and openness to agents. An agent may want to join different institutions in order to fulfill its goals (e.g. either to compare prices, to get the most clients, or to create a total package from the different possibilities offered by different institutions).

We further assume that institutions and agents are developed independently from each other, hence structures are needed to support and guide the search and joining process. The greater the level of standardization, the simpler it will be to provide such support. The aim of this work is to give guidance on what information needs to be provided by agents and by institutions, in order to reason about compatibility. We aim to move away from the current situation where agents are hand-crafted to participate in a particular institutional space. Our aim is to move towards agents being able to determine at run time whether they can sensibly participate in a given institution. It may be clear that a "correct" decision about participation is very complex and involves reasoning about the semantics of what the agent and the institution try to achieve and their compatibility. In this paper we will not attempt to give a complete solution for this problem in one step, but rather sketch a way in which the solution to this decision problem can be approximated. This is done by involving more aspects of the problem in different stages and also adding more semantic matchmaking aspects to a basis of more syntactic matchmaking solutions.

While standards facilitate this kind of reasoning and support (and are indeed a kind of baseline for our approach), our aim is to keep the requirements on agents and institutions as minimal (and realistic) as possible. Where possible, we attempt to use existing (W3C) standards, or information that could be expected to fairly readily be made available. Although few real standards have been developed specifically for agents (see FIPA[1] for the state of the art), we can make use of standards such as WSDL[2] for message formats and OWL-S[3] descriptions for message contents, as well as other W3C standardized information such as WS-CDL[4] for protocol descriptions. In the case of institutions there are far fewer examples, and de-facto or decreed standards have not yet developed. ISLANDER is one of the few implemented tools for the specification and management of institutions [2]. It provides a combination of graphical and textual representations of the institution whilst the complete specification can also be obtained as an XML document. Currently it requires that agents are developed specifically to fit within a particular ISLANDER specified institution. However, we use it to explore

[1] http://www.fipa.org/

[2] http://www.w3.org/TR/wsdl

[3] http://www.w3.org/Submission/OWL-S

[4] http://www.w3.org/TR/2004/WD-ws-cdl-10-20041217/

the general issues involved in attempting to incorporate arbitrary agents within such an institution.

In the sections ahead we provide a concrete example of a simple ISLANDER institution representing a travel agency, and an accommodation agent previously developed for a different project. We explore how it might be determined whether the accommodation agent can participate in the Travel Institution. We provide an architecture that minimizes the requirements on both agents and institutions by introducing a third party service to reason about compatibility. We also identify the kind of information that agents and institutions will need to make available in order for this to work.

2 Application Scenario

In order to test the issues raised in the previous section, we use the domain of travel organizations as an application scenario. The motivations for this choice are twofold. On the one hand, it is a familiar domain, which does not require a lot of background description. Travel applications are widely available on the internet, and the idea of developing agents that can interact seamlessly with several existing applications is a realistic and useful one. On the other hand, we make use of an accommodation agent that was developed as part of a project to provide a testbed of travel and tourism agents, which is implemented using JACK[5]. This agent, which we will refer to as *JACK-acc-agent* in the remainder of this paper, when queried, returns a list of accommodation options. The service description is available in both WSDL and OWL-S and the ontology is defined in OWL-S. The fact that this agent has been developed independently of this project further serves our purpose of analyzing the complexity of interactions in heterogeneous environments.

Since most travel applications existing online are not based on MAS frameworks, we have developed a test institution using the ISLANDER platform [6]. ISLANDER is a graphical tool for the specification and verification of electronic institutions. The core notions of an ISLANDER electronic institution specification are [1]:

Agents and Roles. Agents are the players in the institution, whereas roles are defined as standardized patterns of behavior. Agents within an electronic institution are required to adopt some role(s).

Dialogic framework. Provides the context for interaction, in terms of domain concepts (ontology) and communication language (illocutions).

Scene. Interactions between agents are articulated through agent group meetings, called scenes, with a well-defined communication protocol.

Performative structure. Scenes can be connected, composing a network of scenes that captures the existing (ordering) relations among scenes. Further, it describes how roles can legally move from scene to scene.

Normative Rules. Agent actions may have consequences that either limit or enlarge its subsequent acting possibilities. Such consequences will impose obligations to the agents and affect its possible paths within the performative structure.

[5] JACK is an agent development platform available from Agent Oriented Software, http://www.agent-software.com.au

[6] http://e-institutor.iiia.csic.es/software.html

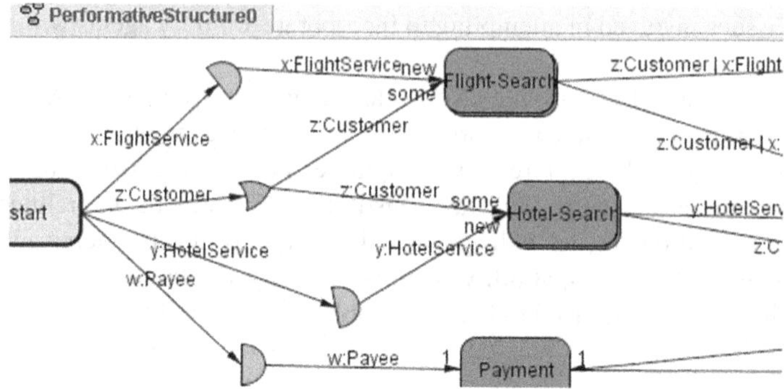

Fig. 1. Partial view of the travel agency in ISLANDER

The travel agency institution facilitates the search, reservation, and purchase of flights and accommodation for potential customers. Some of the possible *roles* within this institution are customer, flight-service, hotel-service and payee (e.g. bank). Agents that enter this institution will take up one or more of these roles. Roles in ISLANDER can be either internal, played by agents within the organization, or external, which can be in principle played by any agent. Our focus in this paper is on these external roles.

The interactions between roles are captured within *Scenes*. For example the *hotel-search-scene* captures the interaction protocol between a customer and a hotel-service. In this scene the customer requests accommodation options from the hotel-service, who in return supplies a list of hotel options. The protocol is defined as a finite state machine. The other scenes of our travel institute include: a *flight-search-scene*, a *reservation-scene* and a *payment-scene*.

The relationships between scenes and the roles that enter and leave particular scenes are captured by the *Performative Structure* in ISLANDER (Figure 1). For example, a customer and a hotel-service may enter the hotel-search-scene and leave this scene with two options: exit the institution or move to the reservation-scene. The performative structure therefore constrains roles to particular scenes and also provides a view of the path an agent or service that enters an institution may take during its stay. As an agent moves between scenes it may well change its role. This is also specified as part of the Performative Structure. For example an agent playing the flight-service role in the flight search scene, may play a payee role in the payment scene. The performative structure specifies the permitted role changes as the agents move between scenes.

The *Ontology* defined in ISLANDER specifies the terms that can be used in the message patterns that can be used by the agents playing roles in a particular scene. The ontology is also used when defining constraints and norms.

As we envisage our travel institution to be an open system, then the accommodation agent *JACK-acc-agent* should be able to determine that it could join this travel institution taking up the role of a *hotel-service*, and participating in the *hotel-search* scene (as long as all conditions were met). Such a process requires two types of abilities. On the one hand, the technical ability of finding and using the API to connect to the institution application, and on the other hand the cognitive ability of determining the applicability of some institutional role to the realization of its goals. Some of the questions that such an agent will need to answer, in order to recognize this opportunity, are:

- What roles will the agent be able to take on in the organization? How does it move between roles and scenes?
- Can the accommodation agent send and receive the right message types for the organization? Will it be able to understand the content of the messages sent by the customer role and vice versa?
- Will it be able to follow the appropriate interaction protocols to conduct its business within the organization?

In the following section we describe an overall architecture to support the kind of open system described in this example. The details in further sections will address the above issues.

3 System Architecture

In order to achieve our aim of having minimum requirements imposed on the agents and on the institutions, we propose an architecture where most of the reasoning about whether a particular agent is equipped to successfully participate in a particular institution, is located in an infrastructure support service, which we conceptualize as a middle agent. The term *middle-agent* has been used to describe various services such as *yellow page agents* [3], directory facilitators[7], brokers, and match-makers [4]. The LARKS system [5] provides a match making between agents based on service descriptions. Although this comes closer to what we propose than something like UDDI (Universal Description, Discovery and Integration) directories[8] it can better be seen as a potential part of our Middle Agent than as an alternative. In our situation we do not only match services, but also protocols and combination of services. To our knowledge, no solution for this type of matchmaking has been proposed yet. We will call this entity an *Institutions Middle Agent (IMA)*.

Similarly to the matchmaker middle agent, the IMA will maintain listings, and provide information regarding compatibility of institutions/agents with requests. Agents and institutions will register with the IMA, providing some information about their structure (such as WSDL descriptions, and other identified information). The IMA will then do the required reasoning to answer the questions identified in our example. An overview of the architecture is given in Figure 2.

It is important to note here that this figure represents the simplest IMA architecture, consisting of only one middle agent. In practice, more than one IMA may be necessary (e.g. to avoid bottlenecks) which will be interconnected. From the perspective of the agents and institutions using the IMA layer, this difference should be irrelevant. That is, whether one or more IMAs are present in the mediation layer, its basic overall functionality is as depicted in figure 2. The interaction of multiple IMAs is the subject of future research.

[7] http://www.fipa.org/specs/fipa00023/SC00023K.html

[8] http://www.uddi.org

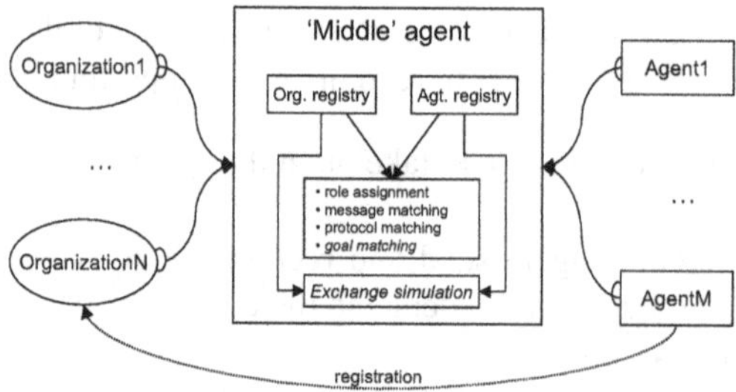

Fig. 2. Institutions Middle Agent (IMA) Architecture

The functionalities of the IMA are divided over a number of levels of complexity. The lower levels require fewer assumptions of the required input and are meant to be used in situations where only simple standards exist and agents and institutions have little reflexive capabilities (i.e. cannot provide much information about the way they function). At the highest level more input is needed and the reasoning involves some very hard and complex issues, but also more guarantees can be given about the actual match between an agent and an institution.

Assign agents to roles within an institution. In order to do this the institution must register with the IMA some list of roles, and the messages and protocols associated with each role. On this most basic level the IMA checks whether the agent can play a role in the institution based on role names. This is explored further in section 4.

Check for message compatibility. On the next level of compatibility, the IMA will require some knowledge of the messages understood and expected by both the agent and the institution. Besides checking for message format compatibility, this also includes a kind of ontology matching on the content of the messages (which might in turn be outsourced to specialized ontology matchers). This is explored further in section 5.

Check for protocol compatibility. Even if the messages are compatible, if the expected pattern of message exchange is not compatible then successful interaction cannot be guaranteed. This is further discussed in section 6.

Perform goal related reasoning. On top of these basic compatibility issues the IMA can further check whether the goals of the agent and the institution are compatible. Is one institution better for the agent to achieve its goals than another? This level of reasoning could be supported if agents and institutions carried a protocol representation that included interaction goals. A possible way to achieve this is suggested by Cheong and Winikoff [6], but (due to space restrictions) will not be discussed further in this paper.

Simulate a run of interactions. The highest level of compatibility can be ensured through a simulated run of interactions. This allows to check not only whether the protocols are compatible but also whether they bring about the desired outcome. Space limitations do not allow us to elaborate on this issue.

4 Agents and Roles

The concept of *role* plays a central role in organizational theory, describing patterns of conduct, that is, expectations, identities, and social positions. Agents can play roles, which potentially give them authority over other agents playing other roles. Empowerment and authority are recognized as critical aspects, since these identify which roles (and hence which agents) are enabled to perform which actions. From the perspective of system design, roles have the advantage that they abstract from the specific design and internal specification of individual agents. Roles in an institution identify the activities and services necessary to achieve social objectives and enable to abstract from the specific individuals that will eventually perform them [7]. From the perspective of institution design, roles are the building blocks for the agent architecture, providing placeholders for the actual agents. The concept is concerned with the specification of patterns of conduct, that is, expectations, identities, and social positions; and with context and social structure. From the agent design perspective, roles specify the expectations of the society with respect to the agent's activity in the society. I.e. a role can be seen as a 'job description' whose conditions the agent wants to negotiate to better match its interests. Roles also define normative behavioral repertoires for agents [8]. In the current practice of MAS design, roles take different functions in different approaches to open agent systems. Some define roles as a class that defines a normative behavioral repertoire of an agent, others see roles as the representation of the 'expectations' of the institution for that position, while others take a more (linguistic) interaction perspective and use roles to represent the different participants in a conversation or protocol.

One of the first problems one encounters when considering the take up of institutional roles by external agents is that tools currently used to implement agents do not contain the concept of a role to represent the position (i.e. place holder) of the agent in the institution. Although agents might be designed to fill a role in the system, they are not aware of these roles at run-time! As such, messages used by agents in these systems always require specific agent IDs as the sender or recipient of the message and cannot be addressed to any agent fulfilling a role. Considering the fulfilment of those roles in an institution that is open for external agents (e.g. the role of seller), the primary functionality for the IMA is thus to enable agents to take up a role in an institution[9]. There are two activities necessary to achieve this aim: (1) Check compatibility between agent and role, and (2), Provide operational support for agent activity as role enactor within the institution.

At the most basic level, a compatibility check can be done by comparing the semantic meaning of the agent's identifier with that of the role identifier. Such a check is obviously not enough but it gives an initial idea of possible compatibility. E.g. a *buyer* agent may probably not be able to perform a *hotel-service* role. Of course, some ontological knowledge is required for this function. At this stage we assume this service to be provided by an ontology mapping service. Another possibility checks which roles an agent may be able to play by looking at the messages that the agent can send and receive, and

[9] Here we assume that the way an institution describes a role indicates possible pre-conditions or requirements on the agents that can take up that role. This can become quite complex, involving a negotiation process between the institution and the potential candidate agents [9].

comparing them against the message interface of the roles. We will elaborate further on this in section 5.

In the specific case of ISLANDER, roles describe a specific position in one dialogic scene. That is, in ISLANDER an agent probably has to take up several roles as it moves into different scenes in the performative structure of an institution (e.g. the agent playing the role of customer in the *hotel-search-scene*, may later have to play the role of payer in the *payment* scene). From the agent's perspective it would make more sense to think of all these roles together as the customer role. This extends the desired functionality of the IMA to create one institutional role to be taken up by one agent to move from entrance to exit of the institution. For ISLANDER this role is composed of the union of scene roles that form a coherent path through the dialogical framework of the institution.

After the IMA has determined that an agent is compatible with a role in an institution, the next step is to help the agent enter into that institution. In ISLANDER execution of electronic institutions is regulated by AMELI [2]. AMELI provides *governor* agents which mediate all interaction with external agents, and thus are able to enforce compliance with the institution's protocols and performative structure. However, other proposals for institution modeling relax this constraint by defining participation negotiation protocols, in which an agent can negotiate its institutional activity[10] to best fit its capabilities [9]. The range of negotiation is defined by the institution so as to limit it to parameters and values that do not endanger institutional norms and objectives.

In this paper, we will limit ourselves to determining the necessary preconditions for an agent to take up a role (in terms of messages and protocol fulfillment). However this still does not say anything about the sufficient preconditions for role enactment. That is, why should the agent take up this role, how does an agent choose which role to perform, or is this the optimal role (and the optimal institution) for the aims of the agent? E.g. should an agent take up a role of *accommodation-service* or of *trip-service*? The definition of sufficient preconditions for role enactment must therefore include the matching of the goals of the agent to those of the role. Given that we cannot assume any level of introspection from the agents, and in fact most existing agent platforms do not enable introspection, it is clear that this is a field that requires much more study.

5 Message Compatibility

In the following, we assume that both agents and institutions are able to provide a WSDL description of their message types. It must be noted, that this is not something that can be generally expected of all current agent platforms. A possible way to solve this, is to develop dedicated services that are able to transform a specific message type representation into a standard such as WSDL. Such services can be used by the IMA to convert message specifications.

Considering our example, messages used by the accommodation agent *JACK-acc-agent* are specified as follows:[11] (a # before a field name indicates that the field is optional)

[10] That is, activity by the agent that is done in order to fill a role in the context of an institution.

[11] The actual WSDL is too lengthy. This provides the relevant conceptual information, with modified syntax.

```
<complex type      AccomodationInfo: "accommodationContactInfo" type=string;
                   "#Name" type=string; "#facilities" type=string; "#maxPrice" type=cost; "#minPrice" type=cost;
                   "#region" type=string; "#paymentMethods" type=string; "address" type=string;/>
<message input:    "#Name" type=string; "#facilities" type=string; "#maxPrice" type=cost;
                   "#minPrice" type=cost; "region" type=string />
<message output:   "AccommodationResult" type=ListOfAccomodationInfo />
```

The following description of messages is extracted from the ISLANDER specification of the *hotel-search* scene:

```
<complex type    AccomodationInfo: "accommodationContactInfo" type=string;
                 "#Name" type=string; "address" type=string; "#region" type=string; "#maxPrice" type=cost;
                 "#minPrice" type=cost; "#paymentMethods" type=string;/>
<message         from role: customer to role: hotel-service "#Name" type=string; "region" type=string;
                 "maxPrice" type=cost; "minPrice" type=cost;/>
<message         from role: hotel-service to role: customer "AccommodationResult" type=ListOfAccomodationInfo />
```

Given a WSDL style specification, such as that above, one of the functionalities of the IMA is the determination of message-level compatibility between the accommodation agent *JACK-acc-agent* and the institutional role of *hotel-service*. In open systems, exact matches are highly unlikely. In fact, the level of similarity in the example above, even though it is not an exact match, is much higher than what is likely to be found between compatible message sets in an open system. In our example, the lack of exact matching has to do with optional and mandatory fields, and with ordering of fields. Another important lack of matching is at the level of sender and receiver fields: while ISLANDER uses role names, the agent does not specify any receiver. As discussed in section 4, the IMA must keep track of the agent's role and the roles of the agents it interacts with, and possibly add this information to the messages being passed within the institution.

In order to realize that the accommodation agent *JACK-acc-agent* is compatible with the role of hotel-service, the IMA needs to determine (a) that all messages sent to the hotel-service role can be transformed into messages compatible with available input messages of the Accommodation Agent, and (b) that all output messages of the Accommodation Agent can be transformed into messages compatible with the messages that the hotel-service role can send.

Determining compatibility of one message specification with another requires ascertaining whether the sent message can be type-cast into what is expected by the receiver. In order to ensure that all instances of sent messages will be able to be transformed into something that is acceptable to the receiver we require that every mandatory field in the received message be compatible with a mandatory field in the sent message. Optional fields can be matched in the same way as mandatory ones, but if no match is found they can be ignored.

Where there is not an exact match between fields within a message we attempt to determine compatibility. Compatibility of compound fields requires compatibility of all their mandatory parts. Compatibility of (atomic) fields requires what we call *field name compatibility* and *value type compatibility*. Two atomic fields are *value type compatible* if the type of the field in the sent message is a subset of the type of that field in the received message. For example, if the sent message contains an integer, but a floating point number is expected to be received.

However, value type compatibility alone is not likely to yield semantic compatibility. Typically the name of a field carries semantic value. We refer to this level of compatibility as *field name compatibility*. For analysis of the semantic compatibility of two field names we require an ontology, and the ability to reason over that ontology. The ontology could be provided by the agent, by the institution, or could be an external ontology, or a combination of these. In our initial implementation, we make the simplification that the ontology matcher returns *true* only if there is an exact match of field names. However the more general case requires some form of ontological reasoning. We envisage this reasoning being done by a separate module (the "ontological reasoner") which could use more sophisticated reasoning to return true/false, or a probability representing the degree of a match. Malucelli *et al.* [10] propose such an ontological reasoning service to facilitate participation of agents in institutions.

In the example above we would hope that if the field "#region" type=string in the institutional message was replaced by "#suburb" type=string, it could still be matched by the ontological reasoner with the field "#region" type=string in the agent message, as region subsumes suburb. We do note however that this kind of ontological representation and reasoning is fraught with difficulty. The existence of agreed ontologies within an application domain can be expected to simplify the problem somewhat.

Finally, it is possible that an agent may need to transition through a number of scenes to obtain a successful outcome. Therefore, the institution will need to provide to the IMA the full set of messages involving the initial role, and all roles it can transform into within necessary scenes. For simplicity, at this stage role transformations should be mapped back to the name of their first occurrence.

6 Protocol Compatibility

A protocol defines the "rules of procedure" for a conversation, that is, describes possible sequences of messages that interacting agents must follow in order to achieve their goals. Given that agents can send and receive the right types of messages, the next step is to check whether they send these messages in the right order, that is, whether their protocols are compatible. For example, protocol checking should detect an incompatibility if agent A can send m_1 followed by m_2, but the recipient expects m_2 followed by m_1.

In order to check protocol compatibility we need a notation to capture protocols. This notation must be expressible in a machine-readable form that can be used by the IMA. A number of notations could be used, including BPEL4WS, WS-CDL, and AUML[12]. In fact, for our discussion we do not make any assumptions about the notation. We use AUML because it is the de-facto standard for describing agent interactions, because its representation is compact, and because it has a machine-readable form [11].

Roughly speaking, the intuition behind protocol compatibility checking is the same as for message compatibility checking: it is the sender who has the choice of what to send, and thus the receiver needs to handle anything that the sender can send. For example, if at a given point in the interaction the sender can send two messages, *Confirm flight* and *Decommit flight*, then the recipient needs to be able to handle either option, and may handle additional messages. However, if the recipient cannot handle, say, *Confirm flight* then the interaction may fail if the sender chooses to send *Confirm flight*. The generalization of this intuition yields a definition of protocol compatibility: an agent's

[12] Agent UML: http://www.auml.org

protocol is compatible with the institution's protocol if at any point in the interaction, the agent's protocol provides the agent with fewer options for messages that it can send, and with more options for messages that it can receive with respect to the institution's protocol. Very similar ideas have also been developed independently in [12] and can also be found in [13,14]. In [15] the notion of common protocols in open environments, and ways to achieve common protocols have also been discussed.

We can formalize the above intuitions by using R_I (respectively R_A) to denote the institution's (respectively agent's) protocol messages that the agent can receive at a given point. Similarly, using S_I (respectively S_A) to denote the institution's (respectively agent's) protocol messages that the agent can send at a given point in the interaction. The above definition of protocol compatibility can be formalized as requiring that at each point in the interaction $S_A \subseteq S_I$ and $R_I \subseteq R_A$.

We now briefly consider four cases where, at a given point in the interaction, there are differences between the protocols. If $S_A \subset S_I$ then the agent follows a sub-protocol of the one provided by the institution. For example, let the agent be a flight service that uses the protocol in Figure 3a while the institution uses protocol 3b. At the end of the protocol $S_A = \{\text{Confirm flight X}\}$ and $S_I = \{\text{Confirm flight X, Decommit flight X}\}$. This is OK, as long as the sub-protocol allows the agent to get from an entrance state to an end state in the institution, which is the case in this example. However, if the agent cannot get to an end state because it misses a necessary branch of the protocol then the agent's protocol is not suited.

If $R_I \subset R_A$ then the agent is able to handle more messages than can be sent, and this does not constitute a problem.

If $S_I \subset S_A$ then, at that point in the interaction, there are messages that the agent's protocol permits the agent to send which are not permitted by the institution's protocol, and which will not be expected by the message's recipient, thus making the protocols incompatible. Similarly, if $R_A \subset R_I$ then the protocols are incompatible because at that point in the interaction the institution's protocol indicates that the agent needs to be able to handle certain messages which are missing in the agent's protocol. For example, if the institution has the protocol in Figure 3b and the customer agent has protocol 3a then the customer agent does not expect a decommitment at the end, and will not be prepared to handle it.

Note that incompatibility does not mean that any interaction will *necessarily* fail, just that it *may* fail. It is quite possible, for example, that the flight service might choose to send a commit message, which the customer agent can handle, rather than a decommit, which it cannot.

More generally, instead of merely checking whether two protocols are compatible as-is, it is possible to determine what constraints would make the protocols compatible. For example, if the flight service is willing to accept a constraint that prevents it from sending a decommit message, then the two protocols (3b at the institution and 3a at the customer agent) become compatible. In order to be willing to adopt constraints, other constraints may need to hold. For example, if the institution guarantees that all transactions are performed within 1 minute then all options provided by the flight service are still available when chosen by the customer, and a decommit is unnecessary.

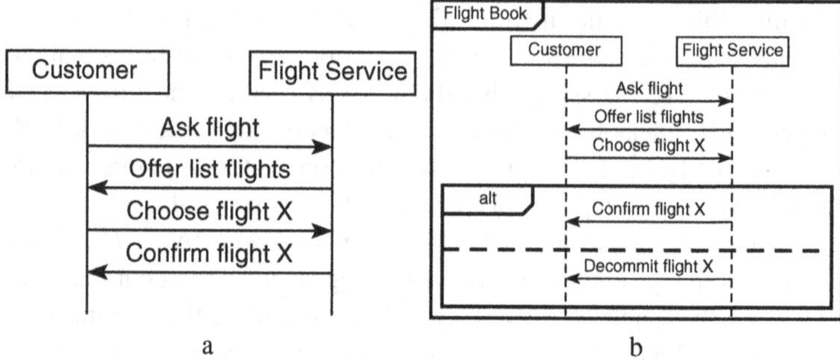

Fig. 3. Example protocol

The discussion of compatibility so far has focused on a "pointwise" comparison between states. We now briefly consider compatibility if the two protocols are not of the same length. For example, if one protocol has a sub-sequence of messages not present in the other. If this sub-sequence is optional then this case is captured above. Otherwise, if the sub-sequence occurs in the middle of a protocol then the protocols are not compatible.

However, if the sub-sequence occurs at the start or end of the protocol then the protocols may be compatible if the sub-sequence can be skipped because it is only important for the agent. For example, if a customer starts with choosing a flight without first asking for a list of possibilities. However, if the sub-sequence is important for the institution then it cannot be skipped. For example, if the institution needs an identification of the customer agent before interacting with it further.

Concluding this brief sketch of protocol compatibility issues we can state that there are some cases in which the protocols are not identical, but interactions might still be successful. Sometimes, this also depends on the content of the messages and sometimes on the internal architecture of the agent. As usual, the more knowledge one has, the more can be done. However, even with limited knowledge gained from standard descriptions a rudimentary check can be made that could suffice for the majority of the cases in practice.

7 Related Work

Open systems assume that the heterogeneous agents are designed and run independently from each other and use their own motivations to determine whether to join an existing institution or another interaction space. However, currently, in most MAS, agents are simply designed from scratch so that their behavior complies with the behavior described by the role(s) it will take up in the society. Comprehensive solutions for open environments require complex agents that are able to reason about their own objectives and desires and thus decide and negotiate their participation in an organization. In [16], the following requirements were identified for the effective design of open agent environments:

1. Formal frameworks are needed for the specification of the society structure and goals with verifiable and meaningful semantics in a way that does not require the formal specification of participating agents.

2. Mechanisms are needed through which prospective participants can evaluate the characteristics and objectives of roles in the society, in order to decide about participation.
3. Tools must be available that support an individual agent to identify specific requirements and particularities of an organization and to adapt their architecture and functionality to the requirements of an assumed role.

That same paper proposed a first step on the road to this solution (cf. [16]) by introducing a formalism to compare the specification of agents and roles and determine whether an agent is suitable to enact a role. This solution is based on the OperA framework [9] that fulfills the first requirement above by providing a formal organizational model that is verifiable without the need to specify specific participating agents.

The work by Sierra et al, in the area of electronic institutions has been highly influential in the area of open agent systems [1]. They also faced the problem of how agents could interact with an institution while the agents and institutions are designed and implemented by different groups. They alleviated this problem by introducing the idea of "skeleton agents" [17]. These skeletons consist of the communication patterns that an agent needs to be able to function in the institution. The idea is that external parties use the skeletons as a basis for developing their agents and thus have an easy way of building agents that fit with the institution. The main restriction is that the agents are still assumed to be developed explicitly for one particular institution.

In [18] an architecture is described in which highly heterogeneous teams are able to cooperate. This is achieved by creating some semi-autonomous proxy agents that take care of the coordination layer between the agents. In fact what this seems to do is extract from the agents the part that they need in order to function within the coordinated team framework. This is similar to what we would like to extract from an agent, but we do not pre-suppose a certain type of interaction pattern as related to teamwork, but rather any type of interaction within an institution.

There is of course also some work done concentrating on the use of "middle agents" within the agent research community. Most notable is the work on RETSINA [19], being one of the first to realize the benefits of using middle agents to connect different parts of a system which each have their own goal and internal structure. The work that comes closest to our purpose for using a middle agent is that of task delegation. The middle agent matches task descriptions of demand and supply. However, in our case we do not match task descriptions but rather interaction patterns and possibly goals

In a similar way the work of [20] is relevant. In that work middle agents were used to manage subscriptions to different types of services. Services could be seen as very simple forms of institutions. The main simplification is that a service has a very simple interaction pattern and the interaction is with only one other party. Therefore, the match between the capabilities and tasks of an agent and a description of what a service can provide is relatively simple.

8 Discussion and Future Work

In this paper we have presented an approach to support open agent environments, where independently created agents can enter suitable institutions, with the assistance of an

IMA. This approach goes beyond the so called "skeleton agents" [17] that assist external parties to build agents that fit a specific institution. We assume standard descriptions such as WSDL and WS-CDL to describe different interaction patterns in order to perform the matching. Based on this, some basic compatibility checks can be made. However, a more semantic matching requires introspection of the agent about its goals and roles. Ontological reasoning also plays an important part in this matching.

The contributions of this paper are: the development of the IMA architecture for facilitating entry of agents into institutions, and the identification and description of reasoning processes (other than the ontological reasoning) which must be done by the IMA, including identification of potential roles the agent can take on, matching of messages between the agent and institution, and checking protocol compatibility.

Further work includes an actual implementation of the IMA other than the basic work done in this paper using one specific agent tool and one specific institution tool, generating plug-ins to extract message and protocol descriptions from agents and institutions' specifications, and exploration of more examples, using either standardized ontologies, or existing ontological reasoners of various types, to better understand what will work well in practice. This paper provides the framework and basis on which such work can be continued. It also identifies some aspects of ISLANDER or similar systems which are necessary for the proposed approach to work, such as institutional management of role (or role name) changes as the agent moves between different scenes within the institution.

Acknowledgments

We would like to acknowledge the support of the Australian Research Council and Agent Oriented Software, under grant LP0453486, the Australian Department of Education, Science and Training, under grant CG040014. We also acknowledge the support of the Netherlands Organization for Scientific Research (NWO), under Veni grant 639.021.509. We thank the Australian Tourism Data Warehouse (ATDW) for the provision of live content for our travel and tourism agents. We also thank Carles Sierra and Juan Antonio Rodriguez for their assistance in understanding and working with ISLANDER.

References

1. Esteva, M., Padget, J., Sierra, C.: Formalizing a language for institutions and norms. In: Meyer, J.-J.C., Tambe, M. (eds.) ATAL 2001. LNCS (LNAI), vol. 2333, pp. 348–366. Springer, Heidelberg (2002)
2. Arcos, J.L., Esteva, M., Noriega, P., Rodríguez, J.A., Sierra, C.: Engineering open environments with electronic institutions. Engineering Applications of Artificial Intelligence 18, 191–204 (2005)
3. Alonso, G., Casati, F., Kuno, H., Machiraju, V.: Web Services: Concepts, Architectures and Applications. Springer, Berlin, Germany (2004)
4. Sycara, K.: Multi-agent infrastructure, agent discovery, middle agents for web services and interoperation. In: Luck, M., Mařík, V., Štěpánková, O., Trappl, R. (eds.) ACAI 2001 and EASSS 2001. LNCS (LNAI), vol. 2086, pp. 17–49. Springer, Heidelberg (2001)

5. Sycara, K., Wido, S., Klusch, M., Lu, J.: Larks: Dynamic matchmaking among heterogeneous software agents in cyberspace. Autonomous Agents and Multi-Agent Systems 5, 173–203 (2002)
6. Cheong, C., Winikoff, M.: Hermes: Implementing goal-oriented agent interactions. In: Programming Multi-Agent Systems, 3rd International Workshop, The Netherlands (2005)
7. Dignum, V., Dignum, F.: Coordinating tasks in agent organizations. or: Can we ask you to read this paper? In: Noriega, P., Vázquez-Salceda, J., Boella, G., Boissier, O., Dignum, V., Fornara, N., Matson, E. (eds.) COIN 2006. LNCS (LNAI), vol. 4386, Springer, Heidelberg (2007)
8. Odell, J., Parunak, H.V.D., Fleischer, M.: The role of roles in designing effective agent organizations. In: Garcia, A.F., de Lucena, C.J.P., Zambonelli, F., Omicini, A., Castro, J. (eds.) Software Engineering for Large-Scale Multi-Agent Systems. LNCS, vol. 2603, Springer, Heidelberg (2003)
9. Dignum, V.: A Model for Organizational Interaction: based on Agents, founded in Logic. SIKS Dissertation Series 2004-1. Utrecht University (2004)
10. Malucelli, A., Cardoso, H., Oliveira, E.: Enriching a MAS Environment with Institutional Services. In: Environments for Multi-Agent Systems II, 2nd International Workshop, The Netherlands (2005)
11. Winikoff, M.: Towards making agent UML practical: A textual notation and a tool. In: First international workshop on Integration of Software Engineering and Agent Technology (ISEAT 2005) (2005)
12. Baldoni, M., Baroglio, C., Martelli, A., Patti, V.: Verification of protocol conformance and agent interoperability. In: Toni, F., Torroni, P. (eds.) CLIMA 2005. LNCS (LNAI), vol. 3900, pp. 265–283. Springer, Heidelberg (2006)
13. Bordeaux, L., Salaün, G., Berardi, D., Mecella, M.: When are two Web Services Compatible? In: Shan, M.-C., Dayal, U., Hsu, M. (eds.) TES 2004. LNCS, vol. 3324, pp. 15–28. Springer, Heidelberg (2005)
14. Yellin, D., Strom, R.: Protocol specifications and component adaptors. ACM Transactions on Programming Languages and Systems (TOPLAS) 19, 292–333 (1997)
15. Paurobally, S., Cunningham, J.: Achieving common interaction protocols in open agent environments. In: AAMAS, Challenges in Open Agent Systems 2003 Workshop, Melbourne, Australia (2003)
16. Dastani, M., Dignum, V., Dignum, F.: Role assignment in open agent societies. In: Proceedings of Second International Joint Conference on Autonomous Agents and Multi-agent Systems (AAMAS), ACM Press, New York (2003)
17. Vasconcelos, W., Sabater, J., Sierra, C., Querol, J.: Skeleton-based agent development for electronic institutions. In: Proceedings of First International Joint Conference on Autonomous Agents and Multi-agent Systems (AAMAS), pp. 696–703. ACM Press, New York (2002)
18. Scerri, P., Pynadath, D., Schurr, N., Farinelli, A., Gandhe, S., Tambe, M.: Team oriented programming and proxy agents: The next generation. In: Dastani, M., Dix, J., El Fallah-Seghrouchni, A. (eds.) PROMAS 2003. LNCS (LNAI), vol. 3067, Springer, Heidelberg (2004)
19. Sycara, K., Paolucci, M., Velsen, M.V., Giampapa, J.: The RETSINA MAS Infrastructure. Autonomous Agents and Multi-Agent Systems 7, 29–48 (2003)
20. Mbala, A., Padgham, L., Winikoff, M.: Design options for subscription managers. In: Proceedings of the 7th International Bi-Conference Workshop on Agent-Oriented Information Systems (AOIS) (2005)

An Agent Framework for Processing FIPA-ACL Messages Based on Interaction Models

Ernesto German and Leonid Sheremetov

Mexican Petroleum Institute, Eje Central Lazaro Cardenas 152, San Bartolo Atepehuacan, Distrito Federal, Mexico
{egerman,sher}@imp.mx

Abstract. Interaction engineering is a key issue to effectively build Multi-Agent Systems. It requires software abstractions, components and control structures to manage interactions among agents and to improve infrastructures at runtime. We propose a framework for automatic processing of interactions generated using FIPA-ACL, a language widely accepted for agent platforms. This framework includes three elements: i) an agent interaction architecture to systematize interaction processing tasks, ii) interaction models to build re-usable validated code used to check different phases of interaction processing associated with message semantics, and iii) components and control structures implementing interaction architecture for a particular agent platform. The paper describes the implementation details of the proposed approach developed within the CAPNET agent platform and illustrates it by example.

Keywords: Interaction architecture, interaction models, FIPA-ACL.

1 Introduction

Interaction among agents is a key feature in agent-based open systems and is being mentioned as a qualitative characteristic of interconnected systems of the future [1]. Agent-oriented interactions generally occur through a high-level declarative agent communication language (typically based on speech act theory). They range from simple semantic interoperation, through traditional client-server interaction, to rich social interactions that should be handled in a flexible manner. Thus, agents need a computational apparatus to make context-dependent decisions about the nature and scope of their interactions and to respond to interactions that were not necessarily foreseen at design time [2].

Recently, much effort has been made towards making agents interoperate in open environments. Though several interaction frameworks like, for instance, goal-based Hermes [3] or role-based BRAIN [4], have been proposed, this goal has not been achieved yet. As a result, a deployment of a worldwide open testbed environment underlined the lack of spontaneous exchanges among agents running in this environment [5]. In most of the applications, agents can only interact with agents they have been designed to interact with and cannot handle messages that are not specified. On the contrary, an agent which could interpret the

M. Luck and L. Padgham (Eds.): AOSE 2007, LNCS 4951, pp. 88–102, 2008.

sense of messages, as defined by their semantics rather than their syntax, could intrinsically support more flexible interaction [6]. Multi-Agent System (MAS) infrastructures usually give abstractions for basic services for communication, interoperability and interaction, supporting only syntactic validation of ACL messages. However, the increasing complexity of MAS integration requires more effective descriptions of interactive behaviors, based on message semantics and pragmatics [7] [8].

Although FIPA-ACL is the most commonly used ACL in MAS agent platforms [9], a relatively little effort has been made to specify the basic agent architecture in order to attend common activities that must be done for processing syntax, semantics and pragmatics derived from each single communicative act and, then, from agents interactions. The interaction architecture has been left open to be a programmer's decision in such way that message processing becomes unstructured, repetitive and prone error task for every agent that is part of a MAS. A lot of code must be written in order to check the same message attributes, for example, validating the content syntax through a given content language, validating the content semantics using ontology and validating the pragmatics of each message. If an agent is to be a part of an open system and if it wants to interoperate with heterogeneous agents, these validation activities are very important and must be carried out at runtime.

The paper is focused on the approach to developing an agent interaction framework introducing convenient software components to manage interactions as well as the control structures supporting them. We try to define guidelines for the specification of first-class processes and components in the agent internals. We define the agent interaction architecture, inspired and guided by the agent communication language like FIPA-ACL, as a basic engineering tool to improve computational infrastructure. The proposed approach includes mechanisms helping to systematize interactions engineering through the modularization and reutilization of programming units called Interaction Models (IM). These models integrate the components that are found implicitly in FIPA-ACL semantics and message structure specification [9] such as dynamic execution of requested actions, content language syntax validation, semantic validation of ontology-based content, and interaction processing being executed at runtime. Proposed architecture and interaction models are general purpose and independent from any MAS infrastructure. Nevertheless, in order to be tested and verified, we have implemented them within the CAPNET agent platform [10]. The rest of the paper is structured as follows. Section 2 contains the description of the proposed agent interaction framework. Section 3 shows technical details of implementation of the framework on the CAPNET agent platform. Section 4 summarizes the results and discusses the related work followed by conclusions.

2 Framework for Agent Interaction

Interactions form a key element of agent behavior; that is why in order to improve MAS interactions engineering, agent interaction architecture should be an essential part of an agent. This architecture should be independent of any particular infrastructure. In this section, a general framework integrating different aspects of interaction processing is proposed. We begin with the basic definitions to make homogeneous the terms involved in the framework.

2.1 Basic Definitions of the Interaction Framework

The structure of a FIPA-ACL message includes attributes specified in the communication model, such as sender, receiver, communicative act, content, content language (CL), ontology, conversation-identifier and interaction protocol (IP). In order to define our framework, based on these concepts, we introduce the following definitions.

Definition 1. *An Interaction Model (IM) represents a modular unit permitting the validation of a simple interaction. A Simple Interaction is a unit of communication composed of a FIPA-ACL message and the interaction space of each participating agent*[1]*. Two or more simple interactions form Composed Interaction where the conversation-identifier and protocol attributes are the same. IM includes modules for programming syntax and semantics content validation, feasibility preconditions, rational effect of messages and the termination condition of the interaction.*

Definition 2. *An Interaction Space (IS) is an environment that the agent can access in order to validate interactions at runtime. It is integrated by the following components: message transport services (MTS) available for interchanging physical messages, a knowledge base (KB), content languages, ontologies, interaction protocols and interaction models. In other words, interaction space stores interaction capabilities of the agent.*

Definition 3. *The Agent Interaction Architecture (AIA) is defined as a component to control creation and processing of interactions through validation of interaction models within the interaction space of an agent.*

2.2 Interaction Architecture

The AIA of an agent enables interaction processing. AIA contains three main layers composed of several components as shown in Fig. 1. Interaction Space stores agent interaction capabilities, which are used during validation activities. Runtime Interaction Process is composed of a set of engines implementing message processing. In the middle of the architecture is the Validation Mechanism. Messages are interchanged through the messaging mechanism. This mechanism connects the MTS and the internal architecture of an agent. For each message, messaging does the following: i) validates message encoding syntax, ii) looks for an IM within the interaction space, taking into account message attributes,

[1] Our definition of the interaction model captures the interaction representation from the agent local view [11].

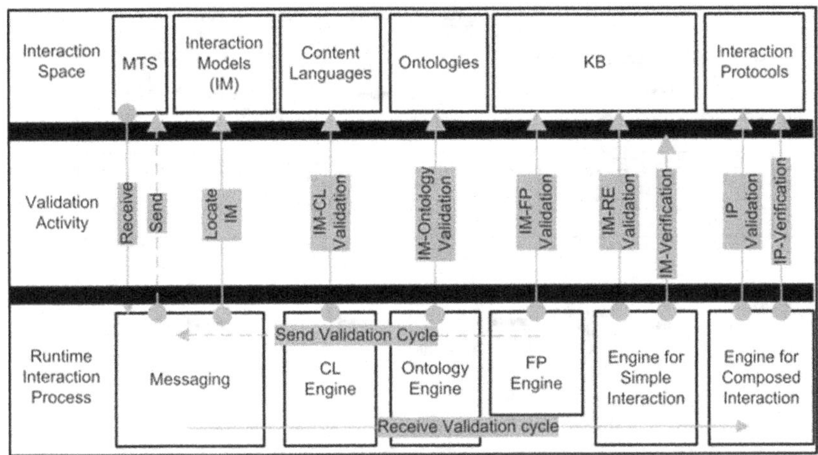

Fig. 1. Agent interaction architecture

content language and ontology, iii) sends the message to the main validation mechanism corresponding to the identified IM activating send or receive validation cycles. Interaction models form the kernel of the interaction process. They implement processing templates composed of validation activities when a new message is being processed. When each engine have to validate an IM, they look for concrete interaction componentes stored in the interaction space which are dynamically instantiated and used. CLs are used to validate syntax of message content and ontologies to validate semantics of message content. For the validation of the Rational Effect (RE) and Feasibility Preconditions (FP) of a message an agent can access the KB where actions, propositions and domain objects are storede and consulted in simple interactions. Finally, IPs could be dynamically instantiated when simple interactions use an explicit protocol.

Validation process is divided into five phases (Fig. 2). Validation activities corresponding to each phase are implemented by IM modules and are invoked by different execution engines. General validation activity is composed of two processes: the first one corresponds to the sender agent where IMs are used to validate content syntax (phase I), content semantics (phase II), feasibility preconditions (phase III) and verification of interaction finalization (phase V). During the receiver agent's process, IMs are used to validate content syntax and semantics (phases I and II), message's RE (phase IV) and conditions of interaction finalization (phase V). The real validation task is implemented and executed in each IM. Special cases are the phases III and IV. During phase III, FPs for the communicative act represented by the IM are checked. This phase is only used in the sender agent and is realized by the FPEngine. In a similar manner, phase IV is executed by the mechanism only in the receiver agent by calling the services from the Engines either for Simple or for Composed Interactions (ESI and ECI in Fig. 2).

The CLEngine is a component designed to apply the syntax validation for each IM. To do this, CLEngine looks for a component that implements the CL

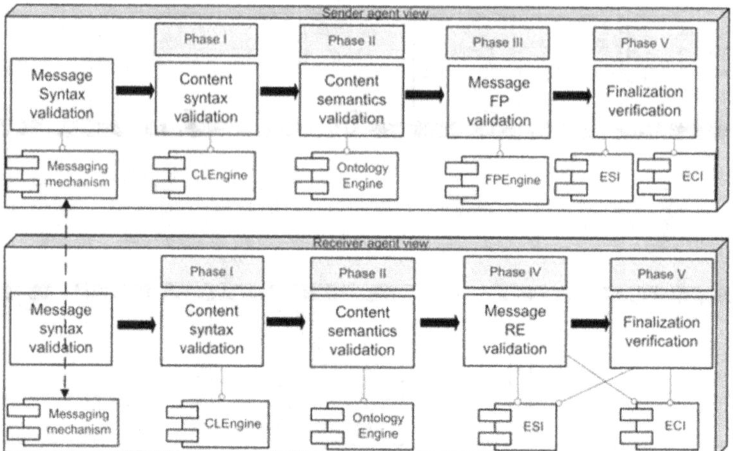

Fig. 2. Validation mechanism

in the interaction space. If a CL is available, it indicates that the agent is capable to understand the syntax of the content represented in such CL. In this case, the engine invokes the CL validation module of the IM that is being processed.

Ontology Engine processes interactions that have an explicit ontology in their messages. It searches for a concrete ontology registered in the interaction space. Then the agent tries to understand the meaning of the entities in the message content. The engine invokes the ontology validation module of the IM that is being processed. The Engine for Simple Interaction implements the validation of message's RE calling the respective RE module implemented in each concrete IM. Due to asynchronous concerns in this type of communication, usually the RE is completed involving other mechanisms and components i.e. the KB, depending on the semantics of each communicative act. When the RE is achieved, this engine passes the control to the Interaction Finalization module to complete the tasks required by the sender to finish the interaction.

Finally, the Engine for Composed Interactions is a component for validating the RE of interactions forming part of a conversation. The main validation process determines if a simple interaction is part of a composed interaction when the related message contains both an IP and conversation-identifier fields. Being this the case, the IM is passed to ECI and not to ESI. This engine is used to check if the interaction protocol is in the interaction space. If so, the engine creates an instance of the concrete component that implements this IP. Then, messages of the conversation are delivered to the concrete IP in order to validate the RE. It is important to mention that ECI should have a special component to store and manage the access to conversations information i.e. IP state and results for both finalized and in-progress conversations. This component is a conversation manager, similar to those known in the MAS infrastructures. The purpose of the conversation manager is to provide an interface between an agent and an application (maybe at user level) enabling checking of composed interaction results in a synchronous way.

As we see, the notion of interaction model is a key concept of this framework. An IM is composed of the modules covering five validation phases: validation of the content structure with a content language, validation of content semantics with ontology, validation of feasibility preconditions, validation of rational effect, and validation of the termination condition.

3 Implementation of the Framework within the CAPNET Platform

The agent interaction architecture is a component of each agent that uses FIPA-ACL. However, interaction engineering requires this component being tested in a concrete computational context. To be implemented, the CAPNET agent platform was selected because it accomplishes with several important characteristics of interaction that we are interested in, such as the availability of different message representations and content languages, along with the facility to build different ontologies and interaction protocols [10].

3.1 Implementation of Agent Interaction Architecture

In CAPNET, the framework has been implemented in the *BasicAgent* class. This class, as well as the entire platform, has been programmed in C#. The AIA is integrated by a set of interconnected components doing different activities related to concurrent interaction processing at runtime (Fig. 3). The messaging mechanism connects the MTS (which encapsulates several transport services) of CAPNET with the AIA through .NET remote objects technology. To send messages, it takes advantage of asynchronous invocation of the MTS remote object. On the contrary to message receiving, an asynchronous remote event has been implemented within the MTS together with a system of delegated methods for each agent. The interaction space is a class which contains a set of tables where concrete object instances are stored at runtime. Each object is an interaction capability of the agent that will be used as a template when necessary, to process interactions with different features. In Table 1, the main classes of objects that were implemented in order to fill the IS and to test the whole architecture are shown.

In CAPNET, each kind of objects used in the IS derives from a generic abstract class implementing the description of basic interfaces and functionality for validating different aspects of the component during the validation cycle. These generic classes bring the AIA the following design and implementation benefits:

- Share the programming interface for inheriting different concrete classes.
- Validation mechanisms can create and access objects in order to apply runtime polymorphism advantages.
- It is easier to implement and add components (CLs, Ontologies, IMs and IPs) by reusing components both at design time and at runtime.

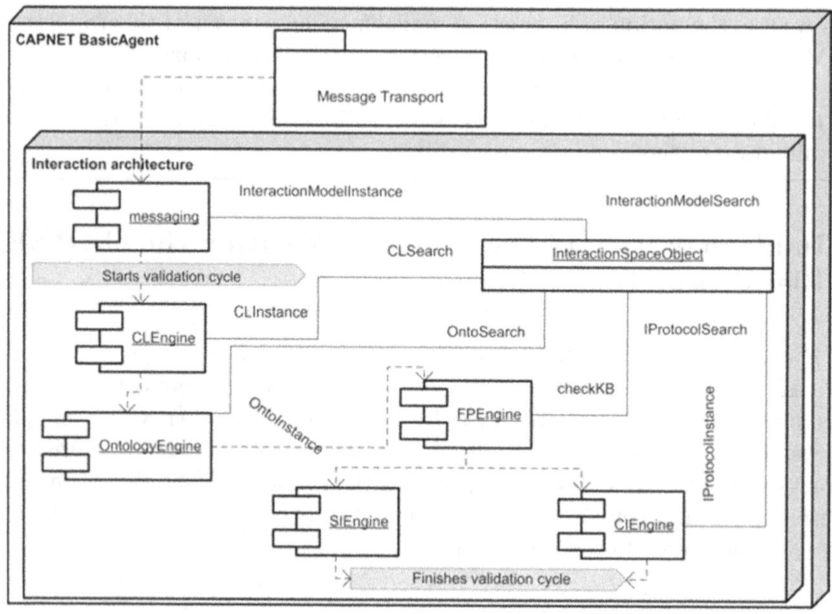

Fig. 3. Interaction architecture on CAPNET

Table 1. Interaction space components

Component	Implementation	Features
Message Transport	HTTPManager TCP-Remoting manager	Table with the objects representing types of services
Content Languages	CAPNET-CL, proprietary CL based on the Knowledge Representation Format described in [12], and SL0.	Table with the objects representing CL types
Ontologies	CAPNETOntology	Table with the objects representing ontologies. The entities are coded with CAPNET-CL
KB	KBManager	Coded with CAPNET-CL
Interaction Protocols	InteractionProtocol FIPARequest FIPA-CNP	Table with the objects representing IP classes
Interaction Models	InformInteractionModel RequestInteractionModel CancelInteractionModel ...	Table with the objects representing IMs.

The mechanism of main validation has been implemented by means of a two-threaded class called InteractionCycle. It holds a single instance of every engine component (CLEngine, OntologyEngine, FPEngine, SIEngine and CIEngine) and two public queues (q-IN, q-OUT). In the main thread, interaction models are received from the messaging component and stored in the q-IN. The second thread actually is dedicated to process validation tasks through different engines, depending on the view (sender o receiver) that the IM requires. When an internal engine fails validating, the respective agent is informed (either by returning false in its send message method to the sender or by sending back a generic not-understood to the receiver). When the IM has been validated successfully, the IM is stored in the q-OUT. Since each engine has the same threading infrastructure, multiple IMs can be validated concurrently and orderly.

3.2 Implementation of Interaction Models

In this section we show by example how the idea of programming interaction models works. For this purpose, CAPNET facilitates the programming of interaction models by giving the *GenericInteractionModel* base class. This class gives virtual methods to implement the interface *IInteractionModel* shown below.

```
public interface IInteractionModel{
bool validateContentLanguage();
bool validateOntology();
bool validateFeasibilityPreconditions();
bool validateRationalEffect();
bool verifyInteractionFinalization();}
```

When specific IMs need to be implemented, developers have to inherit from *GenericInteractionModel* base class and then, override methods of *IInteraction-Model* interface. As an example, we consider an IM of *request* communicative

Table 2. Example of request communicative act

Semantics	Example of message
<i, request (j, a)> FP: FP(a) [i\j] B_i Agent(j, a) $B_i I_j$ Done(a) RE: Done (a)	<fipa-message act=”request”><sender><agent-identifier> <name id=”Coordinator@imp.mx”/><addresses> <href=”http://192.168.142.63:4444/MTSURI”/></addresses> </agent-identifier> </sender><receiver> <agent-identifier><name id=”transport1@provider1”/> <addresses><”href=http://192.168.142.63:4444/MTSURI”/> </addresses></agent-identifier> </receiver> <content><requestContent>”type=CAPNETCLACTION”> <RDF0Action id=”idTransport”><actor>transport1</actor> <act>transportPeople<act/><ActionArguments> <property> <propertyname>workersNum</propertyname><propertytype> System.Int32</propertytype><propertyvalue>200 </propertyvalue></property></ActionArguments> </RDF0Action></requestContent></content> <language>capnetcl</language><content-language-encoding >fipa.acl.rep.xml.std </content-language-encoding> <ontology>emergency</ontology></fipa-message>

act. Its semantics along with an example are shown in Table 2. *Request* semantics indicates that the sender is requesting the receiver to perform some action represented in the message content [9]. Also when a message declares a formal CL and ontology ("capnetcl"' and "emergency" in this case), both sender and receiver agents must have (in their interaction spaces) concrete classes for these CL and ontology along with an IM implemented with these features. In the case of the example, the IM class is called *RequestInteractionModel*. First, the *validateContentLanguage* module instantiates "capnetcl"' from the interaction space. The AIA can get the CL as a generic object (*GenericContentLanguage*) and then uses its function to validate the syntax of the specific action (*requestCO.validate*). A *validateOntology* module works in a similar way. Internally, CAPNET-CL and CAPNET-Ontology classes do the validation of the action *"transportPeople"* to check its representation and parameters. In the next code example CL validation is shown:

```
public override bool validateContentLanguage(){
  bool val=false;
  Hashtable _clTable=ISpace.getCL();
  GenericContentLanguage cl=null;
  if (_clTable.ContainsKey(this.CLName)){
   cl=(GenericContentLanguage)_clTable[this.CLName];
   val=cl.requestCO.validate(this.message.getContent());}
  return val;}
```

The FP validation module has to check if the sender agent believes that the receiver agent can do the action *"transportPeople"*. A way to do this is searching the requested action in the CAPNET-DF before sender sends the message as shown in the code example below:

```
public override bool validateFeasibilityPreconditions(){
   //Gets the type of the implementation class
   Hashtable  _clTable=ISpace.getCL();
   GenericContentLanguage cl=null;
   cl=(GenericContentLanguage)_clTable[this.CLName];
   val=cl.requestCO.validate(this.message.getContent());
   if (searchActionON_CAPNETDF(cl.requestCO.MyAction))
    return true;
   return false;}
```

The *validateRationalEffect* module is encouraged to check whether the requested action is executed or refused. This functionality almost always depends on specific application rules but in the most general way (using CAPNET-CL action and request content object validation functions), we supose by default that the receiver agent is always ready to execute the requested action as follows:

```
public override bool validateRationalEffect(){
  CAPNETRDFO.CAPNETRDFORequestCO requestCO=new
```

```
CAPNETRDFO.CAPNETRDFORequestCO();
CAPNETRDFO.RDFOAction action=null;
if (requestCO.validate(_content)){
 action=requestCO.getAction();
 this.ia.SIEngine.PendingActions.Add(_action);
 return action.execute();}}
```

When the action is executed, the results are stored into internal structures of the class *RDF0Action*. Then, in the *verifyInteractionFinalization* module, receiver agent analyzes the internal structure of the executed action in order to determine whether the action finished successfully or failed. In the former case, an *inform* message is generated to indicate the finalization of the original request interaction. In the latter case, a *failure* message is created and sent back to the sender agent. In both cases, agents obviously must also have IMs to implement inform and failure in order to be sure that the interaction has finalized. For coordinating activities, in CAPNET the AIA uses attributes of messages to determine whether other messages are used to finalize previous interactions. In order to make this mechanism operational, the developers must specify each interaction capability (CL, ontology, IP, IM) in the interaction space to make them available at runtime.

3.3 Example of the Validation Process

When a single message is received by messaging (either for sending or receiving) firstly, the message structure is validated using the message parsers available for CAPNET (string and XML parsers). Then, if it is correct, the mechanism looks for an interaction model in order to satisfy the message requirements (related to the type of communicative act, name of CL and name of ontology). If an IM is registered in the IS, it clones the registered object and returns the IM copy to messaging. In the following we illustrate the main computation process of the interaction architecture for the scenario of the *request* message described above.

Messaging gets an instance of the *RequestInteractionModel* class because it has been implemented in accordance with the *capnetcl* content language and the *emergency* ontology. It depends upon the agent's role what validation cycle the architecture will follow. In the case of the message sender, the send validation cycle is activated in order to process the message before it is sent. The interaction model is passed to the CLEngine component. This component enqueues the interaction model and invokes its *validateContentLanguage* asynchronously. The results of the validation are stored in the CLEngine and are made available for the validation cycle. If the interaction model validation fails then the message is not sent because it does not accomplish with the syntax of that content language. If validation is successful then the interaction model is passed to the ontology engine component where the *validateOntology* module is invoked and the *emergency* ontology is used to validate the *transportPeople* action.

Next, the request interaction model is given to the FPEngine component. At this moment, the *validateFeasibilityPreconditions* is executed. After this validation, the send validation cycle has to decide whether the message is sent or not.

When the message is sent, the *verifyInteractionFinalization* module is called to make the agent aware of the finalization of the interaction. On the contrary, when the message is not sent, it indicates that something was wrong in the validation process. For example, the content of the message can simply has a bug. This processing is very useful while designing and debugging the content of agent interactions before the agent is released. In other cases, at least one feasibility precondition is not fulfilled at runtime. While receiving a message, the process is very similar to the send validation cycle in the first two phases. However, for the third phase, the validation process invokes the interaction model *validateRationalEffect* module. The receive validation cycle finishes when the *verifyInteractionFinalization* is executed. For composed interactions, the processing mechanism is similar since each simple interaction is processed but when the rational effect is validated, the interaction model is delivered to the engine for composed interactions in order to be managed by an interaction protocol.

We have implemented 18 interaction models and also have been testing the framework on CAPNET through the implementation of an open MAS prototype. There, heterogeneous agents interact to realize operations and interchange information to evacuate oil platforms [13]. We have designed platform, hotel and transport agents and consider the case that hotel and transport agents are implemented by third parties. In the context of these agents, we have reused and extended interaction models, by sharing CAPNET-CL and three different ontologies represented with CAPNET-Ontology (emergency, accommodation and transport). In each evacuation experiment different platform, hotel and transport agents could interact using the implemented interaction models.

4 Discussion and Related Work

In open environments, agents are designed by different vendors and their internal structures are different too. When agent interactions are based on the same ACL, it seems to be necessary that agents behave according to their interaction capabilities. The proposed approach is developed within the open research lines which refer to interaction validation and verification models [14] [15] [16] and agent architectures and infrastructures for open systems [17]. We have tried to stand out the importance of engineering agents from two perspectives: autonomy and heterogeneity to guarantee successful interactions at runtime. Autonomy is understood in the sense that agents are able to determine by themselves whether they can process unforeseen messages at runtime depending on their own interaction capabilities. On the other hand, heterogeneity refers to the agent's ability to take into account at runtime the interaction capabilities of the others, without any interaction between software developers.

Agent platforms, such as JADE [18], usually provide a limited support for autonomy within their basic functionality. Moreover, they lack support for interoperability because they do not take into account the semantics of the agent communication language. The mechanisms to support interactions are based on simple routing of ACL messages by defining strategies to deliver messages to execution units. The programming of message processing consists in associating messages to a specific unit (task, action, node, behavior and so on). However, there are no mechanisms to do interaction validation to assure the correct meaning and the context of the message at runtime. Such common activities as structure and meaning analysis of the content, semantic concerns of communicative acts and reasoning about a concrete interaction protocol typically are left to the developer. From the interaction engineering point of view, this freedom makes it difficult and inflexible the implementation of the architecture of interactions when agents try to process and understand the meaning of communications.

Several approaches have been developed to bring together BDI-like frameworks with FIPA compliance communication (JADEX [19] and FIPA-JACK [20]. A very close approach to our framework is PARADE [21]. The goal behind is to provide the agent developer with a goal-oriented agent architecture capable of promoting inter-operability and supporting autonomy exploiting the semantics of FIPA ACL. A strong limitation of PARADE is the underlying mental states theoretic model and its relation with messages content entities. Another limitation is that it considers interactions based on protocols but not on single interactions. The main difference with our framework is that the PARADE architecture does not implement a concrete message validation process. Another related approach is developed in the RICA framework [7] which is focused on the reuse of communicative components by specifying different communicative roles and interactions in order to encapsulate application-dependant functionality. Similar to our approach, RICA pretends to relieve programmers from tasks associated with the management of interactions by separating interaction concerns through special reusable and extensible software modules. The main difference is that RICA focuses exclusively on the pragmatics of the FIPA-ACL messages.

The Semantic Agent framework is an extension for the JADE platform [6] where the developed agents not only automatically interpret the incoming messages according with their formal meaning but they also automatically send proper messages in response to the interpretation. Still, there are three main differences with the proposed agent interaction architecture. First, that approach is only focused on two semantic issues (feasibility preconditions and rational effect) encapsulated into Semantic Interpretation Principles modules compared to the five phases of validation included in our framework. The second difference with that work is related to its so called Semantic Representation. It means that agents only can interact with a particular content language, while our framework is designed to resolve at runtime what content language is required to check the structure of the content. Finally, the third difference is the lack of support of explicit ontologies during interactions. The last two aspects of Semantic agents for JADE are strong limitations in comparison with our framework.

In CAPNET, the agent architecture is designed to build heterogeneous agents using generic classes for interaction that can be reused or extended in any MAS. Other frameworks can provide their own implementation of the agent architecture so that their agents are able to share interaction capabilities using different programming tools and even different software technologies. Having interaction models and an AIA processing them, has three advantages. Firstly, the level of agent autonomy is improved. Whenever an agent interacts with other heterogeneous agents, it will be able to process interactions automatically. Success of processing messages will be a task done by AIA depending on the interaction capabilities at runtime. Secondly, interaction engineering is improved. In the example of request communicative act we implemented the IM in such a way that an agent could reuse it in any request-type interaction. This IM implementation can be shared to implement different agents participating in open MAS without any change. This facilitates the development of new heterogeneous agents. Obviously, if requirements of interactions are different (for example new FP or RE are part of the interaction) developers only need to override the modules that require these changes.

The proposed framework requires less code written. Without AIA and IM each validation must be done by developers for each interaction at design time. As usual, while using available MAS infrastructures, developers have to consider all the scenarios of interaction that agents could participate in. This technique is very limited and inflexible for open and heterogeneous MAS. In contrast, our framework helps interaction engineering by reducing and automating significantly the number of code lines dedicated to interaction processing because the IMs are implemented only once for each communicative act and can be reused for different CLs and ontologies that share the generic classes. The AIA and engines are able to do the real validation tasks so that programmers can concentrate more on the design and implementation of MAS application than on routine tasks for interaction processing.

Although our framework has been tested for FIPA-ACL, it can be applied to interaction among agents that use similar agent communication languages such as KQML [22] where the interactions are defined in terms of speech acts, content languages, ontologies, preconditions and post-conditions. In concrete implementation of agent interaction architecture, an important issue is how to manage messages when interactions are out of the scope of the interaction space. In such a case, agents must have an inter-built support to process those messages and developers have the obligation of implementing message processing. Another concern about our framework is how to build dynamic interaction protocols. Several specific methodologies like AUML [23] and approaches like enlisted in [24] could be implemented as software components in a suitable way that the Engine for Composed Interaction could use.

5 Conclusions

In this paper we described a framework to process FIPA-ACL messages. The message processing is divided into five interaction phases covering the most common aspects of FIPA-ACL: syntax validation of content, semantic validation of content, validation of message feasibility preconditions, validation of message rational effect and validation of termination conditions. We introduced the notions of i) interaction model as a key programming unit to encapsulate the code for each interaction phase and ii) interaction space as a part of the environment where agent interaction capabilities are stored and accessed at runtime. Interaction models are processed at runtime within the agent interaction architecture composed of several validation engines enabling concurrent message processing. A computational implementation for this framework was developed within the CAPNET agent platform.

Our framework gives a structured and automatic way to process interactions that not only known at design time, but also could occur at runtime in open agent systems. We give the capabilities and components to manage several phases of interactions and then, with the AIA, we enable agents with capabilities to analyze messages and then decide if they can be processed in accordance with the requirements. This ability provides a runtime autonomy in understanding interactions based on FIPA-ACL communicative acts and conversations. In the future, we are going to focus on coordination and scalability concerns in order to build a more robust and complete agent architecture for open MAS.

Acknowledgement. The first author would like to thank CONACYT and the IMP for supporting the Ph.D. studies that originated this research.

References

1. Zambonelli, F., Van Dyke Parunak, H.: Signs of a Revolution in Computer Science and Software Engineering. In: Petta, P., Tolksdorf, R., Zambonelli, F. (eds.) ESAW 2002. LNCS (LNAI), vol. 2577, pp. 13–28. Springer, Heidelberg (2003)
2. Ciancarini, P., Wooldridge, M. (eds.): Agent-Oriented Software Engineering, 1st edn. Springer, Heidelberg (2001)
3. Cheong, C., Winikoff, M.: Hermes: Designing goal-oriented agent interactions. In: Müller, J.P., Zambonelli, F. (eds.) AOSE 2005. LNCS, vol. 3950, pp. 16–27. Springer, Heidelberg (2006)
4. Cabri, G., Ferrari, L., Leonardi, L.: Supporting the Development of Multi-Agent Interactions via Roles. In: Müller, J.P., Zambonelli, F. (eds.) AOSE 2005. LNCS, vol. 3950, pp. 154–166. Springer, Heidelberg (2006)
5. Willmott, S. (ed.): Technical Input and Feedback to FIPA from Agentcities.RTD and the Agentcities Initiative. Agentcities Task Force Technical Note 00003, ISSN 1465-3842 (2003), `http://www.agentcities.org/note/00003/`
6. Louis, V., Martinez, T.: The Jade Semantic Agent: Towards Agent Communication Oriented Middleware. AgentLink News Journal (18) (2005)
7. Omicini, A., Ossowski, S., Ricci, A.: Coordination Infrastructures in the Engineering of Multiagent Systems. In: Bergenti, F., et al. (eds.) Methodologies and Software Engineering for Agent Systems - An AgentLink Perspective, Kluwer, Dordrecht (2004)
8. Serrano, J.M., Ossowski, S.: On the Impact of Agent Communication Languages on the Implementation of Agent Systems. In: Klusch, M., Ossowski, S., Kashyap, V., Unland, R. (eds.) CIA 2004. LNCS (LNAI), vol. 3191, pp. 92–106. Springer, Heidelberg (2004)
9. Foundation for Intelligent Physical Agents. FIPA Communicative Act Library Specification `http://www.fipa.org/specs/fipa00037/` and FIPA ACL Message Structure Specification (2003), `http://www.fipa.org/specs/fipa00061/`

10. Contreras, M., German, E., Chi, M., Sheremetov, L.: Design and Implementation of a FIPA Compliant Agent Platform in.NET. Journal of Object Technology 3(9), 5–28 (2004) (Special issue: .NET Technologies)
11. Platon, E., Sabouret, N., Honiden, S.: Modelling Interactions in Assistant Teams. In: International Conference on Active Media Technologies, pp. 383–388 (2005)
12. Sheremetov, L., Batyrshin, I., Filatov, D., Martínez-Muñoz, J.: An Uncertainty Model for Diagnostic Expert System Based on Fuzzy Algebras of Strict Monotonic Operations. In: Gelbukh, A., Reyes-Garcia, C.A. (eds.) MICAI 2006. LNCS (LNAI), vol. 4293, pp. 165–175. Springer, Heidelberg (2006)
13. Sheremetov, L., Contreras, M., Valencia, C.: Intelligent Multi-Agent Support for the Contingency Management System. Int. J. of Expert Systems with Applications 26(1), 57–71 (2004)
14. Colombetti, M., Fornara, N.: A Commitment-Based Approach to Agent Communication. Applied Artificial Intelligence 18, 853–866 (2004)
15. Agerri, R., Alonso, E.: Normative Pragmatics for Agent Communication Languages. In: Akoka, J., Liddle, S.W., Song, I.-Y., Bertolotto, M., Comyn-Wattiau, I., van den Heuvel, W.-J., Kolp, M., Trujillo, J., Kop, C., Mayr, H.C. (eds.) ER Workshops 2005. LNCS, vol. 3770, pp. 172–181. Springer, Heidelberg (2005)
16. Viroli, M., Ricci, A.: Instructions-Based Semantics of Agent-Mediated Interaction. In: Jennings, N.R., et al. (eds.), pp. 102–109. ACM Press, New York (2004)
17. Luck, M., McBurney, P., Shehory, O., Willmott, S.: Agent Based Computing. Agent Technology Roadmap. In: European Coordination Action for Agent-Based Computing (IST-FP6-002006CA) (2005)
18. Bellifemine, F., Bergenti, F., Caire, G., Poggi, A.: JADE - a java agent development framework. Multi-Agent Programming: Languages, Platforms and Applications. In: Bordini, R., et al. (eds.) Multiagent Systems, Artificial Societies, and Simulated Organizations, vol. 15, pp. 125–148 (2005)
19. Pokahr, A., Braubach, L., Lamersdorf, W.: Jadex: A BDI Reasoning Engine, Multi-Agent Programming. In: Bordini, R., et al. (eds.), pp. 149–174. Springer Science, Business Media Inc. (2005)
20. Kenichi, Y.: FIPA JACK: A plug-in for JACK intelligent agents. Technical report, RMIT University (September 2003)
21. Bergenti, F., Poggi, A.: A development toolkit to realize autonomous and interoperable agents. In: International Conference on Autonomous Agents, pp. 632–639 (2002)
22. Finin, T., Labrou, Y.: KQML as an agent communication language. In: Bradshaw, J.M. (ed.) Software Agents, pp. 291–316. MIT Press, Cambridge (1997)
23. Odell, J., Nodine, M., Levy, R.: A Metamodel for Agents, Roles, and Groups. In: Odell, J.J., Giorgini, P., Müller, J.P. (eds.) AOSE 2004. LNCS, vol. 3382, pp. 78–92. Springer, Heidelberg (2005)
24. Chen, B., Sadaoui, S.: A Generic Formal Framework for Multi-agent Interaction Protocols. Technical Report TR 2004-05 ISBN 0-7731-0483-6 Department of Computer Science, University of Regina, Regina SK, Canada (2004)

A Methodology for Developing Multiagent Systems as 3D Electronic Institutions

Anton Bogdanovych[1], Marc Esteva[1], Simeon Simoff[1], Carles Sierra[2], and Helmut Berger[3]

[1] Faculty of IT, University of Technology Sydney, Australia
{anton,esteva,simeon}@it.uts.edu.au
[2] Artificial Intelligence Research Institute (IIIA), CSIC, Campus UAB, Spain
sierra@iiia.csic.es
[3] ECommerce Competence Center, Vienna, Austria
helmut.berger@ec3.at

Abstract. In this paper we propose viewing Virtual Worlds as open Multiagent Systems and propose the 3D Electronic Institutions methodology for their development. 3D Electronic Institutions are Virtual Worlds with normative regulation of interactions. More precisely, the methodology we propose here helps in separating the development of Virtual Worlds based on the concept of 3D Electronic Institutions into two independent phases: specification of the institutional rules and design of the 3D interaction environment. The new methodology is supplied with a set of graphical tools that support the development process on every level, from specification to deployment. The resulting system facilitates the direct integration of humans into Multi-Agent Systems as they participate by driving an avatar in the generated 3D environment and interacting with other humans or software agents, while the institution ensures the validity of their interactions.

1 Introduction

The field of Multiagent Systems (MAS) focuses on the design and development of systems composed of autonomous entities which act in order to achieve their common or individual goals. Several methodologies based on the MAS paradigm have been proposed in the recent years (see [1,2,3] for reviews). Although humans can be seen as autonomous entities most of the MAS methodologies do not consider direct human participation. In general, human role is limited to acting behind the scenes by customising templates of the agents that participate in the system on humans' behalf. Moreover, existing MAS methodologies that consider direct human participation have not developed the necessary tools to facilitate human inclusion.

One of the few areas where direct human participation is considered is the domain of open systems [4], which with the expansion of Internet have been identified as the most important area of application of MAS [5]. Those are systems where participants are assumed to be heterogeneous and self interested

M. Luck and L. Padgham (Eds.): AOSE 2007, LNCS 4951, pp. 103–117, 2008.

and cooperative behaviour can not be expected from them. Hence, methodologies for open systems should not commit to a particular agent architecture or programming language, and should provide mechanisms to deal with agents with self-interested behaviours.

Two of the most prominent methodologies for open systems based on the MAS paradigm are Gaia [6] and Electronic Institutions [7]. In Gaia the system is designed as a set of organizations where agents participate playing different roles. However, Gaia methodology only covers the specification of the system and does not offer any technological support in regards to system execution. In Electronic Institutions the design of the system focuses on specifying a set of institutional rules which establish possible behaviour of the agents. The Electronic Institutions methodology covers all the steps from the specification, to the deployment and execution of the system. Furthermore, the steps of the methodology are supported by a set of provided software tools.

An Electronic Institution can be regarded as a mediator between participants that verifies the validity of their interactions against the set of rules, protocols and norms specified by the systems designers. No assumptions are made about the internal architecture of participating agents and it is only required for an agent to be able to connect to the institution and communicate with it. Thus, Electronic Institutions form a perfect playground for the development of human centered Multiagent Systems and open new horizons to the research in human-agent collaboration. Despite this fact participation of humans in Electronic Institutions have not been well studied and the facilities for their integration have not been properly developed.

In order to solve this problem we propose using 3D Virtual Worlds, which is one of a very few technologies that provides all the necessary means for direct human inclusion into software systems. 3D Virtual Worlds are software generated environments which follow the metaphor of architecture and emulate real world using 3-dimensional visualisation. Humans participate in those environments represented as graphical embodied characters (avatars) and can operate there using simple and intuitive control facilities, which are more or less similar throughout the whole variety of the different Virtual Worlds present on the market. We advocate that 3D Virtual Worlds technology can be successfully used for "opening" Multiagent societies to humans.

In this paper we present a methodology for 3D Electronic Institutions, a concept that appeared from the combination of Electronic Institutions and 3D Virtual Worlds. This methodology focuses on the development of normative environments inhabited by software and human agents. At this aim, the methodology extends the Electronic Institution methodology to generate a representation of the Electronic Institution in 3D Virtual Worlds and to define the necessary elements to successfully integrate both technologies. Hence, humans participate in the institution by controlling an avatar on the generated Virtual World. The methodology is supplied with a set of software tools which give support to all the stages of its development.

Apart from opening MAS to humans the research in 3D Electronic Institutions can also benefit the Virtual World community, which is looking for mechanisms to incorporate social rules into Virtual Worlds in order to control and structure participants' interactions. The design and development of Virtual Worlds has emerged as a phenomenon shaped by a home computer user rather than by research and development activities at universities or companies. As a result, Virtual Worlds are more or less unregulated environments and continue to be developed on an ad hoc basis. Despite the fact that active support of human interactions is one of the key characteristics that set Virtual Worlds apart from other technologies, there are no flexible facilities to control these interactions. As the number of inhabitants of the artificial societies established in Virtual Worlds grows, the level of immersion increases and participants become more and more involved with the experience, the need for structuring their interactions becomes more explicit. Lacking clear mechanisms for doing it, users try introducing some of the convenient social rules from the real world. Doing so, however, in a system that was built without a methodology centered on structuring users' interactions is a very challenging task. One of the consequences of this is that Virtual Worlds are mostly used in computer games, where structuring the interactions of participants is not necessarily useful and the consequences of errors in the code are not dramatic. In order to extend the scope of Virtual Worlds technology to be applied to a wider range of problems, exploit the benefits brought by the Virtual Worlds and deal with their growing complexity, methodologies that regulate the interactions of participants and improve the reliability and security issues need to be applied. We believe that Virtual Worlds have much greater potential and can be used for a broader spectrum of problems. New economical circumstances and conceptual similarity with open systems create a need for Virtual Worlds to be used in domains like E-Commerce, online travel etc. The aforementioned problems of the Virtual Worlds can clearly be solved by applying the 3D Electronic Institutions methodology to their development.

The remainder of the paper is structured as follows. In section 2 we present the conceptual model behind the 3D Electronic Institutions metaphor. Section 3 outlines the steps that 3D Electronic Institutions Methodology utilization requires to be followed and gives the detailed overview of the technical aspects and tools supplied with 3D Electronic Institutions. Next, in section 4 we describe the deployment architecture, while in section 5 we summarize the contribution and present some concluding remarks.

2 3D Electronic Institutions

Conceptually speaking, *3D Electronic Institutions are Virtual Worlds with normative regulation of interactions.* More precisely, we propose to separate the development of 3D Electronic Institutions into two independent phases: specification of the institutional rules and design of the 3D Interaction environment. Such separation is widely used in architecture [8], whose metaphor inspires Virtual Worlds. We are convinced that having it in Virtual Worlds would also be highly beneficial.

For the purpose of the rule specification we suggest employing the Electronic Institutions methodology [9], which is able to ensure the validity of the specified rules and their correct execution. In contrast to Electronic Institutions and Gaia, the normative part of a 3D Electronic Institution does not represent all the activities that are allowed to be performed in a Virtual World. The normative part can be seen as defining which actions require institutional verification assuming that any other action is allowed. Not every Virtual World requires such an approach as well as not every institution requires 3D visualization. Only systems that have a high degree of interactions and those interactions need to be structured in order to avoid violations may need institutional intervention. And only the institutions where 3D visualization of active components is possible and beneficial should be visualized in Virtual Worlds.

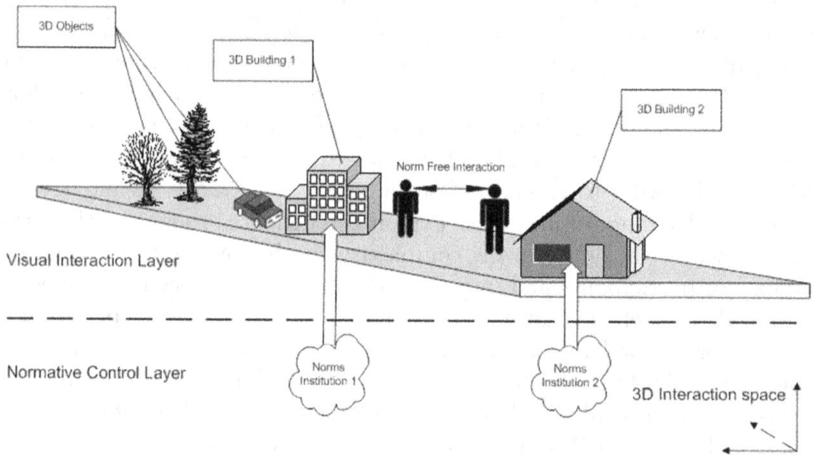

Fig. 1. 3D Electronic Institutions Concept

For those systems that can benefit from both 3-dimensional visualization and institutional control of the specified rules we suggest using the following *conceptual model.* A 3D Electronic Institution is visualized in terms of a 3D Virtual World. We call this Virtual World a 3D Interaction Space. Inside the 3D Interaction Space an institution is represented as a building, and participants are visualized as avatars. Once they enter the building their actions are validated against the specified institutional rules. The institutional buildings is divided into a set of rooms, which are separated from each other by doors. The doors are open or closed for a participant depending on the role she/he is playing, the institutional rules and the current execution state. Figure 1 outlines the brief idea behind the 3D Electronic Institutions concept presented so far. Next we describe the components of the conceptual model in more details.

3D Interaction Space. It represents the generated 3D Virtual World, and there is no possibility for participants to move beyond it. The only way to leave it is by disconnecting from the Virtual World. Once someone enters it, he/she will become embodied as an avatar and will be physically located inside. To enhance the believability of the visualization the space is usually populated with a number of various 3D Objects. The most typical case is that a 3D Interaction Space is decorated as a garden, where the objects enhancing the believability are trees, bushes, cars etc. A special type of objects within the space are the buildings. Each of the buildings metaphorically represents an institution. Anywhere outside the institutional building interactions among participating avatars are not regulated and every event that happens inside this space is immediately visualized without any prior validation.

Institutional Building. An institution is represented as a building in the 3D Interaction Space, and the interactions within the building are regulated by the specified institutional rules. Every event that a participant requests by pressing keys on the keyboard or operating with the mouse are first sent to the institutional infrastructure for validation. If the institution permits event's execution – the corresponding action is visualized, otherwise the event is ignored. It is also possible for the institution to provide context based explanations of the reasons why a particular event can not be processed. The institutional building has a single entrance door, through which the participants can enter it.

Avatars. The participants of the 3D Interaction Space are visualized as avatars. We distinguish between the following two types of avatars: avatars for users and avatars for the institutional employees. For the users' avatars an initial set of default appearances is provided, but those appearances can be changed later. The institutional employees are usually represented by autonomous agents that play internal roles in the corresponding Electronic Institution. They are assumed to have similar appearance which goes inline with the dress code of the institution they are employed with. While outside the institutions the avatars are free to execute any possible actions and their communication is not moderated by any of the institutions. Once they enter an institutional building they can only execute the actions that are permitted by the corresponding institution. In some of the rooms it is allowed by the institution to split the user into several alteroids (avatars), to participate simultaneously in different activities. Each time a new alteroid is created the user should decide which to choose to control and a new autonomous agent is executed to take control over the other ones. This functionality allows a user to employ autonomous agents for performing some routine tasks on user's behalf, while the user may be involved into some other activities.

Rooms. Every institutional building consists of a set of rooms, each one representing a different activity. The number of rooms within a building and the activity going on in each one is determined by the institution specification. Rooms are represented as a set of rectangular boxes closed by walls from every side. Agents can enter and leave a room by traversing one of the doors embedded in their walls connecting it with other rooms.

Doors. The Doors are used to connect different rooms in the institutional building. The institutional rules and the execution state determine which agents depending on their role can progress through the door. This is strictly controlled by the Electronic Institution.

Map. In order to simplify the navigation of the users, every institution is supplied by the map of the building. The map usually appears in the upper-right corner of the screen as a semitransparent schematic plan. Each of the available rooms is shown on the map and the human-like figures show every user the positions of all the alteroids a user is associated with. While moving through the institution the positions are updated accordingly.

Backpack with obligations. While acting in an institution a user may acquire some commitments. An example of such a commitment may be that a user who just won the auction will not be able to directly leave the institution, but is committed to visit the payment room before leaving. These commitments are expressed in the specification of the underlying Electronic Institution and are fully controlled by the system. In order to have a simple way to present those commitments to a user we use the metaphor of a backpack used in many computer games. The backpack is usually present in the lower right part of the screen and a user may decide to hide it or show it back after hiding. Clicking on the backpack will result in a user being presented with the textual list of the acquired commitments.

Events/Actions/Messages. Although, we anticipate that the users may use all sorts of different devices for navigating virtual worlds, in a standard case a participant of a 3D Interaction Space is able to control the avatar and change the state of the Virtual World by pressing keyboard buttons, moving a mouse or clicking mouse buttons. Those physical actions executed by a user in the real world generate events inside the Virtual World, which are then visualized as actions executed within the 3D Interaction Space. The events that a user is trying to execute inside an institutional building are not directly visualized. Before visualization every event is transformed into a message understandable by the institution and send to the institutional infrastructure for validation. Only if the given message is consistent with the current state of the institution and the institutional rules, the action is performed and visualised.

3 3D Electronic Institutions Methodology

In the previous section we presented the metaphor of 3D Electronic Institutions. Here we describe the methodology that facilitates their development and show how this new methodology embeds the Electronic Institutions methodology. We want to remark that this methodology covers the development of a single institution. In order to have an Interaction Space populated by several institutions, the methodology has to be applied to each one of them.

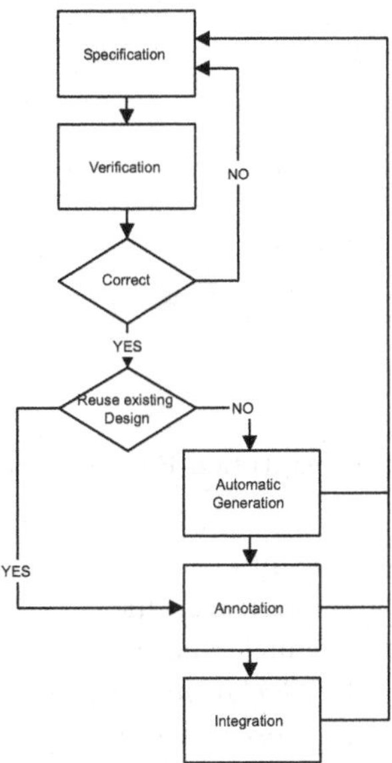

Fig. 2. Methodology steps

Applying 3D Electronic Institutions methodology requires 5 steps to be accomplished:

1. Specification of an Electronic Institution using ISLANDER [7].
2. Verification of the specification.
3. Automatic Generation of the corresponding 3D environment (if needed).
4. Annotation of the Electronic Institution specification with components of the 3D Virtual World.
5. Integrating the 3D Virtual World into the institutional infrastructure.

Figure 2 presents the overview of each of the steps and their sequence. The detailed explanation of each of them follows next.

Step 1 – Specification. The specification step is the same as in the Electronic Institutions methodology [7]. It establishes the regulations that govern the behaviour of the participants. This process is supported by ISLANDER which permits to specify most of the components graphically, hiding the details of the formal specification language and making the specification task transparent. The institutional regulations are established by three types of conventions.

Conventions on language, the *Dialogical Framework*. It defines a common ontology and communication language to allow humans with different cultural backgrounds, as well as, agents to exchange knowledge. This ontology and language for humans will be further transformed into actions that are allowed to be executed in the Virtual World. Those actions are connected to 3D models in the environment, the affordances of which will help in eliminating the cultural barrier. Due to the further provided translation of the communication language

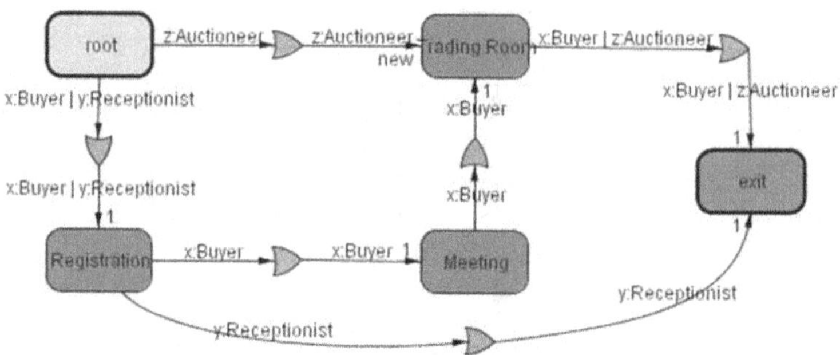

Fig. 3. Trading Institution Performative Structure

into actions and vice-versa, the agents will be able to interact with humans and understand their actions. The dialogical framework also fixes the organizational structure of the society, that is, which roles can participants play.

Conventions on activities, the *Performative Structure.* This dimension determines in which types of dialogues users can engage. For each different activity, interactions among participants are articulated through group meetings, called scenes, which follow well-defined interaction protocols. The protocol of each scene is specified by a graph where the states represent the different interaction states and arcs are labeled with messages of the communication language or timeouts. Participants in a scene can change over time and at this aim, a set of access and exit states per role are defined. Finally, role populations are specified by establishing the minimum and maximum number of participants that must or can play each role. More complex activities are specified by establishing connections among scenes. The resulting, network of scenes, the *Performative Structure*, defines how agents can legally move among scenes depending on their role. This transit of participants between scenes is regulated by special (simple) scenes called transitions, which allow expressing synchronization, parallelization and choice points. In their transit among scenes users are allowed to change their role. The Performative Structure contains two special scenes, the initial and final scene, which does not model any activity and must be regarded as the institution entrance and exit. Participants entering the institution are initially placed in the initial scene, while reaching the final scene means leaving the institution.

Conventions on behavior, the *Norms.* Norms determine the consequences of user actions. These consequences are modeled as commitments that participants acquire as a consequence of their actions and have to fulfill later on. These commitments may restrict future activities of the users.

In order to illustrate the different steps of the methodology, we use a very simple Trading Institution. This institution can be enacted by the agents playing the *receptionist*, *auctioneer* and *buyer* roles. Figure 3 shows the performative structure of the Trading Institution, where rectangles represent different scenes and triangular shapes are transitions. Apart of the root and exit scenes which just represent the entrance and exit, the institution contains the *Registration*, *Meeting* and *Trading Room* scenes. In the *Registration* scene buyers register by communicating their login and password to an agent playing the receptionist role. In the *Meeting* scene buyers can meet and freely interact, while in the *Trading Room* buyers can acquire products auctioned by an agent playing the auctioneer role. The arcs connecting scenes and transitions are labeled with the roles that can progress through them. Notice that buyer agents are required to go to the Registration scene before moving to the meeting room to interact with other buyers. From the Meeting scene, they can proceed to the Trading Room to participate in the auctions. Receptionist can only go to the Registration scene, while agents playing the auctioneer role can only access the Auction Room from the root scene.

Step 2 – Verification. One of the advantages of the formal nature of the 3D Electronic Institutions methodology is that the specification produced on the previous step can be automatically verified for correctness by ISLANDER. The tool verifies the scene protocols, the role flow among the different scenes and the correctness of norms. This verification starts with the validation of the correctness of the protocol defined by each scene. This includes checking that for each state there is a path from the initial state to a final state that passes through the current state, and that the messages of the arcs are correct with respect to the communication language. At the Performative Structure level it is verified that agents will not get blocked at any scene or transition. Thus, it is checked that from each scene and transition users have always a path to follow, that each of them is reachable from the initial scene and that from each scene and transition exists a path to the final scene that will allow participants to leave the institution. Finally, ISLANDER checks that norms are correctly specified and that participants can fulfil their commitments. As commitments are expressed as actions that users have to carry out in the future, it is verified that those actions can be performed by agents.

The verification permits to detect errors in the specification before starting the design and development of the 3D visualization. If such errors are found, the developers should go back to step 1 to correct them. If the specification contains no errors, there are two options. If the 3D Visualization of the environment is already created (reuse of the existing design) then the developers may skip the next step and continue with Step 4. Otherwise, the generation step, Step 3, should be executed.

Step 3 – Generation of the visualization. The institutional specification does not only define the rules of the interactions, but also helps to understand which visualization facilities are required for participants to operate in the institution. Most elements of the specification have conceptual similarities with basic concepts of 3D Virtual Worlds, which makes it possible to create an automatic mapping between those. In our metaphor scenes and transitions, correspond to rooms, connections (arcs) in the Performative Structure graph become doors, and the number of participants allowed in a scene determines the size of a room. The performative structure corresponds to the map of the institution and the

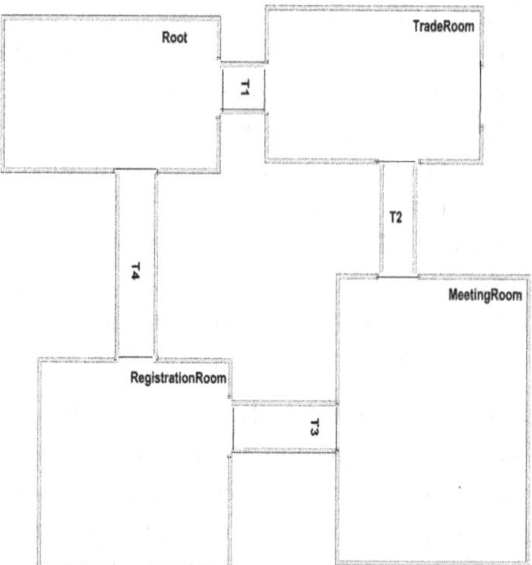

Fig. 4. Trading Institution floor plan

backpack with obligations is a visual way to communicate the normative obligations to the users.

Having this mapping serves two conceptual purposes: explaining the Electronic Institutions metaphor in terms of Virtual Worlds using the concepts familiar to most of the humans and explaining the Virtual Worlds in terms of the institutional specification of the underlying processes. Practically it helps to generate a part of the visualization in a fully automatic way (see [10] for details). The generation can function in two different modes: Euclidean and non-Euclidean. In the first case the rooms on the generated floor plan are positioned so, that each scene and transition connected in the Performative Structure are physically placed next to each other and there is a door between them. In the non-Euclidean case the rooms may be located anywhere and are not necessarily involved in any sort of spatial relationship. The movement between connected rooms in the non-Euclidean approach will then be conducted using teleportation[1].

Next, all the rooms are resized to be able to include the maximum number of participants allowed in the corresponding scene. Another outcome of this step is the schematic plan (map) of the institution.

Figure 4 depicts the automatically generated floor plan for the Trading Institution. Notice that there is a room for each scene and transition of the performative structure shown in Figure 3, except for the output scene (the output scene does not model any interaction and it only represents the exit point of the institution). This is expressed in the figure by the doors (represented by thin lines) in the registration and trading room that are not connected to any other room. Once an agent traverses one of these doors – the agent leaves the institutional building and appears inside the uncontrolled part of the 3D Interactions

[1] The process of moving objects from one place to another instantaneously, without passing through the intervening space.

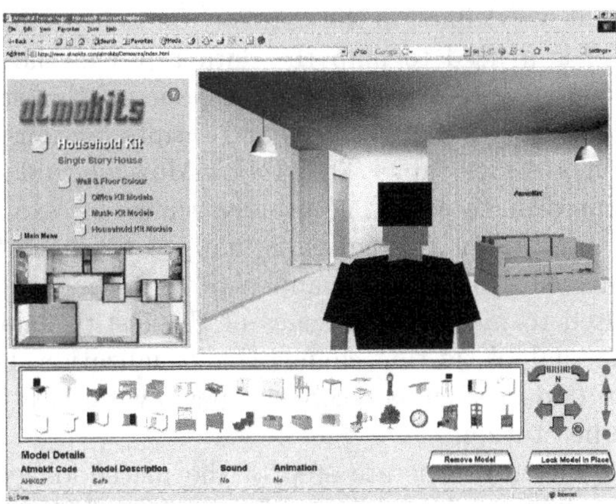

Fig. 5. Annotating the rooms with Atmokits

Space. Transitions are the rooms with names Ti, where i ranges from 1 to 4. The connections among rooms are established through doors, positions of which are determined by the arcs connecting scenes and transitions in the performative structure of the Trading Institution. Although two rooms can be connected by a door, only the agents playing the roles that label the corresponding arc will be allowed to progress through the corresponding door.

Step 4 – Annotation. Although a part of the visualization of a 3D Electronic Institution can be automatically generated there is usually not enough information present in the specification to produce an appealing visualization. To enrich the generated visualization we use the Annotation Editor tool. This tool helps to change the textures, colors and add additional objects inside each of the rooms. In the current implementation we use the Atmokits software[2] for this purpose. It is supplied with a set of standard objects and textures that can be used to enrich the design of the rooms. Figure 5 shows the interface of Atmokits. Left side of the figure shows the map of the institution and the right part displays the 3-dimensional representation of one of the rooms with an avatar inside. The bottom part outlines a set of objects that can be inserted and the control buttons that are used for precise object positioning.

After the annotation step the user can return to step 1, if for any reason he/she wants to modify the specification, or move to step 5.

Step 5 – Integration. On the integration step the execution state related components are specified. This includes the creation of the set of scripts that control the modification of the states of the 3D Virtual Worlds and mapping of those scripts to the messages, which change the state of the Electronic Institution. Firstly, the scripts that correspond to the messages from the agent/institution protocol need to be defined. These include entering scene, leaving scene, entering transition, leaving transition etc. Next, the scripts that correspond to the

[2] http://www.atmokits.com

specific messages that are defined in the ontology on the specification step must be created. If there is a need to map the data types in the ontology to 3D objects in the Virtual World it should also be done on this step. At the end, the correspondences between the messages and scripts (actions) are created by filling in the Action/Message table. The Action-Message table for the trading institution is presented in Table 1. The table specifies, for example, that when an avatar collides with a door this action is mapped to an *ExitScene* message, while the action of raising a hand is mapped to a *Bid* message. Furthermore, the table is also used to map the messages of the institutional infrastructure to actions in the Virtual World that change the visualization. For instance, if a *EnteredAgentInstitution* message is received a new avatar will be shown in the initial scene of the institution.

Making the integration a separate step of the methodology stimulates the development of the scripts in the form of design patters, that are generic enough to be reused in other systems.

After accomplishing this step the generated 3D Virtual World is ready to be visualized and the 3D Electronic Institution infrastructure will be executed to take care of the validity of interactions between participants, verify the permissions of participants to access different scenes and will make sure that all the institutional norms and obligations are imposed.

Table 1. Action-Message Table

Action	Message
addNewAvatar	EnteredAgentInstitution
doorCollideFromScene	ExitScene
roomEnter	MoveToScenes
doorCollideFromTransition	ExitTransition
transitionEnter	MoveToTransition
raiseHand	Bid
removeAvatar	ExitedAgentInstitution

4 Deployment

For deployment of 3D Electronic Institutions created by the proposed methodology, we use a 3-layered infrastructure presented in Figure 6.

First layer is the *Electronic Institution Layer*. It uses the AMELI system [7] for enforcing the institutional rules established on the specification step. AMELI keeps the execution state of the institution and uses it along with the specification to guarantee that participants' actions do not violate any of the institutional constraints.

Second layer is the *Communication Layer*. Its task is to causally connect [11] the institutional infrastructure with the visualization system transforming the actions of the visualization system into the messages, understandable by the institutional infrastructure and the other way around. This causal connection

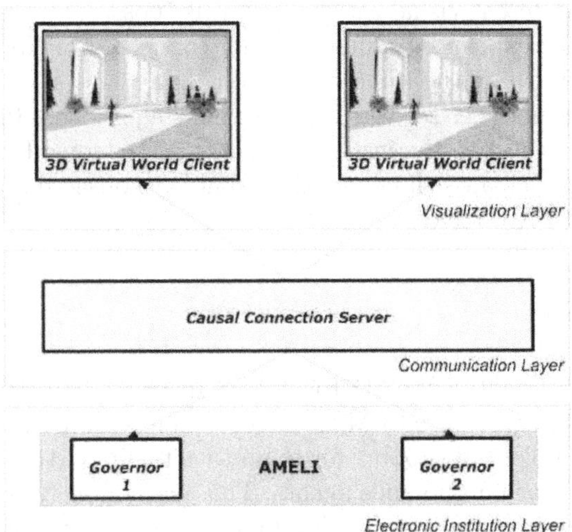

Fig. 6. Runtime Architecture

is done via the Causal Connection Server, which uses the Action-Message table created on the integration step. The causal connection is happening in the following way: an action executed in the 3D Virtual World (that requires institutional verification) results in a change of the institutional state in the AMELI layer, as well as every change of the institutional state is reflected onto the 3D Virtual World and changes its state. The Communication layer conceptually and technologically connects two metaphors: Electronic Institutions and Virtual Worlds and we see it as one of our major scientific contributions.

The third layer is called *Visualization Layer*. It is used to visualize the 3D Virtual World for the users. Currently, we are employing the Adobe Atmosphere[3] technology for this task, however, due to the fact that it was discontinued we are making a transition to Second Life[4].

A clear separation of the runtime architecture into three different layers has a number of advantages:

1. The interactions inside the 3D Virtual World become structured, secure and predictable, as everything that needs control is verified by AMELI and will happen as specified.
2. The Visualization Layer can be easily replaced (i.e. when a more advanced visualization platform appears on the market) with minimal changes in the rest of the system.
3. The changes in the Electronic Institution Layer will be automatically reflected onto the Visualization layer or will require minimal manual adjustment.

[3] http://adobe.com/products/atmosphere
[4] http://secondlife.com

4. A number of different visualization platforms (possibly implemented via different technologies) can be simultaneously connected to the Causal Connection Server and share the same institution.
5. Some participants (i.e. software agents) can bypass the 3D Virtual World and directly connect to the institution via the Electronic Institutional layer, while other participants (humans) will be able to observe their presence and actions in the 3D Virtual World.

5 Conclusion

In this paper we presented the 3D Electronic Institutions methodology, which supports human integration into MAS-mediated environments and provides all the necessary technological support for them to actively participate and interact with other humans or autonomous agents. This methodology is supplied with a set of tools that facilitate the design, development and execution of such environments. We would like to stress that, to our knowledge, 3D Electronic Institutions is the first methodology that is specifically concerned with the developments of Virtual Worlds with normative regulations of interactions. Its formal nature has a number of advantages. Firstly, it forces the designer to follow a structured and formal approach, having to analyse the system in detail before implementing it. This permits designers to detect the critical points and possible problems at an early stage. Furthermore, the methodology clearly distinguishes between the design of the institutional rules and the design of its visualization in Virtual Worlds, which proved to be an efficient way to develop real world designs. Another advantage of using this methodology is that the supplied tools make the development faster, helping to achieve some tasks automatically. Moreover, due to the distributed architecture possible updates of the system can be accommodated in an easy way. Notice, that the development process is independent of the particular Virtual Worlds technology used for the visualization of the system. This in combination with the execution infrastructure permits a quick and easy portability of the system to new visualization platforms.

The proposed architecture also supports an efficient collaboration between humans and agents. There is always a software agent assigned to every human participating in the institution and either of them can control the avatar. When the human is driving the avatar the agent observes and records the actions of the principal. This information is used later on, when the agent is in control of the avatar for achieving its goals and expressing believable human-like behaviour. The immersive nature of 3D Virtual Worlds creates better possibilities to observe human behaviour without a need to overcome the embodiment dissimilarities, while institution control of the interactions helps the agent to reduce the number of possible behaviours and hence, to learn faster. Furthermore, when the agent is driving the avatar the human is supplied with convenient interface to observe its actions and intervene when necessary. In this way the behaviour of the agent acting on user's behalf can be easily controlled, increasing the trust and confidence of the humans in the agent.

Acknowledgements

The research reported in this paper is partially supported by the ARC Discovery Project DP0451692 "The Evolution of Business Networks in Virtual Marketplaces" and the Spanish projects "Autonomic Electronic Institutions" (TIN2006-15662-C02-01) and "Agreement Technologies" (CONSOLIDER CSD2007-0022, INGENIO 2010).

References

1. Iglesias, C., Garijo, M., González, J.: A Survey of Agent-Oriented Methodologies. In: Rao, A.S., Singh, M.P., Müller, J.P. (eds.) ATAL 1998. LNCS (LNAI), vol. 1555, pp. 317–330. Springer, Heidelberg (1999)
2. Wooldridge, M., Ciancarini, P.: Agent-Oriented Software Engineering: The State of the Art. In: Ciancarini, P., Wooldridge, M.J. (eds.) AOSE 2000. LNCS, vol. 1957, pp. 55–82. Springer, Heidelberg (2001)
3. Gómez-Sanz, J., Pavón, J.: Methodologies for developing multi-agent systems. Journal of Universal Computer Science 10(4), 359–374 (2004)
4. Hewitt, C.: Offices are open systems. ACM Transactions on Office Information Systems 4(3), 271–287 (1986)
5. Wooldridge, M., Jennings, N.R., Kinny, D.: A methodology for agent-oriented analysis and design. In: Proceedings of the third annual conference on Autonomous Agents (AGENTS 1999), pp. 69–76. ACM Press, New York (1999)
6. Zambonelli, F., Jennings, N., Wooldridge, M.: Developing multiagent systems: The gaia methodology. ACM Transactions on Software Engineering Methodology 12(3), 317–370 (2003)
7. Arcos, J.L., Esteva, M., Noriega, P., Rodriguez-Aguilar, J.A., Sierra, C.: An Integrated Developing Environment for Electronic Institutions. In: Agent Related Platforms, Frameworks, Systems, Applications, and Tools. Whitestein Book Series, Springer, Heidelberg (2005)
8. Maher, M., Simoff, S., Mitchell, J.: Formalizing building requirements using an activity/space model. Automation in Construction 6, 77–95 (1997)
9. Esteva, M.: Electronic Institutions: From Specification to Development. PhD thesis, Institut d'Investigació en Intel.ligència Artificial (IIIA), Spain (2003)
10. Bogdanovych, A., Drago, S.: Euclidean Representation of 3D electronic institutions: Automatic Generation. In: Proceedings of the 8th International Working Conference on Advanced Visual Interfaces (AVI 2006), pp. 449–452 (2006)
11. Maes, P., Nardi, D.: Meta-Level Architectures and Reflection. Elsevier Science Inc., New York (1988)

Reasoning About Risk in Agent's Deliberation Process: A Jadex Implementation

Yudistira Asnar, Paolo Giorgini, and Nicola Zannone

Department of Information and Communication Technology
University of Trento, Italy
{yudis.asnar,paolo.giorgini,zannone}@dit.unitn.it

Abstract. Autonomous agents and multi-agent systems have been proved to be useful in several safety-critical applications. However, in current agent architectures (particularly BDI architectures) the deliberation process does not include any form of risk analysis. In this paper, we propose guidelines to implement Tropos Goal-Risk reasoning. Our proposal aims at introducing risk reasoning in the deliberation process of a BDI agent so that the overall set of possible plans is evaluated with respect to risk. When the level of risk results too high, agents can consider and introduce additional plans, called treatments, that produce an overall reduction of the risk. Side effects of treatments are also considered as part of the model. To make the discussion more concrete, we illustrate the proposal with a case study on the Unmanned Aerial Vehicle agent.

1 Introduction

Agent technology is becoming more and more an emergent alternative to build safety-critical systems [1, 2]. Humans are replaced by autonomous agents in high risk situations or safety-critical missions, such as reconnaissance and battle-combat. However, developing autonomous agents for such tasks require to introduce and consider risk and related problems within the agent's deliberation process.

Many models dealing with agent's mental states have been proposed in literature [3,4,5]. Most of them describe agent's mental states in terms of Belief, Desire, and Intention (the BDI model). The BDI model has been initially introduced by Bratman [6] and then refined by Rao and Georgeff [7,4] for real implementation in agent based systems, such as Procedural Reasoning System (PRS) and distributed Multi Agent Reasoning System (dMARS). Currently, agent tools and frameworks, such as Jack [8], Jadex [9], and Jason [10], use effectively the BDI model in their implementations. Here the deliberation process of an agent is supported by a meta-level reasoning, where the most appropriate plan for achieving a given goal is selected on the basis of specific criteria such as priority and beliefs. Unfortunately, these implementations do not consider uncertain events and, in particular, risks (i.e., uncertain events with negative impacts [11]) as integral part of the meta-level reasoning. On the other hand, several approaches have been proposed in literature to reason about uncertainty [12, 13], but often their complexity made almost impossible the implementation in real agent-based applications [12, 14].

In this paper, we adopt and adapt Tropos Goal-Risk (GR) Framework [15] within the deliberation process of a BDI agent. The GR framework extends the Tropos Goal

M. Luck and L. Padgham (Eds.): AOSE 2007, LNCS 4951, pp. 118–131, 2008.

Model [16] adopting the idea of the three layers analysis introduced by Feather et al. [17] in their Defect Detection and Prevention (DDP) framework. The GR framework consists of three layers: goal, event/risk, and treatment. These three layers are used to reason about uncertain events that obstruct goals and the plans that can be used to achieve them, and evaluate the effectiveness of treatments. In particular, the GR framework provides an agent with the capability to choose a strategy (i.e., a combination of plans and treatments) to pursue a goal, whose risk and cost are acceptable by the agent. In this paper, we propose an implementation of this framework in Jadex [9]. The idea is to encode the GR framework into the Jadex platform so that the deliberation process of an agent takes into account risks and associated costs.

The paper is structured as follows. Section 2 provides a brief description of the Unmanned Aerial Vehicle agent that will be used as an example to explain the whole framework. Section 3 explains the Tropos Goal-Risk framework, and Section 4 details its implementation in Jadex. Finally, Section 5 discusses related work and Section 6 gives final remarks.

2 Unmanned Aerial Vehicle

An Unmanned Aerial Vehicle (UAV) is an aircraft without pilot, that either is controlled remotely or flies autonomously. UAVs are typically used in a number of critical missions, such as decoy, reconnaissance, combat, and even for research and civil purposes.

In the early time, UAVs were called drones because they were not more than aircraft remotely controlled by human. Recently, several efforts have been made to apply intelligent agents to control aircraft [18, 19, 20]. Attempts to use intelligent agents in managing UAVs are addressed to avoid the risk of human life loss. In this setting, agents can respond to event occurrences autonomously without waiting for instructions from the ground control. This capability results to be essential in critical and dangerous missions (e.g., reconnaissance, decoy, and combat) where the response time has to be as short as possible. For instance, if a drone understands that it has been detected by the enemy, it informs the ground control about the danger. However, it will still proceed with the mission according to the previous plan until it receives new instructions from the ground control. It is possible that these new instructions are sent to the UAV too late for ensuring the success of the mission. The ambitious objective of the agent paradigm is to provide UAV with facilities to react autonomously and so to take countermeasures in the appropriate time.

There are still open problems for completely replacing human with agents. For instance, a human pilot can learn from past experience so that it can adopt adequate measures when a new occurrence of events is detected. This paper aims at improving software agents with such a capability.

3 Tropos Goal-Risk Model

Tropos is a software engineering methodology that adopts the concept of agent and its related mentalistic notions (e.g., goal, plan, and resource) along the whole software development process [21]. The Tropos Goal-Risk (GR) framework [15, 22] enhances the

Tropos goal model by extending the conceptual model with constructs and relations specific to risk analysis. Basically, a GR model is represented as a graph $\langle \mathcal{N}, \mathcal{R} \rangle$, where $\mathcal{N}$ are nodes and $\mathcal{R}$ are relations. $\mathcal{N}$ is comprised of goals, plans, and events, and $\mathcal{R}$ consists of decomposition (AND/OR), contribution, and means-end relations. *Goals* are defined as strategic interests that an agent may have, while an *event* is an uncertain circumstance/state of affair that may affect (positively or negatively) the achievement of a goal. Typically, events are out of agents' control. A *plan* is a course of actions, which can be used to achieve a goal or to reduce/treat/mitigate the effects of an event. To distinguish between the plans used to achieve a goal (hereafter plan) and the ones for mitigating the risk, we call mitigating plans *treatments*.

Goals, plans, treatments, and events are characterized by two attributes: satisfaction (SAT) and denial (DEN). SAT represents the evidence that an agent has about the achievement of a goal, the execution of a plan, or the occurrence of an event. DEN represents the evidence about the failure in fulfilling a goal, executing a task, or the occurrence of an event. Though they have similar intuition with probability theory, SAT and DEN are not related and cannot be derived one from the other. The values of attributes are qualitatively represented as $\{F\}$*ull*, $\{P\}$*artial*, and $\{N\}$*one*, with intended meaning $F > P > N$. For instance, $Sat(G) = P$ means that there is (at least) partial evidence that goal G will be achieved, whereas $Den(G) = N$ means that there is no evidence about the failure in achieving goal G. For plans and treatments, these attributes are used to calculated the *success-rate* that represents how likely a plan or a treatment will be successfully executed. Besides success-rate, plans and treatments has also attribute *cost* that specifies how many efforts are needed to execute them. In the UAV scenario, for instance, it may refer to the power consumed to execute a plan. SAT and DEN are also used to compute the likelihood of an event, following the idea of the Theory of Evidence proposed by Dempster and Shaffer [23]. In a GR model $\langle \mathcal{N}, \mathcal{R} \rangle$, relations in $\mathcal{R}$ are represented as $(N_1, \ldots, N_n) \stackrel{r}{\longmapsto} N$, where r is the type of the relation, $N_1, \ldots, N_n$ are called *source nodes* and N is the *target node*. The formal framework adopts the axioms for the semantic of relations from [24]. This framework is presented in [22] together with the rules used to propagate evidence from source nodes to the target node.

A GR model is composed of three different layers: goal layer, event layer, and treatment layer. The **goal layer** models the strategic interests of an agent (i.e., goals) along with the plans to obtain them. For instance, Fig. 1 shows the GR model of the UAV agent (goals are represented as ovals and plans as hexagonal). The UAV agent has as main goal to investigate the enemy area (G_1) which is AND-decomposed into define the flight airways to the target (G_4), fly to the target (G_5) based on the defined airways, identify the target (G_6) whether it is a relevant target or just a decoy, and take the picture of target (G_7). According to the rules, which is adopted from [24], the SAT value for G_1 is calculated as the minimum of all SAT values of subgoals G_4, G_5, G_6, and G_7. Inversely, the DEN value for a target goal is calculated as the maximum of all DEN values of its subgoals. Differently, for OR-decomposition the achievement of a subgoal implies the achievement of its root goal. For instance, to achieve goal take the picture of target (G_7), the UAV agent can use take-store schema (G_8) or use take-transmit schema (G_9). The refinement process terminates when all leaf goals are tangible, i.e., for each leaf goal there is at least a plan that can be used to achieve it.

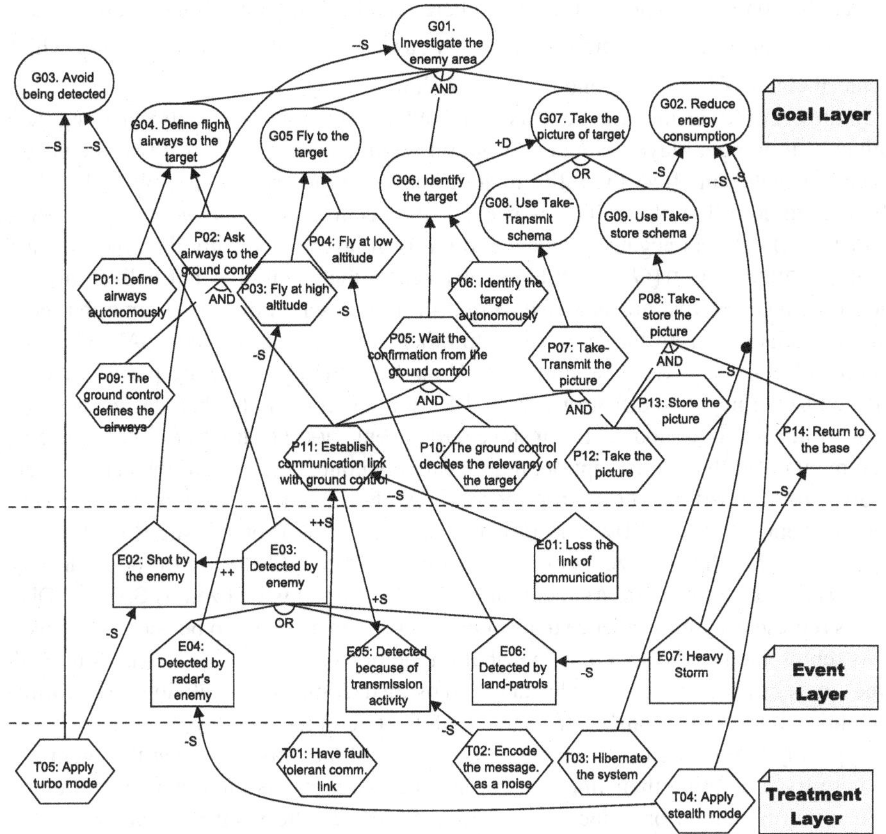

Fig. 1. Goal-Risk model of the UAV Agent

For instance, to achieve goal fly to the target (G_5), the UAV can adopt two alternative plans: fly at high altitude (P_3) or fly at low altitude (P_4). These plans are connected to their end G_5 through means-end relations (indicated as $P_3 \longmapsto G_5$ and $P_4 \longmapsto G_5$, respectively). Each plan may further be refined using decomposition relations.

Additionally, there are situations where the achievement of a goal can contribute positively or negatively (denoted by $+, ++, -, --$) to the achievement of other goals. In our example, goal use take-transmit schema (G_9) requires more energy and so it negatively contributes ($-_S$) to the satisfaction of goal reduce the energy consumption (G_2) (indicated as $G_9 \overset{-S}{\longmapsto} G_2$). Essentially, the contribution $-_S$ states that the SAT value of the source goal is propagated to the DEN value of the target goal with the maximum value *Partial*. $--_S$ has a similar semantics but they can contribute till *Full*. Negative contribution relations for denial ($--_D$ and $-_D$) have dual propagation rules. Similar considerations can be applied to positive contribution. For instance, the denial of goal identify the target (G_6) contribute positively ($+_D$) to the denial of goal take the picture of target (G_7) since the UAV has to decide whether or not the target is relevant before taking the picture. Similar rules apply for positive contribution relations for satisfaction ($++_S$ and $+_S$). Finally, there could be situations where both $+_S$ and $+_D$ are required for the same goals. In this case, we simply use $G_x \stackrel{+}{\longmapsto} G_y$ which means that both $G_x \stackrel{+_S}{\longmapsto} G_y$ and $G_x \stackrel{+_D}{\longmapsto} G_y$ hold.

In the **event layer** uncertain events (depicted as pentagons) are analyzed along their influence to the goal layer using contribution relations (Fig. 1). Notice that the occurrence of events can affect the fulfillment of goals and the execution of plans, but their absence do not affect them. This is because the occurrence of an event (e.g., heavy storm (E_7)) delivers negative evidence to the goal layer (especially the goal reduce energy consumption (G_2)), while the absence of the event does not deliver any evidence neither positive nor negative. Based on this observation, we assume that contribution relations from the event layer to other layers propagate only SAT evidences (denoted by $++_S$, $+_S$, $--_S$, and $-_S$). Though in this paper we are particularly interested to the negative effect of event (risk), the GR model also handles events with positive impacts over goals.[1] For instance, the event heavy storm (E_7) can cause an increment of the fuel consumption, that negatively contributes ($-$) to the achievement of goal reduce energy consumption (G_2). At the same time, E_7 reduces the likelihood of being detected by land-patrols (E_8). As in the Probabilistic Risk Analysis (PRA) [25], we characterize an event with two attributes: *likelihood* of its occurrence and *severity* once it occurs. As mention before, likelihood is realized as SAT and DEN values representing the evidence that support or prevent an event to be occurred. Severity is represented as the sign of a contribution relation (e.g., $+$,$++$,$-$,$--$). As in Fault Tree Analysis [26], an event can be analyzed using decomposition relations. The formal semantics of these relations are the same with the one in the goal layer.

Typically, events are out of an agent's control and the only thing that the agent can do is to try mitigating their impacts. An agent can adopt specific treatments to either reduce the likelihood or reduce the severity of risk. In the **treatment layer** specific plans are introduced and related to the goal and event layer. As shown in Fig. 1, goal apply stealth mode (T_4) technology reduces the likelihood of risk being detected by enemy's radar (E_4). This relation is depicted as $T_4 \stackrel{-}{\longmapsto} E_4$. In case of storm, the UAV agent can hibernate the system (T_3) to reduce the negative impacts of the event E_7 towards the achievement of goal reduce the energy consumption (G_2). This relation is depicted as a line ending with a black circle in Fig. 1 and represented as $T_3 \stackrel{--}{\longmapsto} (E_7 \stackrel{--}{\longmapsto} G_2)$. We call this relation *alleviation relation*, but for sake of simplicity, we do not detail it in this paper. The level of risk effect reduction from a treatment depends on the success-rate of the treatment and the sign of the relation to the event layer.

The overall GR model represents exactly what an agent can do to achieve its goals (i.e., applying the right plans) and to mitigate associated risks (i.e., adopting necessary treatments). Different strategies (i.e., combinations of plans and treatments) can be adopted by the agent to achieve its goals. However, not all possible strategies (i.e., combinations of plans and treatments) may be acceptable by the agent. It wants a strategy whose risk is acceptable and cost (i.e., power consumption) is affordable. Here, the risk of a strategy is defined in terms of SAT and DEN values of the top goals and

[1] Notice that a negative event for an agent, may be positive for another agent.

its cost is defined as the sum of the cost required to execute its plans and treatments. To choose an appropriate strategies, the agent needs to reason on its GR model. To this end, we have employed a risk analysis process (or risk reasoning) [22] that uses forward reasoning [24] on the likelihood of events and the success-rate of plans and treatments. Suppose that an UAV agent must be operated within the maximum risk level (called RISK) and the affordable cost (called COST). The risk analysis process will synthesize a strategy on the basis of GR model $\langle \mathcal{N}, \mathcal{R} \rangle$ such that the agent can satisfies its top goals (e.g., G_1, G_2, and G_3), the risk is below RISK, and the total cost is below COST.

Initially, the agent generates all possible solutions (i.e., sets of leaf subgoals) for achieving top goals in $\langle \mathcal{N}, \mathcal{R} \rangle$. For instance, the UAV agent has top goal G_1 that can be fulfilled by fulfilling two sets of input-goals, $\{G_4, G_5, G_6, G_8\}$ or $\{G_4, G_5, G_6, G_9\}$ (Fig. 1). To find all possible combinations of input-goals that satisfy top goals, we have adopted the solution proposed in [27], where Tropos goal models are encoded into satisfiability formulas. For a given set of input-goals, the agent finds all possible set-of-plans that are means for the input-goals (i.e., a plan that is connected by means-end relation to a goal). For instance, $\{P_1, P_3, P_6, P_{11}, P_{12}\}$ is one of the possible set-of-plans that satisfies the top goal G_1 (Fig. 1).

For each set-of-plans whose cost is affordable (i.e., less than COST), the agent continues to assess the risk. If the risk is also acceptable (i.e., less than RISK), the set-of-plans is adopted as strategy by the agent. Otherwise, if the risk is unacceptable (i.e., higher than RISK), the agent must find applicable treatments to mitigate the risk. For instance, the set-of-treatments $\{T_4, T_5\}$ is one of the possible measures that the UAV can adopt to reduce the risk to be detected by the enemy. Before adding the set-of-treatments as part of the strategy, the agent verifies whether the cost and risk are still affordable. If they are acceptable, the set-of-treatment and the set-of plans are considered as the strategy of the agent; otherwise, the agent restarts the process by analyzing other set-of-plans.

At the end, the risk assessment process returns a strategy that can be used to fulfill top goals and whose level of risk and total cost are within established thresholds. In this paper, we assume that the reasoning process always finds a strategy.

4 Framework Realization

Several agent infrastructures based on BDI concepts, such as Jack [8], Jadex [9], and Jason [10], have been proposed in the last years. Typically, agent platforms follow the Reactive Reasoning and Planning (PRS) computational model [28] to implement their reasoning engine. PRS-like systems are event-based where events[2] are used to denote incoming messages, a new goal to be processed, or a change in the state of an existing goal. Once an event is generated, the agent dispatches the event to the deliberation mechanism (called meta-level reasoning) to choose the most appropriate plan to handle it. In some PRS-system, like Jack and Jason, goals are represented as special type of event, called goal-event. Thus, agents implemented in Jack or Jason platform do not know the current pursuing goals. They execute the plan only as a response to the occurrence of an event.

[2] The notion of event supported by agent platforms is a different from the one in Tropos.

On the contrary, the notion of goal plays a key role in the Jadex platform. This has spurred us to choose Jadex as platform to implement the GR framework. Jadex requires to specify agents' goals explicitly. These goals must be related to the plans that provide means to achieve them. Jadex represents agents' beliefs as Java objects and stores them in the beliefbase, that is, the database of agents' beliefs. Moreover, Jadex allows one to specify the plan that has to be executed when a belief is changed. Those BDI descriptions are represented in an XML file, called *Agent Definition File* (ADF) by a Jadex agent. The Jadex reasoning engine starts the deliberation process by considering the goals requested by the agent. To this end, it adopts the goals stored in the database that contains all adopted goals by the agent, called the agent's goalbase. To distinguish between just adopted and actively pursued goals, Jadex distinguishes a goal into three states: option, active, and suspended. When a goal is adopted, it becomes an option goal in the agent's goalbase. Once the agent pursues the goal, it becomes active and a goal-event is triggered. The event is then dispatched to the meta-level reasoner in order to find the most appropriate plan to achieve the goal.

The process to implement the GR models of the UAV agent into the Jadex platform starts by defining its beliefs (Fig. 2(a)). The agent's beliefs include: the thresholds of risk level and cost (line 2-7) that are acceptable for the UAV agent; the current cost and risk level of adopted strategies are encoded in (line 8-10) and (line 11-13) respectively. The success rate for plans, the likelihood of events, and the success rate for treatments, which are depicted as Goal-Risk labels, are also included as the beliefs (line 17-32). We also provide the agent with facilities for risk analysis by representing the GR model as a Java object and storing it as a belief (line 14-16). We also specify assess_risk plan (line 2-9 in Fig. 2(b)) in case there is a change in these belief values. Essentially, assess_risk calculates the risk level and cost of adopted strategy (i.e., plans and treatments) using a Jadex implementation of *Forward Reasoning* [24].

To contain the risk level and cost, the UAV agent needs to introduce two additional goals: maintain_risks (line 2-9 in Fig. 2(c)) below the risk threshold and maintain_costs below the cost threshold. If such goals are denied, plan re-planning (line 10-15 in Fig. 2(b)) is executed to recover the desired conditions. Essentially, re-planning is the Jadex implementation of *Risk Reasoning* and is used to synthesize a strategy on the basis of the current beliefs. As mentioned previously, we assume that there is always a strategy for each re-planning attempt.

We also need to represent goals, plans, and treatments of the GR model in the ADF, so that the Jadex implementation of the agent behaves accordingly to the GR model at execution time. Goals are declared in the ADF goal-base, while plans and treatments are depicted as plans section of ADF. This transformation starts by declaring all goals, plans, and treatments occurring in the GR model as XML entries in the ADF (Fig. 2(c) and Fig. 2(b)). Additional Jadex-goals and Jadex-plans may be introduced to mimic the behaviors supported by the GR framework, that are missing in the Jadex platform. A Jadex-plan can introduce a new goal, rather than only representing a sequence of actions (as denoted in Jadex-Legend Fig. 3).

Goals, plans and treatments in Tropos can be AND/OR-decomposed, while in Jadex a goal can only be AND-decomposed. Indeed, Tropos decompositions represent the knowledge of agents about the relations between goals. On the other hand, Jadex

```
<beliefs>
<belief name="thres_cost" class="double">
<fact>2000000</fact>
</belief>
<belief name="thres_risk" class="char">
<fact>P</fact>
</belief>
<belief name="cost" class="double">
<fact>1000000</fact>
</belief>
<belief name="risk" class="char">
<fact>N</fact>
</belief>
<belief name="gr_model" class="GRmodel">
<fact>new GRmodel("uav.grmodel")</fact>
</belief>
<beliefset name="goals" class="GRlabel">
<fact>new GRlabel(G1,N)</fact>
...
</beliefset>
<beliefset name="plans" class="GRlabel">
<fact>new GRlabel(P1,F)</fact>
...
</beliefset>
<beliefset name="events" class="GRlabel">
<fact>new GRlabel(E1,P)</fact>
...
</beliefset>
<beliefset name="treatments" class="GRlabel">
<fact>new GRlabel(T1,N)</fact>
...
</beliefset>
...
</beliefs>
```

(a) Beliefs

```
<plans>
<plan name="assess_risk">
<body>new RiskAssessment()</body>
<trigger>
<beliefsetchange ref="events"/>
<beliefsetchange ref="plans"/>
<beliefsetchange ref="treatments"/>
</trigger>
</plan>
<plan name="replanning">
<body>new Replanning()</body>
<trigger>
<goal ref="maintain_risk"/>
</trigger>
</plan>
<plan name="P-G01">
<body>..</body>
<trigger>
<goal ref="G01"/>
</trigger>
</plan>
<plan name="chooseG07">
<body>new RiskReasoning()</body>
<trigger>
<goal ref="choose_planG07"/>
</trigger>
</plan>
<plan name="P7">
<body>..</body>
<trigger>
<goal ref="G8"/>
</trigger>
</plan>
...
</plans>
```

(b) Plans

```
<goals>
<maintaingoal name="maintain_risk">
<maintaincondition>
\$beliefbase.risk < \$beliefbase.risk.thres_risk
</maintaincondition>
<targetcondition>
\$beliefbase.risk < \$beliefbase.risk.thres_risk
</targetcondition>
</maintaingoal>
<achievegoal name="G01">
...
</achievegoal>
...
<achievegoal name="G07">
...
</achievegoal>
<metagoal name="choose_planG07">
...
<trigger>
<goal ref="G07"/>
</trigger>
</metagoal>
<achievegoal name="G08">
...
</achievegoal>
...
</goals>
```

(c) Goals

Fig. 2. UAV agent description in Jadex-ADF

introduces subgoals as a result of a plan. For instance, G_1 is AND decomposed into G_6 and G_7 (left-side in Fig. 3). To realize this behavior during execution of a Jadex agent (right-side in Fig. 3), we need to introduce an additional plan P-G01. This plan

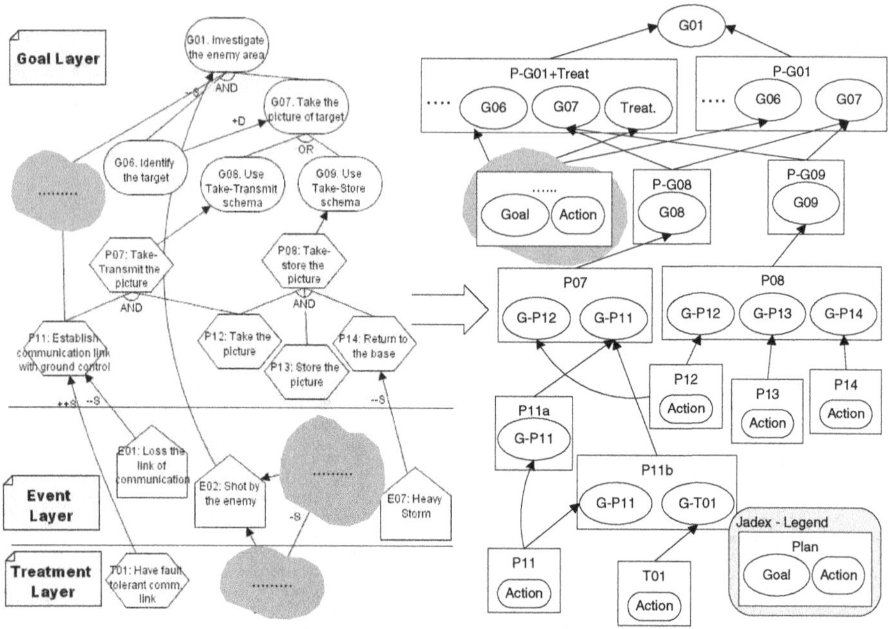

Fig. 3. Goal-Risk model to Jadex

introduces (and later dispatches) subgoals G_6 and G_7, as depicted in the right-side of Fig. 3. P-G01 is means to achieve G_1 (depicted by arrow line), and the ADF description is shown in Fig. 2(b) (line 16-21). However, both Tropos and Jadex require the fulfillment of all AND-subgoals for having evidence about the fulfillment of upper-level goal. AND-decompositions of plans/treatments have a similar intuition, with introducing additional goals to activate the subplans. For instance, plan P_8 will introduce additional goals (i.e., G-P12, G-P13, and G-P14) that later activate subplans P_{12}, P_{13}, and P_{14}.

To mimic goal OR-decompositions, we introduce additional plans where each plan is used to activate a new subgoal. These plans represent alternative means that an agent can adopt to achieve the upper-level goal. For instance, G_7 is OR-decomposed into G_8 and G_9 (Fig. 3). This is represented in the ADF by introducing the additional plans P-G08 and P-G09 that respectively activate G_8 and G_9, as ways to achieve goal G_7. The agent will perform meta-level reasoning on meta-goal of G_7 (called choose_planG07 in Fig. 2(c) line 17-22) to decide which plan should be adopted. In other words, we override the Jadex meta-level reasoning by defining a new plan (chooseG07 in Fig. 2(c)) to determine the least risky alternative. Such a plan has body RiskReasoning which is a Java implementation of *Risk Reasoning*. OR-decompositions of plans/treatments can be mimicked by defining a task that introduces an additional goal, and all subplans are defined as means to achieve the such a goal. Similarly to what we have done for goal OR-decomposition, the Jadex meta-level reasoning is overridden with a plan that uses RiskReasoning.

Finally, we need to represent Tropos means-end relations in a Jadex agent. Means-end relations correspond to the trigger mechanism in Jadex. For instance, $P_7 \longmapsto G_8$ is represented by adding G_8 as the trigger of P_7 in the ADF (line 30-32 in Fig. 2(b)) or denote by relating P07 to G08 with an arrow line (right-side in Fig. 3). This implementation of the Tropos means-end into the Jadex platform holds if the plan is not related with any treatments (i.e., direct or indirectly through the event layer). On the contrary, if the plan is related with a treatment, the mapping schema is slightly different because several combinations of plans and treatments can be used to achieve the goal (e.g., it can adopt only the plan, the plan with a treatment, the plan with some treatments, or the plan and all treatments). For instance, the success of plan establish communication with ground control (P_{11}) is obstructed by the risk due to loss the link of communication (E_1) (Fig. 3). In this setting, the UAV agent can adopt treatment have fault tolerant communication link (T_1) for retention purpose. The agent may adopt only P_{11} (or P11a in Fig. 3 (right-side)), whereas in others it needs to adopt P11b, which is the combination of P11 and T1, for ensuring the success of P_{11} execution. This implementation in the Jadex platform is getting more complicated when several treatments can be applied since the number of combinations of plans and treatments to achieve a goal is exponential $(Numb(plan) \times 2^{Numb(treatment)})$. For instance, if G_1 is obstructed by E_2 directly and by E_3 indirectly and the agent knows a single plan to achieve G_1 and three treatments (e.g., T_2, T_4, and T_5) to mitigate E_2 and E_3, the agent has eight possible strategies to achieve goal G_1.

The proposed Jadex-implementation allows an agent to perform meta-level reasoning using GR framework. In particular, we have taken advantages of combining GR and Jadex reasoning facilities. The Tropos approach explores all alternative solutions and chooses an acceptable (and optimal) sequence of plans and treatments, whose execution allows the agent to achieve the top goals from the current condition. Conversely, Jadex reasoning only elicit a plan to achieve the goal, and later could be the case that the plan will introduce other goals or trigger the execution of other plans. We have implemented *Risk Reasoning* using Jadex approach. Thus, the agent keeps performing *Risk Reasoning* each time there are some applicable plans, though *Risk Reasoning* has already provided a strategy for pursuing a goal. In other words, the reasoning mechanism is executed to define the baseline strategy, and the reasoning will be executed again considering the changes in the agent's beliefs (especially the evidence about events) to revise the existing strategy.

5 Related Work

In artificial intelligent community, a lot of effort has been devoted to develop reasoning mechanisms dealing with uncertainty [12, 14, 13]. Here, the focus was on determining how subtle uncertainties affect the reasoning mechanisms. Differently, the autonomous agent community is mainly focusing on how to implement agent platforms (e.g., Jack, Jason and Jadex) with reasoning mechanisms to deal with existing event and situation [29,30,20].

Helpern [12] proposes a framework to reasons about uncertainty from a single agent viewpoint and multi-agent environments. An environment (i.e., entities outside the agent) is treated as black boxes, with no structure. Therefore, the likelihood of events is viewed as a collection of random variables. In the multi-agent framework, the environment can be structured on the basis of the interactions among agents. The framework also models uncertainty values in terms of functions of time.

Markov Decision Process (MDPs) [13] is a mathematical framework to model a decision-making process where outcomes are partly random and partly controlled by agents. MDPs address optimization problems, represented as tuples $\langle S, A, P, R\rangle$, where S is a set of possible states, A is a set of actions that caused state transitions, P is a set of probabilities of action occurrences, and R is a set of rewards that are gained if an action is executed. This framework uses value iteration algorithms to determine the set of actions that minimize and maximize the reward. If risks are encoded as rewards, the agent can use such algorithms to identify the least risk strategy by searching the solution with minimal reward. Moreover, Samari and Parson [31] investigated on the relation between MDPs and BDI architectures. Their results open the way for using MDPs as reasoning mechanisms in the BDI architecture.

Another proposal is the Abstract Agent Programming Language[3] (3APL), a cognitive agent programming language that employs logical representation and reasoning features based on the BDI model. In this setting, the beliefs are assumed to be certain, either true or false. Kwisthout and Dastani [14] propose an extension of 3APL that allows an agent to reason about uncertain beliefs. The authors recognized that 3APL is not sufficient to reason about uncertain beliefs that result essential for dealing with many real cases. This extension uses Dempster-Shafer theory [23] to model uncertainty in agent's beliefs. Those reasoning frameworks are really sufficient for reasoning about uncertainty, even sometime it is too complex, but those frameworks does not specify how an agent must react to deal with the effects of uncertainty. Finally, these approaches appear to be sophisticated to model uncertainties in a reasoning mechanism of an agent. However, they lacks in representing the extent of uncertainty events in affecting agents. This representation is important because reasoning mechanisms should distinguish events by their effect in case they occur, besides only their likelihood/uncertainty.

In the autonomous agent community, there are some proposals [30, 20] that present implementations of the UAV agent (called Wingman) in the Jack platform. The Wingman is provided with basic plans (e.g., flying quietly and at low altitude) in order to achieve its goals (e.g., taking picture of enemy installations). The Wingman is also provided with additional plans (e.g., flying as fast as possible) to deal with malicious events such as being detected by enemy. When a malicious event occurs, the Wingman reasons about its plans and changes the adopted basic plan with an additional plan to guarantee the achievement its goals. However, the Wingman does not try to anticipate the occurrence of malicious events, but it just reacts when they happen. Similar works have been done in [18, 32]. On the contrary, our approach allows the UAV agent to anticipate malicious events by employing treatments when the risk is unacceptable. Another implementation of reasoning in an autonomous agent has been proposed by Braubach et al. [29]. They propose an implementation of the Cleaner World agent in Jadex. Such an agent is designed to pick all wastes and throw them in trash bins. In this implementation, the agent moves to a location once its sensors detect the existence of

[3] http://www.cs.uu.nl/3apl/

wastes. However, it would be more efficient if agent movements are not only driven by the appearance of wastes, but they are anticipated by reasoning about the likelihood of having new wastes in a certain location. In other words, those agent platforms do not predict future events and react accordingly; most of them just react in case a particular event happens.

Conversely, this paper is in the middle between those two approaches. Our work adopts existing reasoning mechanisms in agent platforms (i.e., Jadex), and extends them with the Goal-Risk reasoning mechanism [22]. This approach takes advantages of having the reasoning mechanism implementable in agent platforms and, especially, in the ones based on BDI. Though the proposed reasoning looks trivial compared with the ones proposed in AI community, we remark that the GR framework is not meant to assess the uncertainty precisely. Rather, it aims to support an agent in defining a strategy whose risk and cost are lower than a certain threshold. As consequence, it also allows agents to define a strategy to achieve their goals on the basis of probable events, and not only the current context condition.

6 Conclusions and Remarks

In this paper, we have presented a Jadex implementation of the Tropos Goal-Risk framework. The GR framework and Jadex differ in concepts and reasoning features and their integration was not straightforward. In particular, we have shown that there are limitations in Jadex to adopt all concepts supported by the GR framework, but we have also shown that this mapping does not limit the expressiveness of the intended goal deliberation process.

The initial GR reasoning mechanisms allow agents to perform cost-benefit analysis on a strategy to be adopted, but require an exhaustive knowledge before the agent starts pursuing its goals. On the other hand, the Jadex approach results faster in choosing a strategy for a given goal and more adaptive to the current conditions of the agent. We have taken advances of combining GR and Jadex reasoning features by implementing complete plans and facilities for reasoning about them in the belief of the agent. The intuition is to use complete plans as a baseline for the Jadex reasoning. Then, during the pursuing of its goals, the agent evaluates the baseline by reasoning about risks in the current situation.

We are currently extending the risk reasoning to cope with multi-agent environments. In this setting, an agent should be able to reason about risks when it depends on other agents for the fulfillment of its goals. Yet, treatments may be introduced when risks are unacceptable or when the agent has no alternatives to achieve its goal besides depending on other agents.

Acknowledgments

We thank Jan Sudeikat for many useful discussions on Jadex platform. This work has been partially funded by EU-SENSORIA and EU-SERENITY projects, by FIRB-TOCAI project, and by PAT-MOSTRO project.

References

1. Lauber, J., Steger, C., Weiss, R.: Autonomous Agents for Online Diagnosis of a Safety-critical System Based on Probabilistic Causal Reasoning. In: Proceedings of the The Fourth International Symposium on Autonomous Decentralized Systems (ISADS 1999), Washington, DC, USA, pp. 213–219. IEEE Computer Society, Los Alamitos (1999)
2. Kumar, S., Cohen, P.R.: Towards a Fault-Tolerant Multi-Agent System Architecture. In: Proceedings of the Fourth International Conference on Autonomous Agents (AGENTS 2000), pp. 459–466. ACM Press, New York (2000)
3. McCarthy, J.: Ascribing Mental Qualities to Machines. Technical Report Memo 326, Stanford AI Lab, Stanford (1979)
4. Rao, A.S., Georgeff, M.P.: BDI Agents: From Theory to Practice. In: Proceedings of 1st International Conference on Multi-Agent Systems (ICMAS 1995), pp. 312–319 (1995)
5. Shoham, Y.: Agent-Oriented Programming. Artificial Intelligence 60(1), 51–92 (1993)
6. Bratman, M.: Intention, Plans, and Practical Reason. Harvard University Press (1987)
7. Rao, A.S., Georgeff, M.P.: Modeling Rational Agents within a BDI-Architecture. In: Proceedings of 2nd International Conference on Principles of Knowledge Representation and Reasoning (KR 1991), pp. 473–484. Morgan Kaufmann publishers Inc, San Francisco (1991)
8. Howden, N., Ronnquist, R., Hodgson, A., Lucas, A.: JACK Intelligent Agents-Summary of an Agent Infrastructure. In: Proceedings of the 5th International Conference on Autonomous Agents (AGENTS 2001), ACM Press, New York (2001)
9. Pokahr, A., Braubach, L., Lamersdorf, W.: Jadex: A BDI Reasoning Engine. In: Multi-Agent Programming: Languages, Platforms and Applications, pp. 149–174. Springer Science, Business Media Inc. (2005)
10. Bordini, R.H., Hübner, J.F.: BDI Agent Programming in AgentSpeak Using Jason. In: Toni, F., Torroni, P. (eds.) CLIMA 2005. LNCS (LNAI), vol. 3900, pp. 143–164. Springer, Heidelberg (2006)
11. COSO: Enterprise Risk Management - Integrated Framework. Committee of Sponsoring Organizations of the Treadway Commission (September 2004)
12. Halpern, J.Y.: Reasoning About Uncertainty. MIT Press, Cambridge (2003)
13. White, D.J.: Markov Decision Processes. John Wiley & Sons, Chichester (1993)
14. Kwisthout, J., Dastani, M.: Modelling Uncertainty in Agent Programming. In: Baldoni, M., Endriss, U., Omicini, A., Torroni, P. (eds.) DALT 2005. LNCS (LNAI), vol. 3904, pp. 17–32. Springer, Heidelberg (2006)
15. Asnar, Y., Giorgini, P., Mylopoulos, J.: Risk Modelling and Reasoning in Goal Models. Technical Report DIT-06-008, DIT - University of Trento (February 2006)
16. Giorgini, P., Mylopoulos, J., Sebastiani, R.: Goal-Oriented Requirements Analysis and Reasoning in the Tropos Methodology. Engineering Applications of Artificial Intelligence 18(2), 159–171 (2005)
17. Feather, M.S., Cornford, S.L., Hicks, K.A., Johnson, K.R.: Applications of tool support for risk-informed requirements reasoning. Computer Systems Science & Engineering 20(1), 5–17 (2005)
18. Dufrene Jr., W.R.: Approach for Autonomous Control of Unmanned Aerial Vehicle Using Intelligent Agents for Knowledge Creation. Proceedings of The 23rd Conference on Digital Avionics Systems Conference (DASC 2004) 2, 1–9 (2004)
19. Karim, S., Heinze, C.: Experiences with the Design and Implementation of an Agent-Based Autonomous UAV Controller. In: Proceedings of 4th International Joint Conference on Autonomous Agents and Multiagent Systems (AAMAS 2005), pp. 19–26. ACM Press, New York (2005)

20. Wallis, P., Ronnquist, R., Jarvis, D., Lucas, A.: The Automated Wingman - Using JACK Intelligent Agents for Unmanned Autonomous Vehicles. Proceedings of IEEE Aerospace Conference 5, 2615–2622 (2002)
21. Bresciani, P., Perini, A., Giorgini, P., Giunchiglia, F., Mylopoulos, J.: Tropos: An Agent-Oriented Software Development Methodology. Journal of Autonomous Agents and Multi-Agent Systems 8(3), 203–236 (2004)
22. Asnar, Y., Giorgini, P.: Modelling Risk and Identifying Countermeasures in Organizations. In: López, J. (ed.) CRITIS 2006. LNCS, vol. 4347, pp. 55–66. Springer, Heidelberg (2006)
23. Shafer, G.: A Mathematical Theory of Evidence. Princeton University Press, Princeton (1976)
24. Giorgini, P., Mylopoulos, J., Nicchiarelli, E., Sebastiani, R.: Formal Reasoning Techniques for Goal Models. Journal of Data Semantics (October 2003)
25. Bedford, T., Cooke, R.: Probabilistic Risk Analysis: Foundations and Methods. Cambridge University Press, Cambridge (2001)
26. Stamatelatos, M., Vesely, W., Dugan, J., Fragola, J., Minarick, J., Railsback, J.: Fault Tree Handbook with Aerospace Applications. NASA (2002)
27. Sebastiani, R., Giorgini, P., Mylopoulos, J.: Simple and Minimum-Cost Satisfiability for Goal Models. In: Persson, A., Stirna, J. (eds.) CAiSE 2004. LNCS, vol. 3084, pp. 20–33. Springer, Heidelberg (2004)
28. Georgeff, M., Lansky, A.: Reactive Reasoning and Planning. In: Proceedings of the Sixth National Conference on Artificial Intelligence (AAAI 1987), Seattle, WA, pp. 677–682. Morgan Kaufmann, San Francisco (1987)
29. Braubach, L., Pokahr, A., Lamersdorf, W., Moldt, D.: Goal Representation for BDI Agent Systems. In: Bordini, R.H., Dastani, M., Dix, J., Seghrouchni, A.E.F. (eds.) PROMAS 2004. LNCS (LNAI), vol. 3346, pp. 9–20. Springer, Heidelberg (2005)
30. Karim, S., Heinze, C., Dunn, S.: Agent-Based Mission Management for a UAV. In: Proceedings of the 2004 of Intelligent Sensors, Sensor Networks and Information Processing Conference (ISSNIP 2004), pp. 481–486. IEEE Press, Los Alamitos (2004)
31. Simari, G.I., Parsons, S.: On the Relationship between MDPs and the BDI Architecture. In: Proceedings of 5th International Joint Conference on Autonomous Agents and Multiagent Systems (AAMAS 2006), pp. 1041–1048. ACM Press, New York (2006)
32. Vidolov, B., De Miras, J., Bonnet, S.: AURYON - A Mechatronic UAV Project Focus on Control Experimentations. In: Proceedings of the International Conference on Computational Intelligence for Modelling, Control and Automation and International Conference on Intelligent Agents, Web Technologies and Internet Commerce (CIMCA-IAWTIC 2006), Washington, DC, USA, vol. 1, pp. 1072–1078. IEEE Computer Society Press, Los Alamitos (2005)

Generation of Repair Plans for Change Propagation

Khanh Hoa Dam and Michael Winikoff

School of Computer Science and Information Technology,
RMIT University,
GPO Box 2476V, Melbourne, VIC 3001, Australia
{kdam,winikoff}@cs.rmit.edu.au

Abstract. One of the most critical problems in software maintenance and evolution is propagating changes. Although many approaches have been proposed, automated change propagation is still a significant technical challenge in software engineering. In this paper we present an agent-oriented change propagation framework based on fixing inconsistencies when primary changes are made to design models. A core piece of the framework is a new method for generating repair plans from OCL constraints that restrict these models.

1 Introduction

Software evolution is critical in the life-cycle of successful software systems, especially those operating in highly volatile domains such as banking, e-commerce and telecommunications. A basic operation of software evolution is change: in order to adapt the system to the desired requirements (be they new, modified, or an environmental change) the system is changed [1]. In practice, the software engineer usually starts making some primary changes that he/she can easily identify based on the characteristics of the change requests and/or his/her knowledge and expertise. However, these primary changes are not enough to make the design meet the change requests and may also create inconsistencies. As a result, additional, secondary, changes might be needed.

The process of determining and making secondary changes is termed *change propagation*. Since complex software systems consist of many artefacts, both design and code, and since there are usually many options when making secondary changes, change propagation is a complicated, labour-intensive, and expensive process. Hence, there is a need for tools that provide more effective *automated* support for change propagation. We do not believe that change propagation can be fully automated, since there are decisions that involve tradeoffs where human expertise is required. However, it is possible to provide tool support to assist with tracking dependencies, determining what parts of the system are affected by a given change, and, as in this paper, determining and making secondary changes.

We are basing our work on the conjecture that, given a suitable set of consistency constraints, *change propagation can be done by fixing inconsistencies in a design*. In other words, we propagate changes by finding places in a design where the desired consistency constraints are violated, and fixing them until no inconsistency is left in the design. For example, an agent type is added, and then consequently other agents need to be modified to communicate with the new agent type.

M. Luck and L. Padgham (Eds.): AOSE 2007, LNCS 4951, pp. 132–146, 2008.

According to a survey in [2], handling inconsistencies has received much attention in mainstream software engineering. However, most existing work either fails to advocate effective automation (e.g. [3,4]) or fails to reflect the cascading nature of repairing inconsistencies (e.g. [5]). In agent-oriented software engineering, there has not been much work addressing the maintenance aspect, especially the change propagation issue in the development of agent designs. In our previous work [6], we have shown how an *agent-oriented* approach, specifically the BDI agent architecture, is a suitable approach for performing change propagation and illustrated its capacity to deal with consistency management in the context of the *Prometheus* methodology [7]. In this paper we present a framework for change propagation which extends our previous work (section 3) and introduce a mechanism for automatic repair plan generation from Object Constraint Language (OCL) [8] constraints (section 4). We then discuss some related work (section 5) before concluding and outlining our future work (section 6).

2 A Running Example

Throughout this paper we use a running example which comprises an initial design for a simple stock trading management system (STMS). The design was developed using the Prometheus methodology [7]. Figure 1 shows a system overview diagram of the existing STMS. The system currently has three agents: a "*GUI Agent*" for handling users' requests such as buying stock or adding funds, a "*Funding Agent*" responsible for managing users' funds, and a "*Trading Agent*" for performing transactions such as buying stocks. In addition, "*GUI Agent*" has the "*Handling adding-funds request*" plan triggered by "*Adding Funds Request*" percept and the "*Handling buying-stocks request*" plan triggered by "*Buying Stocks Request*" percept.

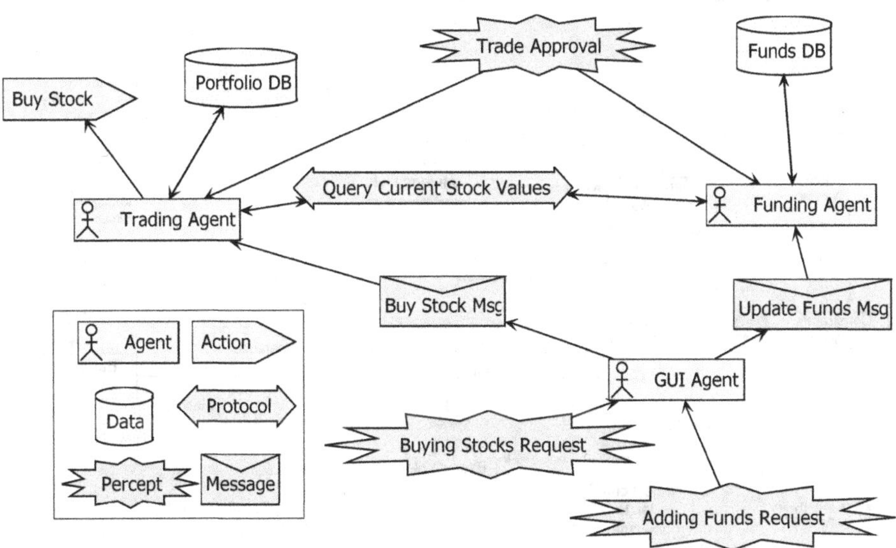

Fig. 1. System overview diagram for a stock trading management system

The initial requirements for the STMS, however, only deal with buying stocks and adding funds. Now suppose that the clients have asked to add a new functionality to the system: *STMS should also allow the users to place selling stock orders*. Assume that the software designer begins making some primary changes by adding a new percept *"Selling Stocks Request"* and assigning the *"GUI Agent"* to handle it. At this point the designer may start wondering what are the next changes that they need to make. The following sections present our change propagation framework and show how it supports the software engineer in propagating changes.

3 Architectural Overview

This section serves to introduce the architecture of the change propagation framework. Figure 2 shows an overview of our architecture as a data flow diagram. At design time, consistency constraints that are created by the repair administrator are input to the change propagation framework along with a meta-model. The meta-model and constraints can be developed by extracting relationships and dependencies from the methodology that we want to apply the framework to. For instance, a Prometheus meta-model and a set of related constraints have been developed in [6]. Normally the meta-model and constraints are developed once for a given methodology (e.g. Prometheus) and then reused: the user (software maintainer) is not required to develop a meta-model or OCL constraints, although in some cases they may desire to add additional domain or application specific constraints. Figure 3 shows an excerpt of the Prometheus meta-model (refer to [6] for a full version) represented as a UML class diagram capturing the relationships between an agent and other entities. The meta-model shows that an agent can contain one or more plans. A plan can send and/or receive messages as well as perform some actions which may include accessing data to handle a percept or to achieve

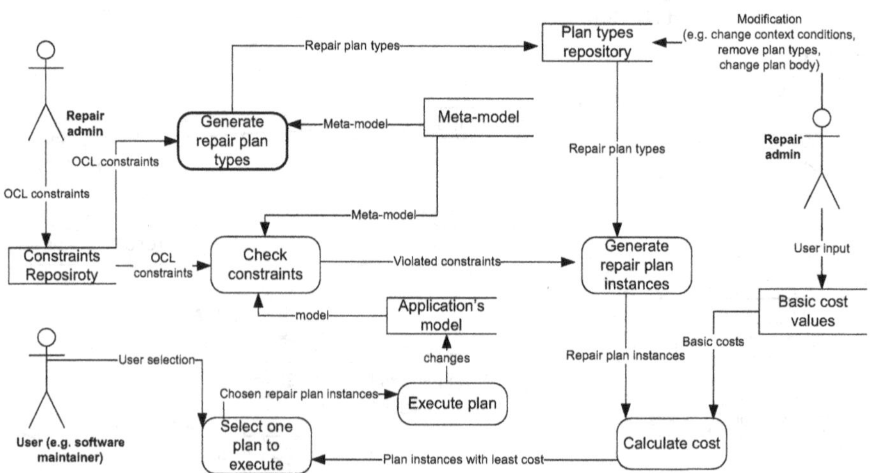

Fig. 2. Change propagation framework

some goals. As a result, agents also have these associations with goals, percepts, actions, messages, and data[1].

The exact relationships between agents, plans and other entities are expressed using a set of Object Constraint Language (OCL) constraints. OCL [8] is part of the UML standards which is used to specify invariants, pre-conditions, post-conditions and other kinds of constraints imposed on elements in UML models. Below is an example of an OCL constraint that defines the semantics of relationships between agents, plans and percepts. In the OCL notation "self" denotes the context node (in this case a Percept) to which the constraints have been attached and an access pattern such as "self.agent" indicates the result of following the association between a percept and an agent, which is, in this case, a collection of agents which handle the percept. OCL also denotes operations on collections such as "$SE \rightarrow$ includes(x)" stating that a collection SE must contain an entity x, or "$SE \rightarrow$ exists(c)" specifying that a certain condition c must hold for at least one element of SE, or "$SE \rightarrow$ forAll(c)" specifying that c must hold for all elements of SE. For detailed information on OCL see [8]. For example, the following constraint, which could be expressed in more traditional form as $\forall a \in \text{self.agent} \exists pl \in a.\text{plan} : \text{self} \in pl.\text{percept}$, states that: considering the set of agents that handle the percept (*self.agent*), for each of the agents (a) if we consider the plans of that agent (*a.plan*) then one of these plans (*pl*) must include the current percept (*self*) in its list of percepts (*pl.percept*).

Constraint 1. *Any agent that handles a percept should contain at least one plan that is triggered by the percept.*

Context Percept inv:
self.agent→forAll(a : Agent | a.plan→exists(pl : Plan | pl.percept→includes(self)))

The repair plan generator takes the constraints and the meta-model as inputs, and returns a parameterized set of event-triggered repair plan types[2] that are able to repair violations of the constraint. Our translation schema guarantees completeness and correctness, i.e. there are no repair plans to fix a violation of a constraint other than those produced by the generator; and any of the repair plans produced by the generator can fix a violation. However, we also allow the repair administrator to use their domain knowledge and expertise to modify generated repair plans or remove plans that should not be executed. In section 4 we discuss this in more detail. The set of repair plan types is created ahead of time and forms the library of plans that the change propagation engine uses to fix constraint violations. Since the library of plans is derived before runtime, the efficiency of deriving it is not crucial.

At runtime, the change propagation engine checks the current design models against the OCL constraints, and any violations of these constraints are fixed using the repair plans. The engine is represented and implemented using the BDI agent architecture.

---

[1] In figure 3, associations marked with an 'A*' are between agent and plan, and goal, percept, action, data, and message. We group and represent them as a single association for readability.

[2] The use of plans which are triggered by events is taken from the well-known and studied Belief Desire Intention (BDI) agent architecture [9], which has been widely implemented within the agents community (e.g. see [10]).

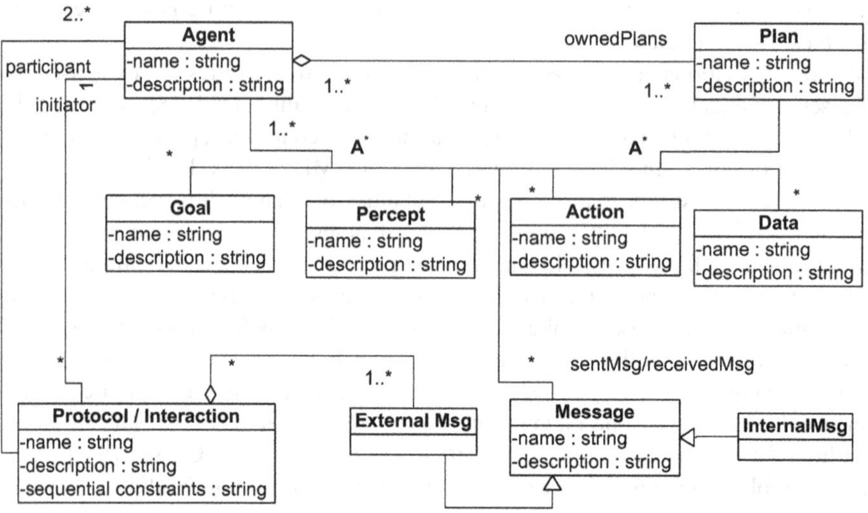

Fig. 3. An excerpt of the Prometheus meta-model

Constraint checking may result in the detection of a number of violated constraints. Each violated constraint is then posted as an event ("ViolationEvent"). A given *ViolationEvent* may trigger a number[3] of possible repair plan instances. In order to help select which repair plan instance to use we calculate the cost of each repair plan instance. We recognize that fixing one violated constraint may also repair or violate others as a side effect, and so the cost calculation algorithm computes the cost of a given repair plan instance as including the cost of its actions (using basic costs assigned by the repair administrator), the cost of any other plans that it invokes directly, and also the cost of fixing any constraints that are made false by executing the repair plan. If there are several equal least cost plans, they are presented to the user, otherwise the cheapest plan is selected. Once a plan is selected, it is then executed to fix the violation, and hence propagate changes. We allow the repair administrator to specify the repair cost for each basic repair action. The repair administrator may use this mechanism to adjust the change propagation process. For example, if he/she wishes to bias the change propagation process towards adding more information then he/she may assign lower costs to actions that create new entities or add entities, and higher costs to actions that delete entities.

The above change propagation framework is currently being implemented. The cost calculation and plan execution components were implemented and used to test some small case studies. At the time of writing this paper, we are at the final stage of completing the implementation of the plan generator component. Due to space limitations, in the remainder of this paper we focus on describing the repair plan generator component of the framework. However, we will also briefly illustrate how the cost calculation component works based on the STMS example.

[3] Which will always be greater than zero, due to the way in which plans are generated (see section 4).

4 Generating Repair Plan Types

Since a large design can contain a substantial number of constraints, the number of repair plans may be very large. In these cases, hand-crafting repair plans for all constraints becomes a labour intensive task. In previous work [6], we encountered this issue when developing repair plans for Prometheus design models. In addition, it is difficult for the repair administrator to know if the set of repair plans which they create is complete and correct. Therefore, we have developed a translation schema that takes as input constraints, expressed as OCL invariants, and generates repair plans that can be used to correct constraint violations.

A similar approach has been proposed in [5] which takes xlinkit rules defining consistency between documents and returns a set of repair actions. One key difference between their work and ours is that we generate abstract, structured, repair plans that are instantiated at runtime.

$$
\begin{aligned}
P &::= E[: C] \leftarrow B \\
C &::= C \vee C \mid C \wedge C \mid \neg\, C \mid \forall x \bullet C \mid \exists x \bullet C \mid \mathit{Prop} \\
B &::= \mathit{true} \mid \mathit{Add\ Entity\ To\ SE} \mid \mathit{Remove\ Entity\ From\ SE} \mid \mathit{Create\ Entity} : \mathit{Type} \mid \\
&\quad\ \mathit{Change\ Property\ to\ Property} \mid \mathit{if\ C\ then\ B} \mid\ !E \mid B_1;\ B_2 \mid \mathit{for\ each\ x\ in\ SE\ B}
\end{aligned}
$$

Fig. 4. Repair plan abstract syntax

Our syntax for repair plans (see figure 4) is based on AgentSpeak(L)[4] [11], but with some differences (most notably in specifying the actions, and in allowing for richer plan bodies). Each repair plan, P, is of the form $E : C \leftarrow B$ where E is the triggering event (conceptually, the name of the constraint P is fixing, subscripted with either t or f to indicate whether the constraint is being made true or false); C is an optional "context condition" (Boolean formula[5]) that specifies when the plan should be applicable[6]; and B is the plan body. The plan body can contain primitive actions such as adding and deleting entities and relationships, and changing properties. The plan body can also contain sequences ($B_1;\ B_2$), conditionals and loops, and events which will trigger further plans ($!E$).

For a given constraint form, for example $c_1 = \mathit{not}\ c_2$, we generate repair plans that repair c_1 (make it true). These plans are defined in terms of other plans that repair sub-constraints. In this example, the plan to repair c_1, i.e. make it true, is defined using plans that make c_2 false. Formally, if we use $\mathcal{R}(c)$ to denote the complete set of repair plans for constraint c, and $\mathcal{P}(c)$ to denote the specific plans for the constraint form, then for a constraint c_1 with sub-constraint c_2 (as is the case for $c_1 = \mathit{not}\ c_2$) we

[4] We chose to use AgentSpeak(L) as a basis because it is a simple and compact notation that captures the essence of BDI-based agent oriented programming languages.

[5] "Prop" denotes a primitive condition such as checking whether $x > y$ or whether $x \in SE$.

[6] In fact when there are multiple solutions to the context condition, each solution generates a new plan instance. For example, if the context condition is $x \in \{1, 2\}$ then there will be two plan instances.

$\mathcal{P}(\mathbf{c} \stackrel{\text{def}}{=} \textbf{SE}\rightarrow\textbf{includes(x)}) =$
$\{c_t \leftarrow$ Add x to SE$\}$

$\mathcal{P}(\mathbf{c} \stackrel{\text{def}}{=} \textbf{SE}\rightarrow\textbf{includesAll(SE')}) =$
$\{c_t \leftarrow$ for each x in (SE' - SE) $!c_t'(\text{x})$,
$c_t'(\text{x}) \leftarrow$ Remove x from SE',
$c_t'(\text{x}) \leftarrow$ Add x to SE$\}$

$\mathcal{P}(\mathbf{c} \stackrel{\text{def}}{=} \textbf{SE}\rightarrow\textbf{excludes(x)}) =$
$\{c_t \leftarrow$ Remove x from SE$\}$

$\mathcal{P}(\mathbf{c} \stackrel{\text{def}}{=} \textbf{SE}\rightarrow\textbf{excludesAll(SE')}) =$
$\{c_t \leftarrow$ for each x in SE $\cap$ SE' $!c_t'(\text{x})$
$c_t'(\text{x}) \leftarrow$ Remove x from SE',
$c_t'(\text{x}) \leftarrow$ Remove x from SE$\}$

$\mathcal{P}(\mathbf{c} \stackrel{\text{def}}{=} \textbf{SE}\rightarrow\textbf{notEmpty()}) =$
$\{c_t : \text{x} \in$ Type(SE) $\leftarrow$ Add x to SE,
$c_t \leftarrow$ Create x : Type(SE) ; Add x to SE$\}$

$\mathcal{P}(\mathbf{c} \stackrel{\text{def}}{=} \textbf{SE}\rightarrow\textbf{isEmpty()}) =$
$\{c_t \leftarrow$ for each x in SE Remove x from SE$\}$

$\mathcal{P}(\mathbf{c} \stackrel{\text{def}}{=} \textbf{SE}\rightarrow\textbf{forAll(c1)}) =$
$\{c_t \leftarrow$ for each x in SE if $\neg$ c1(x) then $!c_t'(\text{x})$,
$c_t'(\text{x}) \leftarrow$ Delete x from SE,
$c_t'(\text{x}) \leftarrow !c1_t(\text{x})\}$

$\mathcal{P}(\mathbf{c} \stackrel{\text{def}}{=} \textbf{SE}\rightarrow\textbf{exists(c1)}) =$
$\{c_t : \text{x} \in \text{SE} \leftarrow !c1_t(\text{x})$,
$c_t : \text{x} \in$ Type(SE) $\wedge$ x $\notin$ SE $\leftarrow$ Add x to SE ; $!c1_t(\text{x})$,
$c_t \leftarrow$ Create x : Type(SE) ; Add x to SE ; $!c1_t(\text{x})$
$\}$

$\mathcal{P}(\mathbf{c} \stackrel{\text{def}}{=} \textbf{c1 or c2}) = \{c_t : \neg\, \text{c1} \leftarrow !c1_t$,
$c_t : \neg\, \text{c2} \leftarrow !c2_t\}$

$\mathcal{P}(\mathbf{c} \stackrel{\text{def}}{=} \textbf{c1 and c2}) =$
$\{c_t : \neg\, \text{c1} \wedge \text{c2} \leftarrow !c1_t$,
$c_t : \neg\, \text{c2} \wedge \text{c1} \leftarrow !c2_t$,
$c_t : \neg\, \text{c1} \wedge \neg\, \text{c2} \leftarrow !c1_t ; !c2_t\}$

$\mathcal{P}(\mathbf{c} \stackrel{\text{def}}{=} \textbf{not c1}) = \{ c_t \leftarrow !c1_f\}$

$\mathcal{P}(\mathbf{c} \stackrel{\text{def}}{=} \textbf{c1 implies c2}) = \{ c_t \leftarrow !c1_f, c_t \leftarrow !c2_t\}$

Fig. 5. Plan generation rules (c_t)

have that: $\mathcal{R}(c_1) = \mathcal{P}(c_1) \cup \mathcal{R}(c_2)$. More generally, if constraint c has sub-constraints $s(c) = \{c_1, \ldots, c_n\}$ then

$$\mathcal{R}(c) = \mathcal{P}(c) \cup \bigcup_{c' \in s(c)} \mathcal{R}(c')$$

Figure 5 gives the definition of the $\mathcal{P}$ function: for each rule the generation of $\mathcal{R}(c)$ will include the given plans, as well as the plans obtained from the sub-constraints. The definition of $\mathcal{P}(c)$ considers, for each case, all the possible ways in which c can be false, and all the possible ways in which it can be repaired. For example, if $c = \text{SE} \rightarrow \text{includes}(x)$ then c is false if and only if x is not an element of SE, and consequently c can be made true only by adding x to SE.

If a constraint has more than one sub-constraint then fixing a sub-constraint might conflict with the plan that repairs the other sub-constraint. For example, if $c = c_1$ and c_2 then fixing c_2 may, depending on the definition of c_2 and c_1, make c_1 false. Therefore, in order to guarantee that the generated repair plans always correctly fix the constraint, we include two top level plans into $\mathcal{P}(c)$. For making a constraint c true, in addition to the definition in figure 5, $\mathcal{P}(c)$ includes {fixC : c $\leftarrow$ true, fixC : $\neg$ c $\leftarrow$! c_t ; ! fixC}.

The figure shows an excerpt of the translation rules from OCL constraints such as *includes*, *includesAll*, *excludes*, *excludesAll*, *isEmpty*, *notEmpty*, and logical connectives (*and*, *or*, *not*, *implies*, *forAll*, *exists*). Note that for each constraint c we generate rules that make that constraint true c_t and rules that make it false c_f, however, for space reasons, figure 5 only shows the c_t rules. Generally speaking the rules for generating c_f follow inverse patterns to those for c_t. For example, for $c = SE \rightarrow \text{includes}(x)$ the rule for c_f is $c_f \leftarrow$ Remove x from SE.

The term "SE" denotes a set expression which can be the name of a collection, or a derived collection, built from another collection using an operator. For example, the set $S_2 = S_1 \rightarrow \text{select}(c)$ includes elements from the set S_1 for which the condition c holds. Although adding an element to a basic collection (or removing it from the set) is a primitive action, adding or deleting elements from derived collections is not a primitive action. Instead, we model addition and deletion from derived collections using additional plans. For example, in order to add the element x to $SE = S \rightarrow \text{select}(c)$ we need to ensure both that x is in S, and that $c(x)$ is true; on the other hand if we want to *remove* x from SE then we can either remove x from S, *or* make $c(x)$ false. Similarly, if $SE = S \rightarrow \text{intersection}(S2)$ then to add x to SE we need to ensure that x is added to both S and $S2$; and to remove x from SE we can either remove it from S or from $S2$. We have developed rules for operations including *select*, *reject*, *union*, *intersection*, *minus* and *symmetricDifference*. The complete set of rules to generate repair plans from OCL constraints can be found in [12].

4.1 Completeness and Correctness

The translation guarantees correctness and completeness since it is developed by considering all the possible ways in which a constraint can be false, and hence all the possible ways in which it can be made true. In this section we provide an excerpt of the proof of correctness and completeness of the plan generator. The full proof can be found in [12].

In order to ease the discussion ahead, we provide here a definition of a *correct* repair plan and a *complete* set of repair plans.

Definition 1 (Correct plan). *A repair plan P correctly fixes a violated constraint c if and only if when P finishes its execution (i.e. all actions are performed and subgoals are achieved), c becomes valid.*

As mentioned earlier, the selection of applicable repair plans is based on the notion of costs. As a result, when repair plans are generated at compile time, we only focus on plans that have no redundant steps in fixing a particular constraint. Such plans are considered as *minimum plans* which are defined as below.

Definition 2 (Minimum plan). *A repair plan P for fixing constraint c is said to be a minimum plan if and only if all of its actions (obtained by running the plan) contribute towards fixing c, i.e. taking out any of the actions results in failing to fix c.*

Given the definitions of correct and minimum plans, a complete set of repair plans is defined as below.

Definition 3 (Complete set of repair plans). *A set of repair plans $\mathcal{R}(c)$ for a constraint c is said to be complete if and only if $\mathcal{R}(c)$ contains all minimum correct repair plans for c.*

Based on the above definitions, the correctness and completeness of our translation scheme are expressed by the following theorem.

Theorem 1. *For any given OCL constraint c the set of repair plans $\mathcal{R}(c)$ produced by the plan generator is correct and complete i.e. it contains all the possible correct minimum plans. In other words, there are no minimum plans to fix c that do not belong to $\mathcal{R}(c)$; and any of the repair plans in $\mathcal{R}(c)$ can fix c and are minimal.*

We will prove, by induction, that the above theorem holds with respect to the translation schema for c_t (figure 5).

First of all, we will prove that theorem 1 holds for all the *basic* OCL constraints that we cover. This is relatively easy since repair plans are generated by considering all the possible ways in which a constraint can be false. In [12], we provide a proof of the theorem for all basic OCL constraints that we consider in figure 5. Due to space limitation, we provide here a detailed proof for a typical example: c $\stackrel{\text{def}}{=}$ SE→includesAll(SE').

The above constraint can be written as:

$$\begin{aligned} c &\stackrel{\text{def}}{=} \forall x \bullet x \in SE' \Rightarrow x \in SE \\ &\stackrel{\text{def}}{=} \forall x \bullet (\neg\, x \in SE') \vee (x \in SE) \\ &\stackrel{\text{def}}{=} \forall x \bullet x \notin SE' \vee x \in SE \end{aligned}$$

Assume that c is violated, i.e. $\neg\, c$ is true, expressed as follows:

$$\begin{aligned} \neg\, c &\stackrel{\text{def}}{=} \neg\, \forall x \bullet x \notin SE' \vee x \in SE \\ &\stackrel{\text{def}}{=} \exists x \bullet \neg\, (x \notin SE') \wedge \neg\, (x \in SE) \\ &\stackrel{\text{def}}{=} \exists x \bullet x \in SE' \wedge x \notin SE \end{aligned}$$

Therefore, to prevent $\neg\, c$ from being true (or c from being false) we either delete x from SE' (to make $x \in SE'$ false) or add x to SE (to make $x \notin SE$ false). In other words, there is *exactly* one way to fix c when it is violated: for each of the elements in SE' but not in SE, either delete it from SE' or add it to SE. This is also the minimum way of fixing c, i.e. it does not involve removing or adding any redundant elements. As can be seen in figure 5, the repair plan set $\mathcal{R}(c)$ is $\{c_t \leftarrow$ for each x in (SE' - SE) !c'_t(x), c'_t(x) ← Remove x from SE', c'_t(x) ← Add x to SE$\}$. The three repair plans exactly address the fixing approach for c that we mentioned earlier. Therefore, we can conclude that $\mathcal{R}(c)$ contains minimum correct plans and that it is complete.

An OCL constraint is ultimately a combination (*and*, *or*, *not*, *xor* and *implies*) of basic constraints. We have proved that theorem 1 holds for all basic constraints. We now use that to prove, by induction, that theorem 1 holds for the basic connectives: *and*, *or*, and *not*. The other connectives (*xor* and *implies*) can be derived from the basic ones. Below is a proof for the *or* connective. For the others, please refer to [12].

For c $\stackrel{\text{def}}{=}$ c1 or c2, assume that theorem 1 holds for $\mathcal{R}(c1)$ and $\mathcal{R}(c2)$, i.e. both of them are correct and complete sets. Now we need to prove that it also holds for $\mathcal{R}(c)$. According to figure 5, we have:

$$\mathcal{P}(c) = \{c_t : \neg\, c1 \leftarrow !c1_t, c_t : \neg\, c2 \leftarrow !c2_t\}$$

and we also have:

$$\mathcal{R}(c) = \mathcal{P}(c) \cup \mathcal{R}(c1) \cup \mathcal{R}(c2)$$

Because of our induction assumption, $c1_t$ and $c2_t$ can fix c1 and c2 respectively. Therefore, plan $c_t : \neg$ c1 $\leftarrow !c1_t$ is able to repair c1 and plan $c_t : \neg$ c2 $\leftarrow !c2_t$ is able to repair c2. Since the constraint c holds if either of c1 or c2 holds, any plan that is able to fix c1 or c2 can fix c. As a result, we can conclude that $\mathcal{R}(c)$ contains plans that correctly fix c. These plans are also minimum because they do not contain redundant repair actions. For instance, plan $c_t : \neg$ c1 $\leftarrow !c1_t$ fixes only c1 when c1 is false, which is just sufficient to repair c without the need to fix c2.

We have proved that $\mathcal{R}(c)$ contains correct and minimum repair plans for c. Now we prove the completeness of the set $\mathcal{R}(c)$. Assume that there is a minimum plan P that fixes c and does not belong to $\mathcal{R}(c)$. Plan P should aim to fix either c1 or c2 and without loss of generality we assume that P aims to fix c1. Therefore, plan P is also the minimum plan for fixing c1, which results in, due to the induction assumption, that P belongs to $\mathcal{R}(c1)$. Since $\mathcal{R}(c)$ contains $\mathcal{R}(c1)$, P also belongs to $\mathcal{R}(c)$, which contradicts our previous assumption. Hence, there does not exist any minimum plan P that fixes c and does not belong to $\mathcal{R}(c)$, i.e. the set $\mathcal{R}(c)$ is complete.

The induction proof above shows that the generated repair plans of a constraint correctly fix the constraint. However, there are special cases in which repair plans for fixing sub-constraints conflict with each other. For instance, for c $\stackrel{\text{def}}{=}$ c1 and c2 the generated repair plans are:

$$\begin{aligned}\mathcal{P}(c) = \{&\mathit{fixC} : c \leftarrow \mathit{true}, \mathit{fixC} : \neg\, c \leftarrow !\, c_t;\ !\, \mathit{fixC},\\ &c_t : \neg\, c1 \wedge c2 \leftarrow !c1_t, c_t : \neg\, c2 \wedge c1 \leftarrow !c2_t, c_t : \neg\, c1 \wedge \neg\, c2 \leftarrow !c1_t;\ !c2_t\}\end{aligned}$$

Assume that c is false because c1 is true and c2 is false, then *fixC* calls the plan aiming to fix c2, i.e. $c_t : \neg$ c2 $\wedge$ c1 $\leftarrow !c2_t$. However, this plan may make c1 become false, which results in c still being false. Since *fixC* is called recursively until c becomes true, the plan aiming to fix c1 is called, i.e. $c_t : \neg$ c1 $\wedge$ c2 $\leftarrow !c1_t$. However, this plan may also make c2 false, in which case the plan aiming to fix c2 is called and this may continue as a loop. In general, if it is not possible to make both c1 and c2 true at the same time, i.e. every plan that fixes c1 violates c2 and vice versa, then c is not satisfiable. If c is satisfiable, then there exists a repair plan that is able to fix c. In this case, our cost algorithm (discussed in section 3) will favor that repair plan over any other repair plans that causes an infinite loop.

Overall, we can conclude that our generated repair plans for a constraint correctly fix it if the constraint is satisfiable. Our cost algorithm is able to detect infinite loops caused by conflict between repair plans fixing sub-constraints.

4.2 Example

Now let us consider a simple example of how repair plans are generated for the constraint previously presented in section 3.

Context Percept inv:
self.agent→forAll(a : Agent | a.plan→exists(pl : Plan | pl.percept→includes(self)))

We denote the above constraint as c(self), and c_t(self) is the event of making c(self) true. We also define the following abbreviations:

$c1(\text{self, a}) \stackrel{\text{def}}{=} \text{a.plan}\rightarrow\text{exists(pl : Plan} \mid \text{pl.percept}\rightarrow\text{includes(self))}$
$c2(\text{self, pl}) \stackrel{\text{def}}{=} \text{pl.percept}\rightarrow\text{includes(self)}$

Our repair plan generator produces the following repair plans for constraint c, since it has the form $SE \rightarrow \text{forAll}(c)$.

$c_t(\text{self}) \leftarrow$ for each a in self.agent if $\neg\ c1_t(\text{self, a})$ then $!c'_t(\text{self, a})$ **(P1)**
$c'_t(\text{self, a}) \leftarrow$ Delete a from self.agent **(P2)**
$c'_t(\text{self, a}) \leftarrow\ !c1_t(\text{self, a})$ **(P3)**

For constraint $c1$ we generate the following plans, since the constraint is of the form $SE \rightarrow \text{exists}(c)$. In the rules of figure 5 "Type(SE)" denotes the type of SE's elements, in this case SE (which is *a.plan*) contains plans, and therefore in P5 the context condition requires that *pl* be an element of the set of all plans, denoted Set(Plan).

$c1_t(\text{self, a}) : \text{pl} \in \text{a.plan} \leftarrow\ !c2_t(\text{self, pl})$ **(P4)**
$c1_t(\text{self, a}) : \text{pl} \in \text{Set(Plan)} \wedge \text{pl} \notin \text{a.plan} \leftarrow$ Add pl to a.plan ; $!c2_t(\text{self, pl})$ **(P5)**
$c1_t(\text{self, a}) \leftarrow$ Create pl : Plan ; Add pl to a.plan ; $!c2_t(\text{self, pl})$ **(P6)**

Similarly, for constraint $c2$ we generate the following plan.

$c2_t(\text{self, pl}) \leftarrow$ Add self to pl.percept **(P7)**

The above repair plan types are instantiated with actual variable bindings at run-time to produce different plan instances. For instance, in our STMS example previously described in section 2, after the software engineer performs the primary changes, the constraint c(self) is violated where *self* is the "*Selling Stock Request*" percept because there is only one agent handling it (*self.agent* = {"*GUI Agent*"}), and that agent contains two plans (*a.plan* = {"*Handling adding-funds request*","*Handling buying-stocks request*"}) but neither of the plans is triggered by the percept. The plans to repair the constraint are either not assigning "*GUI Agent*" to handle the "*Selling Stock Request*" percept (P2), or having one of the agent's plans be triggered by the percept (P3). Plan P3 then produces three alternatives: choosing an existing plan of the agent (which is either "*Handling adding-funds request*" or "*Handling buying-stocks request*) and make the "*Selling Stock Request*" percept be one of its triggers (P4 and P7); or choosing an existing plan in the design other than the two already in the agent and make the percept be one of its triggers (P5 and P7); or creating a new plan, adding it to "*GUI Agent*", and make the percept be one of its triggers (P6 and P7).

As discussed in section 3, we calculate the cost for each repair plan and present a list of equal least cost plans to the user. Let *A* denote the cost of an addition, *C* the cost of creating a new entity, and *D* denote the cost of a deletion. Note that we allow the repair administrator to define these elementary costs. He/she may use this mechanism to adjust the change propagation process as discussed in section 3. Then, considering the tree of plans below, the cost of P7 is the cost of adding the percept to plan pl's percepts (i.e. A), the cost of P4 is just the cost of P7 (i.e. A), the cost of P5 is the cost of P7 plus the cost of adding plan pl to the plans of agent a (i.e. $2 \times A$), and the cost of P6 is that plus the cost of creating a new plan (i.e. $C + 2 \times A$). Since any of P4, P5 or P6 can be used to fix $c1_t$, and the system picks the cheapest, the cost of $P3$ is the cost of P4 (i.e. A). The cost of P2 is D, and if we assume that deletion is more expensive than addition, then the cost of P1 is A, and the repair plan selected involves P1, P3, P4 and P7 (indicated in bold).

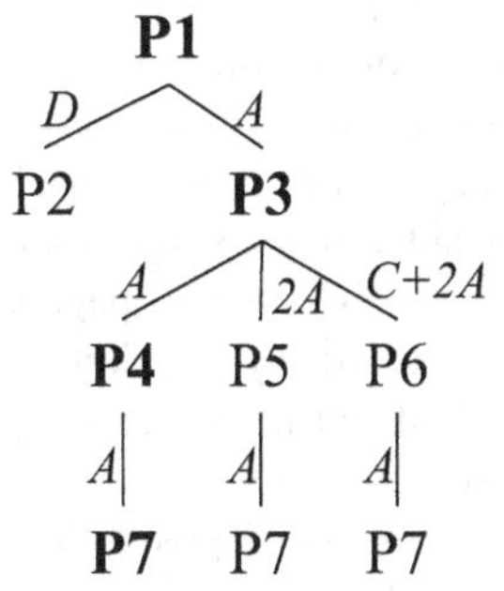

P1
D A
P2 **P3**
A $2A$ $C+2A$
P4 P5 P6
A A A
P7 P7 P7

All plan types generated by our repair system are stored in a repository. As we have noted earlier, the repair administrator is able to modify the generated repair plan types, including modifying the plans' context conditions, modifying the plans' body or even adding additional plans or removing generated repair plans. For example, the repair administrator may think that it does not make sense in practice to have a percept that is not handled by any agent. Therefore, he/she may add a context condition into plan P2 specifying that it is applicable only if the set *self.agent* contains at least two elements.

5 Related Work

The issue of assisting software engineers to deal with software changes has received much attention in the areas of software evolution and maintenance. Change impact analysis has been extensively investigated, but is only loosely related to our work. Change impact analysis techniques [13] aim to assess the extent of the change, i.e. the artefacts, components, or modules that will be impacted by the change, and consequently how costly the change will be. Our work is more focused on *implementing* changes by propagating changes between design artefacts in order to maintain consistency as the software evolves.

There has been a range of work using a *rule-based* approach to detect and resolve inconsistencies (or constraint violations) both in the areas of databases and software engineering. In these approaches, rules are defined in terms of constraints and actions in such a way that if a constraint is violated, actions will be performed to repair the violation. The work in the area of databases focuses on integrity constraint maintenance [14], i.e. making changes to transactions or databases to recreate a state of integrity. There has been some work which addresses how repair actions can be automatically generated from constraints expressed in first order logic in relational, active and deductive databases [15,16,17]. One key difference between their work and ours is that we generate abstract, structured, repair plans that are instantiated at runtime. The approaches proposed in [15,16] are similar to ours in which they involve user intervention in selecting repair actions. In contrast, in [17] a system is described that generates actions from closed, range-restricted first order logic formulae. Since the repair algorithm relies on the rules of the database and the closed-world assumption, it can automatically find repairs for violated existential formulae without user intervention.

In [5], constraints between distributed documents are expressed in xlinkit, a combination of first order logic with XPath expressions. The paper also presents a framework which automatically derives a set of repair actions from the constraints. In [4], such rules form the knowledge base of an expert system. However, these approaches tend to consider only a single change and consequently do not explicitly address the cascading nature of change propagation.

Consistency checking is an area clearly related to our work. Our framework can be built on top of existing (UML) consistency checking approaches. However, note that the iterative nature of cascading changes ideally requires incremental consistency checking as proposed in ArgoUML[7] and xlinkit [18]. Advanced event-driven consistency checking approaches such as Egyed's [19] can be integrated in our framework as the constraint checking component.

Several other approaches implement the change support mechanism based on some underlying mathematical formalism. For example, the formalism of graph rewriting has been used to deal with change propagation [3] and model synchronization [20]. In [21] and [22], they propose to transform (UML) specifications to Petri-Nets and Description Logic respectively. These approaches then exploit existing consistency checks that have been defined for the mathematical formalism. However, it is not clear to what extent these approaches suffer from the traceability problem: that is, can a reported inconsistency be traced back to the original model? Furthermore, the identification of transformations that preserve and enforce consistency still remains a critical issue [21]. By contrast, our approach deals directly with UML models without any transformation and thus does not suffer from that issue.

6 Conclusions and Future Work

In this paper we have presented an approach for change propagation in design models. Our framework takes as input a meta-model and well-formedness constraints (in OCL), and makes use of repair plans to propagate changes by fixing inconsistencies. A key feature is that these repair plans are generated automatically from the OCL constraints, in a way that is sound and complete. We use a design of a stock trading management system developed using the Prometheus methodology as an illustrative example showing how the framework works. Our proposed framework is generic and can be applied to object-oriented methodologies as well, indeed, we have already applied it to the object-oriented UML design of an ATM system, which contains a class diagram (18 classes such as ATM, Bank, Transaction) and 10 sequence diagrams (corresponding to 10 use cases such as GetPIN, PrintReceipt). We then introduced several realistic requirement changes and applied our framework to propagate changes. Although the results have shown the applicability and scalability of our framework, more complex case studies are needed to evaluate it.

Some specific areas for future work that we intend to investigate are: (1) Implementing the repair plan generator (2) Investigating how to extend our approach to deal with programming language code as well as design artefacts. (3) Dealing more efficiently with plan recipes with a context condition of the form $x \in \mathit{Type}(SE)$ by being

[7] http://argouml.tigris.org/

lazy: instead of creating a plan instance for each possible value, defer the choice and use subsequent constraints to narrow down the range of possible values for x. (4) Performing a more extensive case study, in order to better ascertain the *scalability* of our approach; and also conducting more evaluation to better ascertain the *effectiveness* of the approach. There are two measurements that we should take into account when we evaluate the framework. We plan to choose an existing, reasonable-size, system and then define a classification of changes. We then input these to our framework and analyze the accuracy of what our framework recommends. In addition, we investigate how our framework deals with different system sizes to measure its efficiency.

Acknowledgments

This work is supported by the Australian Research Council under grant LP0453486, in collaboration with Agent Oriented Software. The authors would also like to thank Lin Padgham for discussions relating to this work.

References

1. Swanson, E.B.: The dimensions of maintenance. In: ICSE 1976: Proceedings of the 2nd international conference on Software engineering, Los Alamitos, CA, USA, pp. 492–497. IEEE Computer Society Press, Los Alamitos (1976)
2. Spanoudakis, G., Zisman, A.: Inconsistency management in software engineering: Survey and open research issues. In: Chang, K.S. (ed.) Handbook of Software Engineering and Knowledge Engineering, pp. 24–29. World Scientific, Singapore (2001)
3. Rajlich, V.: A model for change propagation based on graph rewriting. In: Proceedings of the International Conference on Software Maintenance (ICSM), pp. 84–91. IEEE Computer Society, Los Alamitos (1997)
4. Sourrouille, J.L., Caplat, G.: Checking UML model consistency. In: Jézéquel, J.-M., Hussmann, H., Cook, S. (eds.) UML 2002. LNCS, vol. 2460, Springer, Heidelberg (2002)
5. Nentwich, C., Emmerich, W., Finkelstein, A.: Consistency management with repair actions. In: ICSE 2003: Proceedings of the 25th International Conference on Software Engineering, pp. 455–464. IEEE Computer Society, Los Alamitos (2003)
6. Dam, K.H., Winikoff, M., Padgham, L.: An agent-oriented approach to change propagation in software evolution. In: Proceedings of the Australian Software Engineering Conference (ASWEC), pp. 309–318. IEEE Computer Society, Los Alamitos (2006)
7. Padgham, L., Winikoff, M.: Developing intelligent agent systems: A practical guide. John Wiley & Sons, Chichester (2004)
8. Object Management Group: Object Constraint Language (OCL) 2.0 Specification (2006)
9. Rao, A.S., Georgeff, M.P.: An abstract architecture for rational agents. In: Rich, C., Swartout, W., Nebel, B. (eds.) Proceedings of the Third International Conference on Principles of Knowledge Representation and Reasoning, San Mateo, CA, pp. 439–449. Morgan Kaufmann Publishers, San Francisco (1992)
10. Bordini, R.H., Dastani, M., Dix, J., El Fallah Seghrouchni, A. (eds.): Multi-Agent Programming: Languages, Platforms and Applications. Springer, Heidelberg (2005)
11. Rao, A.S.: AgentSpeak(L): BDI agents speak out in a logical computable language. In: Perram, J., Van de Velde, W. (eds.) MAAMAW 1996. LNCS, vol. 1038, pp. 42–55. Springer, Heidelberg (1996)

12. Dam, K.H., Winikoff, M.: An agent-based approach to change propagation. Technical Report TR-06-04, RMIT University (2006)
13. Arnold, R., Bohner, S.: Software Change Impact Analysis. IEEE Computer Society Press, Los Alamitos (1996), ISBN 0-818-67384-2
14. Mayol, E., Teniente, E.: A survey of current methods for integrity constraint maintenance and view updating. In: Proceedings of the Workshops on Evolution and Change in Data Management, Reverse Engineering in Information Systems, and the World Wide Web and Conceptual Modeling, London, UK, pp. 62–73. Springer, Heidelberg (1999)
15. Ceri, S., Fraternali, P., Paraboschi, S., Tanca, L.: Automatic generation of production rules for integrity maintenance. ACM Trans. Database Syst. 19(3), 367–422 (1994)
16. Gertz, M., Lipeck, U.W.: An extensible framework for repairing constraint violations. In: Proceedings of the IFIP TC11 Working Group 11.5, First Working Conference on Integrity and Internal Control in Information Systems, pp. 89–111. Chapman & Hall, Ltd, Boca Raton (1997)
17. Moerkotte, G., Lockemann, P.C.: Reactive consistency control in deductive databases. ACM Trans. Database Syst. 16(4), 670–702 (1991)
18. Nentwich, C., Capra, L., Emmerich, W., Finkelstein, A.: xlinkit: a consistency checking and smart link generation service. ACM Transactions on Internet Technology 2(2), 151–185 (2002)
19. Egyed, A.: Instant consistency checking for the UML. In: ICSE 2006: Shanghai, China (May 2006)
20. Ivkovic, I., Kontogiannis, K.: Tracing evolution changes of software artifacts through model synchronization. In: Proceedings of the 20th IEEE International Conference on Software Maintenance (ICSM), pp. 252–261. IEEE Computer Society, Los Alamitos (2004)
21. Engels, G., Kuster, J.M., Heckel, R., Groenewegen, L.: Towards consistency-preserving model evolution. In: Proceedings of the International Workshop on Principles of Software Evolution (IWPSE), pp. 129–132. ACM Press, New York (2002)
22. Van Der Straeten, R., Mens, T., Simmonds, J., Jonckers, V.: Using description logics to maintain consistency between UML models. In: Stevens, P., Whittle, J., Booch, G. (eds.) UML 2003. LNCS, vol. 2863, pp. 326–340. Springer, Heidelberg (2003)

An Expressway from Agent-Oriented Models to Prototypes

Kuldar Taveter and Leon Sterling

Department of Computer Science and Software Engineering
the University of Melbourne
Vic 3010, Australia
{kuldar,leon}@csse.unimelb.edu.au
http://www.csse.unimelb.edu.au

Abstract. Agent-oriented software engineering can be viewed as applying software engineering principles to agent-oriented development or applying agent-oriented principles to software engineering. In this paper, we are more concerned with the second view. We describe how prototype systems can be efficiently created from agent-oriented domain and design models. We propose a conceptual space that accommodates model transformations described by the Model-Driven Architecture. We explain agent-oriented domain models and platform-independent design models and show how the first can be mapped to the latter. We demonstrate how design models can be turned into the implementation of an agent-based prototype on a specific platform. The approach has potential for accelerating the process of rapid prototyping.

1 Introduction

Agent-oriented software engineering can be viewed as applying software engineering techniques and principles to the development of agent-oriented systems, but also as applying agent-oriented principles to developing software. In the latter spirit, we believe that agent-oriented modelling techniques are not just useful for designing systems consisting of software agents, i.e. multi-agent systems. Agent-oriented modelling can, and should, be more generally utilized for designing distributed open socio-technical systems. It can accommodate Web services and component-based systems. What makes agent-oriented modelling suitable is distinguishing between active entities — agents — and passive ones — objects.

Model-Driven Architecture (MDA) [1] by Object Management Group (OMG) is an approach to using models in software development that separates the domain model of a socio-technical system from its design and implementation models. The MDA proposes three types of models: Computation-Independent Models (CIM), Platform-Independent Models (PIM), and Platform Specific Models (PSM). In MDA, a *platform* denotes a set of subsystems and technologies that provide a coherent set of functionalities through interfaces and specified

M. Luck and L. Padgham (Eds.): AOSE 2007, LNCS 4951, pp. 147–163, 2008.

usage patterns. Some examples of platforms are CORBA, Java 2 Enterprise Edition, Microsoft.NET and JADE.

In addition to defining model types at different abstraction layers, the MDA also introduces the term "Model transformation" which is the process of converting one model to another model of the same system. It defines mapping between models as a "specification of a mechanism for transforming the elements of a model conforming to a particular metamodel into elements of another model that conforms to another (possibly the same) metamodel" [1]. To that end, different techniques like model marking as described by MDA, and using templates and mapping languages have been proposed. The MDA focuses on transformation between PIM and PSM, because executable PSM models can be easily generated from PIM models. This is not the case for mapping from CIM to PIM, which are conceptually more separated. To support mapping from CIM to PIM, we propose an appropriate set of CIM and PIM concepts that can be mapped from one another.

As represented in Figure 1, the modelling abstractions we advocate in CIM include *goals* and *roles*, which appear in most agent-oriented methodologies with a similar — though often not identical — meaning. In addition, *social policies* are constraints on interaction and behaviour of agents playing the roles. *Domain entities* define the basic concepts of the problem domain at hand.

For PIM, we have chosen *activities* that are triggered by *rules* as key notions. Both activities and rules are rooted in activity theory [16]. We prefer them to capabilities and plans because activities and rules represent more naturally the nature of activities by human and man-made agents and are free from the bias towards any specific agent architecture like BDI [6]. According to Figure 1, goals and roles can be mapped to *activity types* and *agent types*, respectively. *Social policies* can be mapped to *rules* and *domain entities* to *knowledge* items. Activity types, in turn, consist of *action types*.

The mappings explained do not imply the losing of knowledge of higher abstraction levels at lower abstraction levels. For example, the knowledge of roles can still be retained and utilized at the PIM level and goals after they have been assigned to activities for achieving them can still be explicitly represented in PIM.

The platform-independent notions *action types, rules*, and *agent types*, along with *perception types* and *knowledge items* can be mapped into the corresponding *concrete action types, behavioural construct types*, and *concrete agent types* as well as *event types* and *concrete object types* of some specific platform like JADE [13].

The mappings outlined in Figure 1 can be used for rapid obtaining of prototypes. In some cases, also final implementations can be obtained, but usually design decisions are restricted by commercially available and *preferred* technology.

In addition to the horizontal dimension of modelling, which is represented by Figure 1, there is also a vertical dimension. In [9], the first author has performed a thorough study of various software engineering methodologies and modelling approaches and has concluded that agent-oriented models should address a problem domain from six perspectives: informational, organisational, interactional,

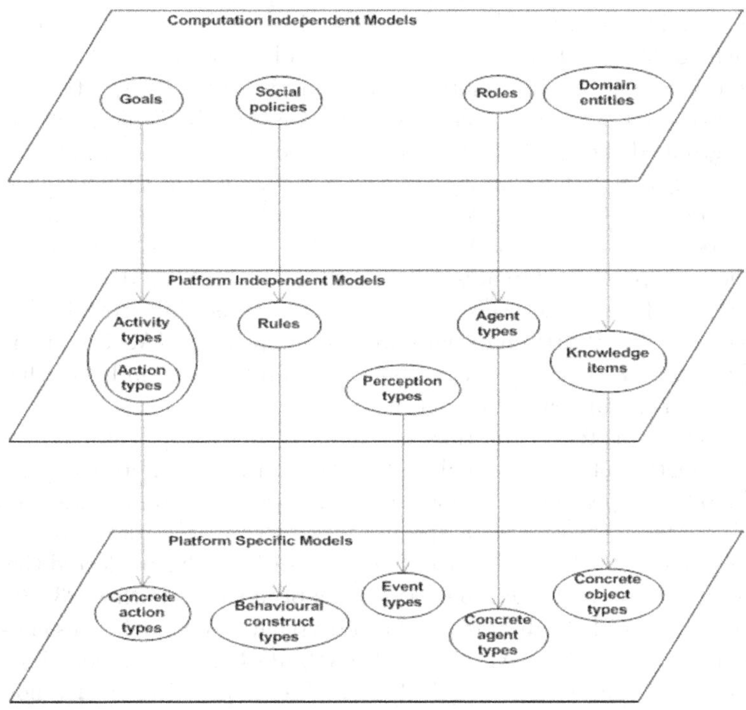

Fig. 1. The Conceptual Space of transformations between different layers of MDA

Table 1. The Viewpoint Modelling Framework

Viewpoint models	***Viewpoint aspect***		
Abstraction layer	*Organisation/ Interaction*	*Information*	*Motivation/ Behaviour*
Computation independent domain analysis (CIM)	Role Models (ROADMAP)	Domain Model (ROADMAP)	Goal Models (ROADMAP)
Platform independent computational design (PIM)	Interaction Models (RAP/AOR)	Information Model (RAP/AOR)	Behaviour Models (RAP/AOR)
Platform specific design and implementation (PSM)	Class and Sequence Diagrams (UML)	Class Diagrams (UML)	Class and Sequence Diagrams (UML)

functional, motivational, and behavioural. In [11], we have identified informational, interactional, and behavioural perspectives as the most crucial ones for agent-oriented design. On the other hand, it can be concluded from [3], [4], and [17] that organisational, informational, and motivational perspectives are the most relevant ones for agent-oriented domain analysis. In Table 1, we have accordingly grouped the perspectives explained above as three viewpoint aspects. This table can be populated in many ways. For example, at the CIM level, motivation models are featured in MaSE [18] as Goal Hierarchy Diagrams, domain models have been proposed as Environment Models in GAIA [19], and organisation models appear as Organisation Diagrams in MESSAGE [20]. Similarly, at the PIM level, behaviour models are represented as Multi-Agent Behaviour Descriptions in PASSI [21], information models appear in MAS-CommonKADS [22] as Expertise Models, and interaction models are featured in Prometheus [14] as Interaction Diagrams and Interaction Protocols.

The structure of Table 1 is thus not associated with any specific software engineering methodology but provides a universal framework for classifying the kinds of models appearing in various methodologies and approaches. However, we have populated Table 1 in a specific way to cater for the needs of rapid prototyping addressed by this article. In other words, we have selected the types of models appearing in Table 1 because it has been shown earlier [23] that this combination of models facilitates rapid prototyping. The model types chosen by us originate in the ROADMAP [3,4] and RAP/AOR [11] methodologies and in the Unified Modelling Language (UML) [12]. Please note that UML models as such are not platform-specific but can be used for modelling platform-specific issues.

In the next section we present types of models at the three abstraction layers — computation independent modelling, platform independent computational design, and platform specific design and implementation — by using an example of creating a system for ordering take-away food, which has been borrowed from [2].

2 Computation Independent Modelling

According to MDA [1], the models created at the computation independent modelling stage should be capable of bridging the gap between experts about the domain and its requirements on one hand, and experts about the design and construction of the socio-technical system on the other. The models should address *motivation* for the system to be designed, *organisation* of the system, and the *environment* in which the system is to be situated. Our experience with industry reported in [23,27], as well as with students in our graduate Agents class at the University of Melbourne, has proven that motivation for the system can be effectively communicated by Goal Models, organisation of the system — by Role Models — and the environment — by Domain Models.

Our goal and role models have been described in [3] and [4], and we review here for completeness. The Goal Model provides a high-level overview of system requirements. Its main objective is to enable both domain experts and developers to pinpoint the *goals* of the system and the *roles* the system needs to fulfil in order to meet those goals. Design and implementation details are not described at all, as they are not addressed during requirements analysis. The Goal Model contains three components: goals, quality goals, and roles. A *goal* represents a functional requirement of the system. A *quality goal*, as its name implies, represents a non-functional or quality requirement of the system. A *role* is some capacity or position that the system requires in order to achieve its goals. As Figure 2 shows, goals and quality goals can be decomposed into smaller related sub-goals and sub-quality goals, allowing hierarchical structure between a goal and its sub-goals. The resulting hierarchy is by no means an "is-a" or generalisation relationship as is common in object-oriented methodologies. Rather, the hierarchical structure is just to show that the sub-component is an *aspect* of the top-level component.

Figure 2 represents the Goal Model of a socio-technical system to be designed for ordering take-away food. In the diagram, the root goal is to 'provide meal'. This goal is associated with the roles Customer, Ordering Centre, and Restaurant. The role Customer represents the stakeholders whose needs the socio-technical system is to satisfy. The system itself consists of actors playing the roles Ordering Centre and Restaurant. The goal to 'provide meal' can be decomposed into the following four sub-goals: to 'take order', 'provide waiting estimate', 'confirm order', and 'deliver meal'. The goal to 'provide meal' is characterized by the quality goal 'customer happy'. There are also the quality goals 'fast reply' and 'fast delivery' pertaining to the sub-goals to 'provide waiting estimate', 'confirm order', and 'deliver meal'. Quality goals represent social policies, which can be anything from access rights, to social norms, to obligations [17]. Please note that the order in which the sub-goals are presented in Figure 2 does not per se imply any chronological order in which they are to be achieved.

The Role Model describes the properties of a role. The Role Model consists of the role name, textual description, and the specifications of its responsibilities

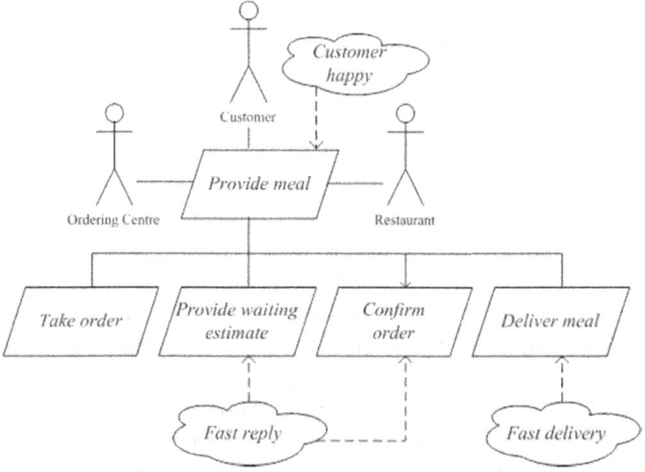

Fig. 2. The Goal Model for the take-away food ordering system

and constraints. Clearly, this is analogous to the delegation of work through the creation of positions in a human organisation. Every employee in the organisation holds a particular position in order to realise business functions. Different positions entail different degrees of autonomy, decision-making, and responsibilities. Taking this analogy, the Role Model is the "position description" for a particular role. Table 2 shows the Role Model created for the role Restaurant shown in the Goal Model in Figure 2.

Table 2. The Role Model for the Restaurant

Role Name	Restaurant
Description	Provides the time estimate for delivery and delivers the meal
Responsibilities	Receive the order Estimate the time required for cooking Inform the ordering centre about the time required Accept the confirmation by the ordering centre Deliver the meal to the customer
Constraints	The deliverer must use an electronic signature device to register the delivery

The Domain Model represents agents' knowledge about their physical and conceptual environments. It can be viewed as an *ontology* providing a common framework of knowledge for agents playing the roles of the problem domain. For example, a take-away food ordering system requires the domain entities Cook, Dish, and Order. The first describes the kinds of agents in the system's physical environment, the second — a particular kind of food and the third — a particular order. The Domain Model can be initially expressed as a list of domain entities showing for each of them with which role(s) it is associated. For example, the domain entities Dish and Order are associated with all three roles — Customer, Ordering Centre, and Restaurant — while the domain entity Cook is associated with just the role Restaurant. Relationships between domain entities, such as generalisation and aggregation, can be represented by using a UML-like notation.

3 Platform Independent Design

According to MDA [1], platform independent modelling focuses on the operation of a system while hiding the details necessary for a particular platform. The resulting models are suitable for use with a number of different platforms of a similar type. The models should address *interactions* between agents of the system to be designed, *information* that those agents require for operating, and *behaviours* of the agents.

Since our models can be used for designing Web services as well as agent-based systems, we are interested in goal-oriented rather than goal-governed agents [5]. *Goal-governed agents* refer to the strong notion of agency, that is, they are agents with some forms of cognitive capabilities, making possible explicit representation of their goals that drive the selection of agent actions. An example class of goal-governed agents are BDI-agents [6]. *Goal-oriented agents* refer to the weak notion of agency, that is, they are agents whose behaviour is directly designed and programmed to achieve some goal, which may not be explicitly represented. Goal-oriented agents generalize over a wide range of software components rather than just over software agents. An example goal-oriented agent architecture is AGENT-0 by Yoav Shoham [7]. Agents of both kinds can be derived from the Goal Models, Role Models, and Domain Models.

We view goal-oriented agents as being engaged in various *activities*. Based on activity theory [16], we consider activities as fundamental units of human and man-made agent behaviour. Activity is started by a *rule* when the activity's triggering conditions are true. Activity is triggered by some event perceived by an agent and/or by some value associated with an object in the agent's knowledge base.

We have chosen as the goal-oriented agent architecture of PIM *Knowledge-Perception-Memory-Commitment* (KPMC) agents, proposed in [8] and extended by [9]. KPMC-agents can be graphically modelled by using diagrams included by the Radical Agent-Oriented Process / Agent-Object-Relationship (RAP/AOR) methodology of software engineering and rapid prototyping, which was introduced in [11]. Before introducing PIM models of the case study of ordering take-away food, we briefly explain the notation that will be used.

An *external* (that is, modelled from the perspective of an external observer) *Agent-Object-Relationship (AOR) diagram* specified by Figure 3 enables the representation in a single diagram of the types of human and man-made (for example, software) agents of a socio-technical system, together with their beliefs about instances of "private" and external ("shared" with other agents) object types. There may be attributes and/or predicates defined for an object type and relationships (associations) among agent and/or object types. A predicate, which is visualized as depicted in Figure 3, may take parameters.

Figure 3 reflects that our graphical notation distinguishes between an *action event* (an event perceived by one agent that is created through the action of another agent, such as a physical reception/delivery of a meal) *type* and a *non-action event type* (for example, types of temporal events or events created by natural forces). We further distinguish between a *communicative* action event (or *message*) type and a *non-communicative* (physical) action event type like providing the customer with a meal.

The first thing to be done at the design stage is mapping the abstract constructs from the analysis stage — *roles* — to concrete constructs — *agent types.* Each agent type may be assigned one or more roles and the other way round. In our simple example, assigning the roles to agent types is straightforward. All three roles — Customer, Centre, and Restaurant — are mapped to the respective man-made agent types `CustomerAgent`, `CentreAgent`, and `RestaurantAgent`. There may be several instances of `CustomerAgent` and `RestaurantAgent`, and there is exactly one `CentreAgent`.

In [11], three complementary modelling perspectives are identified for agent-oriented design. The resulting models can be represented as just one diagram of the kind shown in Fig. 3. We will now treat platform independent design from each of the three perspectives — *interaction design, information design*, and *behaviour design*. As stated above, interaction design models capture interactions between the agents of the system, information design models represent information that those agents require for operating, and behaviour design models specify behaviours of the agents.

In our view, the mapping between CIM and PIM cannot be fully formalized because of the intangible nature of CIM models. What is important is that the mapping is traceable in the sense that it can be seen how CIM modelling constructs relate to the PIM models. The mapping should be supported by tools no matter what degree of automation can be achieved. In the next three sections, we also explain the rationale of deriving a design model of each kind.

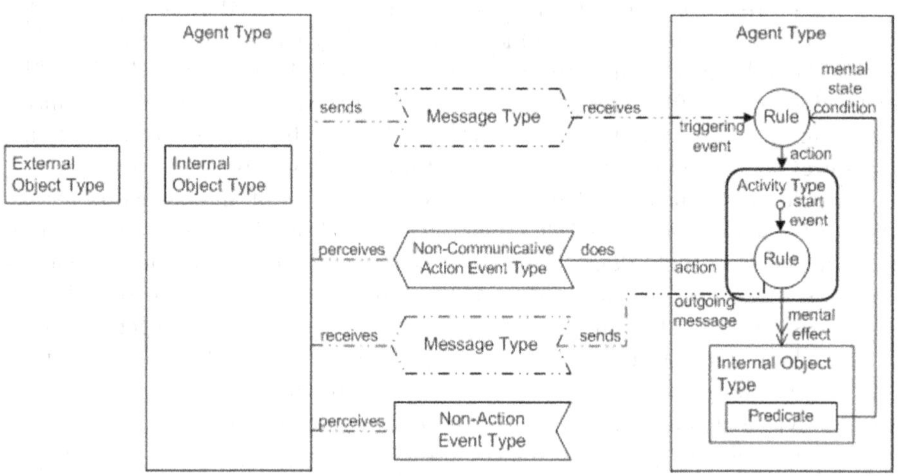

Fig. 3. The belief structure and behaviour modelling elements of external AOR diagrams

3.1 Interaction Design

After determining agent types, we can capture interactions between agents of those types with the Interaction Model represented as an interaction-frame diagram. Interactions can be derived from responsibilities included by Role Models. The interaction frame diagram depicted in Figure 4 consists of two *interaction frames* that have been derived from the Role Model shown in Table 2: one between the agents of a customer and the ordering centre, and the other one between the agents of the ordering centre and a restaurant. Messages in interaction frames have four modalities: "request", "inform", "confirm", and "reject". With a message of the "request" modality, an agent requests another agent to perform a certain action, which can be a communicative action — sending a message — or a physical action. A message of the "inform" modality serves to inform another agent on something. The last two modalities explain themselves. Messages of different modalities can be combined. For example, with a message of the type `request inform time-estimate(Dish(?DishName))`, an agent requests another agent to inform it about the expected time required to prepare and deliver the meal described by a serialized object of the type `Dish`. An argument preceded by a question mark appearing in message content, such as `?DishName`, denotes a string. The interaction represented at the bottom of Figure 4 models a physical action of the type `provideDish(Order(?OrderID))` that occurs between agents of the types `RestaurantAgent` and `CustomerAgent`. This action is naturally only registered rather than performed by the corresponding software agents. This can be accomplished by an electronic device incorporating both an actuator and a sensor where the action is pushing a button by the deliverer and the event is signing by the customer.

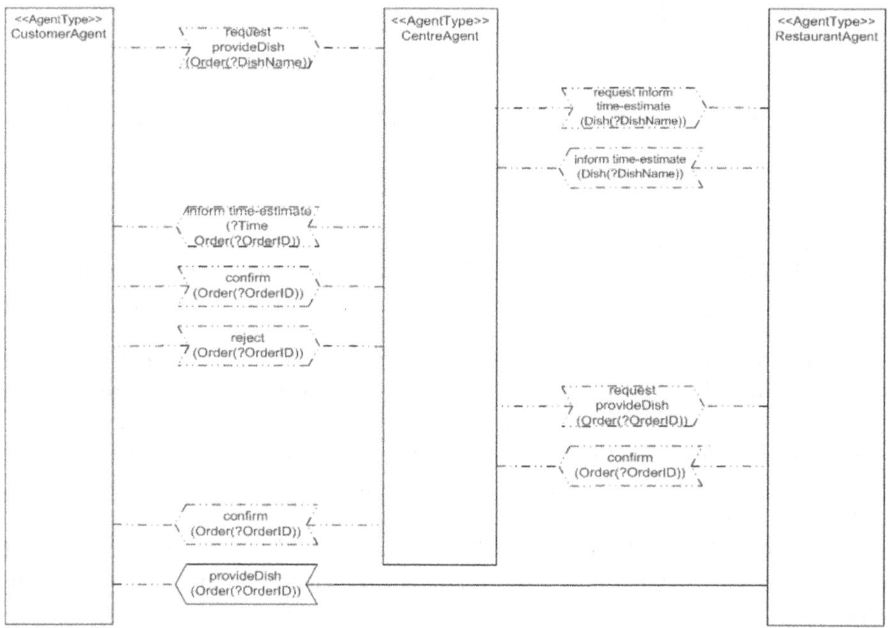

Fig. 4. The Interaction Model for the take-away food ordering system

3.2 Information Design

In information modelling, we further extend and formalize the *ontology* providing a common framework of knowledge for the agents of the problem domain. Recall that the initial version of this ontology — the Domain Model — was created at the stage of domain analysis. Each agent can see only a part of the ontology; that is, each agent views the ontology from a specific perspective. We represent the resulting Information Model as the *AOR agent diagram* shown in Figure 5.

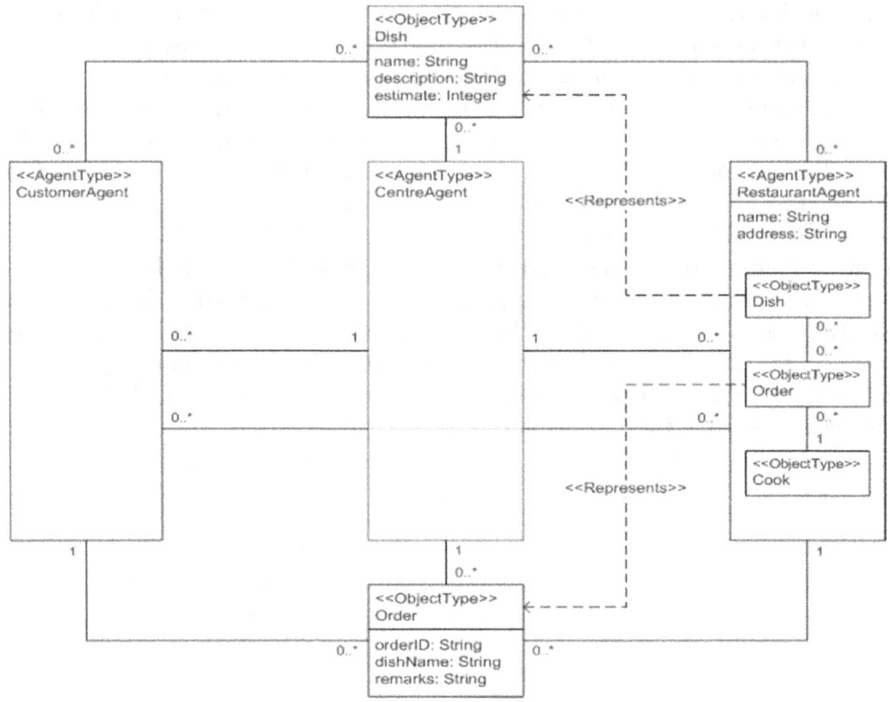

Fig. 5. The Information Model for the take-away food ordering system

In the figure, an agent of the type `CustomerAgent`, representing a customer, has knowledge about one agent of the type `CentreAgent`, which represents the ordering centre, and about several agents of the type `RestaurantAgent` representing restaurants. The `CentreAgent`, in turn, is aware of agents of both other types. Each restaurant agent is aware of the `CentreAgent` and of agents of its customers served by the restaurant.

Additionally, the Information Model depicted in Figure 5 represents that agents of all three types may have a shared knowledge about one or more instances of the object types `Dish` and `Order`. The model also shows that a restaurant agent has private knowledge about inter-related instances of the object types `Dish` and `Order`. Atomic information elements are described as *attributes* rather than objects. As is reflected by Figure 5, an agent of the type `RestaurantAgent` has the attributes `name` and `address` that characterize the restaurant represented by it. Objects of the types `Dish` and `Order` are also described by their respective attributes.

3.3 Behaviour Design

Under behaviour design, goals of CIM are mapped to activity types of PIM. An activity of a given type accomplishes a goal from the Goal Model. For example,

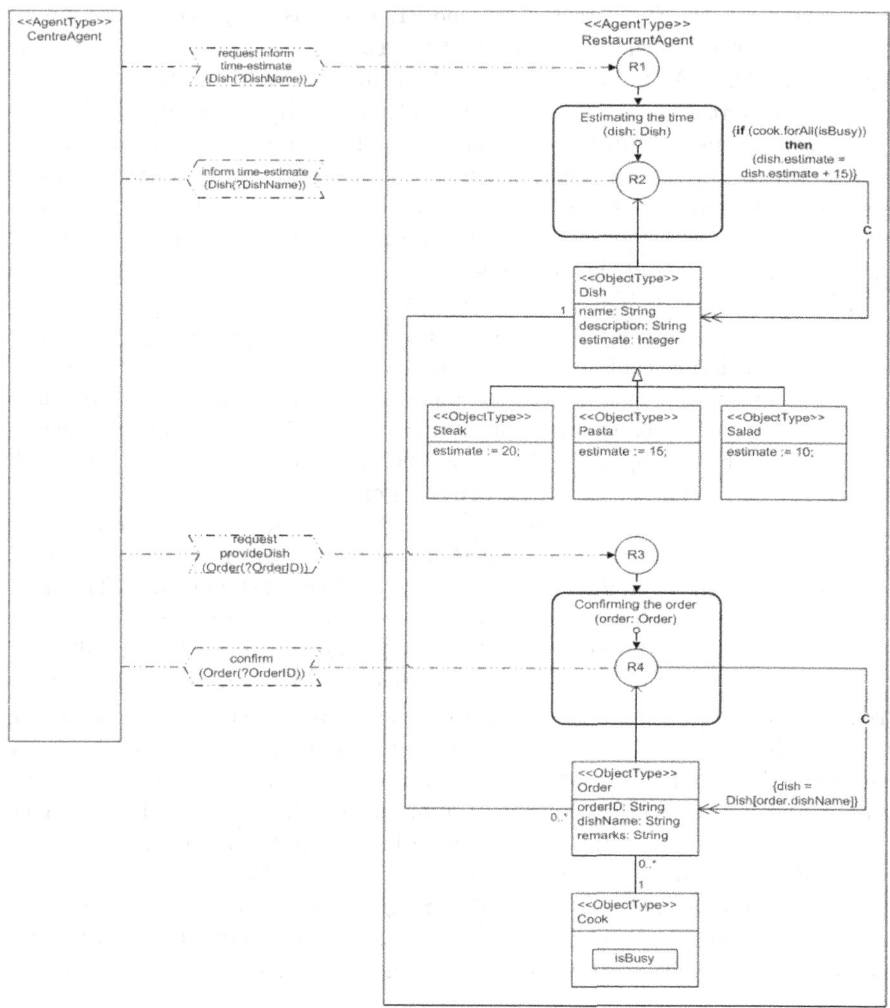

Fig. 6. The Behaviour Model for an agent representing a restaurant

an activity of the type "Estimating the time" represented in Figure 6 achieves a goal to 'provide waiting estimate' modelled in Figure 2. *Rules* determine when, by whom, and under which conditions an activity is invoked. For example, rule `R1` specifies that an activity of the type "Estimating the time" is started by the `RestaurantAgent` upon receiving from the `CentreAgent` a request to provide the waiting estimate. Rules also carry out social policies. For example, rules `R1`, `R2`, `R3`, and `R4` shown in Figure 6 realize the social policy "Fast reply".

Figure 6 represents the Behaviour Model of a `RestaurantAgent` type in the scenario of ordering take-away food. The behaviour involves the activity types "Estimating the time" and "Confirming the order". An activity of the type

"Estimating the time" is started by rule R1, which is triggered by a communicative action event (message) of the type request inform time-estimate (Dish(?DishName)). As has been pointed out in Section 3.1, with this message, the CentreAgent requests the RestaurantAgent to inform it about the estimated waiting time required to prepare and deliver the meal that is identified by a serialized object of the type Dish. Rule R2 prescribes an instance of the object type Dish to be created from the serialized object. As there can be three different types of dishes in our example, an instance of Dish created by rule R2 always belongs to one of the subtypes Steak, Pasta, or Salad. It can be seen in Figure 6 that each of them is modelled with the respective value of the attribute estimate. Additionally, there is an Object Constraint Language (OCL) [12] clause specifying that if all the cooks are busy at the time of creating an instance of Dish, represented by the predicate isBusy of the RestaurantAgent's private object type Cook, the value of the attribute estimate should be increased by 15. Rule R2 further specifies that a modified instance of the object type Dish should be serialized and sent to the CentreAgent.

An activity of the type "Confirming the order" is started by rule R3. This rule processes a serialized instance of the object type Order, which is included by a message of the type request provideDish(Order(?OrderID)). The message means that the CentreAgent requests the RestaurantAgent to perform a physical action of the type provideDish(Order(?OrderID)) according to the enclosed order. Rule R4 prescribes an instance of the internal object type Order to be created from the serialized object. At the creation of an Order instance, the value of its identifying attribute orderID will be automatically generated. The OCL clause dish = Dish[order.dishName] specifies the creation of the association link between the order and the corresponding instance of Dish. Rule R4 further expresses through its connection to the message type confirm(Order(?OrderID)) that a modified instance of the object type Order should be serialized and sent to the CentreAgent. In a later stage of the business process of ordering take-away food, an association between the order and the object representing the cook to which the order is allocated will be created.

4 Platform Specific Design and Rapid Prototyping

Finally, the modelling constructs of PIM are mapped to the corresponding constructs of PSM. It has been shown in [9] that external AOR diagrams can be straightforwardly mapped into the programming constructs of the Java Agent Development Environment (JADE, http://jade.cselt.it/) agent platform. The JADE agent platform [13] is a software framework to build agent-based systems in the Java programming language in compliance with the standard proposals for multi-agent systems by the Foundation for Intelligent Physical Agents (FIPA, http://www.fipa.org/). The mapping principles are more particularly addressed in [9].

Table 3. Mapping of notions of KPMC agents to the object classes and methods of JADE

Notion of KPMC agent	Object class in JADE	Object method of JADE
Object type	java.lang.Object	-
Agent type	jade.core.Agent	-
Elementary activity type	jade.core.behaviours. OneShotBehaviour	-
Sequential activity type	jade.core.behaviours. SequentialBehaviour	-
Parallel activity type	jade.core.behaviours. ParallelBehaviour	-
Execution cycle of a KPMC agent	jade.core.behaviours. CyclicBehaviour	-
Waiting for a message to be received	jade.core.behaviours. ReceiverBehaviour	-
Starting the first-level activity	jade.core.Agent	public void addBehaviour (Behaviour b)
Starting a sub-activity	jade.core.behaviours. SequentialBehaviour	public void addSubBehaviour (Behaviour b)
Starting a parallel sub-activity	jade.core.behaviours. ParallelBehaviour	public void addSubBehaviour (Behaviour b)
Start-of-activity event type	jade.core.behaviours. OneShotBehaviour	public abstract void action()
Start-of-activity event type	jade.core.behaviours. SequentialBehaviour, jade.core.behaviours. ParallelBehaviour	public abstract void onStart()
End-of-activity event type	jade.core.behaviours. Behaviour	public int onEnd()
Agent message	jade.lang.acl.ACLMessage	-

Table 3 shows how various modelling notions of KPMC agents can be mapped to the corresponding object classes and methods of the JADE platform. In particular, activity types and the execution cycle of a KPMC agent map to JADE *behaviours*. Rules are not included in Table 2 because they are mapped to various constructs represented in Java. The programs resulting from the mappings are complemented by simple graphical user interfaces and thereafter executed, as is exemplified by a snapshot shown in Figure 7.

Table 3 does not include the mapping of OCL clauses. We used OCL clauses for representing pre- and post-conditions, which specify the state of the world before and after triggering a rule without considering *how* the desired state of the world will be achieved. This feature of being "side-effect free" is one of the basic features of OCL. The particular way of changing the world state is specified

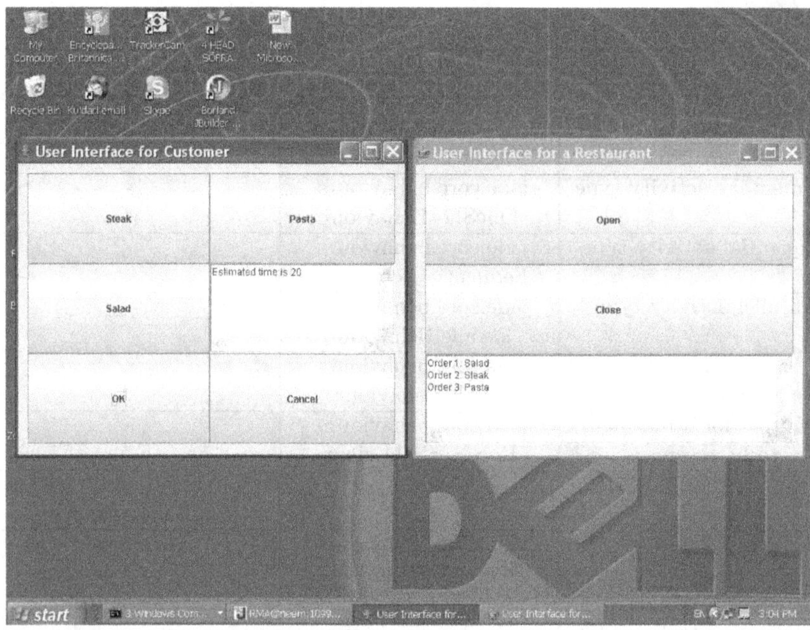

Fig. 7. A snapshot of the prototype created from the CIM and PIM models

only at the PSM level in terms of the constructs of a particular platform, which in our case study was JADE.

The first author has shown in earlier work [11,27] how to represent external AOR diagrams by a graphical tool, enabling mappings into equivalent XML-based representations that are then interpreted and executed by software agents. Since the authors of this paper no longer have access to that tool, we have mapped manually the models for the case study of the take-away food ordering system. However, this was not hard because of the intuitiveness and straightforwardness of the mappings under discussion.

5 Related Work and Conclusions

We have described a technique that maps models of a problem domain into the platform-independent design models of a socio-technical system created for that domain, and from the design models to the a system implementation on a specific platform. The mappings are straightforward, which has been achieved by making use of agent-oriented analysis and design models, as well as of an agent-based implementation platform. Representing the design models in a single diagram increases the transparency of the mappings.

This paper was triggered by the approach to prototyping described in [2]. While the message sequence charts used in [2] are claimed to represent requirements, we believe they are essentially design models. Our technique, on the contrary, starts with modelling requirements at a high level of abstraction that is understandable to both domain experts and software engineers. We acknowledge that we fall short of [2] in fully automated generation of models from design models. However, as has been shown in [11,27], this is not hard to accomplish with our approach, which we plan to do in the near future.

We emphasise that the contribution is that we can generate prototypes rapidly from high-level requirements prior to commitments to detailed design decisions. Other agent-oriented methodologies tend to concentrate on an ultimate agent implementation, and have not focussed on early rapid prototyping. While in principle this may be possible, for example, generating prototypes from Prometheus system overview diagrams [14], not all information such as agent beliefs have been identified or are available during requirements analysis and high level design.

Because of limited space, we confine specific comparisons with related work to other MDA-related model mapping techniques. CIM models employed in [15] represent agent component types, such as belief, trigger, plan, and step. Jayatilleke et al.'s approach assumes from the very beginning that a system will be implemented as a software agent system. However, in our view this is a *design decision*, which should be postponed until the design phase. Considering this, the starting point for our approach entails technology-independent notions of goals, roles, social policies, and domain entities. Differently from us, the approaches described in [28] and [29] address only mapping from PIM to PSM in the context of software agent systems, while our approach has a more generic software engineering stance.

In [25], agents in domain modelling are described in terms of their capabilities, which are then mapped into plans consisting of activities. Differently from [25], we view activities as fundamental concepts. This enables to distinguish between *contextual, goal-oriented, and routine activities.* The notion of norms used in [26] is roughly equivalent to what we mean by rules. However, we think that the work reported in [26] could benefit from the precise modelling of actions and events adopted by us.

In summary, our technique can be used for rapid production of prototypes from agent-oriented models. The technique has been used in industry-related projects of business-to-business electronic commerce [11,27], manufacturing simulation [24], and future home management [23]. We are currently applying the technique in a research project with industry dealing with airport simulation and optimisation.

References

1. MDA Guide Version 1.0.1. Retrieved February 3, 2007, from `http://www.omg.org/cgi-bin/doc?omg/03-06-01`
2. Barak, D., Harel, D., Marelly, R.: InterPlay: Horizontal scale-up and transition to design in scenario-based programming. IEEE Trans. Soft. Eng. 32(7), 467–485 (2006)
3. Juan, T., Sterling, L.: The ROADMAP meta-model for intelligent adaptive multi-agent systems in open environments (Revised Papers). In: Giorgini, P., Müller, J.P., Odell, J.J. (eds.) AOSE 2003. LNCS, pp. 826–837. Springer, Heidelberg (2004)

4. Kuan, P.P., Karunasakera, S., Sterling, L.: Improving goal and role oriented analysis for agent based systems. In: Proceedings of the 16th Australian Software Engineering Conference (ASWEC 2005), Brisbane, Australia, 31 March – 1 April 2005, pp. 40–47. IEEE Computer Society Press, Los Alamitos (2005)
5. Castelfranchi, C., Falcone, R.: From automaticity to autonomy: The frontier of artificial agents. In: Hexmoor, H., Castelfranchi, C., Falcone, R. (eds.) Agent Autonomy, pp. 103–136. Kluwer Academic Publishers, Dordrecht (2003)
6. Rao, A.S., Georgeff, M.P.: Modeling rational agents within a BDI architecture. In: Allen, J., Fikes, R., Sandewall, E. (eds.) Proceedings of Knowledge Representation 91 (KR-91), pp. 473–484. Morgan Kaufmann, San Francisco (1991)
7. Shoham, Y.: Agent-Oriented Programming. Artificial Intelligence 60(1), 51–92 (1993)
8. Wagner, G., Schroeder, M.: Vivid agents: Theory, architecture, and applications. Journal of Applied Artificial Intelligence 14(7), 645–675 (2000)
9. Taveter, K.: A multi-perspective methodology for agent-oriented business modelling and simulation. PhD thesis, Tallinn University of Technology, Estonia (ISBN 9985-59-439-8) (2004)
10. Henderson-Sellers, B., Giorgini, P. (eds.): Agent-oriented methodologies. Idea Group (2005)
11. Taveter, K., Wagner, G.: Towards radical agent-oriented software engineering processes based on AOR modelling. In: [10], pp. 277–316
12. Unified Modeling Language: Superstructure. Version 2.0 (August, 2003), Retrieved February 5, 2007 from `http://www.omg.org/cgi-bin/doc?ptc/2003-08-02`
13. Bellifemine, F., Poggi, A., Rimassa, G.: Developing multi-agent systems with a FIPA-compliant agent framework. Software - Practice and Experience 31, 103–128 (2001)
14. Padgham, L., Winikoff, M.: Developing intelligent agent systems. John Wiley & Sons, Chichester (2004)
15. Jayatilleke, G.B., Padgham, L., Winikoff, M.: A model driven component-based development framework for agents. Comput. Syst. Sci. & Eng. 20(4) (2005)
16. Kuutti, K.: Activity Theory as a potential framework for human-computer interaction research. In: Nardi, B. (ed.) Activity Theory and Human Computer Interaction, pp. 17–44. MIT Press, Cambridge (1995)
17. Rahwan, I., Juan, T., Sterling, L.: Integrating social modelling and agent interaction through goal-oriented analysis. Comput. Syst. Sci. & Eng. 21(2), 87–98 (2006)
18. DeLoach, S.A., Kumar, M.: Multi-agent systems engineering: An overview and case study. In: [10], pp. 317–340
19. Zambonelli, F., Jennings, N.R., Wooldridge, M.: Multi-agent systems as computational organizations: The Gaia methodology. In: [10], pp. 136–171
20. Caire, G., Coulier, W., Garijo, F., Gomez-Sanz, J., Pavon, J., Kearney, P., Massonet, P.: The MESSAGE methodology. In: Bergenti, F., Gleizes, M.-P., Zambonelli, F. (eds.) Methodologies and Software Engineering for Agent Systems: The Agent-Oriented Software Engineering Handbook, pp. 177–194. Kluwer Academic Publishers, Dordrecht (2004)
21. Cossentino, M.: From requirements to code with the PASSI methodology. In: [10], pp. 79–106
22. Iglesias, C. A., Garijo, M. The agent-oriented methodology MAS-CommonKADS. In: [10], pp. 46–78.

23. Sterling, L., Taveter, K.: The Daedalus Team. Building agent-based appliances with complementary methodologies. In: Tyugu, E., Yamaguchi, T. (eds.) Knowledge-Based Software Engineering: Proceedings of the Joint Conference on Knowledge-Based Software Engineering, Tallinn, Estonia, August 28-31, 2006, pp. 223–232. IOS Press, Amsterdam (2006)
24. Taveter, K., Wagner, G.: Agent-oriented modelling and simulation of distributed manufacturing. In: Rennard, J.-P. (ed.) Handbook of Research on Nature Inspired Computing for Economy and Management, pp. 541–556. Idea Group (2006)
25. Penserini, L., Perini, A., Susi, A., Mylopoulos, J.: From stakeholder intentions to software agent implementations. In: Dubois, E., Pohl, K. (eds.) CAiSE 2006. LNCS, vol. 4001, pp. 465–479. Springer, Heidelberg (2006)
26. Kasinger, H., Bauer, B.: Towards a model-driven software engineering methodology for organic computing systems. In: Hamza, M.H. (ed.) Computational Intelligence: IASTED International Conference on Computational Intelligence, Calgary, Alberta, Canada, July 4–6, 2005, pp. 141–146. IASTED/ACTA Press (2005)
27. Taveter, K.: A Technique and Markup Language for Business Process Automation. In: Proceedings of the Workshop on Vocabularies, Ontologies, and Rules for The Enterprise (VORTE 2006), held in conjunction with the Tenth IEEE International EDOC (The Enterprise Computing) Conference, Hong Kong, 16–20 October 2006, IEEE Computer Society Press, Los Alamitos (2006)
28. Perini, A., Susi, A.: Automating model transformations in agent-oriented modeling. In: Müller, J.P., Zambonelli, F. (eds.) AOSE 2005. LNCS, vol. 3950, pp. 167–178. Springer, Heidelberg (2006)
29. Hahn, C., Madrigal-Mora, C., Fischer, K., Elvester, B., Berre, A.-J., Zinnikus, I.: Metamodels, models, and model transformations: Towards interoperable agents. In: Fischer, K., Timm, I.J., André, E., Zhong, N. (eds.) MATES 2006. LNCS (LNAI), vol. 4196, pp. 123–134. Springer, Heidelberg (2006)

Introduction to AOSE Tools for the Conference Management System

Lin Padgham[1] and Michael Luck[2]

[1] School of Computer Science, RMIT University, Melbourne, Vic 3000, Australia
lin.padgham@rmit.edu.au
[2] Department of Computer Science, King's College London, UK
michael.luck@kcl.ac.uk

Abstract. Over several years, conference management systems have been used as an example to illustrate various aspects of computing, in particular agent-oriented software engineering methodologies. At AOSE in 2007, the conference management system was used as a basis for providing a comparison of different AOSE tools and methodologies from different researchers. This paper provides an overview of the basic system, and an introduction to the papers describing those methodologies and tools that follow.

1 Introduction

In the call for papers for AOSE 2007 we had requested submissions for a comparative designs track. Proponents of AOSE methodologies were asked to design a common system — a conference management system described in the literature, and to submit papers presenting the key aspects of the design using their methodology. The intention of this track was to provide alternative designs of a common system, thus allowing for a more direct comparison between methodologies, and also providing a useful resource to the community — namely a set of designs using different methodologies.

We also invited demonstrations of AOSE tools at AOSE 2007, and decided to combine these two aspects. We invited developers of three prominent AOSE methodologies, MaSE, Prometheus and Tropos, each with well developed toolkits, to demonstrate their respective tools by focussing on the design artefacts produced by the toolkit, in designing the Conference Management System. They were each asked to produce design handouts at the workshop, and to participate in a structured interactive toolkit presentation. Danilo Santos, who responded to the special track on comparative designs then presented his work in a similar way, within this session.

2 The Conference Management System Example

A multiagent conference management system was first proposed as an example by Ciancarini et al. [1] in 1998, and based on work describing conference management systems elsewhere (for example, [5]). It has since been widely used for

M. Luck and L. Padgham (Eds.): AOSE 2007, LNCS 4951, pp. 164–167, 2008.

the elaboration and application of different methodologies within agent-oriented software engineering [9,2,3] as it is suitable for illustrating a variety of aspects of multi-agent system analysis and design. It has also been used for other domains, including the illustration of systems related to mobile computation [4] and coordination systems and languages [6,7,8].

Presenters were referred to the version described in [3], as a focus for their design and toolkit presentations.

The conference management system is described as a multiagent system that supports the management of conferences that require the coordination of several individuals and groups to handle the paper selection process. This process includes paper submission, paper reviews, paper selection, author notification, final paper collection, and the printing of the proceedings. Authors may submit papers to the system up until the submission deadline.

Once the submission deadline has passed, members of the program committee (PC) review the papers by either contacting referees and asking them to review a number of the papers, or by reviewing them themselves. Once all the reviews are complete, a final decision is made on whether to accept or reject each paper. Each author is notified of this decision and authors with accepted papers are asked to produce a final version that must be submitted to the system. All final copies are collected and sent to the printer for publication in the conference proceedings.

As all the presenters were familiar with the conference reviewing process of the AAMAS conference, this also influenced the system designs. AAMAS has a Senior Program Committee each member of which oversees the reviewing of a set of papers by the Program Committee (or reviewers). Individual Senior Program Committee members then make recommendations to the Program Chairs to accept/reject the particular papers, based on the reviews.

3 Comparison of Methodologies and Tools

In particular, the conference management system provides a sufficiently generic problem description that can be used across multiple tools and techniques, yet is also sufficiently detailed to allow these tools and techniques to provide specific details that illustrate their features. In relation to the application of agent-oriented software engineering, there are several potential distinct points of comparison and evaluation, but we describe three key areas next.

Notation or Modeling Language: Among others, a *software methodology* is typically characterised by a *modeling language*, used for the description of models, and for defining the elements of the model together with a specific syntax or notation, and associated semantics. Indeed, accepted methods for industrial development must depend on standardised representations of artifacts supporting all phases of the software life cycle. In particular, these standardised representations are needed by tool developers to provide commercial-quality tools that mainstream software engineering departments need for industrial agent systems development.

Process: A *software methodology* is also characterised by a *software process*, defining the development activities, the interrelationships among the activities, and the ways in which the different activities are performed. In particular, the software process defines phases for process and project management as well as quality assurance. Each activity results in one or more deliverables, such as specification documents, analysis models, designs, code, testing specifications, testing reports, performance evaluation reports, and so on, serving as input for subsequent activities.

Tool Support: Tool support relates to the availability of software for deploying an agent infrastructure or for aiding in the development of agent applications. Agent toolkits aim at providing a significant proportion of the basic building blocks required to support an operational agent-based system. Of course, like development in many other domains, different methodologies will merit different kinds of tool support, often representing the underlying philosophy of the respective methodology developer about how agent-based systems should operate.

4 The AOSE 2007 Session

This session was concerned primarily with tools, but inevitably, other aspects must also be considered for any coherent presentation.

The tools session took place in four iterations, covering System specification, Architectural Design, Detailed Design, and other features/aspects. By iterating between the tools, using the same example, it was easy to see both similarities and differences. While each approach and each tool set has different strengths, there was also a substantial amount of agreement on key processes and design artefacts.

The session was very successful, and provided a valuable means of understanding and evaluating the relative features and benefits of the different approaches; as a result, the developers/presenters of Tropos, Prometheus and MaSE/O-MaSE were invited to contribute papers to this volume. These papers, together with the original paper from Santos et al., are contained in this section.

References

1. Ciancarini, P., Niestrasz, O., Tolksdorf, R.: A case study in coordination: Conference Management on the Internet (1998), `ftp://cs.unibo.it/pub/cianca/coordina.ps.gz`
2. Ciancarini, P., Omicini, A., Zambonelli, F.: Multiagent System Engineering: the Coordination Viewpoint. In: Jennings, N.R. (ed.) ATAL 1999. LNCS, vol. 1757, pp. 250–259. Springer, Heidelberg (2000)
3. DeLoach, S.: Modeling organizational rules in the multi-agent systems engineering methodology. In: AI 2002: Proceedings of the Fifteenth Conference of the Canadian Society for Computational Studies of Intelligence on Advances in Artificial Intelligence, London, UK, 2002, pp. 1–15. Springer, London (2002)

4. Durán, F., Verdejo, A.: A conference reviewing system in Mobile Maude. In: Gadducci, F., Montanari, U. (eds.) Proceedings of the Fourth International Workshop on Rewriting Logic and its Applications, WRLA 2002. Electronic Notes in Theoretical Computer Science, vol. 71, pp. 79–95. Elsevier, Amsterdam (2002)
5. Mathews, G.J., Jacobs, B.E.: Electronic management of the peer review process. In: Proceedings of the fifth international World Wide Web conference on Computer networks and ISDN systems, pp. 1523–1538. Elsevier Science Publishers B. V, Amsterdam, The Netherlands (1996)
6. Montangero, C., Semini, L.: Composing Specifications for Coordination. In: Ciancarini, P., Wolf, A.L. (eds.) COORDINATION 1999. LNCS, vol. 1594, pp. 118–133. Springer, Heidelberg (1999)
7. Rossi, D., Vitali, F.: Internet-based coordination environments and document-based applications: A case study. In: Ciancarini, P., Wolf, A.L. (eds.) COORDINATION 1999. LNCS, vol. 1594, pp. 259–274. Springer, Heidelberg (1999)
8. Scutellà, A.: Simulation of conference management using an even-driven coordination language. In: Ciancarini, P., Wolf, A.L. (eds.) COORDINATION 1999. LNCS, vol. 1594, pp. 243–258. Springer, Heidelberg (1999)
9. Zambonelli, F., Jennings, N.R., Wooldridge, M.: Organizational abstractions for the analysis and design of multi-agent system. In: Ciancarini, P., Wooldridge, M.J. (eds.) AOSE 2000. LNCS, vol. 1957, pp. 235–251. Springer, Heidelberg (2001)

Developing a Multiagent Conference Management System Using the O-MaSE Process Framework

Scott A. DeLoach

Department of Computing and Information Sciences, Kansas State University
234 Nichols Hall, Manhattan, KS 66506
sdeloach@cis.ksu.edu

Abstract. This paper describes how the Organization-based Multiagent Systems Engineering (O-MaSE) methodology can be applied to an exemplar multiagent system, the Conference Management System. First, a custom process for the CMS application is created using the O-MaSE Process Framework. Then, each task identified in the O-MaSE compliant process is performed and the appropriate models are generated. For the CMS system, we begin by creating a Goal Model via the Model Goals and Goal Refinement tasks. Once the Goal Model is complete, we create an Organization Model to capture all the interfaces to external actors and systems. After that, a Role Model is created to capture the functionality and the logical architecture of the system. Next, based on the Role Model, an Agent Class Model is created. The details of the agents and protocols identified in the Agent Class Model are further refined into several Protocol Models and Agent Plan Models.

1 Introduction

The purpose of this paper is to describe how the Organization-based Multiagent Systems Engineering (O-MaSE) methodology [4] can be applied to a particular example multiagent system, the Conference Management System, which is described earlier in the volume.

The Organization-based Multiagent System Engineering (O-MaSE) methodology is actually a process framework that helps process engineers to create customized agent-oriented software development processes. O-MaSE consists of three basic structures: (1) a metamodel, (2) a set of methods fragments, and (3) a set of guidelines. The O-MaSE metamodel defines the key concepts needed to design and implement multiagent systems. The method fragments are operations or tasks that are executed to produce a set of work products, which may include models, documents, or code. The guidelines define how the method fragments are related to one another. Because O-MaSE is really a framework for creating custom multiagent systems development processes and not a single process, the first step is to define an appropriate O-MaSE compliant process. The O-MaSE

M. Luck and L. Padgham (Eds.): AOSE 2007, LNCS 4951, pp. 168–181, 2008.

compliant process described in this paper is presented in Section 2. Once our custom process is defined, we present each step of the process in Section 3. Finally, we conclude in Section 4 with our conclusions and future work.

2 O-MaSE Process

The first step in using O-MaSE to define a CMS system is the creation of an appropriate custom process for the CMS application using the O-MaSE Process Framework [4]. As a detailed discussion of the task selection criteria is beyond the scope of this paper, it should be pointed out that the CMS system is made up of agents representing specific humans playing specific roles in the organization and thus, there is no requirement for an autonomously adaptive system. Thus, the definition of individual capabilities of the roles and agents are not required.

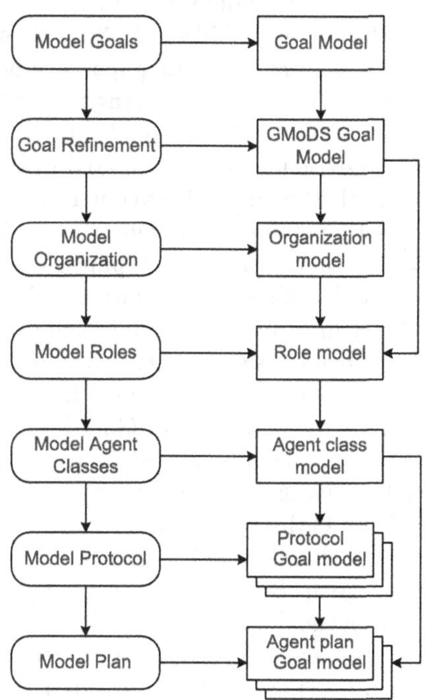

Fig. 1. CMS O-MaSE Compliant Process

The process defined for designing the CMS system is shown in Figure 1. Assuming there exists some kind of system requirements or system definition, we begin by creating a goal tree and refining it into a GMoDS Goal Model via the Model Goals and Goal Refinement tasks. Once the Goal Model is complete, we create an Organization Model to capture all the interfaces to external actors and systems. Once the Organization Model is complete, it and the GMoDS Goal

Model are used to create the initial Role Model. Based on the Role Model, an Agent Class Model is created. The details of the agents and protocols identified in the Agent Class Model are further refined into several Protocol Models and Agent Plan Models. While we chose to define the Protocol Models based on the Agent Class Model, we could have also defined the protocols after creating the Organization Model or the Role Model, as each of those identifies protocols as well.

3 Modeling CMS in O-MaSE

3.1 Goal Model

The first step in our O-MaSE compliant process is to create an initial Goal Model that captures the essential requirements of the CMS system as defined in the system definition or requirements documents. The initial Goal Model for the CMS system is shown in Figure 2. The Model Goals task uses traditional AND/OR refinement to decompose the top-level CMS goal, `Manage submissions`, into six AND-refined subgoals: `Get papers`, `Assign papers`, `Review papers`, `Select papers`, `Inform authors`, and `Print proceedings`. The UML aggregation notation is used to represent AND-refinement while the UML generalization notation is used to represent OR-refinement. Each goal in the model is annotated by the keyword ≪goal≫. All the subgoals except `Review papers` are further decomposed into subgoals that define what must be accomplished in order to achieve the given goal. For instance, the `Select papers` goal is AND-refined into a `Collect reviews` goal and a `Make decision` goal. Notice that the `Inform authors` goal is OR-refined into an `Inform declined` and `Inform accepted` subgoals. Obviously, the subgoal used to satisfy the `Inform authors` goal is based on the decision made whether to accept or reject the paper.

The Goal Refinement task takes the initial Goal Model and adds additional information to capture the dynamism associated with the CMS system. Specifically, we refine our initial model into a model based on the Goal Model for Dynamic Systems (GMoDS) [6]. GMoDS introduces three concepts into AND/OR goal modeling approaches to handle goal sequencing, the creation of goal instances, and parameterized goals. Sequencing of goals is provided by goal precedence, which specifies that one goal must be achieved before a second goal can be achieved. Goal instances are created based on events that occur during system operation. Goals without a specific trigger are created at system initialization, while other goals are created when specific events occur. Finally, goals can be parameterized to fully define what the purpose of the goal is. For instance, in the CMS system, we have a goal to `Review papers`. However, this goal is ambiguous until we specify which set of papers to be reviewed. Thus, we add a parameter to the goal to specify the papers to be reviewed.

The GMoDS Goal Model for the CMS system is shown in Figure 3. The GMoDS model has the same basic shape as shown in Figure 2, but with additional arrows between goals showing precedence and goal triggering as well parameters for several goals. In the Figure 2, precedence between goals is shown

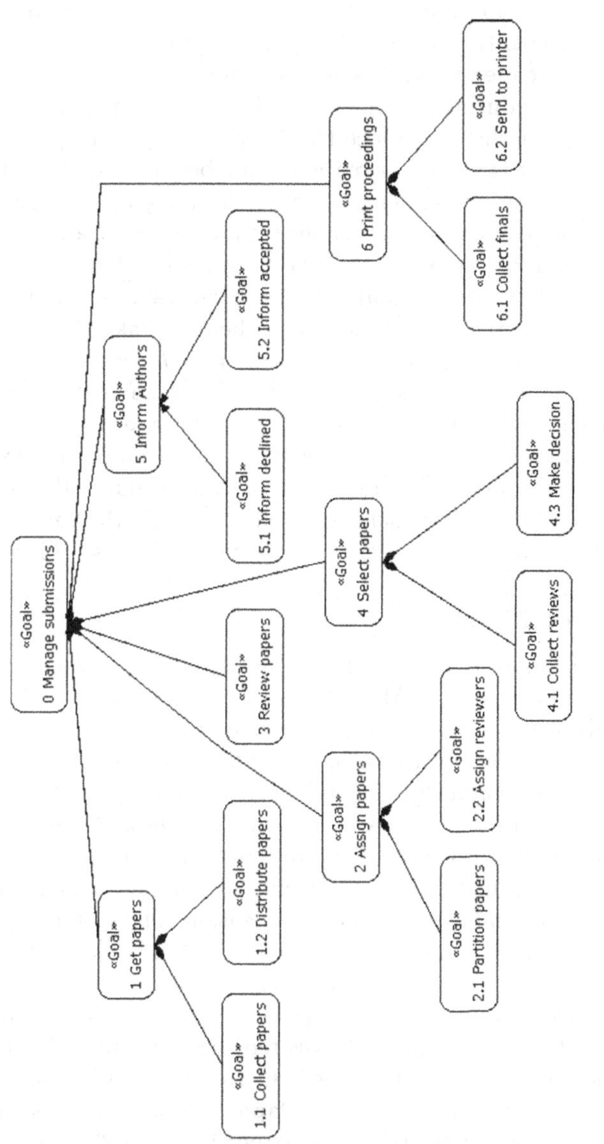

Fig. 2. CMS AND/OR Goal Model

by an arrow labeled with the ≪precedes≫ keyword while triggers are represented by arrows between goals with an event name and a set of parameters in the form *event*($p_1, ...p_n$). Reading Figure 3 we can see that the `Collect papers` goal precedes both the `Distribute papers` and `Assign papers` goals. Thus, once the `Collect papers` goal is achieved, the papers may be distributed and the `Partition papers` goal (a sub-goal of `Assign papers`) can begin. The trigger between `Partition papers` and `Assign reviewers` denotes that each time a set of papers is *created* during the pursuit of the `Partition papers` goal, a new goal is instantiated for that set. Once the `Partition papers` goal is achieved, the pursuit of the `Assign reviewers` goal can begin on each of the `Assign reviewers` goals. As an assignment is made, the *assign(p,r)* trigger creates a new goal to `Review papers` for each paper set and reviewer assigned.

When all the `Review papers` goals have been achieved, the `Select papers` goal can be pursued via its subgoals: `Collect reviews` and `Make decision`. When the `Collect reviews` goal is achieved, then the `Make decision` goal can be pursued. As a decision is made on each paper, a *declined(p,a)* or *accepted(p,a)* event occurs. If a paper is declined, an `Inform decline` goal for that paper is instantiated while if a paper is accepted, both an `Inform accepted` and `Collect finals` goal is instantiated for that paper. Once all the `Collect finals` goals are achieved, then the `Send to printer` goal can be pursued. Assuming the `Inform authors` goals have been achieved, achievement of the `Send to printer` goal achieves all the sub-goals and the overall system goal is achieved.

3.2 Organization Model

The Organization Model is created using the Model Organization task, which takes as input the GMoDS Goal Model derived in the previous task. The aim of this task is to identify system's (which is referred to as the organization) interfaces with external actors. In the case of the CMS system (see Figure 4), the system interfaces with the committee (including the `PC chair` and the `reviewers`), the `Authors`, and the `Printer`. The various ways that the actors interact with the system are modeled as protocols, which are represented by arrows from the initiator of the protocol to the responder. The initiator and responder of an protocol must be either an external actor or the organization. The system is represented as an organization, which is denoted using the ≪Organization≫ keyword.

As stated above, the `CMS` organization interacts with `Authors`, the `PC chair`, `Reviewers`, and the `Printer`. Each of these are shown as actors in Figure 4. Using the system description, the protocols required for interaction between the organization and the actors are identified. In the `CMS` system, an `Author` submits papers to the system using the `submitPaper` protocol. After being reviewed, the `CMS` notifies the `Author` whether their paper is accepted or rejected via the `informAuthor` protocol. If the paper was accepted, the `Author` then submits the final version of the paper using the `submitFinal` protocol. The `PC chair` actor works with the `CMS` by partitioning papers into sets via the `partitionPaper` protocol and then assigns various reviewers to review those sets of papers via the

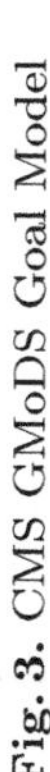

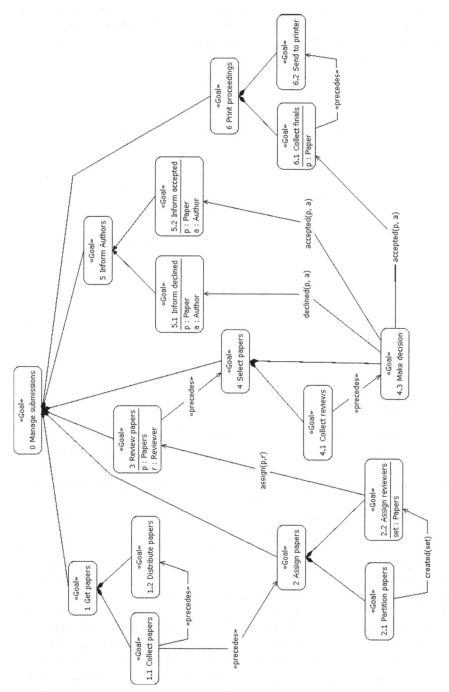

Fig. 3. CMS GMoDS Goal Model

`selectReviewers` protocol. Once the reviews are complete, the `PC chair` makes the final selections via the `selectPapers` protocols. The `Reviewers` accept or reject their assignments via the `getOK` protocol and submit their reviews via the `submitReviews` protocol. Finally, the final papers are sent to the `Printer` for printing via the `printProceedings` protocol.

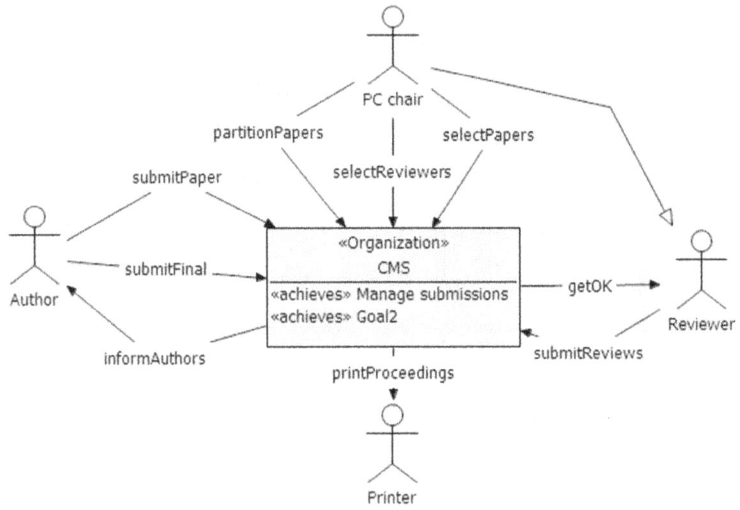

Fig. 4. CMS Organization Model

3.3 Role Model

The Role Model is developed using the Organization Model and the GMoDS Goal Model defined earlier in the process. This focus of the Role Modeling task is to identify the roles required in the organization and their interactions (defined via protocols) with each other. The actors from the Organization Model should show up as actors in the Role Model and the protocols between the actors and the organization must be mapped to protocols between those actors and specific roles in the system. Thus, the Role Model is a refinement of the Organization Model. In addition, each leaf goal in the GMoDS Goal Model must be assigned to a role in the Role Model that can achieve it, as denoted by the ≪achieves≫ keyword in the body of the role. Thus, each role should achieve at least one leaf goal, although in general, a role may achieve multiple leaf goals.

The Role Model for the CMS system is shown in Figure 5. In the CMS system, there are seven roles: the `PaperDB`, the `Paritioner`, the `Assigner`, the `PCreviewer`, the `ReviewCollector`, `FinalsCollector`, and `DecisionMaker`. The `PaperDB` role acts as the collection and distribution mechanism in the CMS. `Authors` submit papers to the `PaperDB`, while the `Partitioner`, `PCreviewer`, and `FinalsCollector` roles access the papers, abstracts, and final versions via protocols with the `PaperDB`. When all the papers have been submitted, the `PC` chair interacts with the Paritioner role to look at the various abstracts and assign them to groups to be assigned reviewers. Once this task is complete, the PC chair interacts with the Assigner role to select reviewers to assign to each set of papers. The Assigner role then interacts with the PCreviewer role via the reviewPapers protocol, which interacts with the Reviewer via the getOK protocol. The Reviewer then reviews the papers and submits them to the PCreviewer role using the writeReviews protocol. The PCreviewer role then sends the reviews to the ReviewCollector role. Once all the reviews have been submitted, the PC chair interacts with the DecisionMaker role to select papers for the conference. The status of the papers are relayed to their authors by the DecisionMaker role via the informAuthors protocol. Once the Author completes the final version, the paper is submitted to the PaperDB via the submitFinal protocol. When all the final papers have been submitted, the papers are then forwarded to the Printer from the FinalsCollector via the printProceedings protocol.

3.4 Agent Class Model

Once the roles have been defined, the analysis phase is complete and the analysis models are transformed into design models that more closely match the final implementation form. For the CMS system, this includes creating an Agent Class Model via the Model Agent Classes task. The goal of this task is to translate the role model, which captures basic system functionality, into a form more amenable to implementation. In short, this means mapping roles to agent classes. The result of this mapping for the CMS system is shown in Figure 6. The roles that each agent has been assigned to play are embedded in the body of the agent classes and are prefixed with the keyword ≪plays≫. The agent classes are denoted by the ≪Agent≫ keyword.

While the assignment of roles to agents is made by the designer, typical software engineering concepts such as coupling and cohesion should be used to evaluate the assignment. In the CMS system, two agent classes play two roles, while the other two classes play a single role each. The PCmember agent has been assigned to play both the Assigner and Paritioner roles and thus interacts with the PC chair. Likewise, the PCchair agent also plays two roles – ReviewCollector and DecisionMaker – while also interacting with the PC chair. The Referee agent plays the PCreviewer role and interacts with the Reviewer, while the Database agent plays the PaperDB role and interacts with the Authors and the Printer. Notice that the protocols between roles in the Role Model have been mapped to protocols between the appropriate agents in the Agent Class Model.

After the Agent Model is complete, the agent classes and protocols have been identified, but not defined. The remaining two tasks – Model Protocols and Model Plans – are used to define the low-level design of the individual agents. The Model Protocols task is performed first, followed by the Model Plans task.

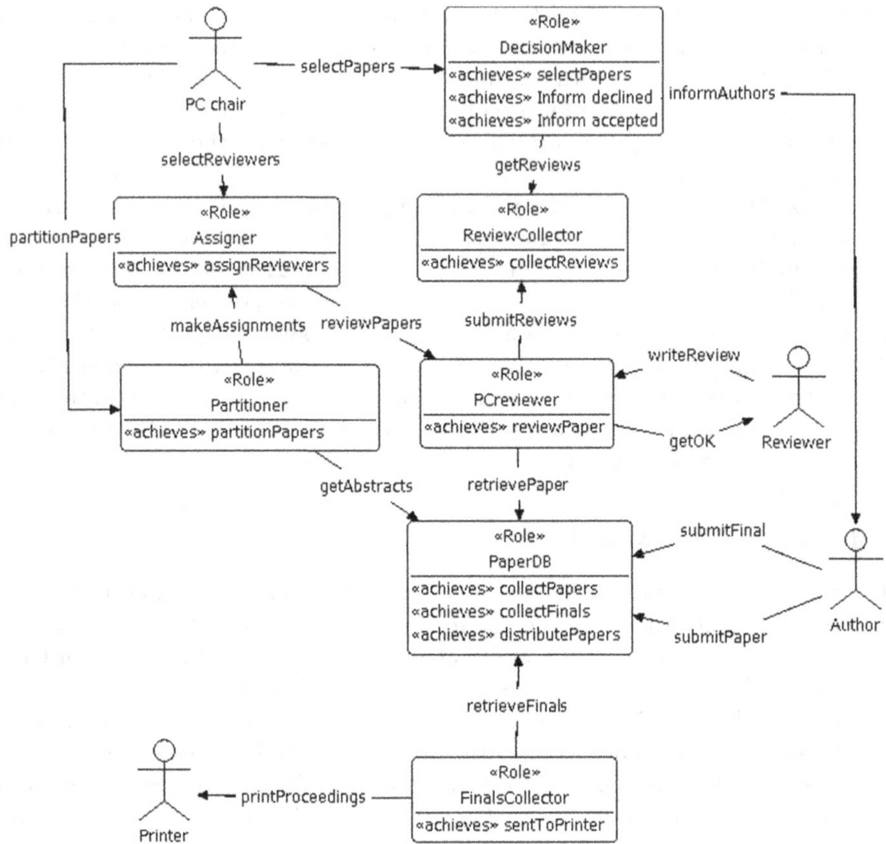

Fig. 5. CMS Role Model

3.5 Protocol Models

The goal of the Model Protocols task is to define the details of the protocols identified in the Role Model and Agent Class Model. The Protocol Model defines the protocol in terms of messages passed between agents or between agents and external actors. As there were 13 protocols identified in the Agent Class Model (Figure 6), we must define each of the 13 protocols with individual Protocol Models. The protocols are modeled using the AUML Interaction Diagrams [5], which allow us to specify message sequences, alternatives, loops, and references to other protocols.

Due to space constraints, we will only present three of the 13 protocol models: `reviewPapers`, `submitReviews`, and `retrievePapers`. Figure 7 shows the `reviewPapers` protocol, which defines the interaction between the `PCmember` and `Referee` agents, which are specified by the ≪Agent≫ keyword (protocols can also be specified between agents and actors using the same method). This protocol is very simple. The `PCmember` sends a `reviewpapers` message with a

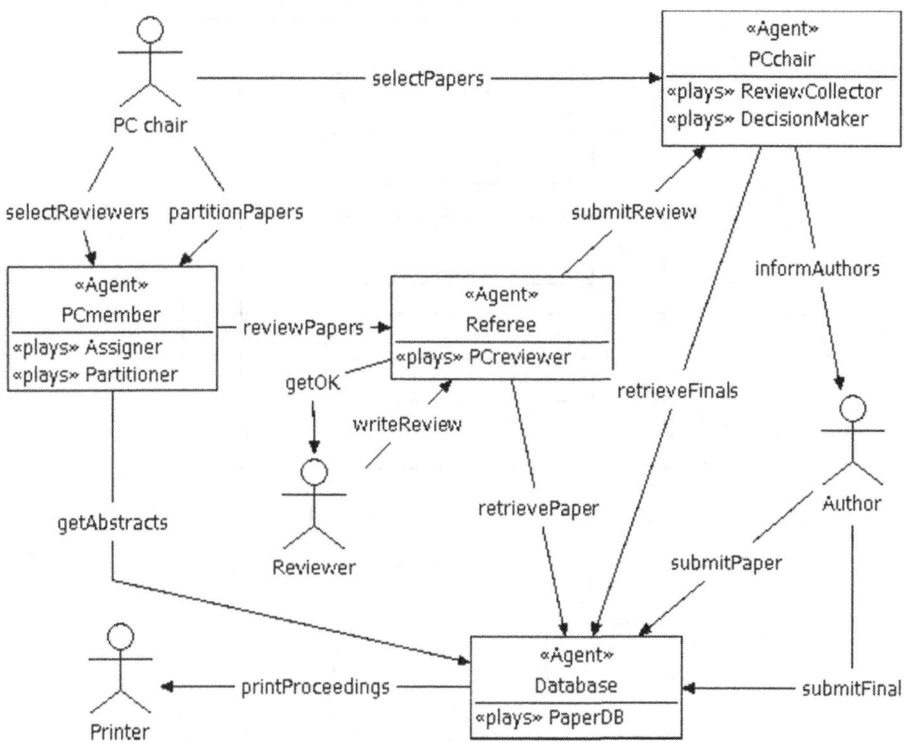

Fig. 6. CMS Agent Model

list of *paperIDs* for the `Referee` to review. The `Referee` may respond by either accepting or declining to review the set using the `accept` and `decline` messages respectively.

Figure 8 shows the `submitReviews` protocol, which defines the interaction between the `Referee` agent and the `PCchair` agent. In this protocol, the `Referee` sends several reviews via a `submit` message to the `PCchair` followed by a `done` message. There is no response by the `PCchair`.

Figure 9 shows the `retrievePapers` protocol, which defines a simple request protocol between the `Referee` and `Database` agents. According to the protocol, the `Referee` issues a request to the `Database` for a set of papers via a `request` message. The `Database` simply responds with the appropriate set of papers in a `receive` message.

3.6 Agent Plan Models

The last design models developed in our O-MaSE compliant process are the Agent Plan Models. Basically, a plan represents a mean by which agents can satisfy a goal in the organization, thus a plan can be viewed as an algorithm for achieving a specific goal. Again, because there are four different agents defined in the Agent Class Model, there should be at least four Agent Plan Models

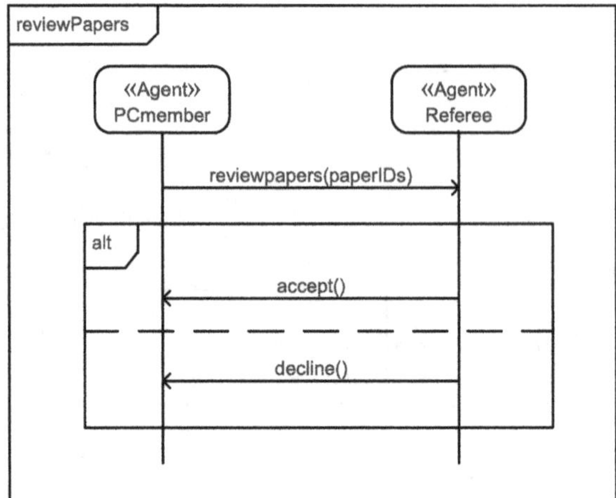

Fig. 7. CMS reviewPapers Protocol Model

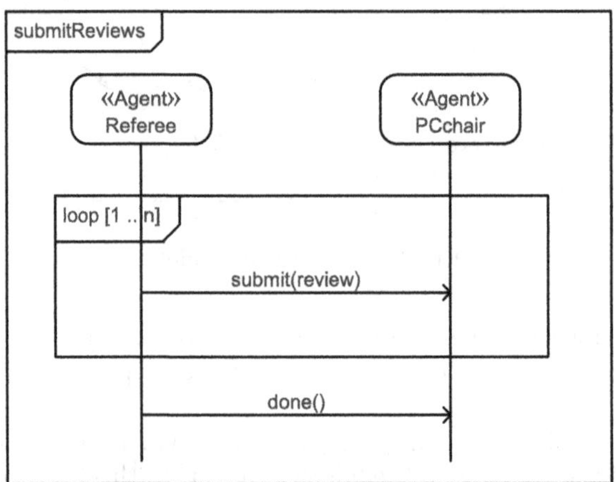

Fig. 8. CMS submitReviews Protocol Model

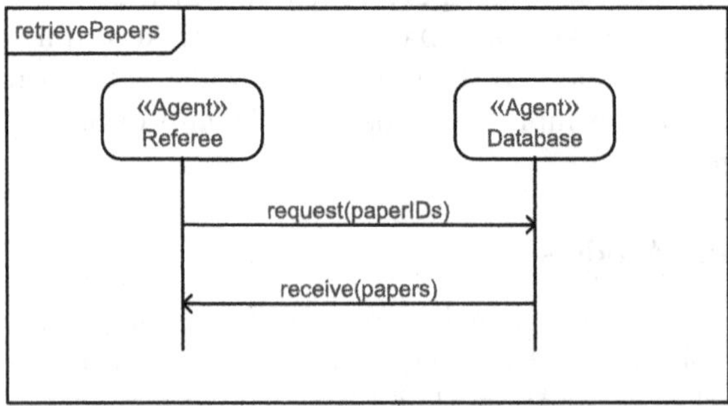

Fig. 9. CMS retrievePapers Protocol Model

developed, one for each agent. Depending on the internal architecture chosen for each agent, we could develop multiple Agent Plan Models for each agent. This might be the case when we wanted a unique plan for each role an agent could play or if we could choose between multiple plans to achieve the same goal. In either case, the agent architecture would be responsible for selecting the appropriate plans and interleaving their execution if required.

O-MaSE plans are modeled using a finite state automata to specify a single thread of control that defines the behavior that the agent should exhibit. As such, each plan has a `start state` and an `end state`. All messages are sent and received on state transitions. For the Plan Model, the syntax of the transitions is `[ guard ] receive(message,sender) / send (message,receiver)`. The `guard` defines a boolean condition that determines if the transition is enabled. The `receive(message,sender)` is a message that is received from the `sender` agent that enables the transition, while the `send(message,receiver)` is a message sent to the `receiver` agent when the transition occurs. Messages are specified in the form $performative(p_1...p_n)$, where the $performative$ is the name of the message and $p_1...p_n$ are the parameters of the message. Each part of the transition is optional and a null transition may exist between two states.

Each state has a (possibly empty) set of actions that are executed sequentially once the state is entered. Each action is represented in the form of a function that returns a value. These actions may represent internal computations of the agent or be part of interactions with objects in the environment. Transitions out of a state are not enabled until all actions have returned their values. The parameters to the actions, the action return values, and all parameters in messages in the plan are considered variables within a single name space, thus a parameter `X` of a message is the same as the return value of an action `X`.

Figure 10 shows the Plan Model for the Reviewer agent. The plan starts upon receipt of a `reviewpapers` message from the `PCmember` agent. Immediately upon receipt of the message, the agent sends a `request` message to the `Database` agent to get the papers identified by the list of paper identifiers, *paperIDs*, and moves into the `Wait` state. When the `Database` returns a list of the *papers* requested, the plan moves into the `Evaluate` state where it interacts with its associated `Reviewer` via the `getOK` action. If the `Review` does not agree to review the set of papers, a `decline` message is sent to the `PCmember` agent and the plan ends. However, if the `Review` does agree to review the set of papers, an `accept` message is sent to the `PCmember` agent and the plan moves to the `Review` state. In the `Review` state, the plan interacts with the `Reviewer` via the `getSelectedPaper` and `getReview` actions. Every time a review is completed, the *review* is submitted to the `PCchair` agent via a `submit` message and the the list of *papers* is reduced in size. Once the *papers* list is empty, the plan moves into the `Done` state and immediately sends a `done` message to the `PCchair` agent.

As the Agent Plan Model implements the protocols identified in the Agent Class Model and defined in the Protocol Models, it is critical that a Plan Model be consistent with all Protocol Models that it is required to implement. Thus, by looking at Figure 6, we can see that `Referee` agent must implement the

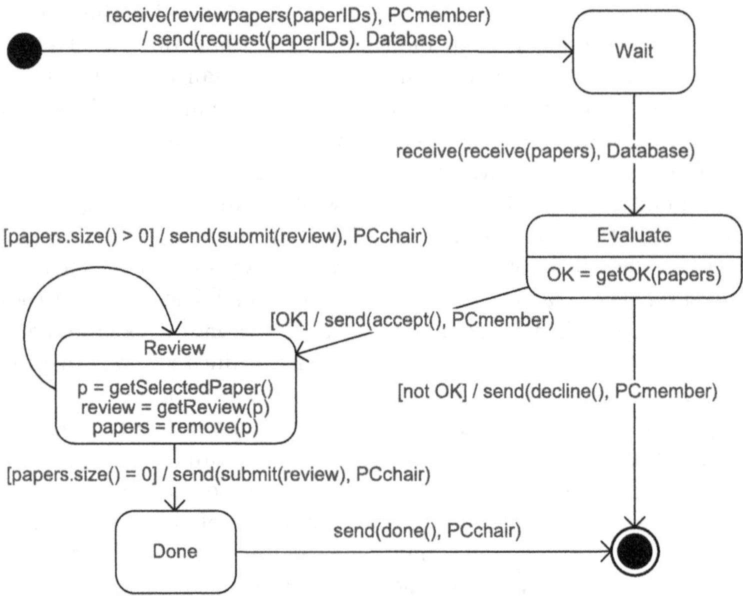

Fig. 10. CMS Plan Model

`reviewPapers`, `getOK`, `writeReview`, `retrievePapers` and `submitReview` protocols. While the `getOK` and `writeReview` protocols interact with the `Reviewer` actor and are implemented as action, we can analyze the `reviewPapers`, `retrievePapers` and `submitReview` protocols with the `Referee` Agent Plan Model to verify that they are indeed consistent.

4 Conclusion and Future Work

This paper has presented an example of an O-MaSE complaint process for the Conference Management System example. After defining a custom process for this example, we showed how to step through each of the tasks to create a set of models that eventually resulted in a set of Agent Plan Model that describe how to implement the set of agents required for the system. While the example showed several of the main O-MaSE tasks and models, it did not include several potentially powerful concepts supported by O-MaSE as defined in [4]. Specifically, we did not use the Define Roles, Model Domain, or Model Policies, tasks. We also did not do detailed design that would have included the tasks of Model Capabilities and Model Actions.

The approach we used also reflected a traditional approach to designing agent systems. That is, we identified a set of roles and then designed specific agent classes to perform those roles. While this approach is straightforward and is very useful for the CMS system, it does not reflect the power of the O-MaSE approach for modeling highly adaptive systems. By incorporating the notion of capabilities within O-MaSE, we allow designers to design much more flexible and adaptive multiagent systems. Instead of assigning roles directly to specific agent classes, we define roles in terms of the capabilities required to carry out that role and agent classes in terms of the capabilities they posses. Role behavior is then specified in terms of a Role Plan Model that uses its required capabilities to implement the actions in the plan. By specifying roles and agents in terms of capabilities required or possessed, the assignment of roles to specific agents can be delayed until runtime. When a goal is instantiated that requires a specific role, the agent that has all the required capabilities of the role can be selected to play that role to achieve a specific goal.

We are continuing to add new tasks and models to O-MaSE to allow it to be even more flexible and useful. We are currently encoding O-MaSE to be used in the Eclipse Process Framework (EPF) tool [7], which allows designers to pick and choose method fragments to create custom processes. While the EPF supports the main concepts we need to define O-MaSE, we are looking into extending EPF to allow us to formally verify that the custom process created is actually O-MaSE compliant.

We are also developing agentTool III (aT3) [2] to support O-MaSE modeling. aT3 is being developed by an Eclipse plugin and will be available at the aT3 web site. The Goal Model, Organization Model, Role Model, and Agent Class Model were all created using a prototype of aT3.

Acknowledgments

This work was supported by grants from the US National Science Foundation (0347545) and the US Air Force Office of Scientific Research (FA9550-06-1-0058).

References

1. DeLoach, S.A.: Engineering Organization-based Multiagent Systems. In: Garcia, A., Choren, R., Lucena, C., Giorgini, P., Holvoet, T., Romanovsky, A. (eds.) SELMAS 2005. LNCS, vol. 3914, pp. 109–125. Springer, Heidelberg (2006)
2. DeLoach, S.A.: Multiagent & Cooperative Robotics Laboratory. agentTool III Home Page (April 2007), `http://agenttool.projects.cis.ksu.edu/`
3. DeLoach, S.A., Mark, F.: Wood and Clint H. Sparkman, Multiagent Systems Engineering, The International Journal of Software Engineering and Knowledge Engineering 11(3), 231–258 (2001)
4. Garcia-Ojeda, J.C., DeLoach, S.A., Robby, O.W.H., Valenzuela, J.: A Customizable Approach to Developing Multiagent Development Processes. In: Luck, M., Padgham, L. (eds.) AOSE 2007. LNCS, vol. 4951, pp. 1–15. Springer, Heidelberg (2008)
5. Huget, M., Odell, J.: Representing Agent Interaction Protocols with Agent UML. In: Proceedings of the Third international Joint Conference on Autonomous Agents and Multiagent Systems. International Conference on Autonomous Agents, Washington, DC, vol. 3, pp. 1244–1245. IEEE Computer Society, Los Alamitos (2004)
6. Miller, M.: A Goal Model for Dynamic Systems. Master's Thesis, Dept. of Computing and Information Sciences, Kansas State University (2007)
7. The Eclipse Foundation. Eclipse Process Framework Project Home Page (April 2007), `http://www.eclipse.org/epf/`

Tool-Supported Development with Tropos: The Conference Management System Case Study

Mirko Morandini, Duy Cu Nguyen, Anna Perini, Alberto Siena, and Angelo Susi

Fondazione Bruno Kessler - IRST
Via Sommarive, 18
38050 Trento, Italy
{morandini,cunduy,perini,siena,susi}@itc.it

Abstract. The agent-oriented software engineering methodology *Tropos* offers a structured development process and supporting tools for developing complex, distributed systems.

The objective of this paper is twofold: first, to illustrate the use of *Tropos* to develop a Multi-Agent System, performing basic analysis and design activities, code generation and testing, with the support of a set of tools; second, to enable the comparison with other, tool-supported, agent-oriented software engineering methodologies through a description of the main steps of these activities and of excerpts of the resulting artefacts, with reference to a common case study, namely, the Conference Management System case study.

1 Introduction

Many Agent-Oriented Software Engineering (AOSE) methodologies have been proposed over the last years [13,7]. This fact motivated research on how to compare and evaluate these methodologies, with the purpose of pointing out differences and complementarities, and of giving criteria for selecting the most appropriate methodology, for a given development scenario [13,5].

While this research field is becoming more mature, a need is emerging for detailed guidelines when applying a methodology along core phases in the software development process, and for supporting tools. This is considered a crucial step towards the adoption of AOSE methodology by industry.

The *Tropos* methodology, proposed in [3], is an agent-oriented methodology for developing complex, distributed systems. A peculiarity of *Tropos* is that it adopts a requirement driven approach to software development, recognizing a pivotal role to the modelling of domain stakeholders and to the analysis of their goals, before generating a design for the system-to-be. System design then consists in specifying software agents who have their own goals and capabilities that are intended to support the fulfilment of stakeholder goals.

M. Luck and L. Padgham (Eds.): AOSE 2007, LNCS 4951, pp. 182–196, 2008.

Further research on the *Tropos* methodology focused on its application in developing specific classes of applications, as for instance distributed knowledge management systems [23]. Moreover, extensions of its modelling language have been proposed to support the analysis of crucial issues in distributed systems, such as trust and security [10]. Several tools have been built as well. *TAOM4e*, for supporting a model-driven, agent-oriented approach to software development [19,17], the T-Tool [9], for performing model-checking of *Tropos* specifications, the GR-Tool for supporting formal reasoning on goal models [12], multi-agent planning for supporting the selection among alternative networks of delegations [4].

The main objectives of this paper are: first, to illustrate how to use *Tropos* to develop a Multi-Agent System (MAS), performing basic analysis and design activities, generating code and performing testing on it, with the support of a set of tools; second, to enable the comparison with other tool-supported AOSE methodologies through a description of the main steps of these activities and of excerpts of the resulting artefacts, with reference to a common case study, namely, the Conference Management System (CMS) case study [6].

The paper is structured as follows. Section 2 recalls basic development activities in *Tropos* and gives a short description of the tools that support them. Requirements analysis is described in Section 3, system design is described in Section 4, code generation and testing in Section 5. Considerations emerged during the development of the CMS case study are discussed in Section 6. Finally, conclusion and future work are presented in Section 7.

2 Tropos Development Process and Tools

The software development process in *Tropos* is structured in five main phases, namely: early requirements analysis that focuses on the understanding of the existing organizational setting where the system-to-be will be introduced; late requirements that deals with the analysis of the system-to-be; architectural design that defines the system's global architecture in terms of subsystems; detailed design that specifies the system agents micro-level; implementation that concerns code generation according to the detailed design specifications.

This development process is model-based, that is, requirements and design models are core artefacts. They are built using a conceptual modelling language, derived from the i* framework [24]. This modelling activity, called Agent-Oriented (AO) modelling in Fig. 1, spans the first four phases in the software development process. Basic concepts of the modelling language are those of actor, goal, plan and dependency for goal achievement.[1] AO modelling can be performed using the *TAOM4e* modelling tool [19]. The tool has been extended to support automatic code generation from the *Tropos* specification into *JADE* [1] or *Jadex* [20] MAS, by exploiting a mapping between the *Tropos* meta-model concepts and the target implementation languages constructs [18,15].

[1] UML activity and sequence diagrams may be used as well for detail design in *Tropos*.

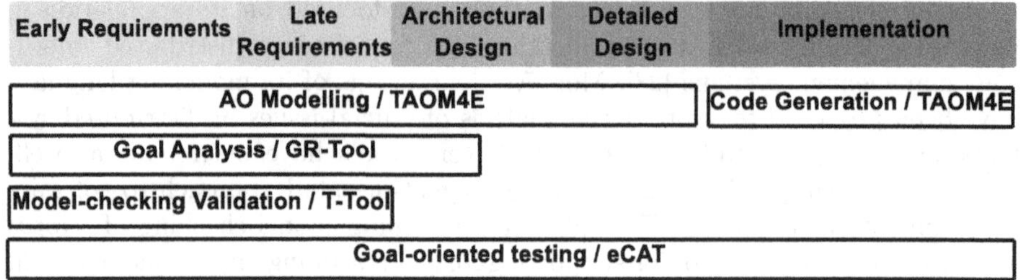

Fig. 1. Development Process Phases: Activities and Supporting Tools

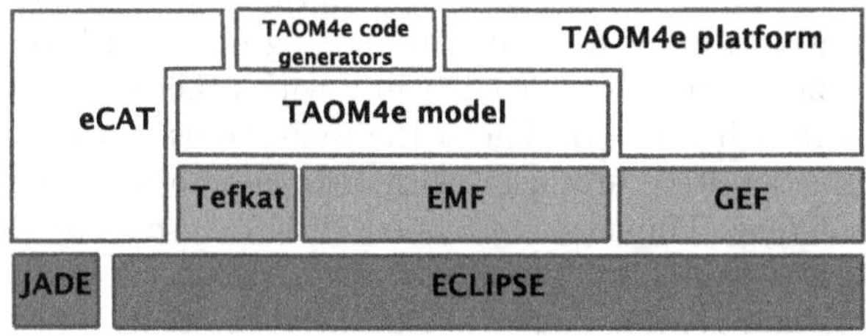

Fig. 2. Architecture of *TAOM4e* and *eCAT*

Other tool-supported analysis techniques are available in *Tropos*, such as validation of requirements specification via model-checking (see T-Tool [9]) or formal analysis on goal models of requirements and system design (see GR-Tool [12]). These types of analysis are particularly useful in case of complex models. They will be not described in this paper.

Goal-Oriented testing has been recently proposed as a complementary activity to AO modelling and code generation activities [16]. The basic idea is that of deriving test cases directly from the AO specifications produced along the development process with the aim to support testing and validation along the process phases. In this paper we will illustrate agent and integration testing as supported by the eCAT tool [16].

A high-level architecture of the tooled environment is described below, while the use of the tools during the development of the CMS system will be illustrated in the following sections.

2.1 TAOM4e and Code Generation Functions

TAOM4e[2] is a graphical *Tropos* modelling framework, which supports modelling in all phases of the *Tropos* process. It is realized as a plug-in for the Eclipse[3] project and extends existing plug-ins, as shown in Fig. 2: the EMF plug-in[4] offers

[2] `http://sra.itc.it/tools/taom4e`

[3] `http://www.eclipse.org`

[4] `http://www.eclipse.org/emf`

a modelling framework and code generation facility for building tools and other applications based on a model specification described in XMI; the Graphical Editing Framework (GEF) plug-in[5] allows to create a graphical editor from an existing application model; the Tefkat plug-in[6] provides a rule-based language to implement model to model transformation.

The *Tropos* metamodel has been implemented on top of EMF (*TAOM4e* model), GEF is used to realize the graphical representation of the model and the different views on it (*TAOM4e* platform), whereas the Tefkat plug-in is used to transform top-level plans and their decompositions into UML activity diagrams. The resulting diagrams can be edited using any UML2 editor and further detailed with sequence diagrams, which define communication protocols among agents.

Fig. 3 shows a screen-shot of the *TAOM4e* GUI.

The *TAOM4e* modeller is enriched with *TAOM4e* generators to derive skeletons of code for the *JADE* and *Jadex* agent platforms, directly from an UML specification of detailed design artefacts or from a *Tropos* goal model. *TAOM4e* generators include *UML2JADE*, *t2x*, and *Tropos2UML*. *Tropos2UML* can be used to generate UML activities diagrams from *Tropos* goal model, while *UML2JADE* can generate *JADE* agent code from UML activity and sequence diagrams that specify *Tropos* plans (capabilities), details are given in [17].

The part of an agent that is responsible for choosing the right plans at runtime in order to reach the desired goals is called *knowledge level*. In an agent's *GM*, the *knowledge level* consists of goals and their decomposition, contributions, dependencies to other agents and means-end relations to plans. These are inputs for the *t2x* (namely *Tropos* to *Jadex*) tool. The tool generates skeletons for agents following the *BDI architecture*, and they are executable on the Jade BDI agent platform [21]. The mapping between *Tropos* goal model elements and *Jadex* construct is described in [18,14].

The generated code skeleton implements the reasoning part of a software agent. It consists of an *Agent Definition File* (ADF), in XML format, which defines goals, plans, beliefs and messages for every system agent in the *GM*. The single plans can be implemented in Java files, which can be associated to the elements in the ADF.

2.2 eCAT

eCAT[7] implements our method for automated continuous testing of MAS, supporting a goal-oriented testing approach [16]. The tool facilitates test suites derivation from goals analysis and generates semi-automatically test suites from goal analysis diagrams produced with *TAOM4e*. It also provides GUIs to help human testers specifying test inputs and oracles. Moreover, *eCAT* can evolve and generate more test inputs during the course of testing, and run these test inputs continuously to test the MAS. In this way, the MAS under test is tested more thoroughly and is stressed more extensively.

---

[5] `http://www.eclipse.org/gef`

[6] `http://tefkat.sourceforge.net`

[7] `http://sra.itc.it/people/cunduy/ecat`

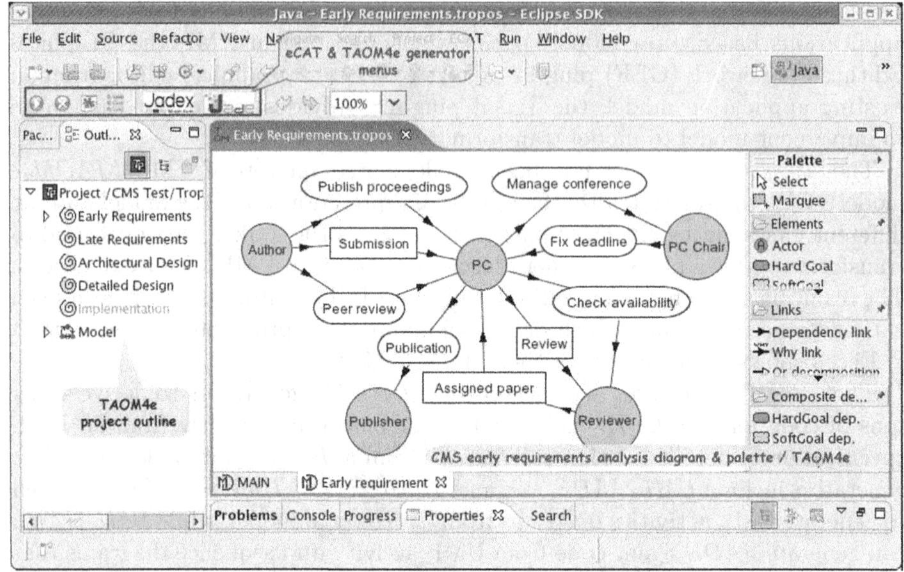

Fig. 3. A snapshot of the TAOM4e's GUI including: the tool's button menu (top); the project's artefacts browser (left); model views, e.g. the Early requirements Actor Diagram (centre); the modeller's palette (right)

eCAT consists of three main components: *Test Suite Editor*, *Autonomous Tester Agent*, and *Monitoring Agents*. Its operation is described as follows:

- Based on agent specifications and design (e.g. outputs of AO modelling with *TAOM4e*), the *Test Suite Editor* generates initial test suites and then provides a GUI for end-users to edit them.
- The *Autonomous Tester Agent* takes those test suites and/or generates other test suites randomly. It then continuously executes them against the multi-agent system under test. During the course of test execution, the *Autonomous Tester Agent* can evolve test suites by applying a mutation and evolutionary technique in order to create more test suites, which aim at revealing more bugs.
- The *Monitoring Agents* assist the *Autonomous Tester Agent* during testing. By monitoring events and interactions happened in the multi-agent system and its environment, it provides useful information to the *Autonomous Tester Agent* in order to judge if a test passes or fails, and a trace to the found bug when failed.

3 Requirements Analysis

Starting software development in *Tropos* using *TAOM4e* requires to create a "*Tropos* project" that will collect all the artefacts generated during the development process, such as models, actor and goal diagrams that represent views on these models, agent code, test cases and logs generated during test execution.

Two models are built in the requirements analysis phases: the **Early Requirements** and the **Late Requirements** models. They are in charge of describing the domain setting as is and the same domain once the system-to-be will have been introduced, respectively.

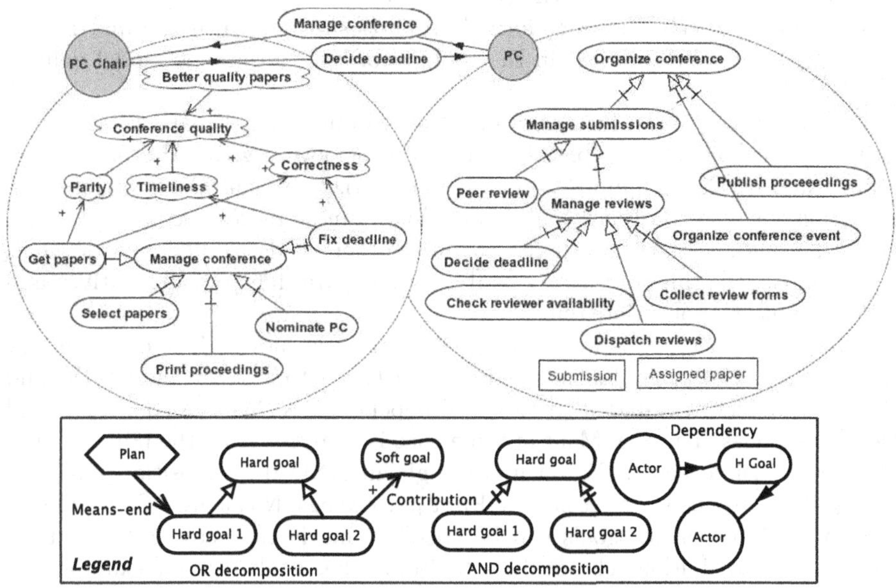

Fig. 4. Early Requirements of CMS: Goal Diagram

A guide to start building the Early Requirements model is given by the following analysis questions: *Who are the stakeholders in the domain? What are their goals and how are they related to each other? What are there strategic dependencies between actors for goal achievement?*

The Conference Management System domain is modelled in terms of its main stakeholders (actors), namely papers' authors, by the actor Author, the conference's program committee and its chair, by the PC and the PC Chair actors respectively, papers reviewers by the actor Reviewer and the proceedings publisher by the actor Publisher. Stakeholders' goals are then identified and, for every goal, the analyst can decide, on the basis of the domain documentation, if the goal is achievable by the actor itself or if the actor has to delegate it to another actor, revealing a dependency relationship between the two actors, such as in the case of the dependency between Author and PC for the achievement of the goal Publish proceedings. An analogous analysis can be carried on for the domain tasks and resources, according to the *Tropos* modelling process described in [11].

In practice, using *TAOM4e*, the Early Requirements model is built by creating a first Actor Diagram into the project and adding actors, goals, etc. into the model using the graphical editor. Fig. 3 shows a view of the Early Requirements model (actor diagram) for the CMS case study. Circles represent actors, ovals the goals, rectangles the resources and the double arrows links between pairs of actors the dependencies between the two actors for the achievement of the goal or resource connected by the two dependency links. For every entity in the model, some properties, such as formal properties related to the Formal Tropos language [8], can be specified in the tool, according to the metamodel defined in [2].

AO modelling can be further pursued by decomposing a goal into sub-goals and by exploring the possible alternatives to achieve a goal. Alternatives are represented by OR-decomposition and characterized by multiple contributions. At this stage, also non-functional requirements can be represented as soft-goals. Choosing one alternative with respect to another, leads to different soft-goals achievement. By this way, it is possible to compare different alternatives and select the most appropriate one.

In Fig. 4, an Early Requirements goal diagram is shown. This diagram represents a (partial) view on the model. Only two actors of the model, PC and PC Chair, are represented with two goal dependencies, Manage conference and Decide deadlines. The goal Manage conference is analyzed from the point of view of its responsible actor, PC Chair, through an AND decomposition into several goals: Get papers, Select papers, Print proceedings, Nominate PC and Decide deadlines. Moreover, softgoals can be specified inside the actor goal diagram, with their contribution relationships to/from other goals (see for example the softgoal Conference quality and the positive contribution relationship from the softgoal Better quality papers).

Goal diagrams can be dynamically created in *TAOM4e*. The tool allows, for every actor in the model, to open (close) their goal diagrams, which appear as balloons attached to the relative actors. This allows to dynamically visualize the internal perspective of each single actor. Notice also that the tool supports the analyst in identifying the elements to be analyzed. For instance, goals that have been delegated to an actor through dependency relationships, appears automatically in the actor goal diagrams, as for instance in the case of the PC Chair actor and the goal Manage conference in Fig. 4.

The results of the first phase are the Early Requirements model and the set of Actor and Goal diagrams produced during its specification.

The Late Requirements phase is intended to capture the changes in the domain caused by the introduction of the system-to-be and the actual properties of the system. The phase starts by introducing in the domain model a new actor representing the system-to-be.

A partial view of the resulting model is shown in Fig. 5 where the CMS System actor is represented. In practice, the analyst creates a new diagram inside the

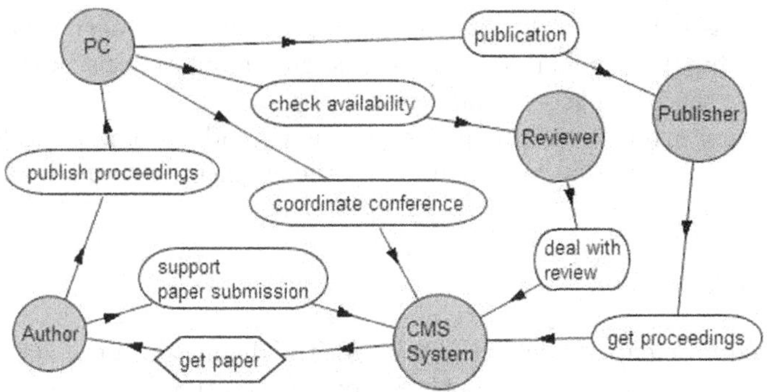

Fig. 5. Late Requirements: Actor Diagram

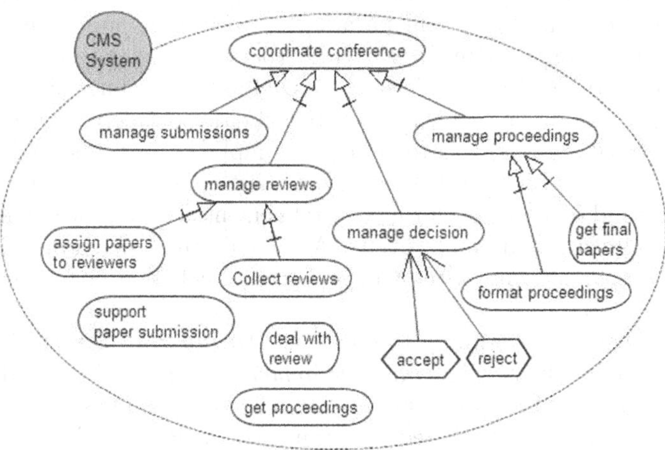

Fig. 6. Late Requirements: Goal Diagram

project that, again, is a view on the model under construction, and adds the new actor. specifying its property of being a system actor.[8]

The driving analysis questions here can be stated as follows: *what are the goals that can be assigned to the system-to-be and which dependencies can be redirected from domain actors to the system?*

According to these questions, several existing or new dependencies can be respectively redirected and established between the other actors in the domain and the new CMS System actor, such as the new goal dependencies Coordinate conference and Manage proceedings.

These goals are then analyzed from the system actor perspective. In Fig. 6, the relative goal diagram is shown. The goals Coordinate conference and Manage proceedings are decomposed in new sub-goals. Moreover, operative plans are

[8] The tool can be customized to show system actors with a different color with respect to domain actor to facilitate model reading.

specified and associated to the system goals as means to achieve them (means-ends relationships), such as in the case of the goal Manage decision that is operationalised by the plans accept and reject.

The resulting artefacts of this phase are the extended domain model and all the Late Requirements diagrams defined by the engineer. The model will be the input for the Design phases.

4 Design

The Late Requirements model is the basis for the definition of the actual system architecture. It is comprised by both the overall multi-agent system structure, and the detailed design for each single agent of the system.

The **Architectural Design** artefact consists of the system's overall structure: it is represented in terms of its sub-systems and of their inter-dependencies. Adopting the multi-agent system paradigm, sub-systems are agents that can act independently and communicate with others through message passing. In order to build the architectural design, the engineer will refine the system actor by introducing sub-actors, which are responsible for actually carrying out the system's top goals. The aim is to split the complexity of the system, which is described in terms of high-level goals, into smaller components, easier to design, to implement and to manage. During this refinement activity, the engineer has to face possible alternative decompositions. Among alternative decompositions, one that results in sub-systems with stronger internal cohesion and lower coupling should be selected.

TAOM4e gives the possibility to create an *Architectural Design* diagram for every system actor defined in *Late Requirements Analysis*. In this diagram, a dashed box associated to the system actor represents the system. In the box, new system agents can be created. Subsequently, a single goal, the whole goal tree or parts of them can be delegated from the system to the new system agents.

Fig. 7 displays the resulting architectural design diagram for the CMS System actor. Analyzing this actor's goal model (see fig. 6), the engineer should be able to extract a proper decomposition into sub-actors. In our example we introduce four new actors. The Conference Manager manages the top-level goal coordinate conference, delegated to the system by the program committee actor PC. The Paper Manager deals with the goal support paper submission from the domain actor Author, moreover some internal agents depend on it to manage papers. To do this, the agent depends on authors to get papers. Similarly, to the Review Manager and Proceedings Manager the corresponding goals are delegated.

Once the sub-actors have been modelled, together with the goals and tasks delegated to them, the next step consists in analyzing and detailing the goal model of these new agents. Similarly to the late requirements analysis phase, the engineer "opens" the balloon of an agent or creates a new view for the agent under consideration, to analyze the goals delegated to it. Goals can be decomposed and plans can be added as means for achieving goals.

Fig. 8 shows an excerpt of the goal models for two of the sub-actors, namely Paper Manager and Proceedings Manager. We focus on the analysis of the goal

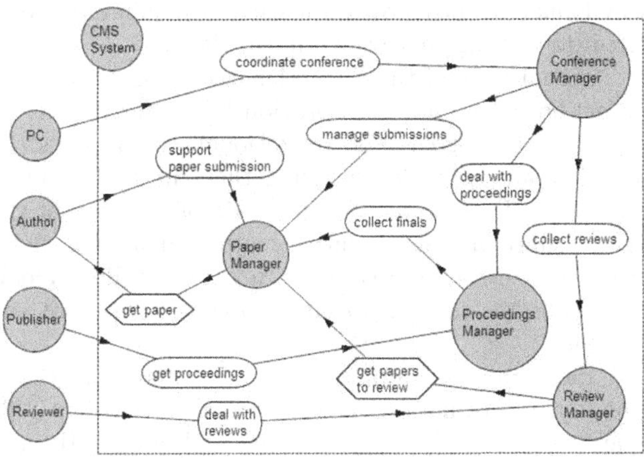

Fig. 7. Architectural Design: CMS System Decomposition into Sub-actors

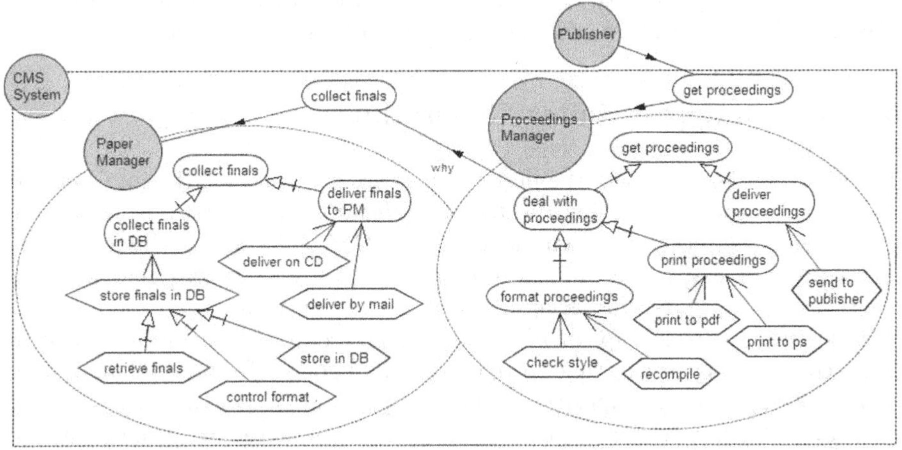

Fig. 8. Architectural Design: Simplified Goal Model of two Sub-actors of CMS

get proceedings delegated from the Publisher actor, and the resulting dependency between the two system actors. The delegated goal is AND-decomposed into sub-goals, which are either operationalised by defining a plan or further decomposed. To be achieved, one of the sub-goals, deal with proceedings, causes the Proceedings Manager to depend on the Paper Manager for the goal collect finals.

Plans are defined as means to achieve the goals that are not delegated to other agents. Defining more than one plan for a goal (as for the goal format proceedings), leads to modelling alternatives. One possible way to format the proceedings is to recompile them, an alternative way is to control the style of posted papers. However, the applicability of the plans can depend on availability of resources (the source files in this example) and the selection of alternatives can be guided by looking at positive and negative contributions to softgoals, for example consistent formatting (not shown in the figure).

Opening the internal view of the PaperManager actor, the engineer can now find the goal collect finals that has been previously delegated to it. This goal can now be decomposed to sub-goals and operationalised by plans. Furthermore, plans can also be detailed, by decomposing them in AND and OR to more concrete sub-plans. See for instance the AND decomposition of the plan store finals in DB into the sub-plans retrieve finals, control format, store in DB, in Fig. 8.

The system design can be completed with the **Detailed Design** artefact that specifies in detail the plans associated to each agent goal and the agent interaction protocols.

UML activity diagrams are automatically generated from the *Tropos* plan diagrams, by model transformation, using the *Tropos2UML* tool. The resulting diagrams can be further detailed and modified with any UML2 editor able to import files in XMI format. Sequence diagrams are associated to activities that contribute to the definition of the communication protocols used. Starting from these diagrams, *JADE* Behaviour code can be generated. These modelling steps are not used in the case study and therefore will be not further detailed in this paper, we focus instead on BDI code generation from goal models.

5 Code and Test Suites Generation

The goal models created in the design phase are the basis for the implementation of software agents. Using the *t2x* tool, *Jadex* agent definition files can be generated by selecting a system agent in the *GM* and starting the automatic generation process. Regarding the present case study, code was generated for the two system agents ProceedingsManager and PaperManager.

The generated code implements the agent's reasoning mechanisms needed to select correct plans at run-time to achieve desired goals. The *t2x* tool analyses a *GM* exploring goal decomposition trees. The goal hierarchy is mapped to *Jadex* goals along with Java files containing the decomposition logic, while plans are implemented in Java files and connected to the relative goals by a *triggering* mechanism. These goal decomposition graphs are also stored in the agent's belief base, together with all contributions to softgoals and dependencies to other agents. Therefore, at run-time the agent can control its behaviour by navigating the modelled goal graph.

The generated code skeleton can be executed on the *Jadex* platform. It exhibits a basic behaviour corresponding to the designed goal model and can be modified and customized as needed. In particular, it can be extended with code, generated by *UML2JADE*, corresponding to the activity diagrams that can be specified at detailed design.

As an example, Fig. 9 briefly shows the generated *Jadex* code, in XML format, of the agent Paper Manager. This fragment of code corresponds to the *Tropos* goal model on the top-left side of the figure, and its reasoning trace at run-time is presented on the bottom-left corner of the figure.

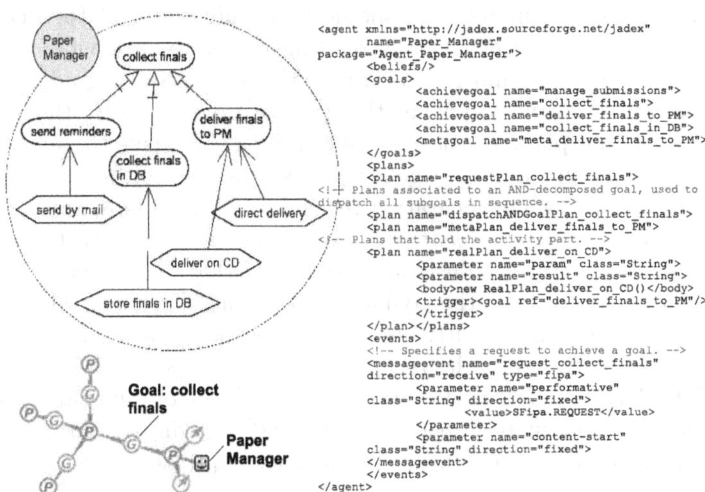

Fig. 9. Simplified goal diagram for PaperManager, part of generated *Jadex* XML code, and example *Jadex* run-time agent instance with activated goals and plans, visualized by the *Introspector* tool provided by the *Jadex* platform

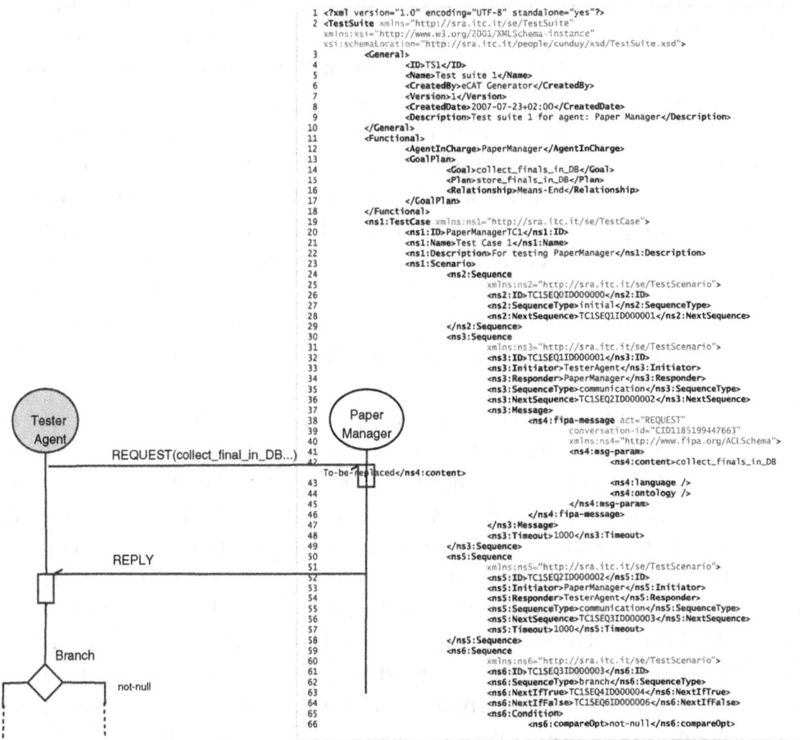

Fig. 10. Example of a Test Scenario. An excerpt of the XML specification is depicted in the right part.

Following the goal-oriented testing methodology presented in [16], *eCAT* generates test suites for every elementary relationship, i.e. relationship between a goal and a plan. The underlining idea is to use the test suite as a guideline for the *Autonomous Tester Agent* to trigger the goal in order to verify the execution of the corresponding plan. In the case of CMS, *eCAT* takes the architectural diagram, Fig. 8, as an input and generate a set of test suites for each agent. Developers can choose when generating test suites which communication protocols the *Autonomous Tester Agent* will use to communicate with the agents of CMS. As an example, Fig. 10 illustrates a test suite that tests whether the agent PaperManager is able to fulfil the goal collect finals in DB or not. The graphical part of the figure gives an intuitive understanding of the test suite, formalized in XML: when executing test, the *Autonomous Tester Agent* will send a request that has "REQUEST" as its performative and the name of the goal collect finals in DB as message content to Paper Manager. Then, it will wait for a reply and decide to finish the test or to continue with other requests.

6 Discussion

For sake of simplicity we have not described iterations along different phases that usually occur in the development process. For instance, iterations along the Early and Late requirements phases, in order to explicit domain entities that are relevant when specifying the impact of the system-to-be in the original organizational setting, and that may have not been captured in the initial Early Requirements model. *Tropos* allows model refinement through iterative steps. This process is managed manually since, up to now, *TAOM4e* does not provide versioning functions. Moreover, formal techniques to support goal analysis and consistency checking of the requirements model have not been exploited.

We shall mention also the fact that the CMS case study offers interesting problems that have not been considered in this paper, due to lack of space. For instance, non-functional requirements, which may emerge in case of large-size conferences and may require more complex MAS architecture, should be taken into account.

Moreover, rules and norms that characterize the CMS domain were not modelled in the case study. For example, rules for manging possible conflicts between the reviewers and the authors of papers to be reviewed should have been modelled. We also have not addressed the rules related to the instances, such as those related to the number of reviews for every paper or the policy of distribution of the papers to the reviewers. Some of these rules can be represented in *Tropos* in the form of Linear Temporal Logics constraints imposed on the entities of the model via the Formal Tropos language. As pointed out in Section 3, *TAOM4e* allows for the representation of these constraints in the form of annotated properties on the model entities. Moreover, starting from the Early requirements phase, the formal annotations give the possibility to formally check the model via model checking techniques as described in [19]. An alternative approach to norm modelling with an AO approach is described in [22].

7 Conclusion and Future Work

This paper illustrated how to use the *Tropos* methodology and a set of supporting tools, to develop a MAS for the Conference Management System case study. In particular, analysis, design, code generation and testing activities have been illustrated together with examples of the resulting process's artefacts.

Work is ongoing to consolidate the tool-supported development process in *Tropos*. In particular, we are deserving particular effort to the integration of requirements and design modelling with the Goal Oriented testing methodology. Moreover, we are studying mechanisms for supporting automatic traceability between process artefacts, e.g. design artifacts and code.

References

1. Bellifemine, F., Poggi, A., Rimassa, G.: JADE: A FIPA Compliant agent framework. In: Practical Applications of Intelligent Agents and Multi-Agents, pp. 97–108 (1999)
2. Bertolini, D., Novikau, A., Susi, A., Perini, A.: TAOM4E: An Eclipse ready tool for Agent-Oriented Modeling. Issue on the development process. Technical report, Fondazione Bruno Kessler - irst (2006)
3. Bresciani, P., Giorgini, P., Giunchiglia, F., Mylopoulos, J., Perini, A.: Tropos: An Agent-Oriented Software Development Methodology. Autonomous Agents and Multi-Agent Systems 8(3), 203–236 (2004)
4. Bryl, V., Giorgini, P., Mylopoulos, J.: Designing cooperative IS: Exploring and evaluating alternatives. In: Meersman, R., Tari, Z. (eds.) OTM 2006. LNCS, vol. 4275, pp. 533–550. Springer, Heidelberg (2006)
5. Dam, K., Winikoff, M.: Comparing Agent-Oriented Methodologies. In: Proceedings of the 5th Int'l Bi-Conference Workshop on AgentOriented Information Systems (AOIS), Melbourne, Australia (2003)
6. DeLoach, S.A.: Modeling organizational rules in the multi-agent systems engineering methodology. In: Cohen, R., Spencer, B. (eds.) Canadian AI 2002. LNCS (LNAI), vol. 2338, pp. 1–15. Springer, Heidelberg (2002)
7. Federico Bergenti, M.-P.G., Zambonelli, F. (eds.): Methodologies and Software Engineering for Agent Systems: The Agent-Oriented Software Engineering Handbook. Springer, Heidelberg (2004)
8. Fuxman, A., Liu, L., Mylopoulos, J., Roveri, M., Traverso, P.: Specifying and analyzing early requirements in tropos. Requir. Eng. 9(2), 132–150 (2004)
9. Fuxman, A., Pistore, M., Mylopoulos, J., Traverso, P.: Model checking early requirements specifications in Tropos. In: IEEE Int. Symposium on Requirements Engineering, Toronto, CA, August 2001, pp. 174–181. IEEE Computer Society Press, Los Alamitos (2001)
10. Giorgini, P., Massacci, F., Mylopoulos, J., Zannone, N.: Modeling security requirements through ownership, permission and delegation. In: Proceedings of the 13th IEEE International Requirements Engineering Conference (RE 2005) (2005)
11. Giorgini, P., Mylopoulos, J., Perini, A., Susi, A.: The Tropos Methodology and Software Development Environment. In: Giorgini, P., Maiden, N., Mylopoulos, J., Yu, E. (eds.) Social Modelling for Requirements Engineering, MIT Press, Cambridge (to appear)

12. Giorgini, P., Mylopoulous, J., Sebastiani, R.: Goal-Oriented Requirements Analysis and Reasoning in the Tropos Methodology. Engineering Applications of Artificial Intelligence 18(2), 159–171 (2005)
13. Henderson-Sellers, B., Giorgini, P. (eds.): Agent-Oriented Methodologies. Idea Group Inc. (2005)
14. Morandini, M.: Knowledge Level Engineering of BDI Agents. Master's thesis, Dept. of Computer Science, University of Trento, Italy (2006), `http://dit.unitn.it/~morandini/resources/ThesisMirkoMorandini.pdf`
15. Morandini, M., Penserini, L., Perini, A., Susi, A.: Refining goal models by evaluating system behaviour. In: 8th International Workshop on Agent-Oriented Software Engineering, AAMAS (May 2007)
16. Nguyen, D.C., Perini, A., Tonella, P.: A goal-oriented software testing methodology. In: Luck, M., Padgham, L. (eds.) AOSE 2007. LNCS, vol. 4951, Springer, Heidelberg (2007)
17. Penserini, L., Perini, A., Susi, A., Mylopoulos, J.: From Stakeholder Intentions to Software Agent Implementations. In: Dubois, E., Pohl, K. (eds.) CAiSE 2006. LNCS, vol. 4001, pp. 465–479. Springer, Heidelberg (2006)
18. Penserini, L., Perini, A., Susi, A., Mylopoulos, J.: From Stakeholder Intentions to Agent Capabilities. In: Sixth International Joint Conference on Autonomous Agents and Multi-Agent Systems (AAMAS 2007), Hawaii, USA, ACM Press, New York (2007)
19. Perini, A., Susi, A.: Agent-Oriented Visual Modeling and Model Validation for Engineering Distributed Systems. Computer Systems Science & Engineering 20(4), 319–329 (2005)
20. Pokahr, A., Braubach, L., Lamersdorf, W.: Jadex: Implementing a bdi-infrastructure for jade agents. EXP - in search of innovation (Special Issue on JADE) 3(3), 76–85 (2003)
21. Pokahr, A., Braubach, L., Lamersdorf, W.: Jadex: A bdi reasoning engine. In: Bordini, J.D.R., Dastani, M., Seghrouchni, A.E.F. (eds.) Multi-Agent Programming, pp. 149–174. Springer Science, Business Media Inc. (2005)
22. Siena, A.: Engineering Normative Requirements. In: Proceedings of the First International Conference on Research Challenges in Information Science, RCIS 2007, Ouarzazate, Morocco, pp. 439–444 (2007)
23. Souza, R.G.-S., Perini, A.: Analyzing requirements of knowledge management systems with the support of agent organizations. Journal of the Brazilian Computer Society (JCBS) 11(1), 51–62 (2005), ISSN 0104-6500
24. Yu, E.: Modelling Strategic Relationships for Process Reengineering. PhD thesis, University of Toronto, Department of Computer Science, University of Toronto (1995)

The Prometheus Design Tool – A Conference Management System Case Study

Lin Padgham, John Thangarajah, and Michael Winikoff

School of Computer Science, RMIT University, Melbourne, Vic 3000, Australia
{lin.padgham,john.thangarajah,michael.winikoff}@rmit.edu.au

Abstract. This paper describes how the Prometheus Design Tool (PDT) is used to support the Prometheus methodology for designing agent systems. This is done by using an exemplar system that has been used previously in the literature, and is briefly described earlier in this volume. This paper presents the development of a design for this system using PDT. By using different tools and methodologies to design the same example system it is easier to observe the similarities and differences between both the methodologies and the tools supporting them. Prometheus and PDT, like the other systems presented in this volume, has specific strengths and features that have been developed to support the design process. However it is also evident that there is a great deal of commonality across agent methodologies that should give developers confidence that there is in fact an emerging agreed understanding as to the important aspects of designing and developing agent systems.

1 Introduction

A large number of methodologies for the analysis and design of agent systems have been proposed [1,2]. Some of the more well-known and arguably better developed methodologies include PASSI [3], MaSE [4], Tropos [5], Gaia [6], and Prometheus [7].

The fact that there are a substantial number of agent development methodologies to choose from can be confusing for developers who simply want direction in using the technology. Detailed working of a common example can provide assistance in understanding both the commonalities and the differences between approaches. This paper presents a design for a conference management system (based on the presentation of [8]), which has been developed using the *Prometheus* methodology [7] and PDT, the Prometheus Design Tool [9]. Because tools are crucial to use of a methodology for designing any real system, we focus on the design process as supported by PDT.

Key aspects of Prometheus include:

- It provides detailed guidance with specific techniques and heuristics for performing steps in the design process; PDT supports and helps structure these steps.
- It is intended to support the detailed design of agent internals as well as the structure and interactions of the agents as a system. It supports (though is not limited to) design of Belief-Desire-Intention (BDI) agents;
- It aims to strike a balance between defined structures, which support some automated reasoning, and free text or diagrams which allow designers freedom.

M. Luck and L. Padgham (Eds.): AOSE 2007, LNCS 4951, pp. 197–211, 2008.

- It covers (to some extent), all phases of development: specification, design, implementation, and testing [10] and debugging [11];[1]
- It is designed to scale to large designs (through the use of a range of abstraction mechanisms, such as protocols and capabilities);

The methodology has been developed over more than 10 years as a result of working with industry partners who are building agent systems and agent development tools. It has also been continually refined and developed through teaching both undergraduate and postgraduate students as well as running industry seminars. The tool support has arisen out of the need to provide this at a reasonable level for building even relatively small systems. For larger systems it is essential in order to maintain consistency even of such simple things as naming. The Prometheus Design Tool (PDT) is freely available from `http://www.cs.rmit.edu.au/agents/pdt/` tool, running under Java 1.5.

The rest of this paper presents the development of the conference management system using PDT and illustrates the way in which the tool supports the different steps in the methodology. All figures in the paper are generated by PDT.

2 Prometheus Design Tool Overview

The Prometheus design methodology consists of 3 stages: system specification (which could be considered as a pre-design stage), architectural design, and detailed design. Figure 1) provides an overview of these three stages and the artifacts produced in each. In developing a Prometheus design the developer produces the design artifacts for each of these stages, which are represented in the upper left pane of PDT (see figure 2). The graphical models produced at each stage of the process are listed in this upper left pane, and are displayed and developed in the upper right pane. These are the core static models of a Prometheus design, and in figure 1 are in the centre of each stage/row.

Each entity in a Prometheus design also has a detailed descriptor with a series of fields, some of which are free text, and others of which are structured. These descriptors are displayed and developed in the bottom right pane of PDT (figure 2), and are indicated on the right hand side of each stage in figure 1. The particular descriptor on display is determined by selecting the relevant entity icon in the graphical model pane, or by selecting the entity from a list of entities in the bottom left pane (figure 2).

The left hand side of each stage in figure 1 shows design artifacts which capture models of the dynamics of a system. The primary artifacts here are *scenarios*, *protocols* and *process diagrams*. The details of scenarios and protocols are developed and displayed in pop-up windows available from the "Entities" menu at the top of the tool.[2] Icons representing these entities appear in the figures in the main graphical models pane. The notation used in PDT is shown in figure 3. The symbols used are somewhat idiosyncratic (as are those in other toolkits) and we are currently working with some of the major groups in the area, to agree a more standardised graphical notation.

---

[1] The testing and debugging are not yet integrated into the publically available version of PDT.

[2] Process diagrams are not currently supported.

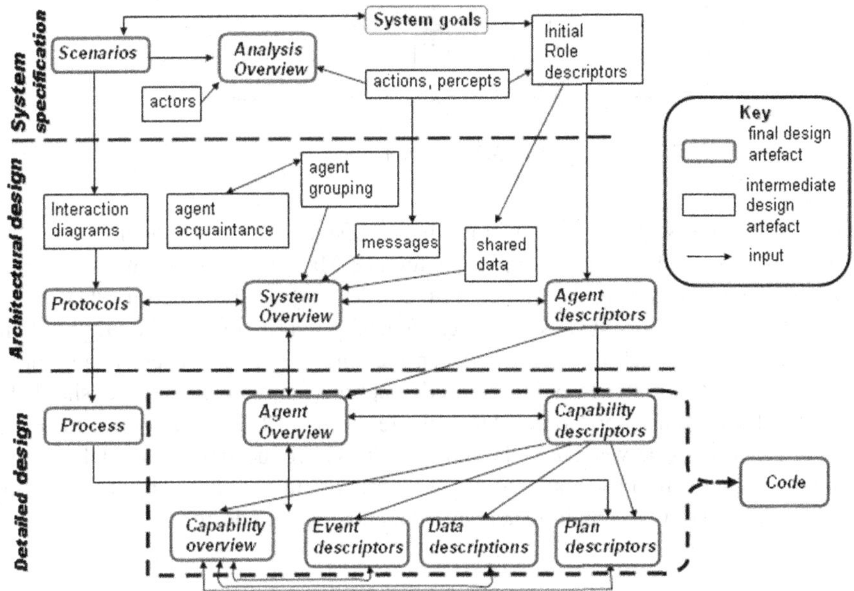

Fig. 1. Overview of Prometheus Methodology and Design Artifacts

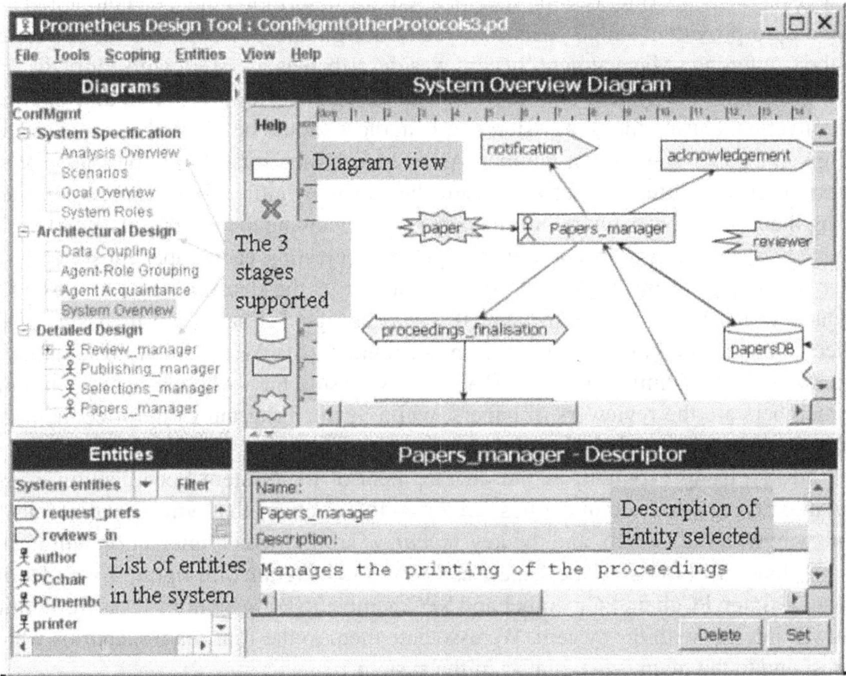

Fig. 2. Overview of PDT

Fig. 3. Entity Notation

In the following sections we illustrate the process of design using PDT, showing the artifacts produced for the example Conference Management system. We present the design linearly covering the models in the order they are provided in PDT. However the design process is always iterative, especially within a particular stage, where typically one moves back and forth between the various models. There is also often some iteration between stages and if required, diagrams from previous stages should be revisited and revised as appropriate. One of the features of PDT is that it does enforce a degree of consistency between models, and so entities introduced in one model or stage, are often automatically propagated to other models or stages where appropriate. This assists the developer in maintaining a consistent and coherent design.

3 System Specification

It is not unusual for the initial ideas for a system to be captured very briefly, possibly in a few paragraphs. During System Specification this description must be elaborated and explored, to provide a sound basis for system design and development. In our example the Conference Management System was described as a system with four "distinct phases in which the system must operate: submission, review, decision, and final paper collection. During the submission phase, authors should be notified of paper receipt and given a paper submission number. After the deadline for submissions has passed, the program committee (PC) has to review the papers by either contacting referees and asking them to review a number of the papers, or reviewing them themselves. After the reviews are complete, a decision on accepting or rejecting each paper must be made. After the decisions are made, authors are notified of the decisions and are asked to produce a final version of their paper if it was accepted. Finally, all final copies are collected and printed in the conference proceedings." [8]. We modified this slightly to assume a structure similar to the AAMAS reviewing structure, where Program Committee members are the reviewers of papers, while Senior Program Committee members make recommendations based on the reviews.

Typically, using Prometheus, the development of the System Specification begins with identifying the external entities[3] (referred to as *actors*) that will use or interact in some way with the system, and the key *scenarios* around which interaction will occur. This is done in PDT using the 'Analysis Overview Diagram'. In figure 4 we identify Author, Printer, PCchair, PCmember and SPCmember (SPC = Senior PC) as the entities that will interact with the system. We associate them to the four main scenarios which correspond to the main functionality of the system.

[3] These may be humans or other software systems.

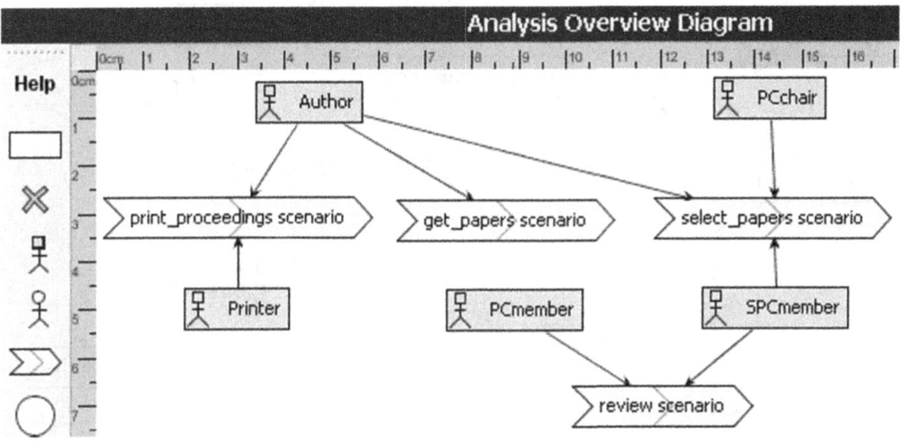

Fig. 4. Initial Analysis Overview Diagram

We then refine this diagram by identifying the *percepts* that are input to each scenario, and the *actions* produced by the system for each scenario, linking them to the appropriate actors as shown in figure 5. For example, an author submits a paper as a percept (input) to the system and the system performs an action of sending an acknowledgement back to the author. The analysis overview diagram thus defines the *interface* to the system in terms of the percepts (inputs) and actions (outputs).

The next step is to specify the details of the scenarios that we identified in the analysis overview diagram. A scenario is a sequence of *structured steps* where each step can be one of: *goal, action, percept*, or *(sub)scenario*. Each step also allows the designer to indicate the *roles* associated with that step, the *data* accessed, and a *description* of the step. These preliminary goals, roles and data that are identified are used to automatically propagate information into other aspects of the design. As steps are defined, the relevant entities are created if they do not yet exist. Figure 6 illustrates the steps of the paper reviewing scenario where the first step is a goal to invite reviewers, associated with the Review_Management role and accesses the ReviewerDB (a data structure to store reviewer details, their preferences, and paper assignments).

By default PDT creates a goal for every scenario, with the same name as the scenario. This is the goal which the scenario is intended to achieve. The name of the goal can be changed, and if desired the same goal can be associated with multiple scenarios, although this is not usually the case at the most abstract level of the Analysis Overview diagram. The goals, created from the scenarios are automatically placed into the 'Goal Overview Diagram', where goal hierarchies further describing the application are developed. For each goal, we identify its sub-goals by asking the question "how can we achieve this goal?". Figure 7 shows the goals of the conference management system. Sub-goals are either "AND"[4] or "OR"[5] branches. By default they are "AND" branches.

[4] Each sub-goal is a part of the parent goal.

[5] Sub-goals are alternative approaches to achieving the parent goal.

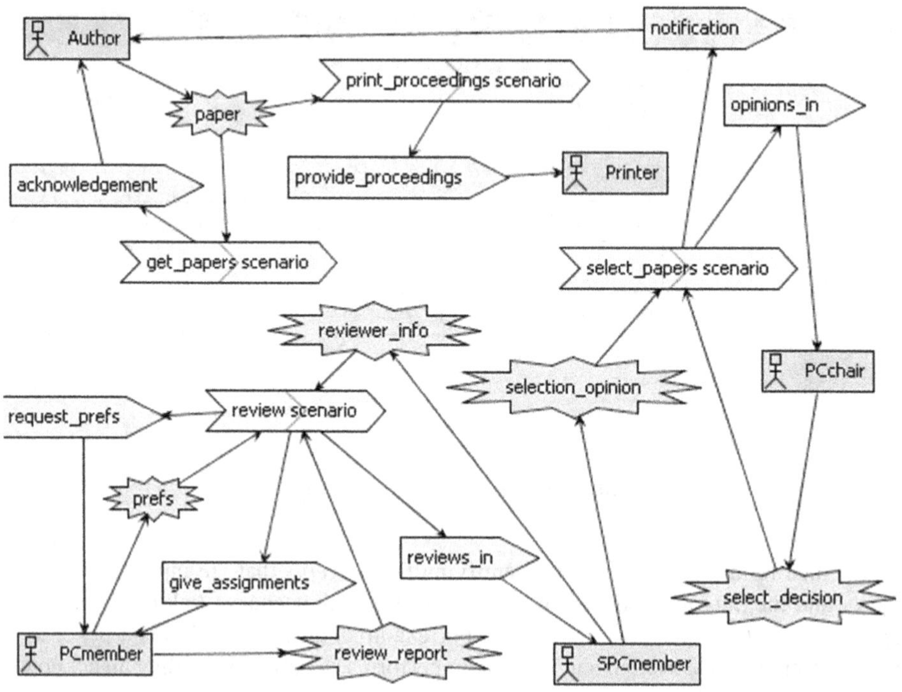

Fig. 5. Refined Analysis Overview Diagram

Edit Scenario - review scenario

	Type	Name	Role	Data	Description
1	G	invite_reviewers	Review_management	ReviewerDB	Invite candidates to join the review panel
2	G	collect_prefs	Assignment	ReviewerDB	Collect the preference of the reviewers
3	G	assign_reviewers	Assignment	ReviewerDB	Assign papers to reviewers based on their prefe...
4	A	give_assignments	Assignment		Send the papers to the allocated reviewers
5	P	review_report	Review_management		Receive the review from the reviewers
6	G	collect_reviews	Review_management	ReviewDB	Collect all the reviews from the reviewers

Insert Step Edit Remove

Close

A -> Action G -> Goal O -> Others P -> Percept S -> Scenario

Fig. 6. Scenario example - Paper Review

There is typically substantial iteration between scenario development and goal hierarchy development until the developer feels that the application is sufficiently described/defined. At this stage goals are grouped into cohesive units and assigned to *roles* which are intended as relatively small and easily specified chunks of agent

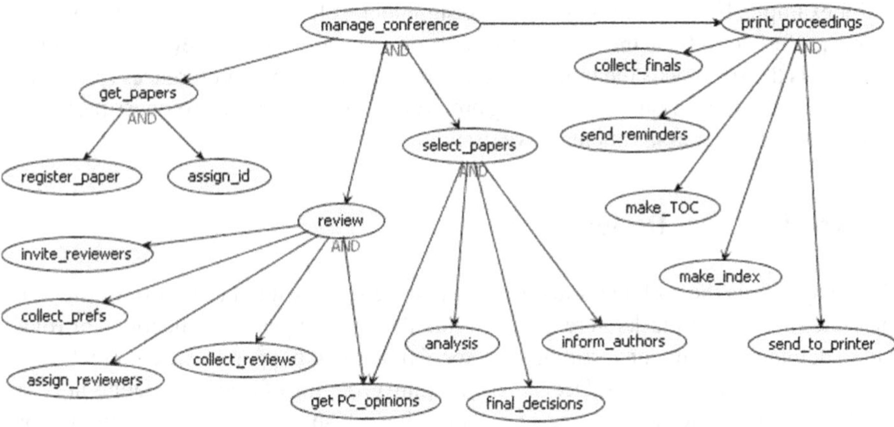

Fig. 7. Goal Overview Diagram

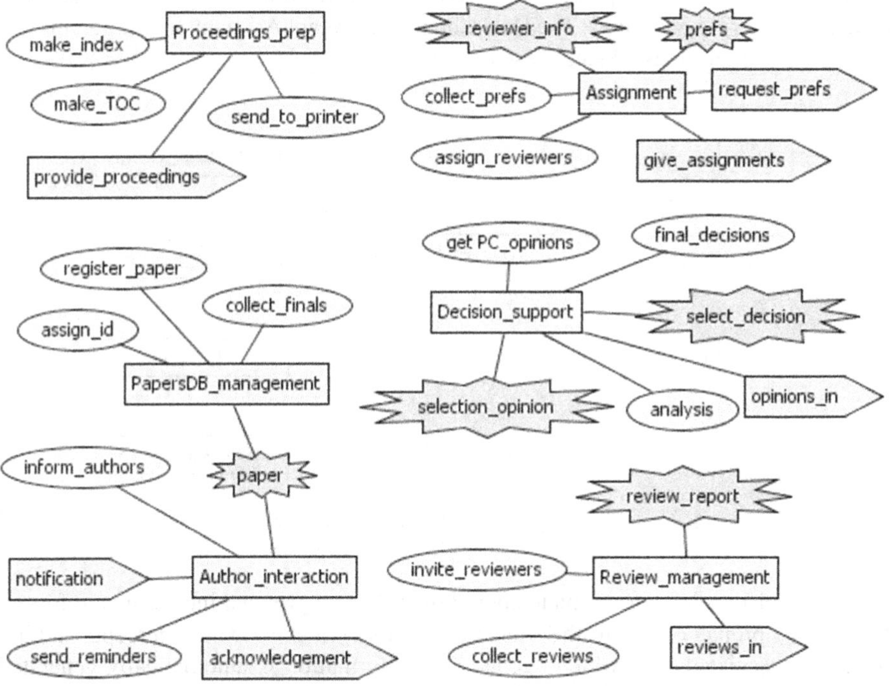

Fig. 8. System Roles Diagram

functionality. The percepts and actions are then also assigned to the roles appropriately to allow the roles to achieve their goals. This is done using the ‘System Roles’ diagram.

For example, Figure 8 shows that the 'Assignment' role is responsible for the goals to collect preferences (from the reviewers) and assign papers (to the reviewers). To achieve these goals the role needs the input (reviewer_info) and reviewer preferences (prefs) and should perform the actions of requesting preferences from reviewers (request_prefs) and giving out the paper assignments (give_assignments).

4 Architectural Design

The next stage is the architectural design where we specify the internal composition of the system. The main tasks here are to decide the agent types (as collections of roles) and to define the agent conversations (protocols) that will happen in order to realise the specified goals and scenarios. Decisions regarding grouping of roles into agents are captured in the 'Agent-Role Grouping Diagram'. Figure 9 shows the roles of assigning papers to reviewers (Assignment) and managing the review process (review_management) as being part of a Review_manager agent. A number of issues must be considered in determining how to group roles into agents, including standard software engineering issues of cohesion and coupling. The relationships of roles to data are also considered in determining role groupings. The Data Coupling anAgent Acquaintance diagrams can assist the designer in visualising these aspects.

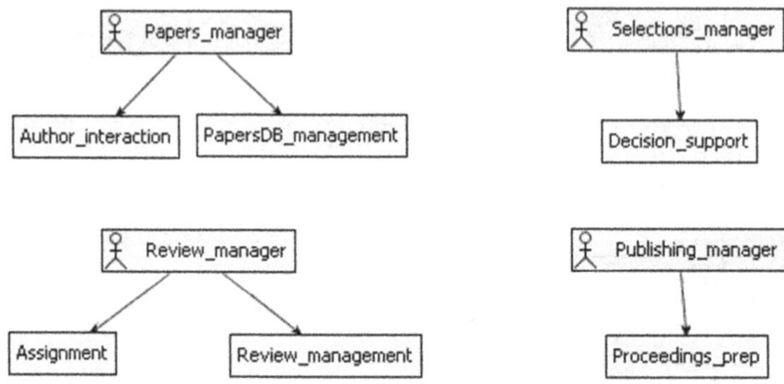

Fig. 9. Agent-Role Grouping Diagram

Once decisions have been made about how roles are grouped into agents, information can be propagated from the role specifications, to show which percepts and actions are associated with which agents. This information is automatically generated into the 'System Overview Diagram' which, when completed, provides an overview of the internal system architecture. What must be done to complete this overview is to define interactions between the agents (protocols), and to add any shared data. Figure 10 shows the system overview for our conference management system design. Observing the 'Papers_manager' agent we can see that it receives papers (percept) from authors and provides an acknowledgment (action) to them. It interacts with the 'Selections_manager' agent via the 'selection_decision' protocol to be able to send authors

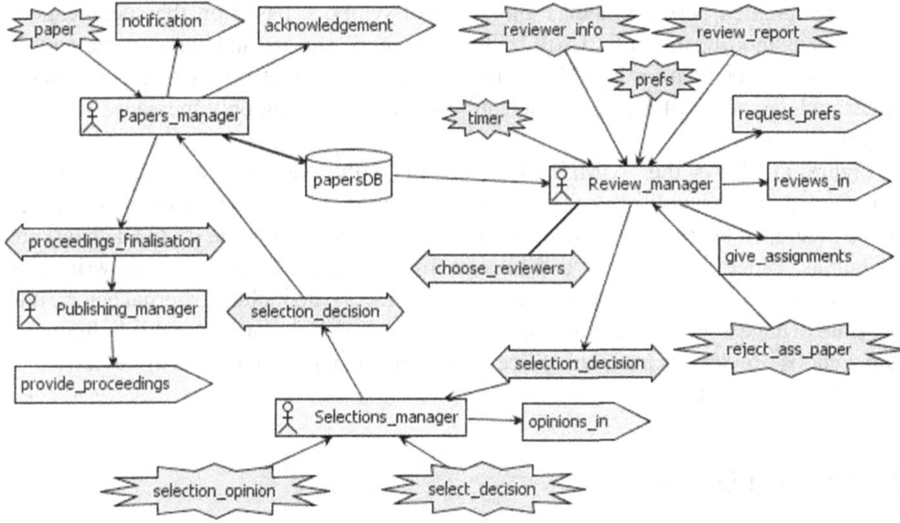

Fig. 10. System Overview Diagram

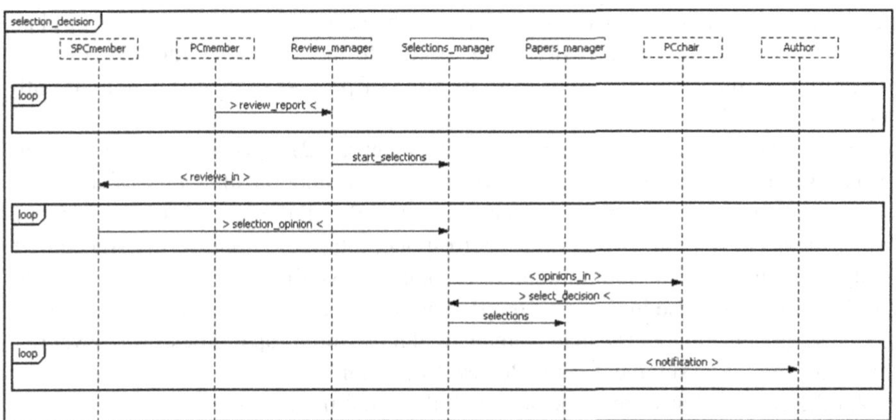

Fig. 11. Selection Decision Protocol Diagram

a notification of accept/reject (action). It also interacts with the 'Publishing_manager' agent via the 'proceedings_finalisation' protocol to provide final versions of papers to publish the proceedings.

In order to link agents with the appropriate protocols, the protocol structure must be specified using the protocol specification window (available from the Entities menu, or by double clicking the icon in the diagram). The structure of message flows is specified using a textual notation for describing a modified AUML2 [12] protocol specification. This can then be displayed as an AUML2 style figure. Any messages (or other entities) specified in the protocol, but not yet existing in the design, are created automatically.

Links are created between agents and protocol symbols, based on the specification. Prometheus modification of AUML2 allows percepts, actions and actors to be part of the protocol specification in addition to messages and agents. This often provides a better understanding of a conversation structure than showing only messages between agents.

Figure 11 shows the AUML2-like diagram of the 'selection_decision' protocol, where interactions involve three agents and four actors (identified by the dotted squares in the diagram). Percepts (which always originate with an actor and go to an agent) are written as ">percept_name<", and actions (from an agent to an actor) are written as "<action_name>". Because conversations, or protocols, do include external actors, it is possible to have a protocol connected to only one agent. An example of this in figure 10 is the choose_reviewers protocol where the review manager interacts with reviewers to give out assignments.

5 Detailed Design

The detailed design stage deals with design of the agent internals, to allow the agent to achieve the goals associated with it (via its roles and associated goals) and to engage in the interactions specified. A generic stage of detailed design describes agents in terms of capabilities, or modules. These capabilities are then finally specified in terms of plans and events, which are of necessity more specific to the implementation paradigm or platform, than the preceding steps. Specification of process diagrams is not currently supported in PDT.

The detailed design section (bottom left of figure 12) consists of a list of agent overview diagrams, one for each agent. Each agent has underneath it a list of capability overview diagrams, one for each capability included in the agent. Often the capabilities of the agent will (at least initially) correspond to the roles that were assigned to it, though roles may also be split into multiple smaller capabilities, or merged into a larger capability. For example in this case the Review_manager agent had two roles assigned to it (Assignment and review_management) and it has three capabilities: 'Reviewer registration', 'Papers assignment' and 'Review Collection'.

All the entities that were associated with the agent in the system overview diagram are propagated to the agent overview diagram, including the individual messages from protocols associated with the agent. Entities in an agent/capability overview diagram that are propagated, form part of the interface to the internals of the agent/capability and are shown as "faded" icons. These interface entities must then be connected to internal capabilities or plans defined to use or generate them. The designer needs to ensure that all the actions, percepts, messages, and data access is accounted for. For example, the 'Reviewer registration' capability handles the percept 'review_info' and modifies data in the 'ReviewerDB'.

Capabilities, which are specified using the 'Capability Overview Diagram' contain the plans which actually do things. Similarly to the agent overview diagram, percepts, messages, actions and data are propagated into this diagram and plans or (sub) capabilities are created to handle the relevant entities. A dotted line from a percept or message to a plan indicates that the percept/message is the trigger of the plan. Figure 13,

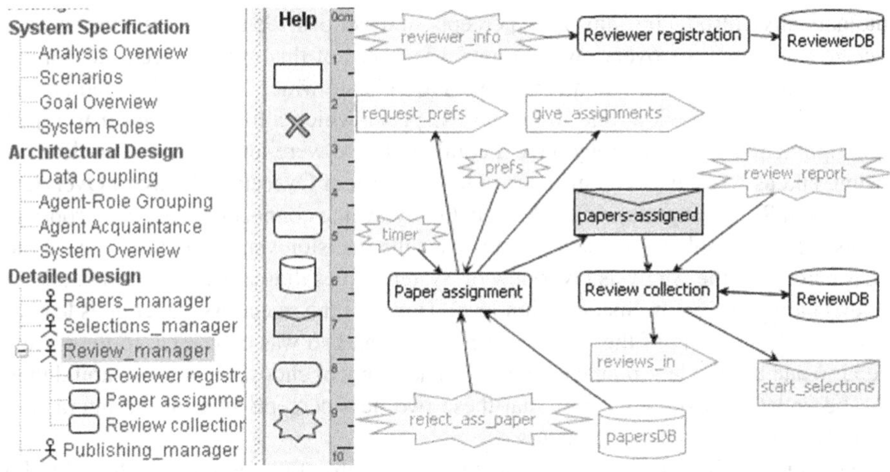

Fig. 12. Agent Overview Diagram for Reviewer_manager

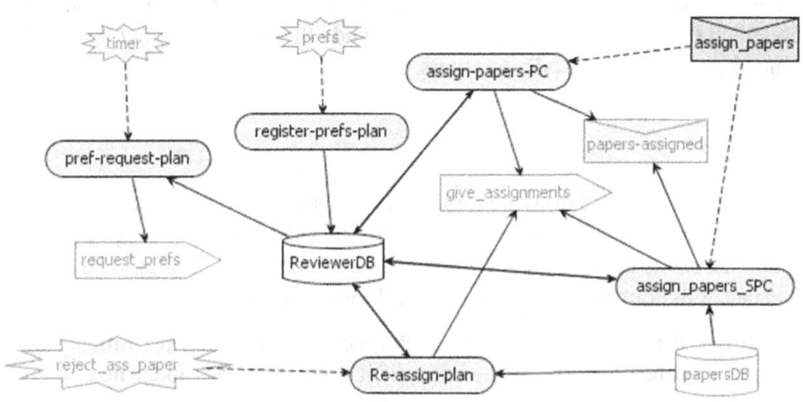

Fig. 13. Capability Overview Diagram for Paper_asignment

outlines the details of the 'Paper assignment' capability. The 'assign-papers-PC' plan is triggered by a message to assign the papers (assign_papers), reads data from 'ReviewerDB' and 'PapersDB', assigns papers to PC members (give_assignments), records the assignments in 'ReviewerDB' and, when all assignments are complete, sends a 'papers-assigned' message.

Plan descriptors allow for additional information such as a description of the plan, a context condition specifying the conditions under which this plan is applicable, a failure condition under which the plan may fail, a failure recovery procedure if the plan fails, and a description of the plan body where the developer may specify pseudocode that can be easily translated to code.

As the details of a design are developed it is very common that one recognises the need for new percepts, actions, messages, and so on. This will inevitably lead to the need to revise slightly the models developed at an earlier stage. PDT supports this by automatically introducing any new percepts and actions identified, into the system overview and analysis overview diagrams. Examples of this in the current design are the timer that is the trigger to ask reviewers to indicate which of the submitted papers they would like to review, and the reject_ass_paper which allows a reviewer to reject an assignment with which they have a conflict. These were identified during detailed design, and as a result were introduced into the System Overview, Analysis Overview and System Roles diagrams. In the System Overview the connections to the appropriate agents were also able to be made. In this case the decision was made to not leave the timer percept in the Analysis Overview or System Roles diagrams, as it did not add to understanding at System Specification level. However the reject_ass_paper does lead to a fuller understanding of the system functionality and so was connected to the review scenario and the Review_management role. The protocol choose_reviewers should then also be updated to show the role that these two new percepts play in the interaction around assigning reviewers to papers.

Once the detailed design is completed it is possible to generate skeleton (JACK) code from the Tools menu. The developer can then add to this code using a text editor. In order to maintain consistency between code and design, any additions or deletions of entities, or relationships between entities should be made in the design tool, and code regenerated on this basis. Code that is added outside that which is generated by PDT is maintained between design code iterations.

6 Features

PDT is more than simply a drawing tool for development of design diagrams. The tool maintains constraints based on the metamodel, and also provides support to prevent such simple errors as generation of unintended entities due to typographical errors. The user interface will continuously prevent the following sorts of errors:

(i) Definition: it is not possible to have references to non-existent entities, since creating a reference will create the entity if it does not exist, and when an entity is deleted all references to it are deleted as well.
(ii) Naming: it is not possible for two entities to have the same name, for example a goal and a plan both called 'assign-Papers-PC'.
(iii) Simple type errors: for example, it is not possible in PDT to connect an action and another action.
(iv) Scope constraints: for example, it is not possible to create an incoming percept to a plan without that percept also being (a) shown on the system overview diagram, and (b) shown as incoming to the agent whose plan it is.
(v) Violations of interface declarations: for example, if an agent is specified as reading a belief set, then it is not possible to create an arrow from one of the agent's plans to the belief set. Similarly, if an agent specifies that it only sends a message, then its plans cannot receive the message, and PDT does not allow the user to violate this constraint.

In addition PDT has a number of additional features available from the tools menu shown in Figure 14 Some of the additional features that the Prometheus Design Tool provides include:

- Crosschecking - this is a consistency check that is performed on demand, generating a list of errors and warnings that can be checked by the developer. Examples of a warning are writing of internal data that is never read, while an example of an error is a mismatch between the interaction protocol specified between two agents and the messages actually sent and received by processes within those agents.
- Code generation - The detailed design specification is close to code, and the tool currently provides a code generation feature that generates skeleton code of the system in the JACK agent language [13]. The skeleton code can then be completed by the developers. The tool supports repeated code generation from the design, preserving any user edited code segments.
- Report generation - One of the very useful features of the tool is its ability to generate an HTML design document. This document contains both figures and textual information, as well as an index over all the design entities. The report can also be customized such that only certain entities are included in the report. The tool can also save printable images of the various diagrams (in PNG format).
- Auto save and Backup - PDT automatically saves the current project at a set time interval (which can be changed) and also allows for creating backup files, which save the current version into a different file specified by the user.

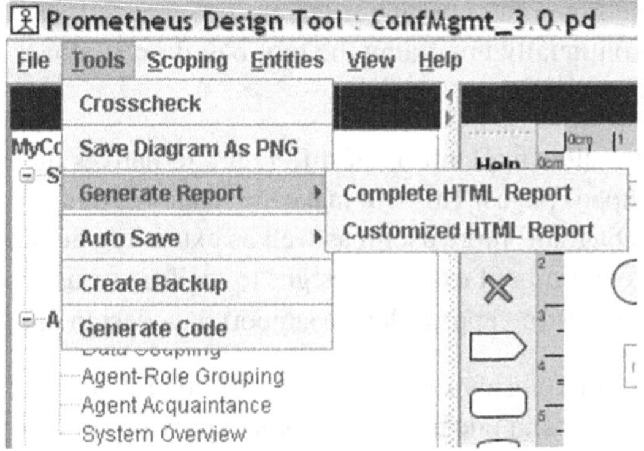

Fig. 14. Tools in PDT

PDT is also available with an Eclipse plugin, enabling it to be used within a broader IDE supporting aspects such as syntax highlighting, version management and so on. Details are available from the PDT home page at `www.cs.rmit.edu.au/agents/pdt`.

7 Future Work

There is a range of ongoing research on extending and refining the Prometheus methodology, and many aspects of this work are gradually being integrated into PDT, as they reach an appropriate stage of maturity, and as their usefulness is verified. These include:

- Testing support: we have developed automated incremental unit testing based on the design model as specified in PDT [10]. This is currently being integrated into the publically available version of PDT and should be available relatively soon.
- Debugging support: there is substantial work on interactive debugging support based on the design models specified in PDT [14,11]. This will eventually be integrated into PDT.
- Interaction development: There has been work on alternative approaches to developing agent interactions, which are more goal centric, and less message centric [15] than AUML2. This may be included into PDT as an alternative approach to interaction specification and development, which also includes detailed design of agent tasks.
- Agent organisations: We have worked with Carles Sierra on integrating an organisation design phase based on Islander, into Prometheus and PDT [16]. Facilities for integrating this design phase into PDT, using the Islander design tool, will be available soon.
- Model based production of fully executable code: A variation of PDT extends the granularity of the detailed design, as well as introducing additional specifications, in order to allow automated production of a fully functional system [17]. Aspects of this work will be incorporated into PDT soon.

In addition to incorporating ongoing research in Agent Software Engineering, into PDT, we are also continually upgrading the tool based on feedback from users. Some improvements currently in process include:

- Functionality to allow exploration of different alternatives during the design process, on "sketchpad" pages. This will make the 'Data coupling Diagram' and 'Agent Acquaintance Diagram' more useful as well as extending flexibility generally.
- Importing and exporting of existing designs to facilitate reuse and group work.
- Incorporation of existing approaches to support data design more explicitly.

We also hope to work closely with developers of other Agent Software design tools and methodologies to try and integrate our efforts to provide simpler access for industry developers and others outside the specialised community.

References

1. Henderson-Sellers, B., Giorgini, P.: Agent-Oriented Methodologies. Idea Group Publishing (2005)
2. Bergenti, F., Gleizes, M.-P., Zambonelli, F.: Methodologies and Software Engineering for Agent Systems. The Agent-Oriented Software Engineering Handbook. Kluwer Academic Publishers, Dordrecht (2004)
3. Burrafato, P., Cossentino, M.: Designing a multi-agent solution for a bookstore with the PASSI methodology. In: Proceedings of the Fourth International Bi-Conference Workshop on Agent-Oriented Information Systems (AOIS-2002), Toronto (2002)
4. DeLoach, S.A.: Analysis and design using MaSE and agentTool. In: Proceedings of the 12th Midwest Artificial Intelligence and Cognitive Science Conference (MAICS 2001) (2001)

5. Bresciani, P., Perini, A., Giorgini, P., Giunchiglia, F., Mylopoulos, J.: Tropos: An agent-oriented software development methodology. Autonomous Agents and Multi Agent Systems 8(3), 203–236 (2004)
6. Zambonelli, F., Jennings, N., Wooldridge, M.: Developing multiagent systems: the gaia methodology. ACM Transactions on Software Engineering and Methodology 12(3) (2003)
7. Padgham, L., Winikoff, M.: Developing Intelligent Agent Systems: A Practical Guide. John Wiley, Chichester (2004)
8. DeLoach, S.A.: Modeling organizational rules in the multi-agent systems engineering methodology. In: Proceedings of the 15th Canadian Conference on Artificial Intelligence, pp. 1–15 (2002)
9. Padgham, L., Thangarajah, J., Winikoff, M.: Tool support for agent development using the prometheus methodology. In: Cai, K.-Y., Ohnishi, A., Lau, M.F. (eds.) Proceedings of the Fifth International Conference on Quality Software (QSIC 2005). Workshop on Integration of Software Engineering and Agent Technology (ISEAT), sep 2005, pp. 383–388 (2005)
10. Zhang, Z., Thangarajah, J., Padgham, L.: Automated unit testing for agent systems. In: 2nd International Working Conference on Evaluation of Novel Approaches to Software Engineering (ENASE-07), pp. 10–18 (2007)
11. Poutakidis, D., Padgham, L., Winikoff, M.: Debugging multi-agent systems using design artifacts: The case of interaction protocols. In: Proceedings of the First International Joint Conference on Autonomous Agents and Multi Agent Systems (AAMAS 2002) (2002)
12. Winikoff, M.: Defining syntax and providing tool support for Agent UML using a textual notation. International Journal of Agent-Oriented Software Engineering 1(2), 123–144 (2007)
13. Busetta, P., Rönnquist, R., Hodgson, A., Lucas, A.: JACK Intelligent Agents - Components for Intelligent Agents in Java. Technical report, Agent Oriented Software Pty. Ltd, Melbourne, Australia (1998), `http://www.agent-software.com`
14. Padgham, L., Winikoff, M., Poutakidis, D.: Adding debugging support to the prometheus methodology. Journal of Engineering Applications in Artificial Intelligence 18(2) (2005)
15. Cheong, C., Winikoff, M.: Hermes: Implementing goal-oriented agent interactions. In: Proceedings of the Third international Workshop on Programming Multi-Agent Systems (ProMAS) (July 2005)
16. Padgham, C.S.J.T.L., Winikoff, M.: Designing institutional multi-agent systems. In: Padgham, L., Zambonelli, F. (eds.) AOSE VII / AOSE 2006. LNCS, vol. 4405, pp. 84–103. Springer, Heidelberg (2007)
17. Jayatilleke, G.B., Padgham, L., Winikoff, M.: A model driven component-based development framework for agents. Computer Systems Science & Engineering 4(20) (2005)

Developing a Conference Management System with the Multi-Agent Systems Unified Process: A Case Study

Danilo Santos, Marcelo Blois Ribeiro, and Ricardo Bastos

FACIN - PUCRS, Av Ipiranga 6681, Porto Alegre, RS, 90619-900, Brazil
dsantos@inf.pucrs.br, {blois,bastos}@pucrs.br

Abstract. Many methodologies appeared in the latest years to deal with multi-agent systems complexity and special development requirements. Each methodology focuses in certain aspects of multi-agent systems development and use different case studies to prove their effectiveness. In order to compare their characteristics it is necessary to use a single case study that requires a complex and distributed solution. This paper presents the development of a very well-known multi-agent systems case study - the Conference Management System - with the Multi-agent Systems Unified Process (MASUP).

1 Introduction

Multi-Agent Systems are gaining attention in the software development area. The quick growth of multi-agent systems development relies on the belief that the agent paradigm is appropriate to explore the possibilities offered by open distributed systems such as the Internet [1]. Due to the growing interest in agent technology in the context of the software engineering, many methodologies were created to support agent-oriented systems development.

An agent-oriented methodology should allow the designers to model the agents common goals and the society workflow. The most natural way to view business process is as a collection of autonomous, problem solving agents which interact when they have interdependencies [2].

In this paper a multi-agent solution to the Conference Management System (CMS) [3] will be presented using the *Multi-agent Systems Unified Process* (MASUP) [4]. The paper aims to present how MASUP captures specific agency characteristics such as organizational rules to create the design of an agent-based solution ready to be implemented. This paper is structured as follows. Section 2 briefly presents MASUP through its phases, models and artifacts. Section 3 shows the artifacts produced by the application of MASUP in the Conference Management System. Section 4 discusses some specific aspects on the case study such as the organizational rules mapping, coordination rules representation and some implementation issues. The latest section presents the conclusion and future work.

M. Luck and L. Padgham (Eds.): AOSE 2007, LNCS 4951, pp. 212–224, 2008.

2 Multi-Agent Systems Unified Process (MASUP)

MASUP is a RUP [5] extension that focuses on multi-agent systems development. The methodology main purpose is to systematically identify the applicability of an agent-oriented solution during the modeling phases [6]. MASUP has the Requirements, Analysis and Design disciplines. The agent solution identification occurs on the analysis and design disciplines through a heuristic over activity diagrams. After the identification that an agent solution is appropriate for the problem at hand, MASUP proposes different diagrams to capture agent characteristics. It is important to notice that the methodology is fully compatible with RUP and thus the non-agent part of the system can be modeled using the traditional RUP techniques. Figure 1 shows the artifacts generated in MASUP grouped by discipline models.

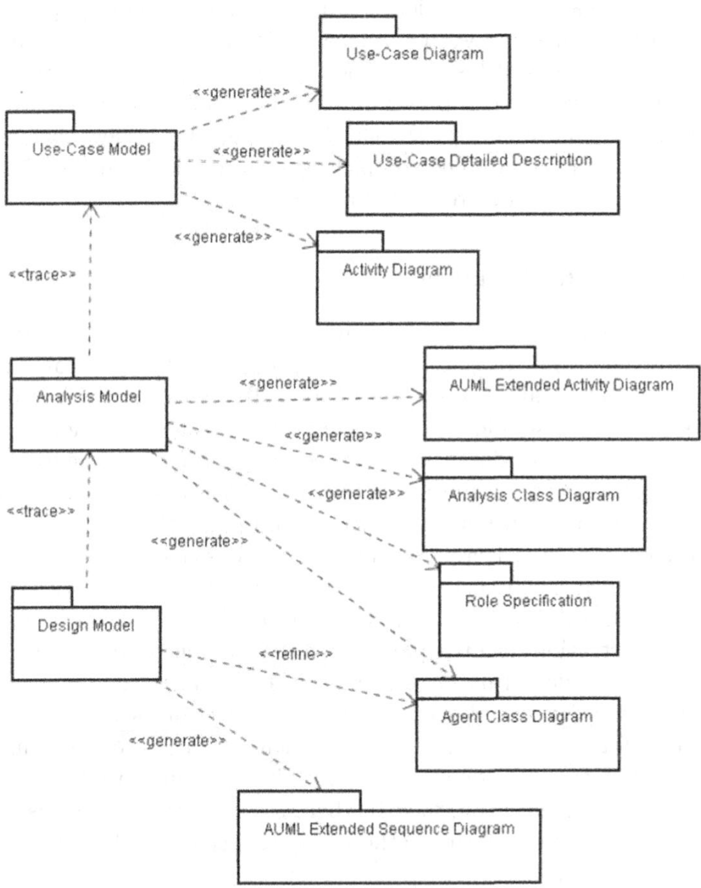

Fig. 1. MASUP models and artifacts

MASUP is being used by under-graduate and graduate in university courses on multi-agent systems and also by researchers in their work every time an agent-oriented solution should be modeled. Since 2005 ate least 10 projects used MASUP offering important information on its practical usage and improvement opportunities.

3 Modeling Organizational Rules in MASUP

This section presents MASUP application in the CMS [7] showing how it structures the solution for the problem from the requirements to the design phases. CMS is an open multi-agent system which supports international conferences paper reviewing management. This kind of system requires the coordination of several individuals and groups. In the original paper, the authors identified seven organizational rules involving the agents in CMS: (i) there must be at least three reviewers for each paper; (ii) a reviewer can not review the same paper more than once; (iii) a paper author does not review his own paper; (iv) a paper author does not collect reviews of his own paper; (v) if a paper is received, it should eventually be reviewed; (vi) a paper must actually be received before a review can be submitted; and finally, (vii) there be at least two reviews before a paper can be accepted or rejected. The complete system modeling using MASUP can be found at http://semanticore.pucrs.br/masup/cms.

3.1 Requirements Workflow

At the Requirements phase it is necessary to identify the people and the functionality involved in the system. For the CMS this discipline generated a use case diagram with 5 actors and 7 use cases (Figure 2). At this stage it is impossible to know if the system should be built using software agents or not.

MASUP uses use cases detailed description and/or activity diagrams for each use case realization. The activity diagram technique allows you to write brief descriptions of each activity state, which should make the textual specification of the workflow obsolete. Here, you need to be sensitive to your audience and the format in which they expect the specification [12]. In this work we are using both notations in order to show how rules can be identified in each one. To keep MASUP demonstration into the paper's size restrictions only the *Assign Paper* use case will be detailed. Table 1 presents the *Assign Paper* detailed description.

In the use case detailed description the rules section is used to capture all business rules for the requirements being elicited. This use case must clearly take into account the rule identified as (i). The rules indicated are required in the description step facilitating their further usage on other diagrams. The rule's ID must be used throughout the methodology and thus should not be replicated on the other diagrams.

The activity diagram for the *Assign Paper* use case showed in figure 3 is the regular UML diagram with a simple annotation over the decision element in order to identify if the decision is derived from a rule (business rule) or not

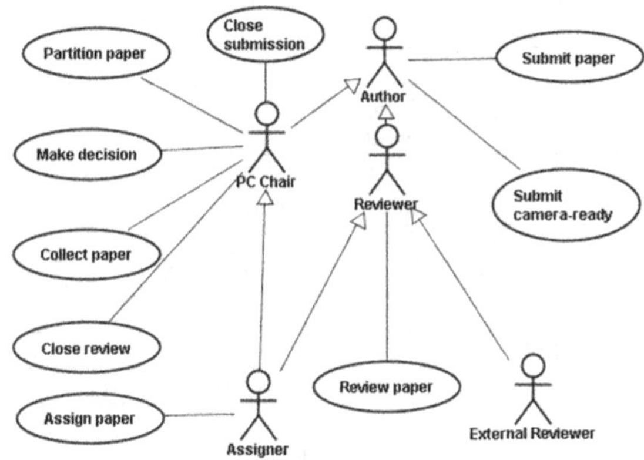

Fig. 2. Use case diagram

(regular consistency checking). This representation allows diagram traceability and checking. These rules will be later used on other diagrams in order to specify which agent role is responsible to guarantee the rule application.

3.2 Analysis Workflow

After the requirements capture it is necessary to create analysis class diagrams to identify the classes needed for use case realization. Five classes were identified for CMS: *paper*, *assigner*, *reviewer*, *review record* and *results record*. In this phase it is possible to check if an agent-solution is suitable for the problem and in which proportion it should be applied (which use cases). A heuristic based on decision making aspects of actors activities in the activity diagram is used for this purpose. It checks all the actors' activities in the activity diagrams. The designer must ask himself if the activity involves decision making capabilities in the actor. If it does, he must investigate if the decision making logic can be modeled computationally. If it can, he must shift the activity from the actor's swimlane to the system's swimlane. This provokes the other activities, directly related to the shifted one, to adapt their specification. The objects connected to these activities may be impacted and turned into roles in the MAS redesigned activity diagram. These roles will have at least the responsibilities indicated by the activities' specification.

Redesigning the Activity Diagrams to Include Analysis Classes. The analysis classes were included in the activity diagrams generated previously as objects that are produced and consumed in each activity. It is necessary to repeat this step for all the activity diagrams. This is a fundamental step since the heuristic used for the agent-oriented solution identification is highly dependable on the classes produced and consumed by each activity. Figure 4 presents the analysis diagram containing the system entities.

Table 1. Assign Paper use case detailed description

Identification:		2	
Use case name:		Assign paper	
Actors:		Assigner	
Preconditions:		Papers partitioned	
Postconditions:		Papers assigned	
EVENTS TYPICAL SEQUENCE			
ID	ACTOR ACTION	ID	SYSTEM ACTION
MAIN SECTION			
1	Request papers.		
		2	Show partitioned papers.
3	Select paper.		
		4	Save selection.
5	Request reviewers.		
		6	Show reviewers.
7	Select reviewer.		
		8	Save the number of reviews it reviewer is responsible for.
		9	Verify if there are at least three reviewers selected for the paper. (i)
10	Confirm assignment.		
		11	Assign paper to reviewer.
		12	Verify if there are more papers to be assigned.
ALTERNATIVE SEQUENCE			
Sequence ID	Alternative ID	Action/alternative answer	
9a	1	There are not three reviewers for the paper selected. (i)	
	2	Return to step 7 in the main section.	
12a	1	There are more papers to be assigned.	
	2	Return to step 3 in the main section.	
RULES			
ID	Description		
(i)	There must be at least three reviewers for each paper.		

Identifying Agent Roles from Use Case Realization. Each activity diagram redesigned in the previous step must be inspected using MASUP heuristic in order to find role candidates among the objects represented. Those objects are than marked as roles using UML stereotype notation for future usage. If an UML diagram contains roles the UML activity diagram is redesigned to capture agency characteristics.

For instance, the activity *Select Reviewer* in the activity diagram *Assign Paper* (Figure 3) requires decision making capabilities from the actor represented as *Assigner* in the swimlane. This indicates that an agent could play a role related to this activity to automate the decision-making process. Since the activity is considered for automation, it must be transferred to the system and the actor's decision criteria must be formalized. The objects linked with the

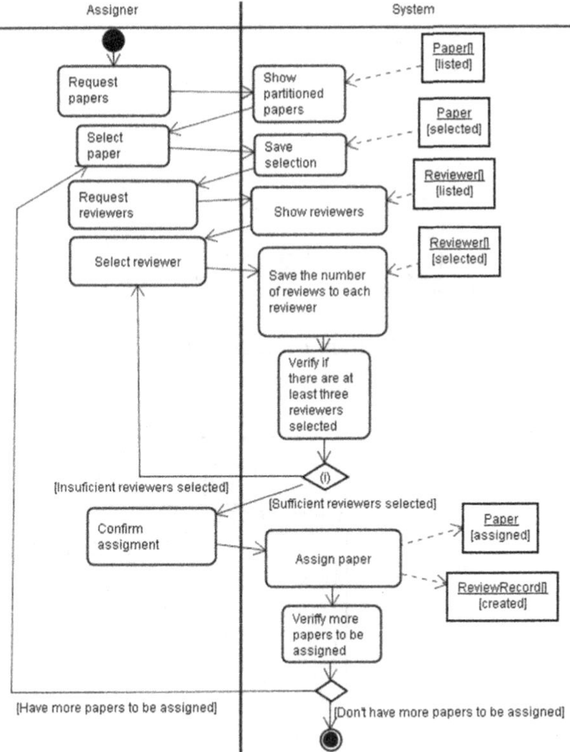

Fig. 3. Assign Paper activity diagram

agentified activity are candidates to be turned into agent roles. If an object is named as simple resource it should be renamed to indicate the role that deals with that resource. In MASUP we use the *Handler* termination for this purpose. In the example, since paper is a resource it is not interesting to have a role named paper. Because of this we used the *paperHandler* identification in the redesigned UML activity diagram (Figure 5). In the redesigned UML activity diagram, the relationship between a role and an activity must be named with UML stereotypes. If a role manages an activity the stereotype << responsible for>> is used and if the role participates in a negotiation to perform an activity the stereotype used is << participate in >>.

Applying the heuristic on all diagrams produced in the requirements phase it was possible to identify four roles for CMS: *paperHandler*, *reviewer*, *assigner* and *resultsHandler*.

Role Specification. Each role identified in the activity diagrams must be detailed in terms of attributions and restrictions. These restrictions include the organizational rules related with the multi-agent system defined in the requirements phase. The organizational rules not related to the roles should be captured

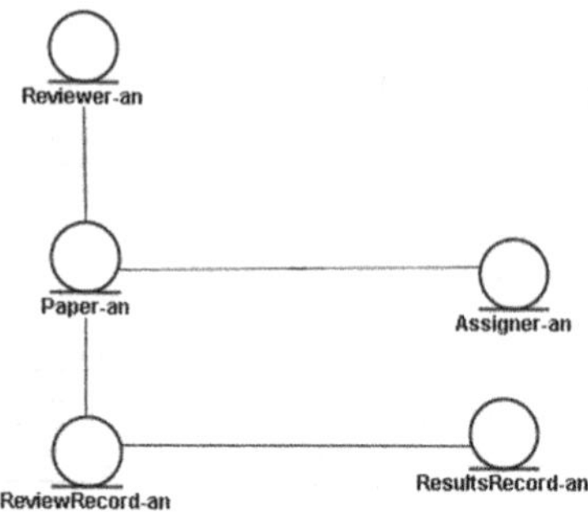

Fig. 4. Analysis Diagram containing the system entities

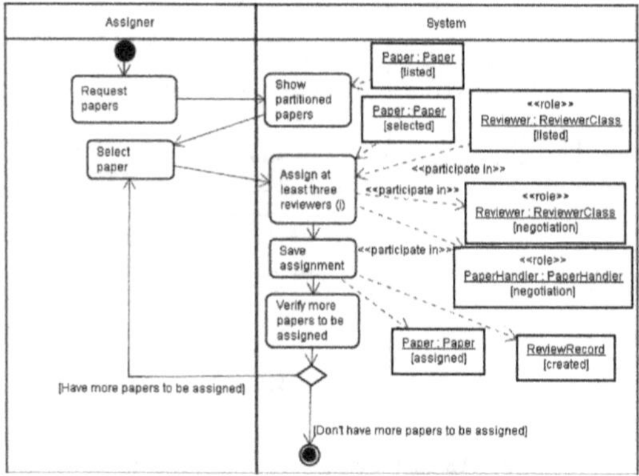

Fig. 5. Assign Paper redesigned UML activity diagram

in the object-oriented portion of the system which will be modeled using the regular RUP disciplines and further integrated with the agent-oriented one.

All CMS rules should be modeled in the multi-agent part of the system. The role *paperHandler* found in the *Assign Paper* redesigned activity diagram has as its attribution the negotiation process to assign papers to reviewers. In this assignment the agent who is playing this specific role must take into account that he must accept at least three reviewing proposals for each paper (rule (i)). The roles specification for *paperHandler*, *reviewer*, *assigner* and *resultsHandler* are presented respectively in tables 2, 3, 4 and 5.

Identifying Agents. Although the designer may aggregate roles into agents freely, it is a good practice to combine the roles sharing common knowledge in a single agent. In other words, roles that consume and produce the same resources will be aggregated in the same agent. For CMS four agents were identified: *PaperHandlerAgent* plays the *paperHandler* role, the *AssignerAgent* plays the *assigner* role, the *ReviewerAgent* plays the *reviewer* role and the *ResultsHandlerAgent* plays

Table 2. PaperHandler role specification

Role: PaperHandler			
Use Case	**Activity**	**Attributions**	**Restrictions**
Assign Paper	Assign at least three reviewers.	- It negotiates and accepts the proposal for the paper to be assigned to reviewers.	- It accepts at least three proposals (i).
Partition Paper	Partition papers.	- It negotiates and accepts the proposal for the paper to be partitioned to assigners.	- Paper abstracts subject must be considerate in the negotiation.
Make Decision	Evaluate papers in ascending order.	- It negotiates and accepts to evaluate a paper. - Notify result to the author.	- Paper is not own (iv). - There are at least two reviews (vii).

Table 3. Reviewer role specification

Role: Reviewer			
Use Case	**Activity**	**Attributions**	**Restrictions**
Assign Paper	Assign at least three reviewers.	- It negotiates and accepts to review a paper.	- Must have the skills to review a paper.
Review Paper	Show papers.	- Present received papers.	- Just the received papers will be presented (vi).
Review Paper	Verify if the paper is already reviewed	- Verify if the paper was already reviewed him/herself.	- Reviewer doesnt review the same paper more than once (ii).
Review Paper	Verify if it is own paper	- Verify if it is own paper.	- Reviewer does not review his own paper (iii).
Review Paper	Verify more papers received	- Verify more papers received.	- If a paper is received, it should eventually be reviewed (v).

the *resultsHandler* role. It was not identified knowledge sharing among roles and thus we used a 1-to-1 mapping between roles and agents.

Defining the Agent Society. MASUP has a diagram to represent the agent society showing communication and authority relationships between the agents. The Agent Class Diagram shows the society related to CMS (figure 6). One *PaperHandlerAgent* may communicate with many *AssignerAgents* as well as many *ReviewerAgents*. The *AssignerAgents* or *ReviewerAgents* decide if it is appropriate to answer *PaperHandlerAgent's* requests based on the matching between the request interests and the agents' expertise. One *PaperHandlerAgent* may also communicate with one *ResultsHandlerAgent* in order to send paper reviews and to receive if the paper it handles was accepted or not for publishing. Figure 6

Table 4. Assigner role specification

Role: Assigner			
Use Case	**Activity**	**Attributions**	**Restrictions**
Partition Paper.	Partition papers.	- It negotiates and accepts to assign a paper.	- Must have the skills to assign a paper.

Table 5. ResultsHandler role specification

Role: ResultsHandler			
Use Case	**Activity**	**Attributions**	**Restrictions**
Make Decision.	Evaluate papers in ascending order.	- It evaluates and accepts papers evaluation.	

also presents the organizational rules linked with the *reviewer* role (ii, iii, v, vi) and the organizational rules that apply to the agent's interactions as (i), (iv) and (vii).

3.3 Design Workflow

The purpose of design workflow is to adapt the analysis results to the constraints imposed by the implementation. In the design workflow MASUP has activities to define the agent interactions and how they will be mapped to implementation structures. Each interaction between agents showed in figure 5 (*paper partition assignment*, *paper review assignment*, *results requisition*) will be detailed in an AUML extended sequence diagram. MASUP does not force the use of any specific implementation platform. Because of this, it uses the notion of infrastructure services to map the implementation platform services, showing how the designed agents will interact with them.

Specifying Agent Interactions Scenarios. The relationships in the Agent Class Diagram show that interactions between the agents must occur in a certain

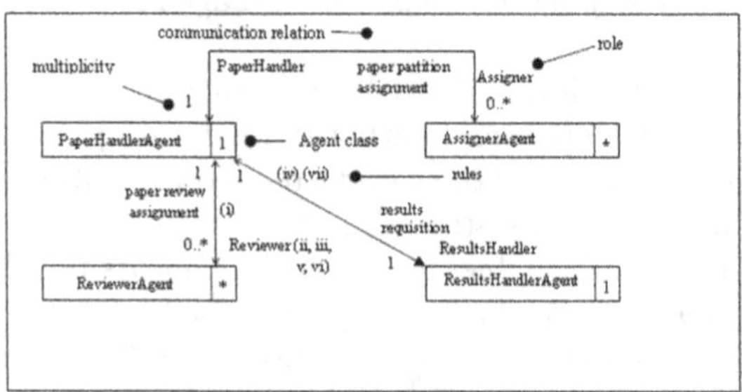

Fig. 6. Agent Class Diagram

time during the system execution. The interaction scenarios are represented in MASUP using the AUML Extended Sequence Diagram [8]. Figure 7 presents the interaction scenario for *Assign Paper*. Due to space limitations just one part of the scenarios is shown. The other dialogs were suppressed but follow the same general template. The *PaperHandlerAgent* sends a broadcast message to all *ReviewerAgents* with the agent's id and name and the paper to be assigned. The interested *ReviewerAgents* send a response with the conversationId, the agent's id and name, their skills (representing the agents expertise) and the number of papers they can review. Finally, the *PaperHandlerAgent* accepts at least three reviewing proposals (i) and sends a message to the chosen *ReviewerAgents*. The others *ReviewerAgents* do not receive a message and wait for a timeout in the communication.

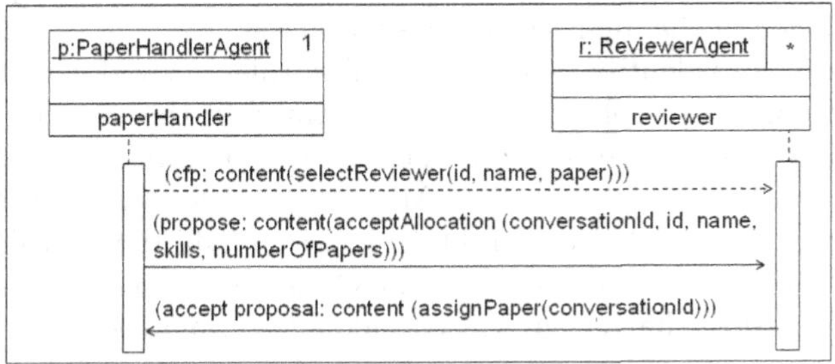

Fig. 7. Assign Paper AUML extended sequence diagram (paper review assignment)

PaperHandlerAgent	1
Id Name Paper ContactAuthor	
(cfp: content(selectAssigner(id, name, paper))) (accept proposal: content(partitionPaper(conversationId))) (cfp: content(selectReviewer(id, name, paper))) (accept proposal: content(assignPaper(conversationId))) (request: content(requestResults(id, name, reviewRecord)))	
paperHandler	
It negotiates and accepts the proposal for the paper to be assigned to reviewers (i). It negotiates and accepts the proposal for the paper to be partitioned to assigners. It negotiates and accepts to evaluate a paper (iv) (vii).	

Fig. 8. Agent Class Specification for the PaperHandlerAgent

Complementing the Agent Class Specification with the Agents' Communication Acts. The interaction scenarios define the communication protocols used by the agents. These protocols are composed by the interaction interfaces. It is necessary to complement the agent class specification with these interfaces for an agent to communicate with the others. Figure 8 presents the agent class specification for the *PaperHandlerAgent* completed with its interaction protocol. This specification describes all the elements that must be implemented in an agent giving a synthetic view of the agent to guide the programmers during the MAS implementation. The other agents have to be specified in the same way.

4 Discussion

Traceability is important issue on any software development methodology. MASUP provides traceability guidance for developing each artifacts based on some previously developed. MASUP treats the integration between the organization and the information system. MASUP does not have a diagram to represent the agent organizational workflow and cooperation rules. It does provide support for rule identification from the requirements phase and their mapping in the artifacts produced in the analysis and design phases.

MASUP naturally identify two types of rules: rules derived from the business rules in the requirements phase (usually annotated in the use case description steps) and coordination rules (usually identified in the pre and post conditions of use cases detailed description). Since MASUP does not assume that an agent-oriented solution is suitable for a problem, it uses a hybrid approach combining agent-oriented modeling and conventional OO modeling. In this paper, only the agent-oriented part of the system was considered and modeled.

Not all the organizational rules will be implemented in the agent-oriented portion of the system and thus must be indicated in the non-MAS one. The integration between the agent-oriented and non-agent-oriented parts of a system is done in the design phase when mapping the agents to infrastructure services such as database management systems, web servers and so on. This mapping is based on the resources consumed and produced by agents which are classes of the non-MAS design architecture.

It is possible to demonstrate that MASUP is a very straightforward methodology with three main differences from the other methodologies in the literature such as Prometheus [9], Tropos [10] and MaSE [11]: (i) it does not assume that an agent solution is suitable for a problem and it uses an heuristic to guide the developers on finding if this is the case based on the decision making required in the activities modeled. Although Tropos does not assume at the first hand that an agent-oriented solution will be applied, it uses concepts of Artifitial Intelligence (such as intentions) that are easier to be mapped to agent-oriented systems; (ii) it uses whenever possible well-known modeling structures such as UML while MaSE uses some isolated UML diagrams; and (iii) it enables the development of large scale systems that use agents only in critical and complex tasks while maintaining the simplicity of ready to use technology on other less critical tasks.

5 Conclusion and Future Work

Agent-oriented software development is a growing research area since there are no standards for agent systems design and implementation. In spite of the lack of standards, there are many interesting works showing a methodological approach for agent system development. This work presented a methodology which extends RUP called MASUP to develop agent-oriented systems and a case study specially chosen for its comparison with other methodologies found in the literature.

The organizational and coordination rules identification and tracing is done in all phases of MASUP. The models produced in each activity of the methodology are specified through successive refinements using use cases as the reference to express the system requirements. The design model takes into account the implementation infrastructure required to implement the solution using a multi-agent approach.

The main contribution of this work is to present the methodology using a reference case study and discussing its strengths and weaknesses to map all the case studys requirements and organizational rules. MASUP is being extended to use diagrams to represent agents organizational workflows and rules. A visual modeling tool is being developed to support MASUP usage and diagram consistency over MASUP workflows.

Acknowledgments. This study was developed by the Intelligent Systems Engineering Group of PUCRS and partially financed by Dell Computers of Brazil Ltd. with resources of Law 8.248/91.

References

1. Wooldridge, M.: An Introduction to MultiAgent Systems. John Wiley & Sons Ltd, Chichester (2002)
2. Jennings, N.R., Faratin, P., Johnson, M.J., O'Brien, P., Wiegand, M.E.: Using intelligent agents to manage business processes. In: Proceedings of First International Conference on The Practical Application of Intelligent Agents and Multi-Agent Technology (PAAM 1996), London, pp. 345–360 (1996)
3. Zambonelli, F., Jeenings, N.R., Wooldridge, M.J.: Organizational Rules as an Abstraction for the Analysis and Design of Multi-Agent Systems. International Journal of Software Engineering and Knowledge Engineering 11, 303–328 (2001)
4. Bastos, R.M., Ribeiro, M.B.: Modeling Agent-Oriented Information Systems for Business Processes. In: Third International Workshop on Software Engineering for Large-Scale Multi-Agent Systems. 26th International Conference on Software Engineering - Workshop, Edinburgh, pp. 90–97 (2004)
5. RUP - Rational Unified Process. RATIONAL Software Corporation. United States (2002)
6. Bastos, R.M., Ribeiro, M.B.: MASUP: An Agent-Oriented Modeling Process for Information Systems. In: Software Engineering for Multi-Agent Systems III: Research Issues and Practical Applications, Springer, Berlin (2005)
7. DeLoach, S.: Modeling Organizational Rules in the Multi-agent Systems Engineering Methodology. In: Proceedings of the 15th Conference of the Canadian Society for Computational Studies of Intelligence on Advances in Artificial Intelligence, pp. 1–15 (2002)
8. Odell, J., Parunak, H.V.D., Bauer, B.: Representing Agent Interaction Protocols in UML. In: Agent-Oriented Software Engineering. 22nd International Conference on Software Engineering (ISCE), pp. 121–140. Springer, Heidelberg (2001)

9. Padgham, L., Winikoff, M.: Prometheus: A Methodology for Developing Intelligent Agents. In: Proceedings of the the Third International Workshop on Agent-Oriented Software Engineering (AAMAS 2002) (2002)
10. Castro, J.F.B., Mylopoulos, J., Kolp, M.: Developing Agent-Oriented Information Systems for the Enterprise. In: Enterprise Information Systems, 2nd edn., Kluwer Academic Publishers, Dordrecht (2001)
11. Deloach, S.A., Wood, M.F., Sparkman, C.H.: Multiagent Systems Engineering. The International Journal of Software Engineering and Knowledge Engineering 11 (2001)
12. IBM Developer Works (Last access in March 14, 2007), `http://www-128.ibm.com/developerworks/rational/library/2802.html`

Author Index

Lecture Notes in Computer Science

Sublibrary 2: Programming and Software Engineering

For information about Vols. 1–4323
please contact your bookseller or Springer

Vol. 4989: J. Garrigue, M.V. Hermenegildo (Eds.), Functional and Logic Programming. XI, 337 pages. 2008.

Vol. 4966: B. Beckert, R. Hähnle (Eds.), Tests and Proofs. X, 193 pages. 2008.

Vol. 4954: C. Pautasso, É. Tanter (Eds.), Software Composition. X, 263 pages. 2008.

Vol. 4951: M. Luck, L. Padgham (Eds.), Agent-Oriented Software Engineering VIII. XIV, 225 pages. 2008.

Vol. 4949: R.M. Hierons, J.P. Bowen, M. Harman (Eds.), Formal Methods and Testing. XIII, 367 pages. 2008.

Vol. 4937: M. Dumas, R. Heckel (Eds.), Web Services and Formal Methods. IX, 169 pages. 2008.

Vol. 4906: M. Cebulla (Ed.), Object-Oriented Technology. VIII, 204 pages. 2008.

Vol. 4902: P. Hudak, D.S. Warren (Eds.), Practical Aspects of Declarative Languages. X, 333 pages. 2008.

Vol. 4899: K. Yorav (Ed.), Hardware and Software: Verification and Testing. XII, 267 pages. 2008.

Vol. 4888: F. Kordon, O. Sokolsky (Eds.), Composition of Embedded Systems. XII, 221 pages. 2007.

Vol. 4880: S. Overhage, C.A. Szyperski, R. Reussner, J.A. Stafford (Eds.), Software Architectures, Components, and Applications. X, 249 pages. 2008.

Vol. 4849: M. Winckler, H. Johnson, P. Palanque (Eds.), Task Models and Diagrams for User Interface Design. XIII, 299 pages. 2007.

Vol. 4839: O. Sokolsky, S. Taşıran (Eds.), Runtime Verification. VI, 215 pages. 2007.

Vol. 4834: R. Cerqueira, R.H. Campbell (Eds.), Middleware 2007. XIII, 451 pages. 2007.

Vol. 4829: M. Lumpe, W. Vanderperren (Eds.), Software Composition. VIII, 281 pages. 2007.

Vol. 4824: A. Paschke, Y. Biletskiy (Eds.), Advances in Rule Interchange and Applications. XIII, 243 pages. 2007.

Vol. 4807: Z. Shao (Ed.), Programming Languages and Systems. XI, 431 pages. 2007.

Vol. 4799: A. Holzinger (Ed.), HCI and Usability for Medicine and Health Care. XVI, 458 pages. 2007.

Vol. 4789: M. Butler, M.G. Hinchey, M.M. Larrondo-Petrie (Eds.), Formal Methods and Software Engineering. VIII, 387 pages. 2007.

Vol. 4767: F. Arbab, M. Sirjani (Eds.), International Symposium on Fundamentals of Software Engineering. XIII, 450 pages. 2007.

Vol. 4765: A. Moreira, J. Grundy (Eds.), Early Aspects: Current Challenges and Future Directions. X, 199 pages. 2007.

Vol. 4764: P. Abrahamsson, N. Baddoo, T. Margaria, R. Messnarz (Eds.), Software Process Improvement. XI, 225 pages. 2007.

Vol. 4762: K.S. Namjoshi, T. Yoneda, T. Higashino, Y. Okamura (Eds.), Automated Technology for Verification and Analysis. XIV, 566 pages. 2007.

Vol. 4758: F. Oquendo (Ed.), Software Architecture. XVI, 340 pages. 2007.

Vol. 4757: F. Cappello, T. Herault, J. Dongarra (Eds.), Recent Advances in Parallel Virtual Machine and Message Passing Interface. XVI, 396 pages. 2007.

Vol. 4753: E. Duval, R. Klamma, M. Wolpers (Eds.), Creating New Learning Experiences on a Global Scale. XII, 518 pages. 2007.

Vol. 4750: M.L. Gavrilova, C.J.K. Tan (Eds.), Transactions on Computational Science I. XI, 181 pages. 2008.

Vol. 4749: B.J. Krämer, K.-J. Lin, P. Narasimhan (Eds.), Service-Oriented Computing – ICSOC 2007. XIX, 629 pages. 2007.

Vol. 4748: K. Wolter (Ed.), Formal Methods and Stochastic Models for Performance Evaluation. X, 301 pages. 2007.

Vol. 4741: C. Bessière (Ed.), Principles and Practice of Constraint Programming – CP 2007. XV, 890 pages. 2007.

Vol. 4735: G. Engels, B. Opdyke, D.C. Schmidt, F. Weil (Eds.), Model Driven Engineering Languages and Systems. XV, 698 pages. 2007.

Vol. 4716: B. Meyer, M. Joseph (Eds.), Software Engineering Approaches for Offshore and Outsourced Development. X, 201 pages. 2007.

Vol. 4709: F.S. de Boer, M.M. Bonsangue, S. Graf, W.-P. de Roever (Eds.), Formal Methods for Components and Objects. VIII, 297 pages. 2007.

Vol. 4680: F. Saglietti, N. Oster (Eds.), Computer Safety, Reliability, and Security. XV, 548 pages. 2007.

Vol. 4670: V. Dahl, I. Niemelä (Eds.), Logic Programming. XII, 470 pages. 2007.

Vol. 4652: D. Georgakopoulos, N. Ritter, B. Benatallah, C. Zirpins, G. Feuerlicht, M. Schoenherr, H.R. Motahari-Nezhad (Eds.), Service-Oriented Computing ICSOC 2006. XVI, 201 pages. 2007.

Vol. 4640: A. Rashid, M. Aksit (Eds.), Transactions on Aspect-Oriented Software Development IV. IX, 191 pages. 2007.

Vol. 4634: H. Riis Nielson, G. Filé (Eds.), Static Analysis. XI, 469 pages. 2007.

Vol. 4620: A. Rashid, M. Aksit (Eds.), Transactions on Aspect-Oriented Software Development III. IX, 201 pages. 2007.

Vol. 4615: R. de Lemos, C. Gacek, A. Romanovsky (Eds.), Architecting Dependable Systems IV. XIV, 435 pages. 2007.

Vol. 4610: B. Xiao, L.T. Yang, J. Ma, C. Muller-Schloer, Y. Hua (Eds.), Autonomic and Trusted Computing. XVIII, 571 pages. 2007.

Vol. 4609: E. Ernst (Ed.), ECOOP 2007 – Object-Oriented Programming. XIII, 625 pages. 2007.

Vol. 4608: H.W. Schmidt, I. Crnković, G.T. Heineman, J.A. Stafford (Eds.), Component-Based Software Engineering. XII, 283 pages. 2007.

Vol. 4591: J. Davies, J. Gibbons (Eds.), Integrated Formal Methods. IX, 660 pages. 2007.

Vol. 4589: J. Münch, P. Abrahamsson (Eds.), Product-Focused Software Process Improvement. XII, 414 pages. 2007.

Vol. 4574: J. Derrick, J. Vain (Eds.), Formal Techniques for Networked and Distributed Systems – FORTE 2007. XI, 375 pages. 2007.

Vol. 4556: C. Stephanidis (Ed.), Universal Access in Human-Computer Interaction, Part III. XXII, 1020 pages. 2007.

Vol. 4555: C. Stephanidis (Ed.), Universal Access in Human-Computer Interaction, Part II. XXII, 1066 pages. 2007.

Vol. 4554: C. Stephanidis (Ed.), Universal Acess in Human Computer Interaction, Part I. XXII, 1054 pages. 2007.

Vol. 4553: J.A. Jacko (Ed.), Human-Computer Interaction, Part IV. XXIV, 1225 pages. 2007.

Vol. 4552: J.A. Jacko (Ed.), Human-Computer Interaction, Part III. XXI, 1038 pages. 2007.

Vol. 4551: J.A. Jacko (Ed.), Human-Computer Interaction, Part II. XXIII, 1253 pages. 2007.

Vol. 4550: J.A. Jacko (Ed.), Human-Computer Interaction, Part I. XXIII, 1240 pages. 2007.

Vol. 4542: P. Sawyer, B. Paech, P. Heymans (Eds.), Requirements Engineering: Foundation for Software Quality. IX, 384 pages. 2007.

Vol. 4536: G. Concas, E. Damiani, M. Scotto, G. Succi (Eds.), Agile Processes in Software Engineering and Extreme Programming. XV, 276 pages. 2007.

Vol. 4530: D.H. Akehurst, R. Vogel, R.F. Paige (Eds.), Model Driven Architecture - Foundations and Applications. X, 219 pages. 2007.

Vol. 4523: Y.-H. Lee, H.-N. Kim, J. Kim, Y.W. Park, L.T. Yang, S.W. Kim (Eds.), Embedded Software and Systems. XIX, 829 pages. 2007.

Vol. 4498: N. Abdennahder, F. Kordon (Eds.), Reliable Software Technologies - Ada-Europe 2007. XII, 247 pages. 2007.

Vol. 4486: M. Bernardo, J. Hillston (Eds.), Formal Methods for Performance Evaluation. VII, 469 pages. 2007.

Vol. 4470: Q. Wang, D. Pfahl, D.M. Raffo (Eds.), Software Process Dynamics and Agility. XI, 346 pages. 2007.

Vol. 4468: M.M. Bonsangue, E.B. Johnsen (Eds.), Formal Methods for Open Object-Based Distributed Systems. X, 317 pages. 2007.

Vol. 4467: A.L. Murphy, J. Vitek (Eds.), Coordination Models and Languages. X, 325 pages. 2007.

Vol. 4454: Y. Gurevich, B. Meyer (Eds.), Tests and Proofs. IX, 217 pages. 2007.

Vol. 4444: T. Reps, M. Sagiv, J. Bauer (Eds.), Program Analysis and Compilation, Theory and Practice. X, 361 pages. 2007.

Vol. 4440: B. Liblit, Cooperative Bug Isolation. XV, 101 pages. 2007.

Vol. 4408: R. Choren, A. Garcia, H. Giese, H.-f. Leung, C. Lucena, A. Romanovsky (Eds.), Software Engineering for Multi-Agent Systems V. XII, 233 pages. 2007.

Vol. 4406: W. De Meuter (Ed.), Advances in Smalltalk. VII, 157 pages. 2007.

Vol. 4405: L. Padgham, F. Zambonelli (Eds.), Agent-Oriented Software Engineering VII. XII, 225 pages. 2007.

Vol. 4401: N. Guelfi, D. Buchs (Eds.), Rapid Integration of Software Engineering Techniques. IX, 177 pages. 2007.

Vol. 4385: K. Coninx, K. Luyten, K.A. Schneider (Eds.), Task Models and Diagrams for Users Interface Design. XI, 355 pages. 2007.

Vol. 4383: E. Bin, A. Ziv, S. Ur (Eds.), Hardware and Software, Verification and Testing. XII, 235 pages. 2007.

Vol. 4379: M. Südholt, C. Consel (Eds.), Object-Oriented Technology. VIII, 157 pages. 2007.

Vol. 4364: T. Kühne (Ed.), Models in Software Engineering. XI, 332 pages. 2007.

Vol. 4355: J. Julliand, O. Kouchnarenko (Eds.), B 2007: Formal Specification and Development in B. XIII, 293 pages. 2006.

Vol. 4354: M. Hanus (Ed.), Practical Aspects of Declarative Languages. X, 335 pages. 2006.

Vol. 4350: M. Clavel, F. Durán, S. Eker, P. Lincoln, N. Martí-Oliet, J. Meseguer, C. Talcott, All About Maude - A High-Performance Logical Framework. XXII, 797 pages. 2007.

Vol. 4348: S. Tucker Taft, R.A. Duff, R.L. Brukardt, E. Plödereder, P. Leroy, Ada 2005 Reference Manual. XXII, 765 pages. 2006.

Vol. 4346: L. Brim, B.R. Haverkort, M. Leucker, J. van de Pol (Eds.), Formal Methods: Applications and Technology. X, 363 pages. 2007.

Vol. 4344: V. Gruhn, F. Oquendo (Eds.), Software Architecture. X, 245 pages. 2006.

Vol. 4340: R. Prodan, T. Fahringer, Grid Computing. XXIII, 317 pages. 2007.

Vol. 4336: V.R. Basili, H.D. Rombach, K. Schneider, B. Kitchenham, D. Pfahl, R.W. Selby (Eds.), Empirical Software Engineering Issues. XVII, 193 pages. 2007.

Vol. 4326: S. Göbel, R. Malkewitz, I. Iurgel (Eds.), Technologies for Interactive Digital Storytelling and Entertainment. X, 384 pages. 2006.